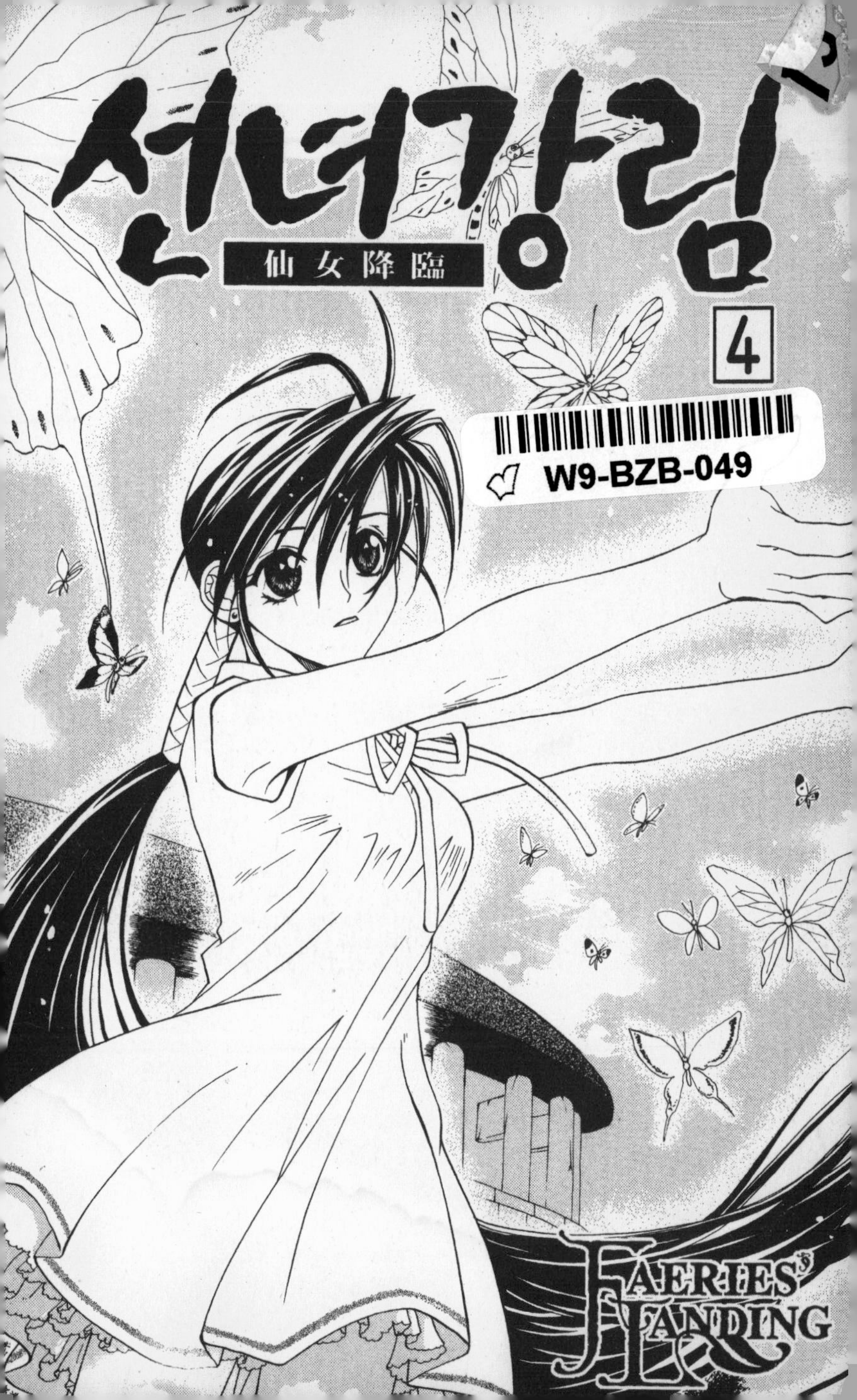
선녀강림
仙女降臨
4
FAERIES' LANDING

Translator - Woo Sok Park
English Adaptation - Tim Beedle
Associate Editor - Tim Beedle
Retouch and Lettering - Jeanine Han
Cover Layout - Raymond Makowski
Graphic Designer - Vicente Rivera, Jr.

Editor - Paul Morrissey
Digital Imaging Manager - Chris Buford
Pre-Press Manager - Antonio DePietro
Production Managers - Jennifer Miller and Mutsumi Miyazaki
Art Director - Matt Alford
Managing Editor - Jill Freshney
VP of Production - Ron Klamert
President & C.O.O. - John Parker
Publisher & C.E.O. - Stuart Levy

E-mail: info@TOKYOPOP.com
Come visit us online at www.TOKYOPOP.com

A  **TOKYOPOP**® Manga

TOKYOPOP Inc.
5900 Wilshire Blvd. Suite 2000
Los Angeles, CA 90036

Faeries' Landing Vol. 4

ISBN: 1-59182-612-8

First TOKYOPOP printing: July 2004

10 9 8 7 6 5 4 3 2 1

Printed in the USA

Volume 4

By
You Hyun

Los Angeles • Tokyo • London • Hamburg

Ryang Jegal

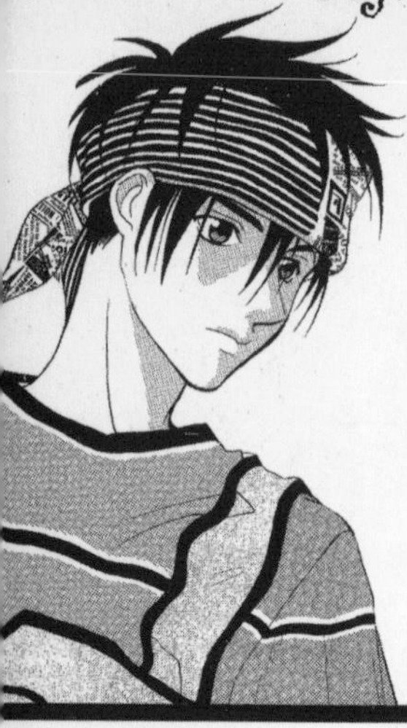

Our hapless bandanna-wearing protagonist. He's harboring Fanta, a fetching faerie grounded on Earth. Due to a magical curse, Ryang must suffer through 108 doomed relationships. This guy's gonna have major girl troubles!

Mungyeong Seong

Ryang's buddy. Boy, is he a sucker for pretty girls.

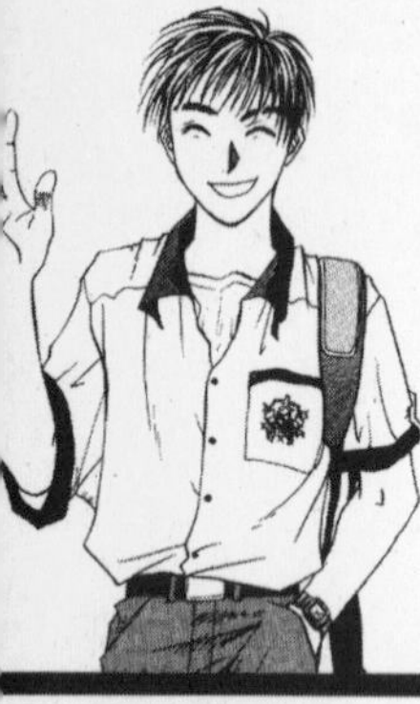

Hun Jegal and Taeyeong

Hun is Ryang's older brother, and Taeyeong is Hun's lovely wife. Ryang currently lives with them.

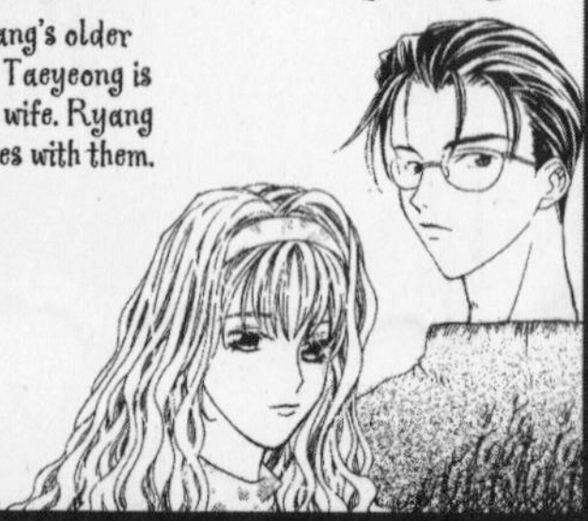

FROM THE REALM OF MAN

Fanta

A gorgeous faerie from the mystical realm of Avalon. She must stay in the human world after her winged gown is torn. Much to Ryang's delight--and frequent dismay--she now lives with him.

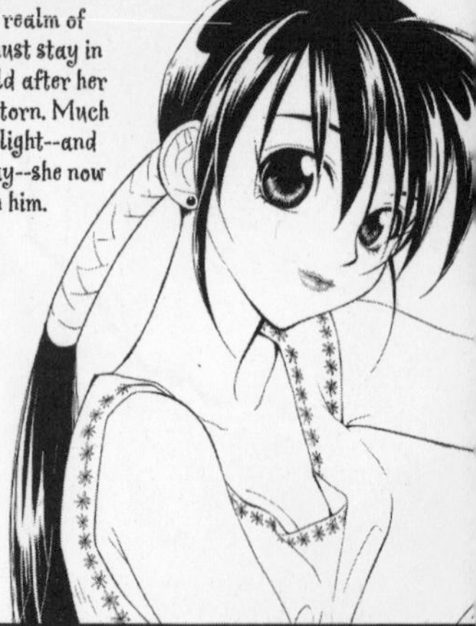

Goodfellow

An impish pan-like creature from Avalon who introduced Ryang to Fanta.

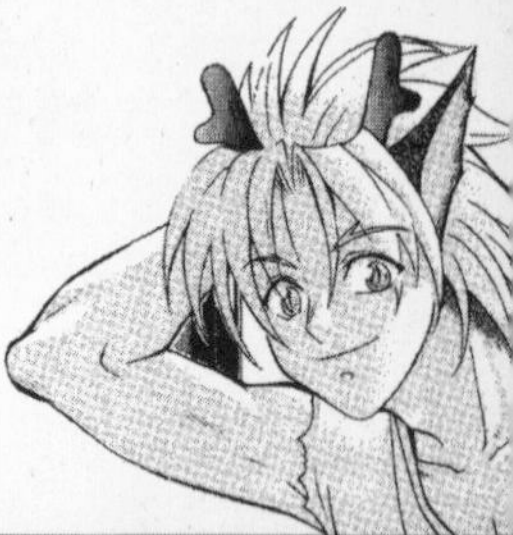

Charon

As the right-hand man of the faerie God, he overlooks all of the important administrative duties in Avalon. He's also Medea's older brother.

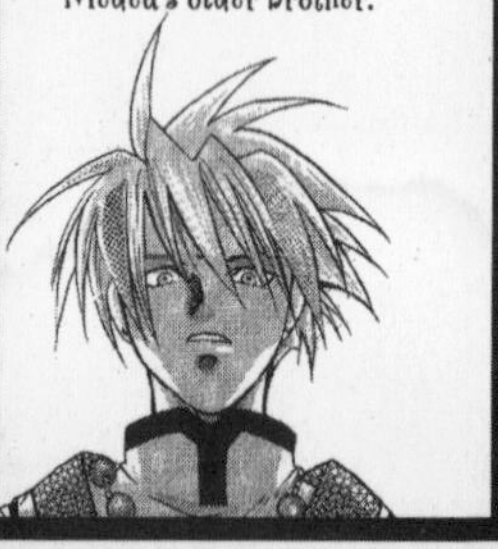

Medea

Fanta's devious and ambitious rival. She aspires to be the queen of Avalon.

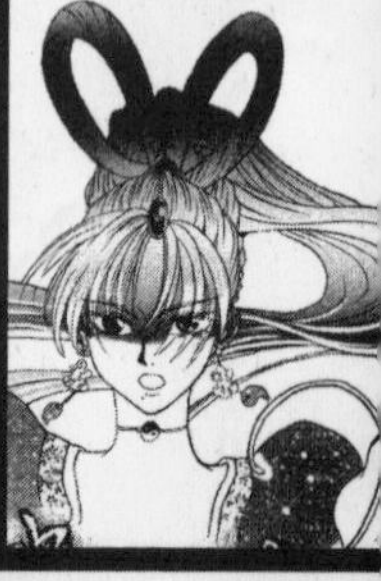

FROM THE REALM OF AVALON

STORY SO FAR...

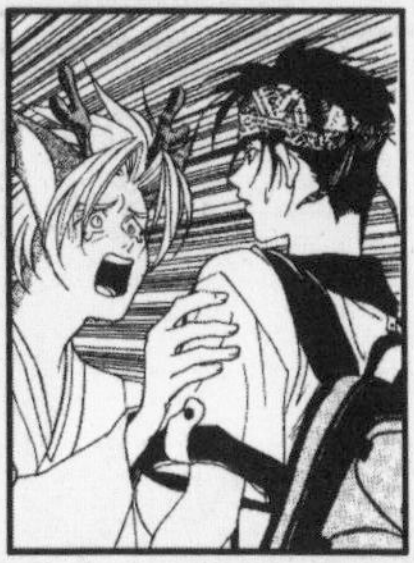

Ryang, a high school freshman, while walking the mean streets, stumbles upon a mysterious character named Goodfellow.

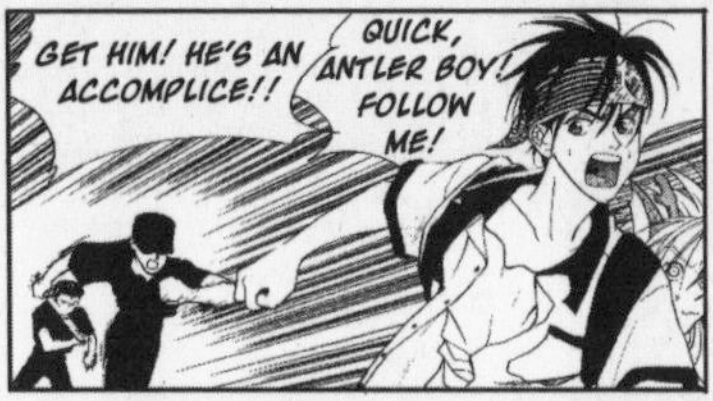
GET HIM! HE'S AN ACCOMPLICE!!
QUICK, ANTLER BOY! FOLLOW ME!

Ryang helps the naughty Goodfellow elude a pack of policemen who are hot on his heels.

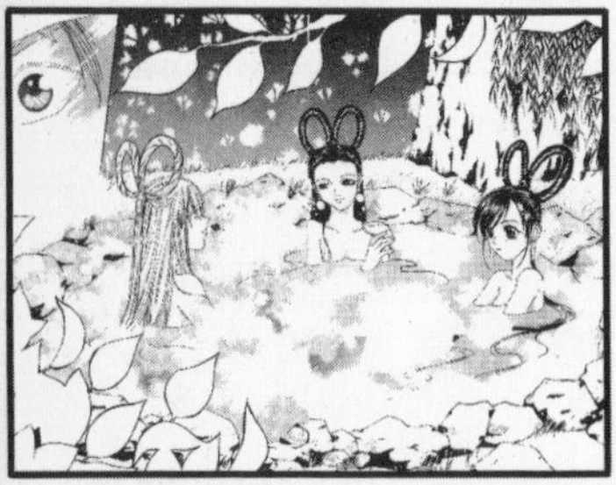

In return, the impishly grateful Goodfellow leads Ryang to an enchanting sight--three gorgeous female faeries taking a bath in a public bathhouse! You would think this would be a common occurrence in a town called "Faeries' Landing," but Ryang is flabbergasted.

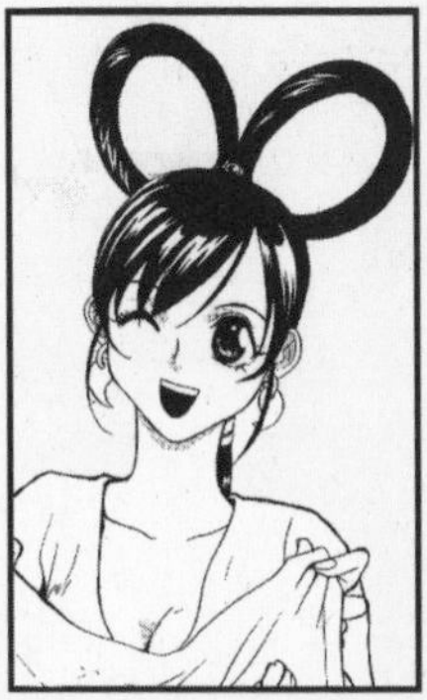

Here, Ryang meets Fanta, a fetching faerie who wants nothing more than to stay in the human world.

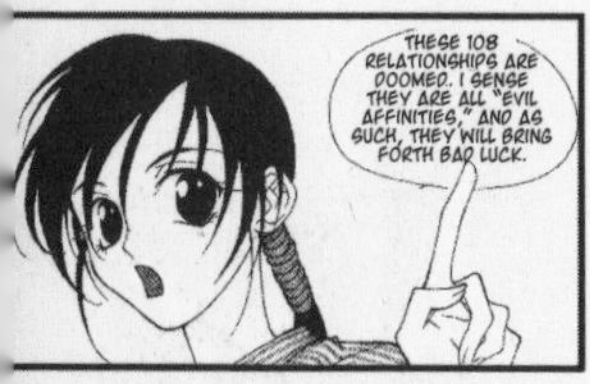
THESE 108 RELATIONSHIPS ARE DOOMED. I SENSE THEY ARE ALL "EVIL AFFINITIES," AND AS SUCH, THEY WILL BRING FORTH BAD LUCK.

One day, Fanta reads Ryang's palm. Uh-oh. Every life must have a little rain. She warns him that he is destined to have 108 "evil affinities" with women. Looks like Ryang's love life is going to be bumpy.

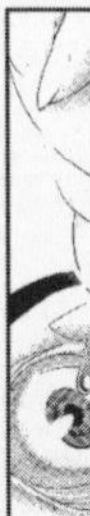

Fanta's cunning faerie rival, Medea, puts a few drops of a magical serum into Ryang's eyes. It's not for his contact lenses, though--it's a curse!

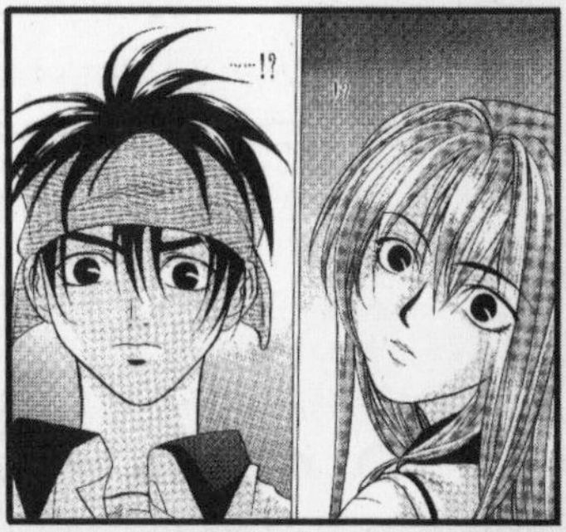
......!?

Now, if a girl makes eye contact with Ryang, she's doomed to become one of Ryang's 108 "evil affinities"! Ryang better have a high tolerance for twisted romance!

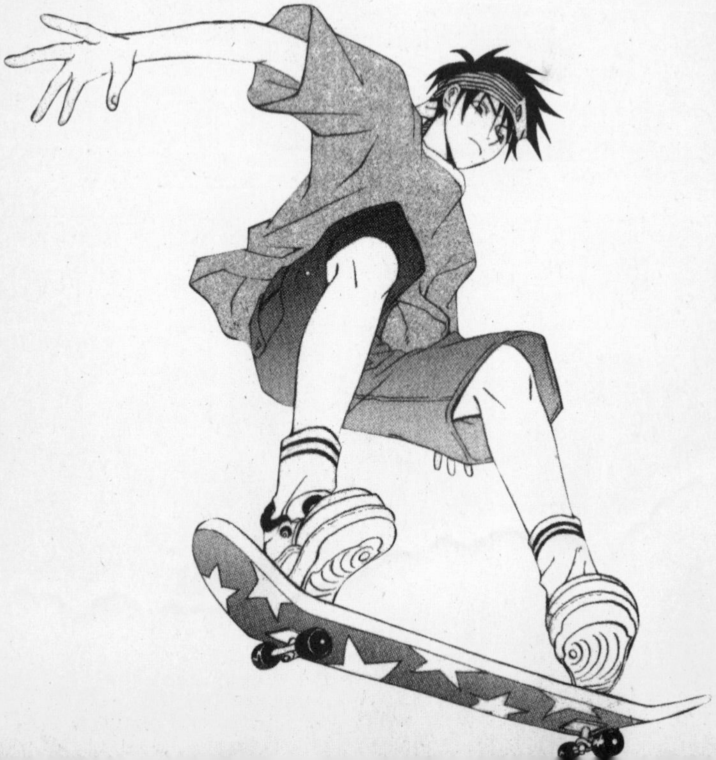

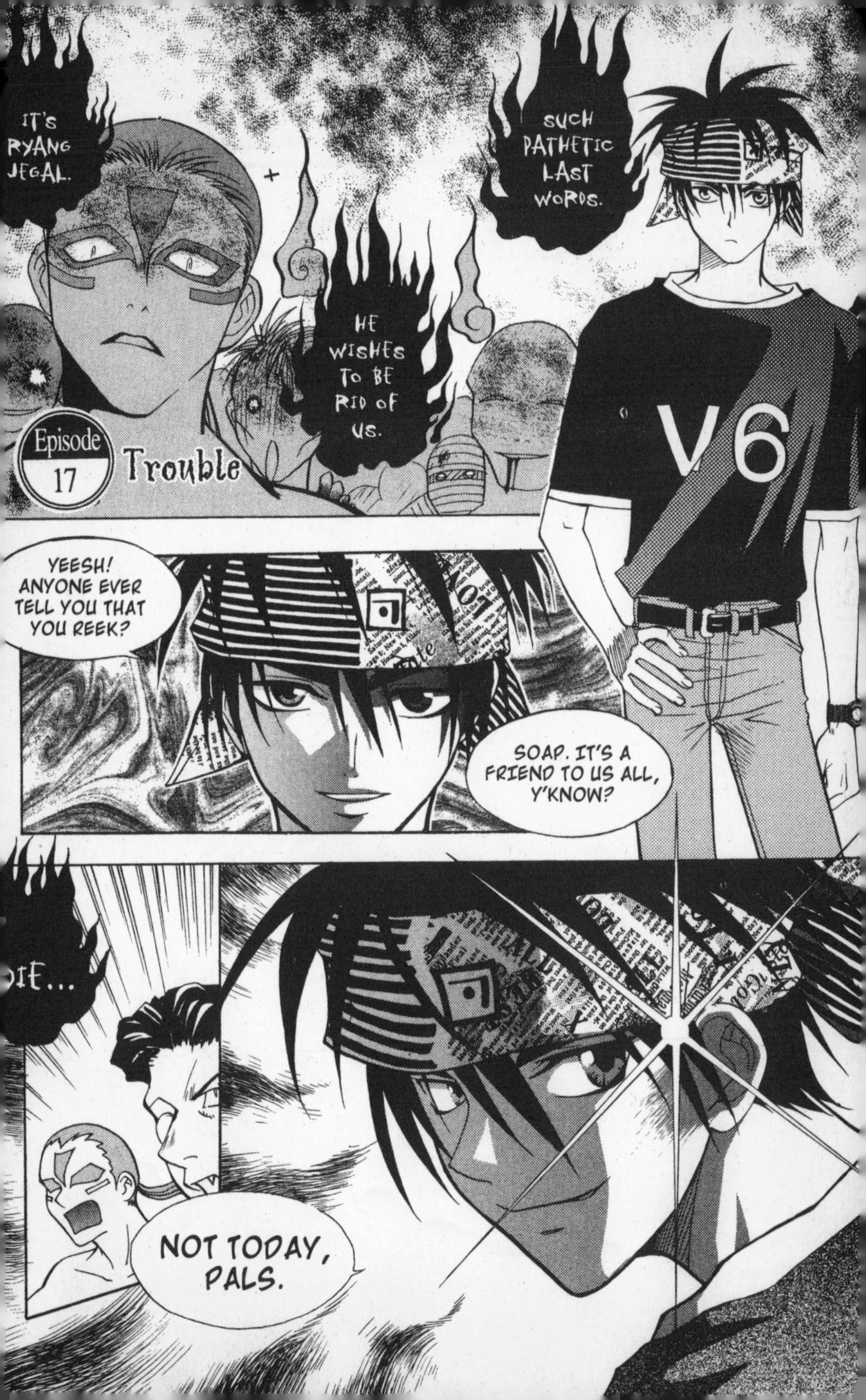
IT'S RYANG JEGAL.
Episode 17 Trouble
HE WISHES TO BE RID OF US.
SUCH PATHETIC LAST WORDS.
YEESH! ANYONE EVER TELL YOU THAT YOU REEK?
SOAP. IT'S A FRIEND TO US ALL, Y'KNOW?
IE...
NOT TODAY, PALS.

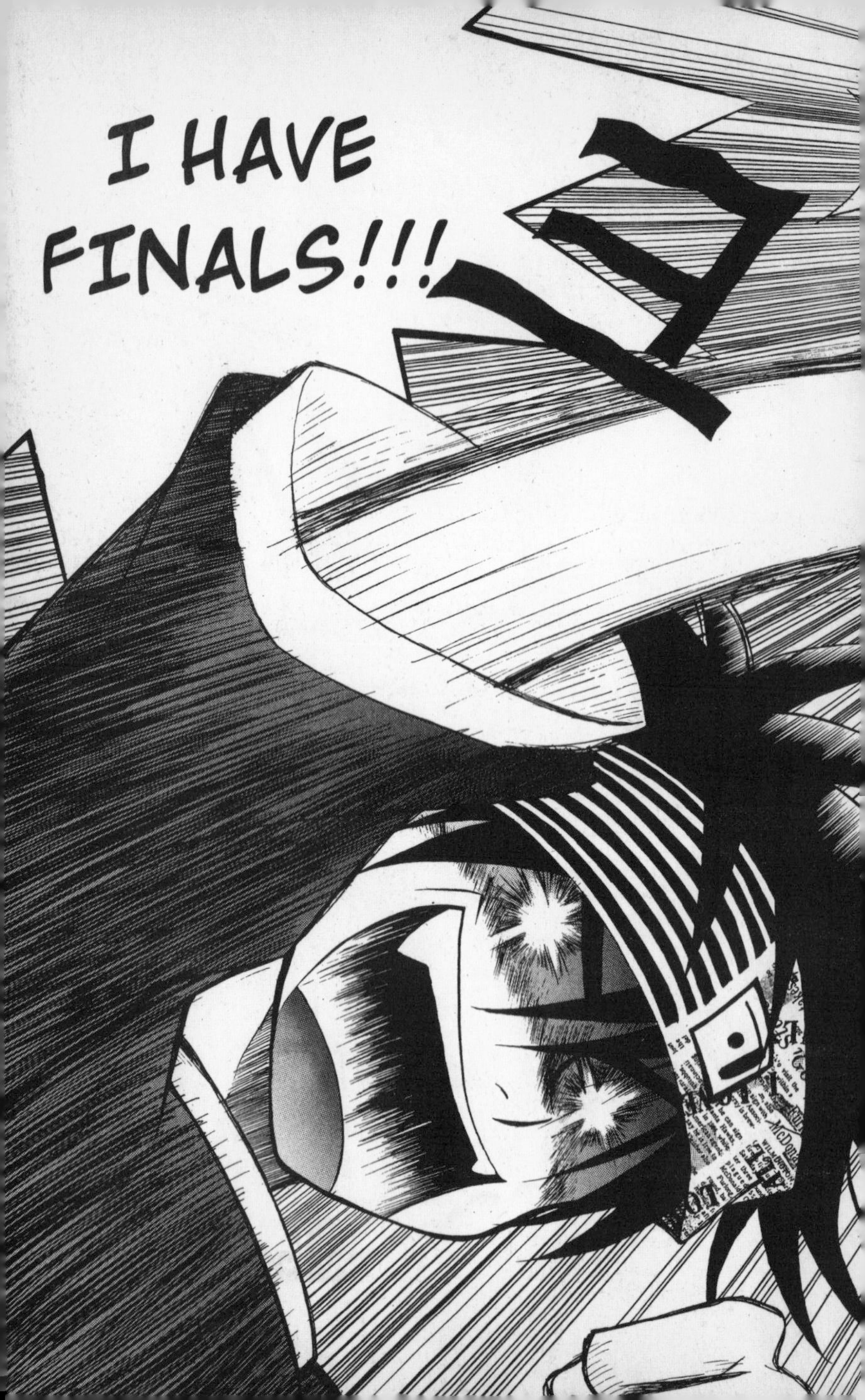
I HAVE FINALS!!!

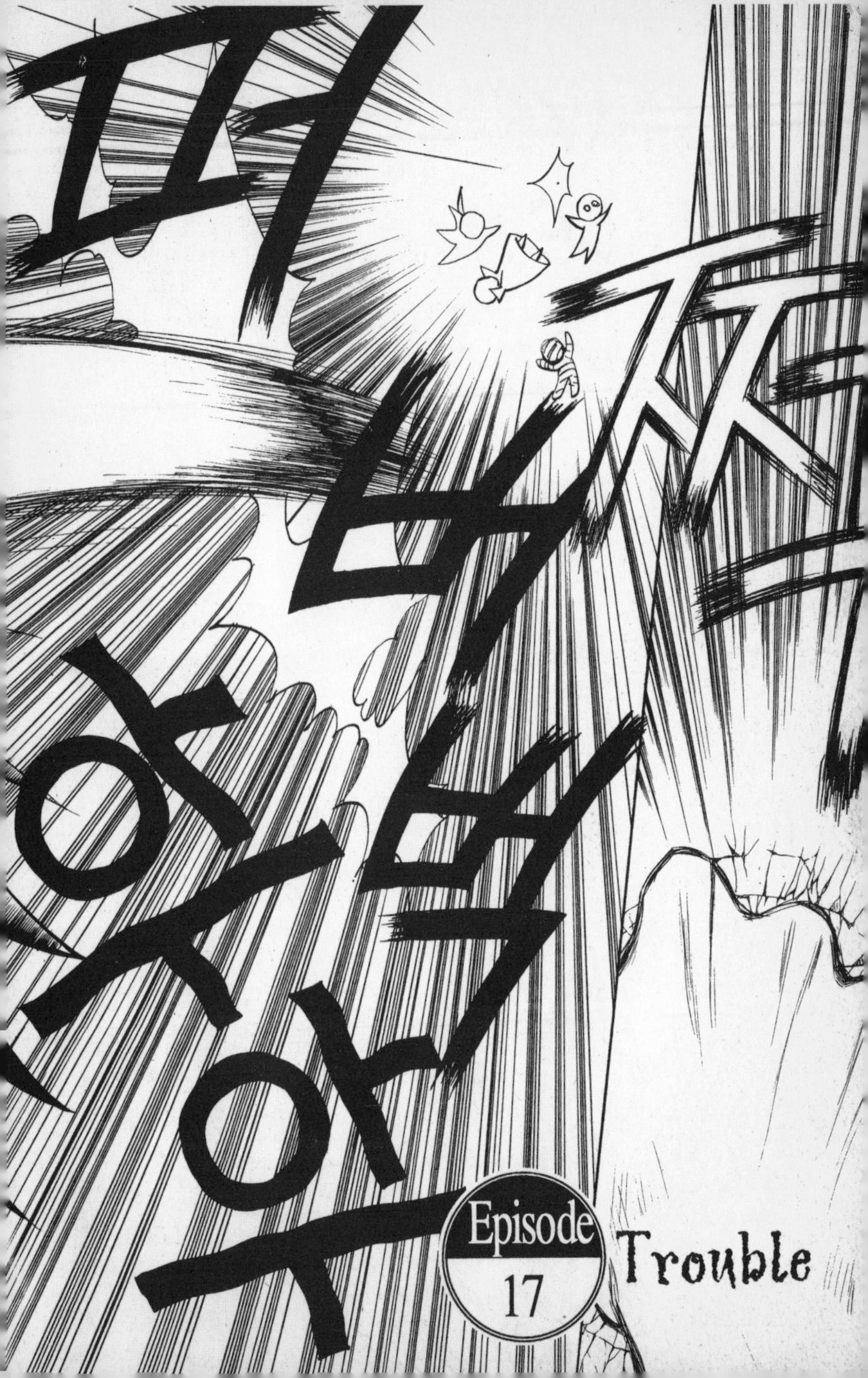
Episode 17
Trouble

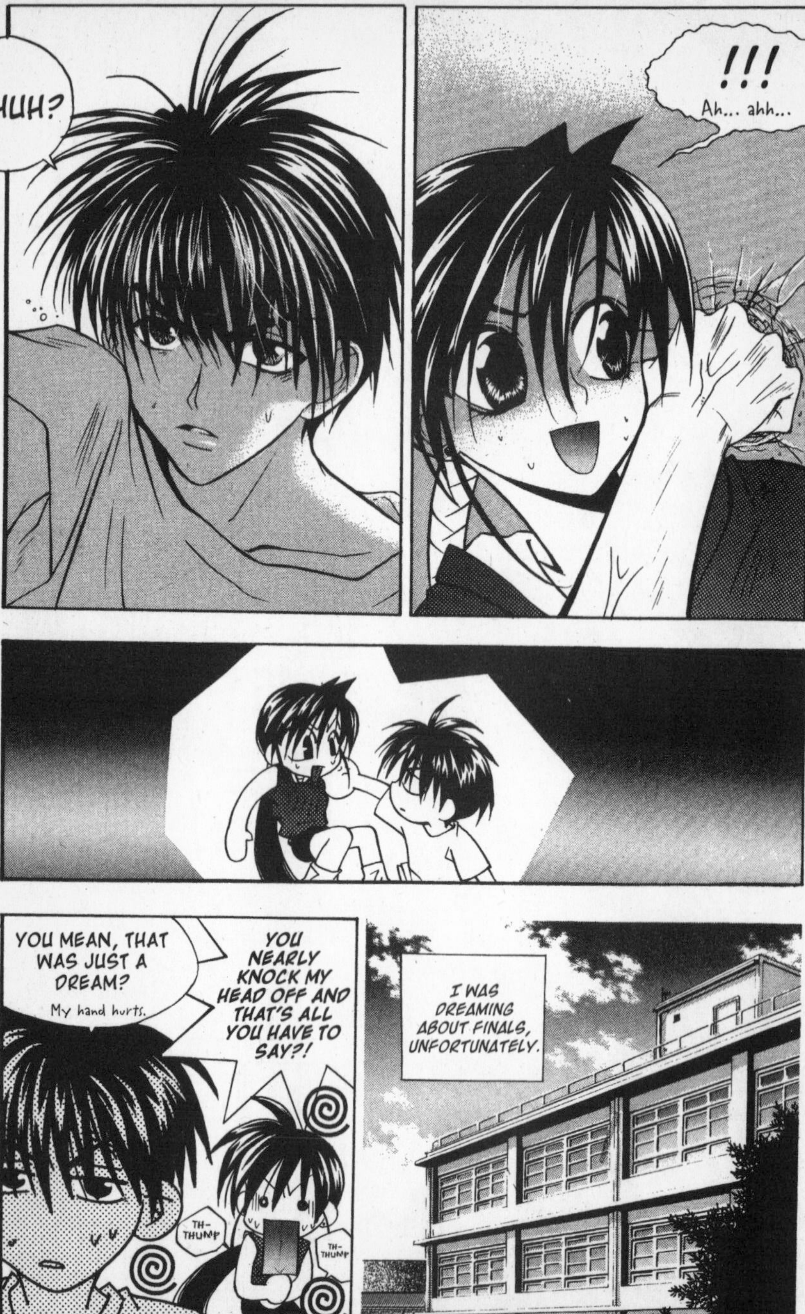
HUH?
!!!
Ah... ahh...
YOU MEAN, THAT WAS JUST A DREAM?
My hand hurts.
YOU NEARLY KNOCK MY HEAD OFF AND THAT'S ALL YOU HAVE TO SAY?!
TH-THUMP
TH-THUMP
I WAS DREAMING ABOUT FINALS, UNFORTUNATELY.

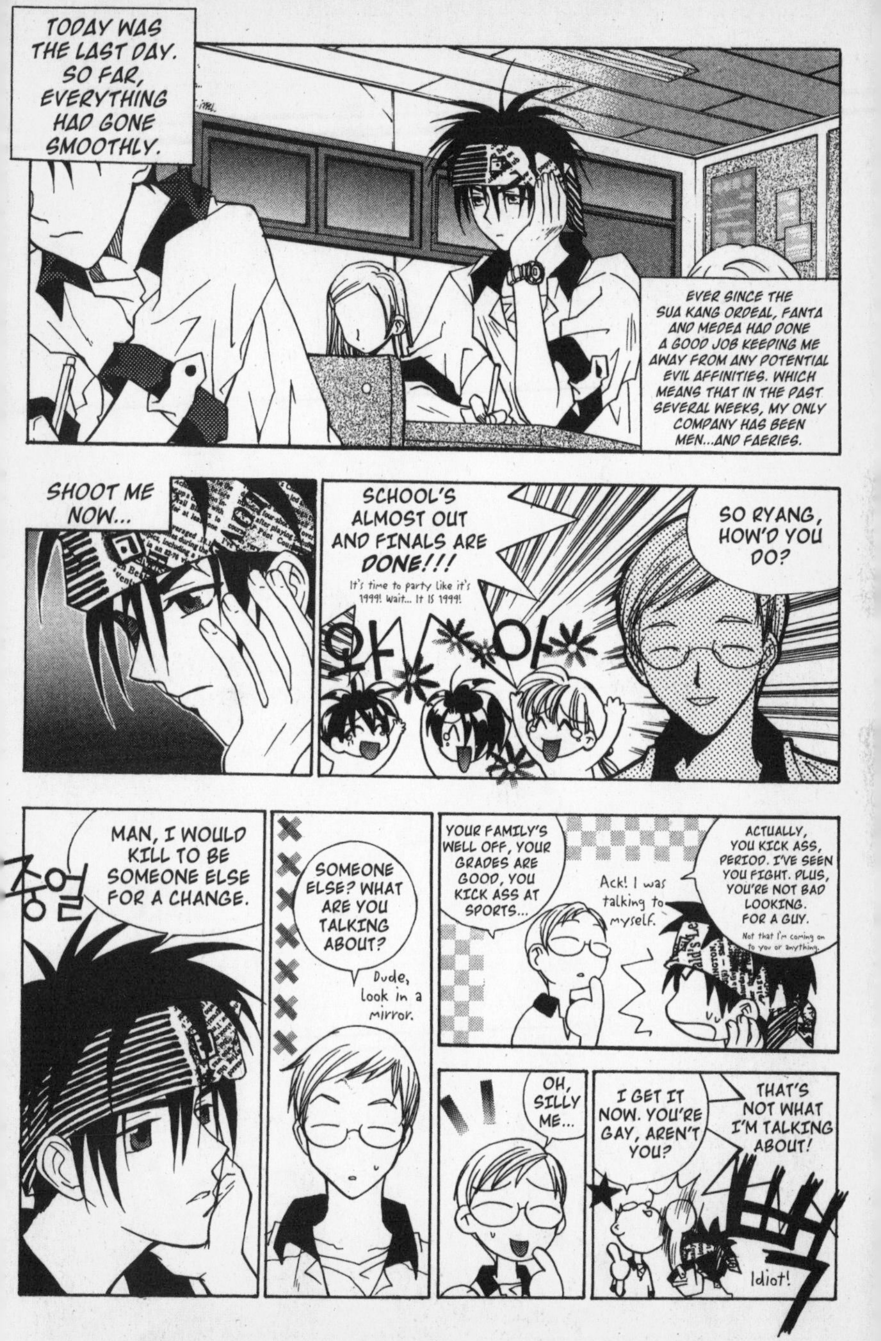
TODAY WAS THE LAST DAY. SO FAR, EVERYTHING HAD GONE SMOOTHLY.
EVER SINCE THE SUA KANG ORDEAL, FANTA AND MEDEA HAD DONE A GOOD JOB KEEPING ME AWAY FROM ANY POTENTIAL EVIL AFFINITIES. WHICH MEANS THAT IN THE PAST SEVERAL WEEKS, MY ONLY COMPANY HAS BEEN MEN...AND FAERIES.
SHOOT ME NOW...
SCHOOL'S ALMOST OUT AND FINALS ARE DONE!!!
It's time to party like it's 1999! Wait... It IS 1999!
와아아
SO RYANG, HOW'D YOU DO?
중얼
MAN, I WOULD KILL TO BE SOMEONE ELSE FOR A CHANGE.
SOMEONE ELSE? WHAT ARE YOU TALKING ABOUT?
Dude, look in a mirror.
YOUR FAMILY'S WELL OFF, YOUR GRADES ARE GOOD, YOU KICK ASS AT SPORTS...
Ack! I was talking to myself.
ACTUALLY, YOU KICK ASS, PERIOD. I'VE SEEN YOU FIGHT. PLUS, YOU'RE NOT BAD LOOKING. FOR A GUY.
Not that I'm coming on to you or anything.
OH, SILLY ME...
I GET IT NOW. YOU'RE GAY, AREN'T YOU?
THAT'S NOT WHAT I'M TALKING ABOUT!
Idiot!

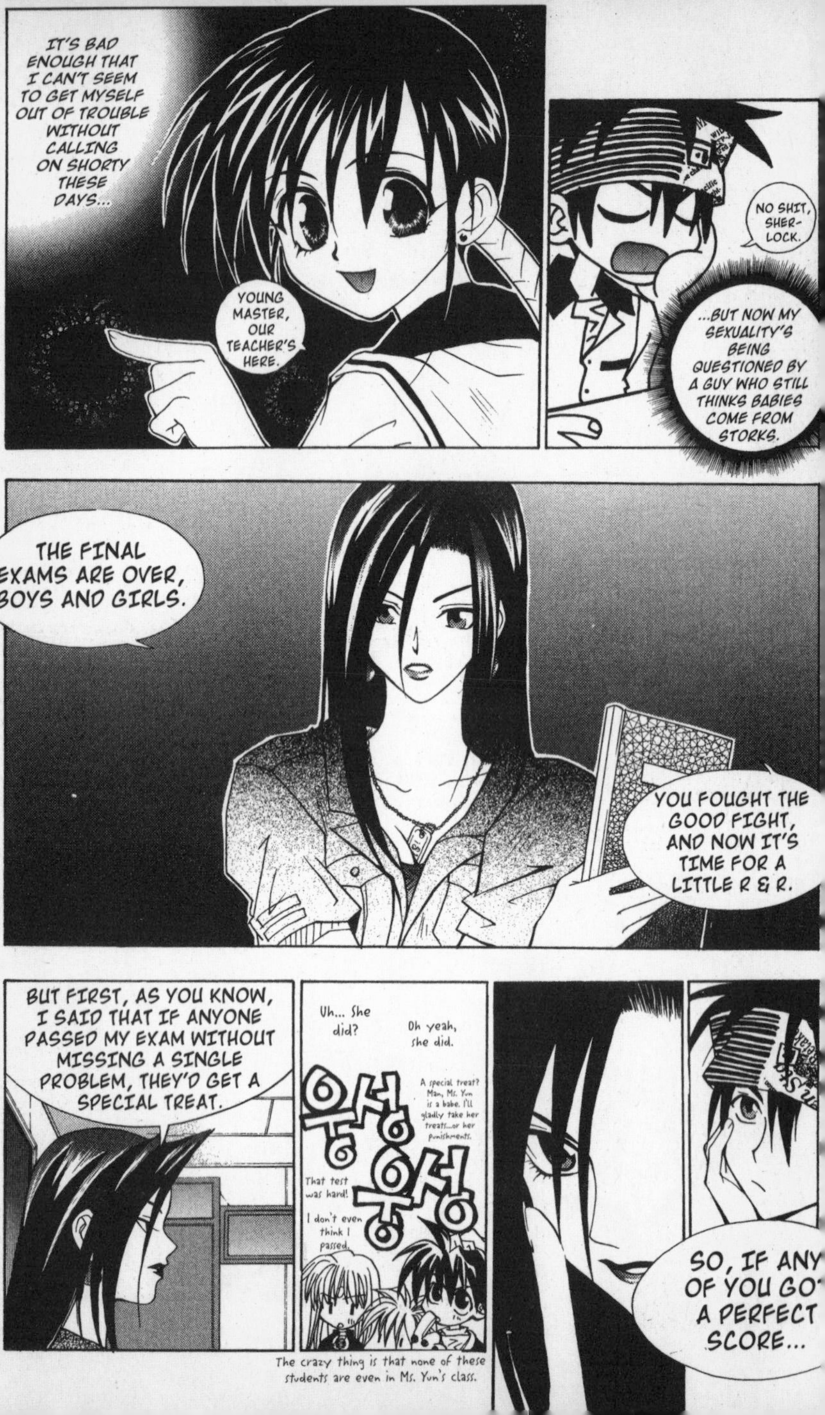
IT'S BAD ENOUGH THAT I CAN'T SEEM TO GET MYSELF OUT OF TROUBLE WITHOUT CALLING ON SHORTY THESE DAYS...
YOUNG MASTER, OUR TEACHER'S HERE.
NO SHIT, SHER-LOCK.
...BUT NOW MY SEXUALITY'S BEING QUESTIONED BY A GUY WHO STILL THINKS BABIES COME FROM STORKS.
THE FINAL EXAMS ARE OVER, BOYS AND GIRLS.
YOU FOUGHT THE GOOD FIGHT, AND NOW IT'S TIME FOR A LITTLE R & R.
BUT FIRST, AS YOU KNOW, I SAID THAT IF ANYONE PASSED MY EXAM WITHOUT MISSING A SINGLE PROBLEM, THEY'D GET A SPECIAL TREAT.
Uh... She did?
Oh yeah, she did.
웅성 웅성
A special treat? Man, Ms. Yun is a babe. I'll gladly take her treats...or her punishments.
That test was hard!
I don't even think I passed.
The crazy thing is that none of these students are even in Ms. Yun's class.
SO, IF ANY OF YOU GO A PERFECT SCORE...

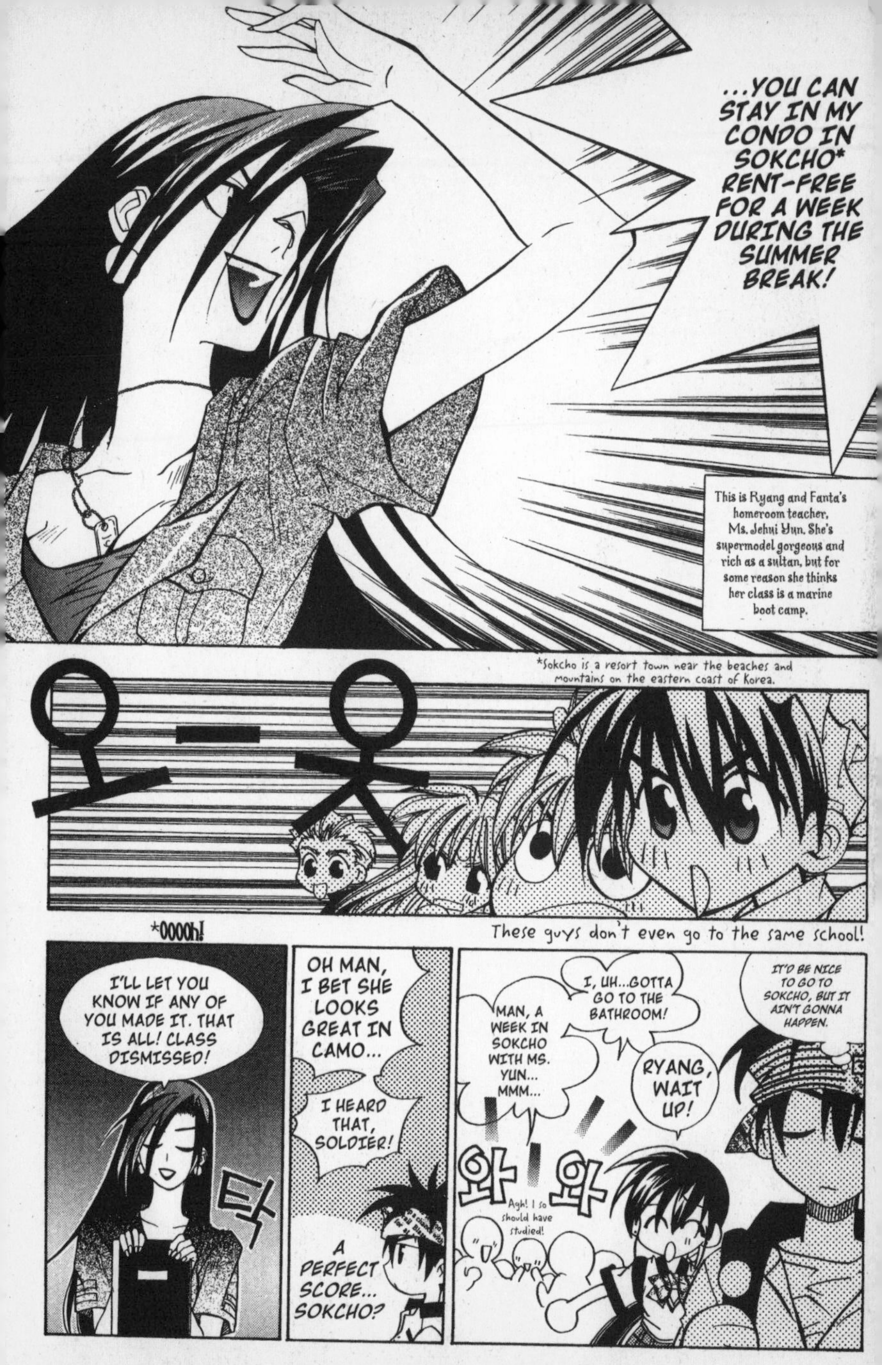
...YOU CAN STAY IN MY CONDO IN SOKCHO* RENT-FREE FOR A WEEK DURING THE SUMMER BREAK!
This is Ryang and Fanta's homeroom teacher, Ms. Jehui Yun. She's supermodel gorgeous and rich as a sultan, but for some reason she thinks her class is a marine boot camp.
*Sokcho is a resort town near the beaches and mountains on the eastern coast of Korea.
오-옷
*Oooh!
These guys don't even go to the same school!
I'LL LET YOU KNOW IF ANY OF YOU MADE IT. THAT IS ALL! CLASS DISMISSED!
탁
OH MAN, I BET SHE LOOKS GREAT IN CAMO...
I HEARD THAT, SOLDIER!
A PERFECT SCORE... SOKCHO?
MAN, A WEEK IN SOKCHO WITH MS. YUN... MMM...
I, UH...GOTTA GO TO THE BATHROOM!
RYANG, WAIT UP!
IT'D BE NICE TO GO TO SOKCHO, BUT IT AIN'T GONNA HAPPEN.
와 와
Agh! I so should have studied!

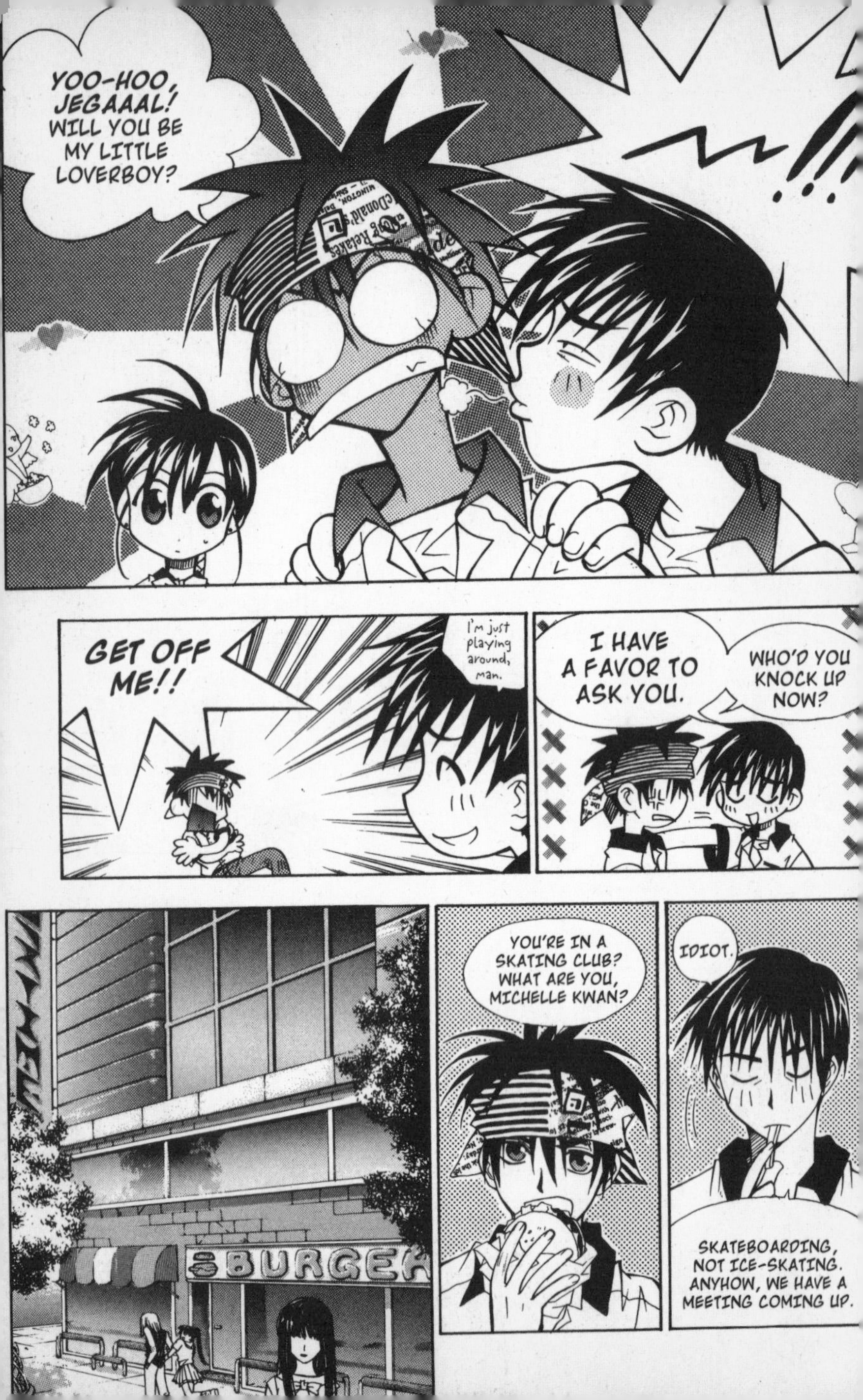

YOO-HOO, JEGAAAL! WILL YOU BE MY LITTLE LOVERBOY?
GET OFF ME!!
I'm just playing around, man.
I HAVE A FAVOR TO ASK YOU.
WHO'D YOU KNOCK UP NOW?
BURGER
YOU'RE IN A SKATING CLUB? WHAT ARE YOU, MICHELLE KWAN?
IDIOT.
SKATEBOARDING, NOT ICE-SKATING. ANYHOW, WE HAVE A MEETING COMING UP.

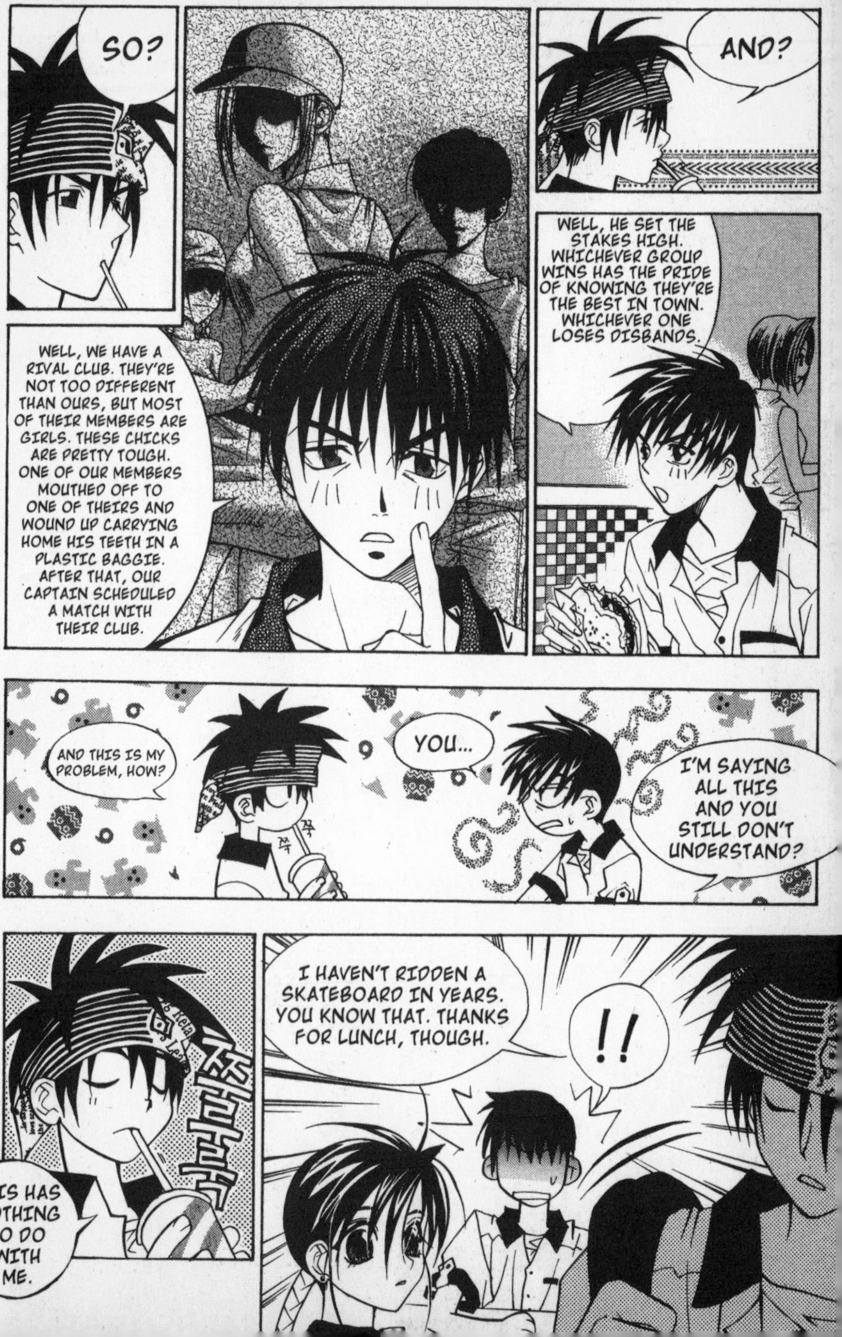
SO?
AND?
WELL, WE HAVE A RIVAL CLUB. THEY'RE NOT TOO DIFFERENT THAN OURS, BUT MOST OF THEIR MEMBERS ARE GIRLS. THESE CHICKS ARE PRETTY TOUGH. ONE OF OUR MEMBERS MOUTHED OFF TO ONE OF THEIRS AND WOUND UP CARRYING HOME HIS TEETH IN A PLASTIC BAGGIE. AFTER THAT, OUR CAPTAIN SCHEDULED A MATCH WITH THEIR CLUB.
WELL, HE SET THE STAKES HIGH. WHICHEVER GROUP WINS HAS THE PRIDE OF KNOWING THEY'RE THE BEST IN TOWN. WHICHEVER ONE LOSES DISBANDS.
AND THIS IS MY PROBLEM, HOW?
YOU...
I'M SAYING ALL THIS AND YOU STILL DON'T UNDERSTAND?
THIS HAS NOTHING TO DO WITH ME.
I HAVEN'T RIDDEN A SKATEBOARD IN YEARS. YOU KNOW THAT. THANKS FOR LUNCH, THOUGH.
!!

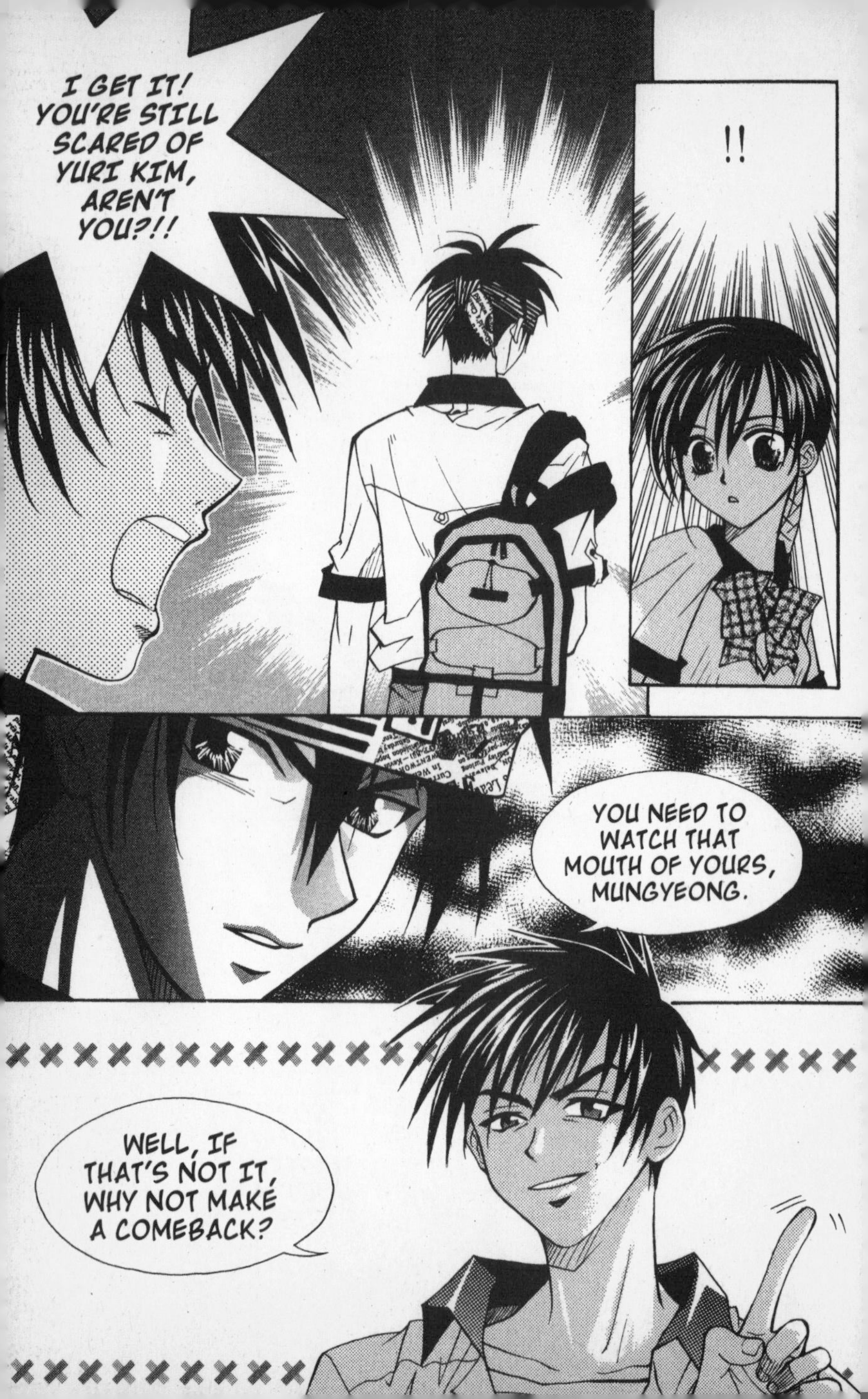
I GET IT! YOU'RE STILL SCARED OF YURI KIM, AREN'T YOU?!!
!!
YOU NEED TO WATCH THAT MOUTH OF YOURS, MUNGYEONG.
WELL, IF THAT'S NOT IT, WHY NOT MAKE A COMEBACK?

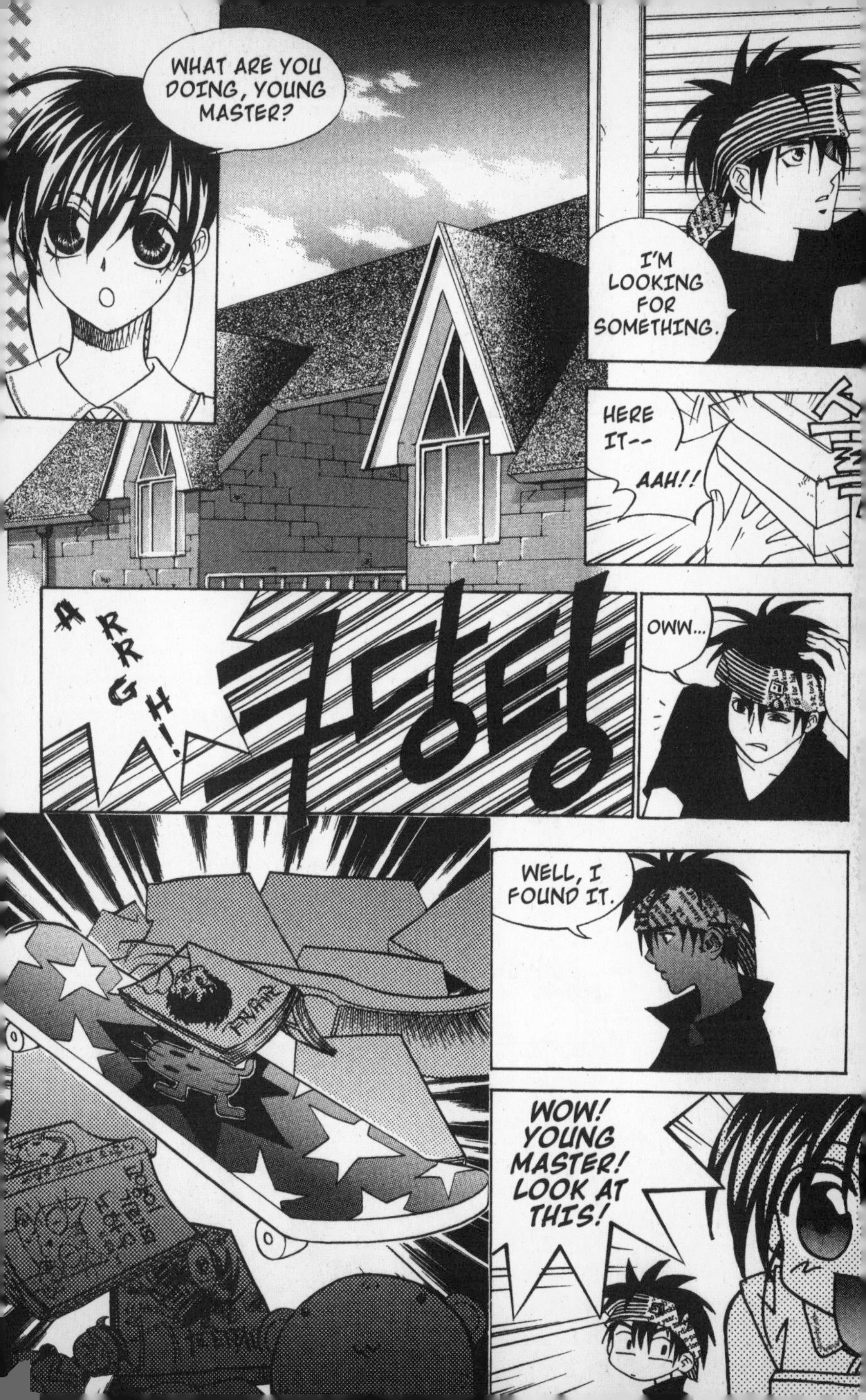
WHAT ARE YOU DOING, YOUNG MASTER?
I'M LOOKING FOR SOMETHING.
HERE IT--
AAH!!
ARRGH!
OWW...
WELL, I FOUND IT.
WOW! YOUNG MASTER! LOOK AT THIS!

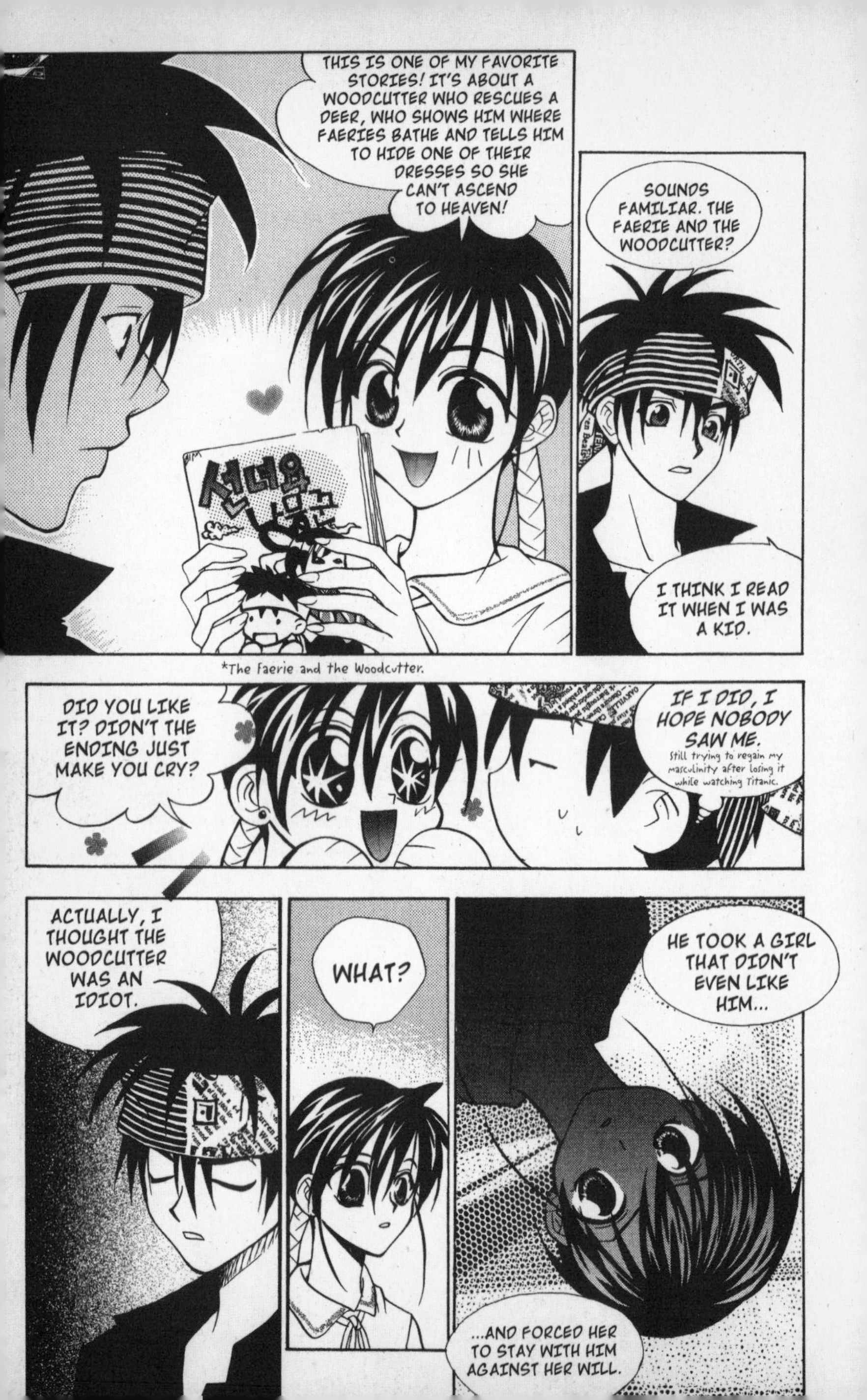
THIS IS ONE OF MY FAVORITE STORIES! IT'S ABOUT A WOODCUTTER WHO RESCUES A DEER, WHO SHOWS HIM WHERE FAERIES BATHE AND TELLS HIM TO HIDE ONE OF THEIR DRESSES SO SHE CAN'T ASCEND TO HEAVEN!
SOUNDS FAMILIAR. THE FAERIE AND THE WOODCUTTER?
I THINK I READ IT WHEN I WAS A KID.
*The Faerie and the Woodcutter.
DID YOU LIKE IT? DIDN'T THE ENDING JUST MAKE YOU CRY?
IF I DID, I HOPE NOBODY SAW ME.
Still trying to regain my masculinity after losing it while watching Titanic.
ACTUALLY, I THOUGHT THE WOODCUTTER WAS AN IDIOT.
WHAT?
HE TOOK A GIRL THAT DIDN'T EVEN LIKE HIM...
...AND FORCED HER TO STAY WITH HIM AGAINST HER WILL.

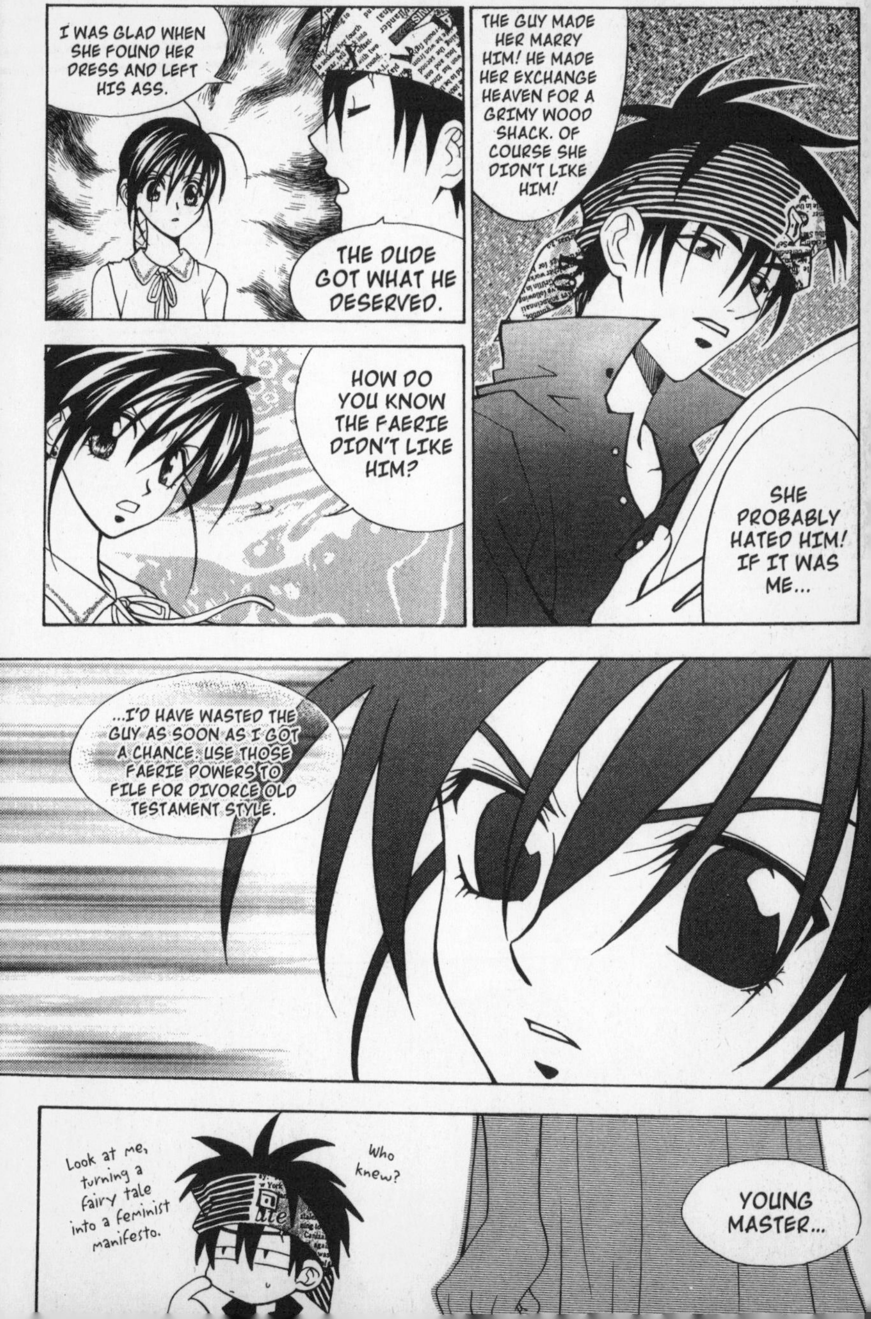
I WAS GLAD WHEN SHE FOUND HER DRESS AND LEFT HIS ASS.
THE DUDE GOT WHAT HE DESERVED.
HOW DO YOU KNOW THE FAERIE DIDN'T LIKE HIM?
THE GUY MADE HER MARRY HIM! HE MADE HER EXCHANGE HEAVEN FOR A GRIMY WOOD SHACK. OF COURSE SHE DIDN'T LIKE HIM!
SHE PROBABLY HATED HIM! IF IT WAS ME...
...I'D HAVE WASTED THE GUY AS SOON AS I GOT A CHANCE. USE THOSE FAERIE POWERS TO FILE FOR DIVORCE OLD TESTAMENT STYLE.
Look at me, turning a fairy tale into a feminist manifesto.
Who knew?
YOUNG MASTER...

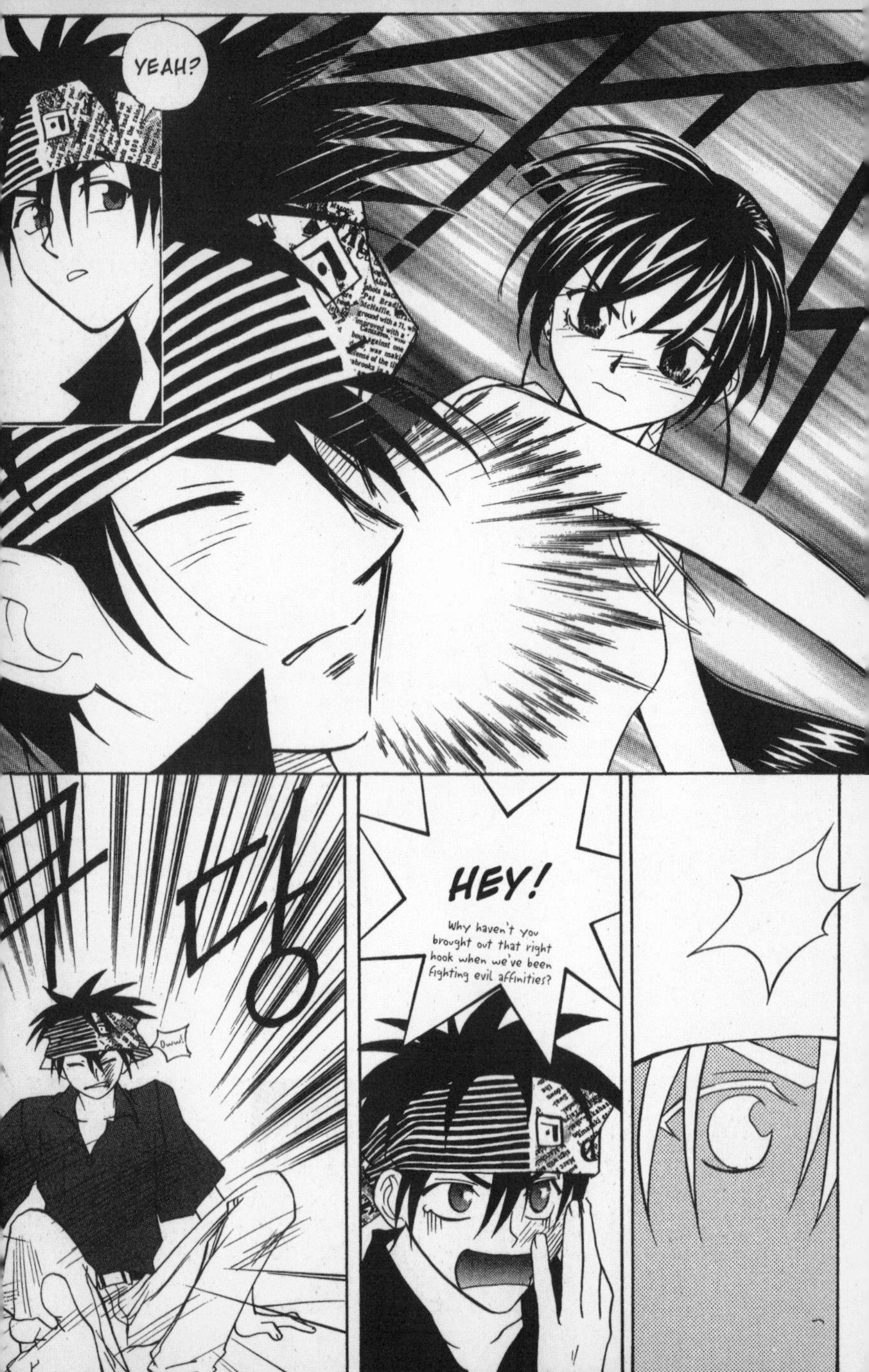
YEAH?
Oww!
HEY!
Why haven't you brought out that right hook when we've been fighting evil affinities?

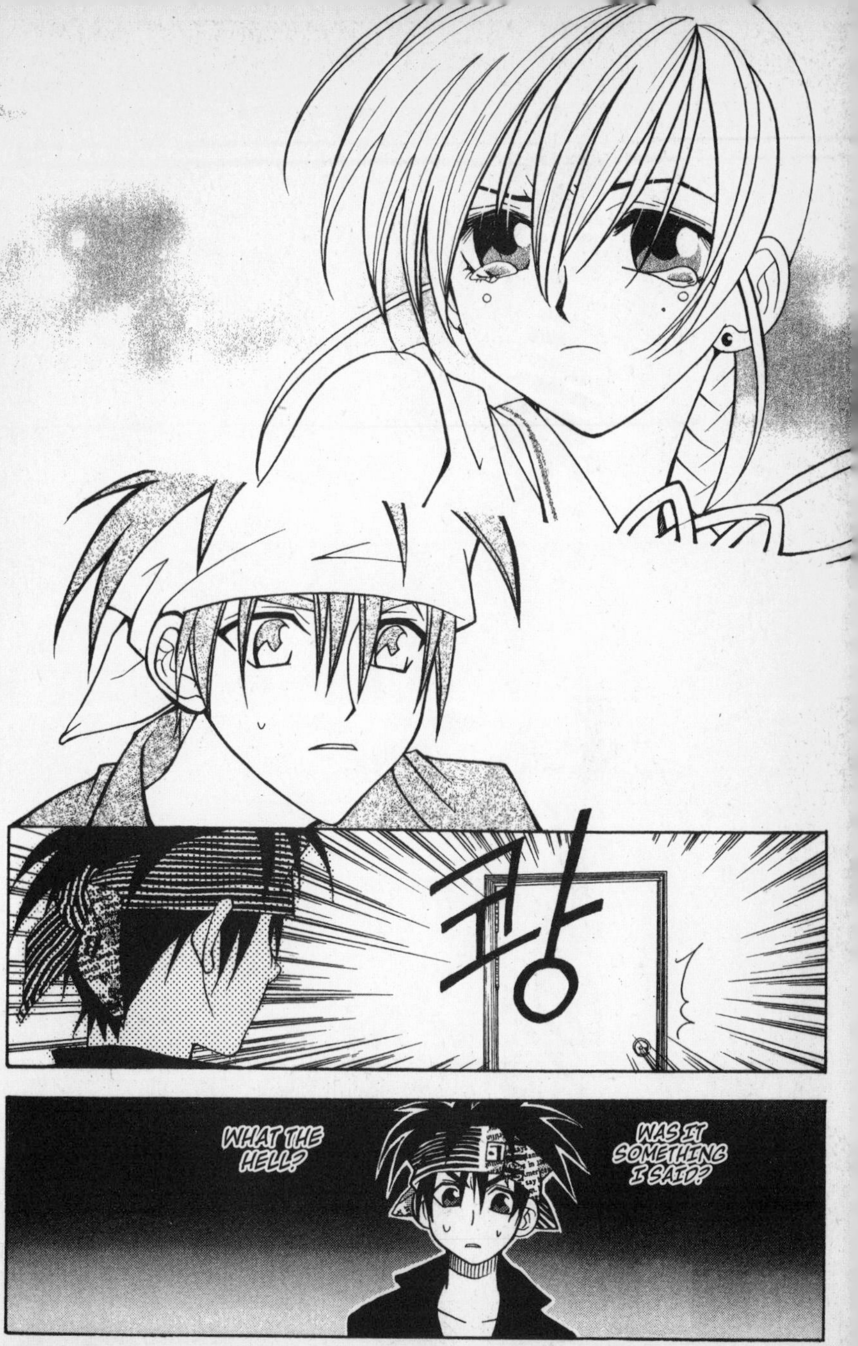
쾅
WHAT THE HELL?
WAS IT SOMETHING I SAID?

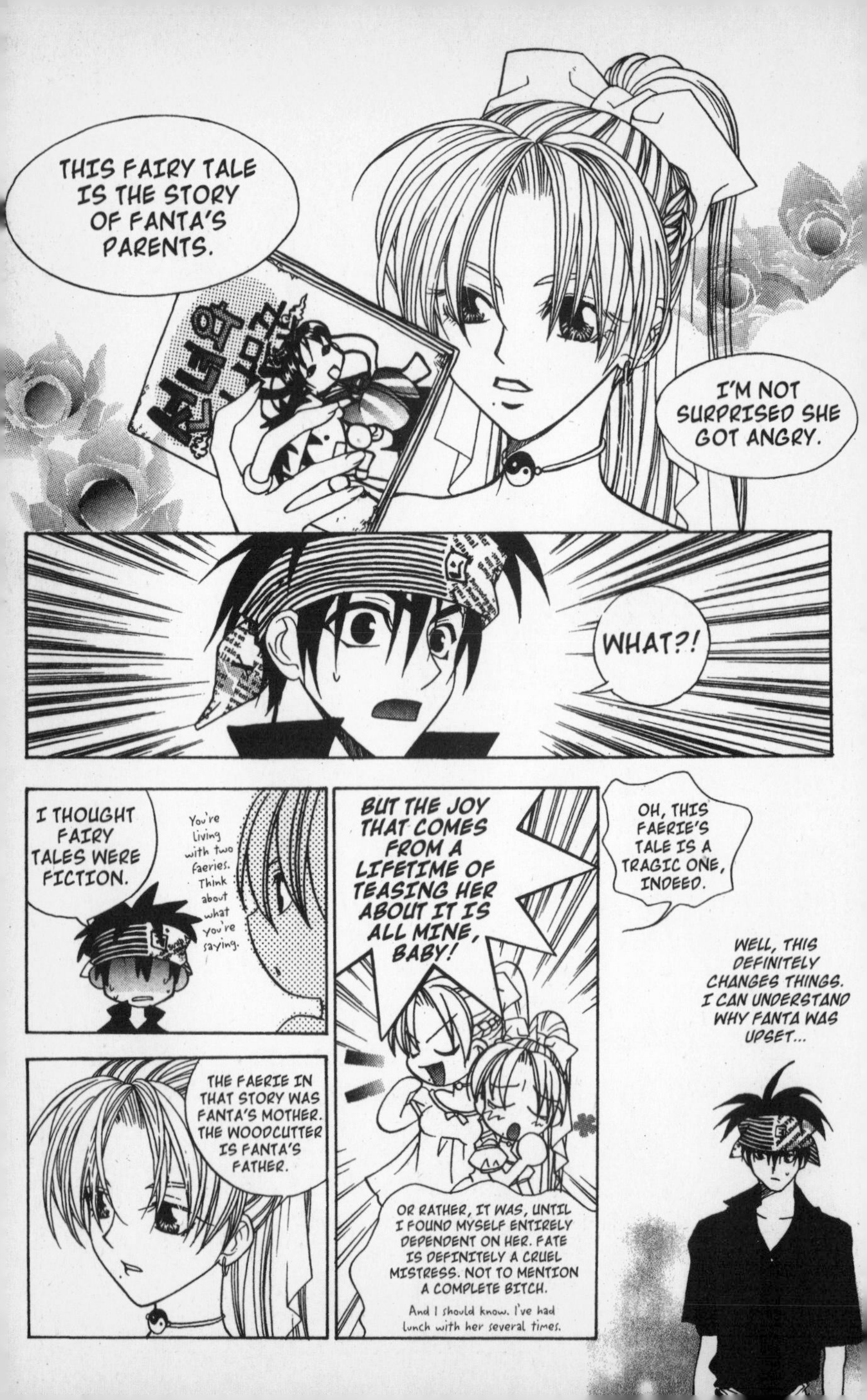
THIS FAIRY TALE IS THE STORY OF FANTA'S PARENTS.
I'M NOT SURPRISED SHE GOT ANGRY.
WHAT?!
I THOUGHT FAIRY TALES WERE FICTION.
You're living with two faeries. Think about what you're saying.
THE FAERIE IN THAT STORY WAS FANTA'S MOTHER. THE WOODCUTTER IS FANTA'S FATHER.
BUT THE JOY THAT COMES FROM A LIFETIME OF TEASING HER ABOUT IT IS ALL MINE, BABY!
OR RATHER, IT WAS, UNTIL I FOUND MYSELF ENTIRELY DEPENDENT ON HER. FATE IS DEFINITELY A CRUEL MISTRESS. NOT TO MENTION A COMPLETE BITCH.
And I should know. I've had lunch with her several times.
OH, THIS FAERIE'S TALE IS A TRAGIC ONE, INDEED.
WELL, THIS DEFINITELY CHANGES THINGS. I CAN UNDERSTAND WHY FANTA WAS UPSET...

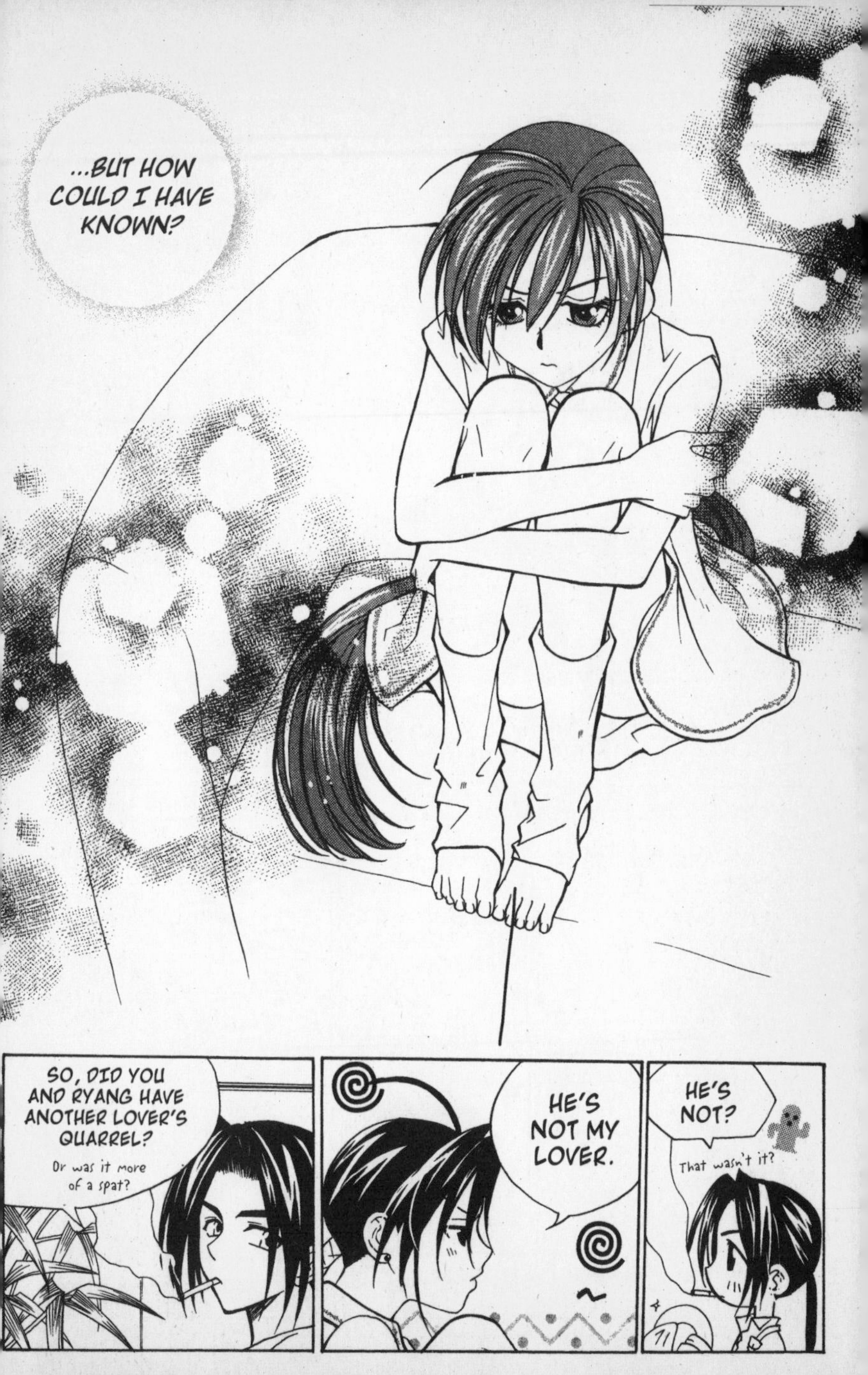
...BUT HOW COULD I HAVE KNOWN?
SO, DID YOU AND RYANG HAVE ANOTHER LOVER'S QUARREL?
Or was it more of a spat?
HE'S NOT MY LOVER.
HE'S NOT?
That wasn't it?

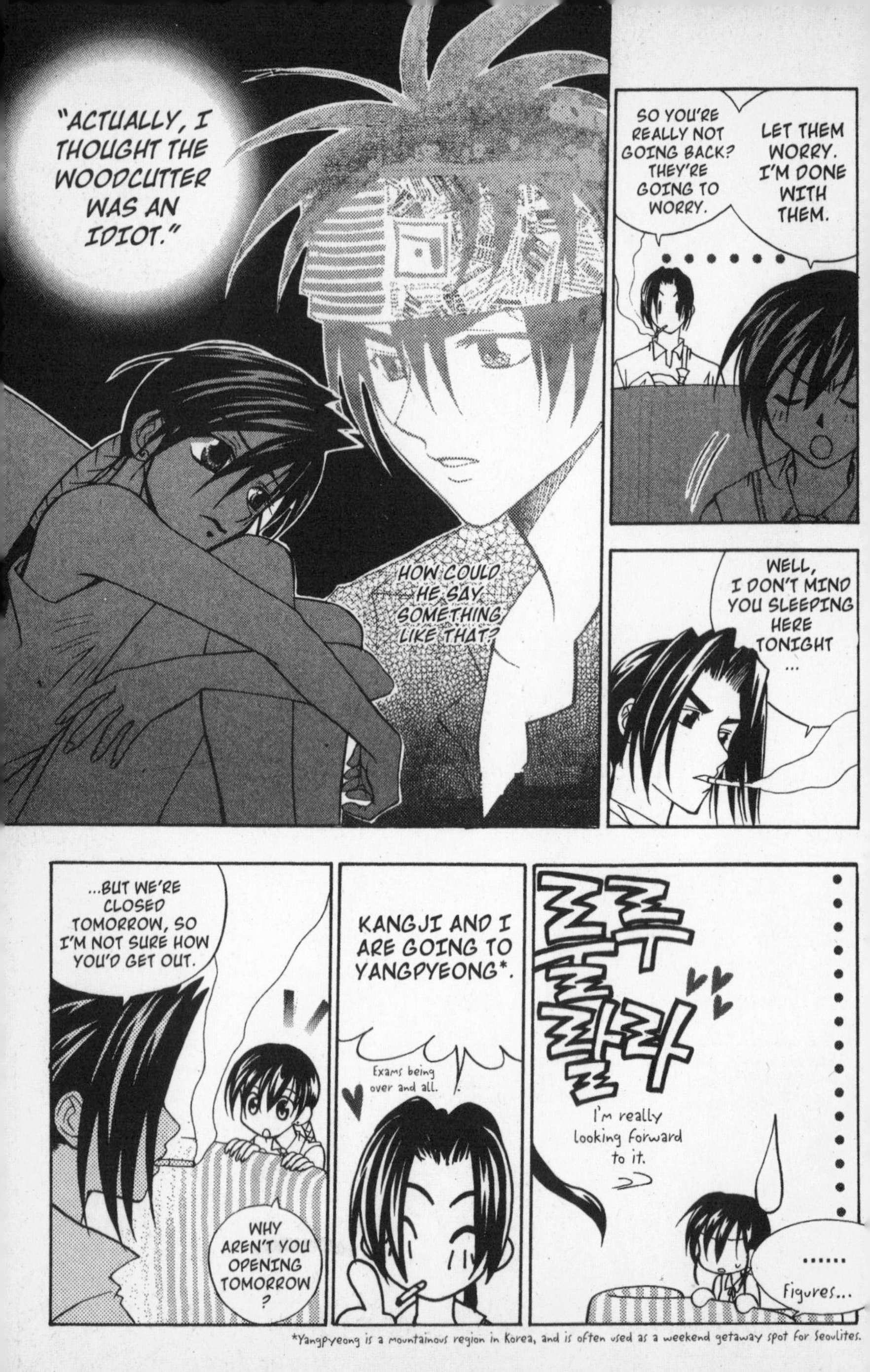
"ACTUALLY, I THOUGHT THE WOODCUTTER WAS AN IDIOT."
HOW COULD HE SAY SOMETHING LIKE THAT?
SO YOU'RE REALLY NOT GOING BACK? THEY'RE GOING TO WORRY.
LET THEM WORRY. I'M DONE WITH THEM.
......
WELL, I DON'T MIND YOU SLEEPING HERE TONIGHT ...
...BUT WE'RE CLOSED TOMORROW, SO I'M NOT SURE HOW YOU'D GET OUT.
WHY AREN'T YOU OPENING TOMORROW ?
KANGJI AND I ARE GOING TO YANGPYEONG*.
Exams being over and all.
I'm really looking forward to it.
......
Figures...

*Yangpyeong is a mountainous region in Korea, and is often used as a weekend getaway spot for Seoulites.

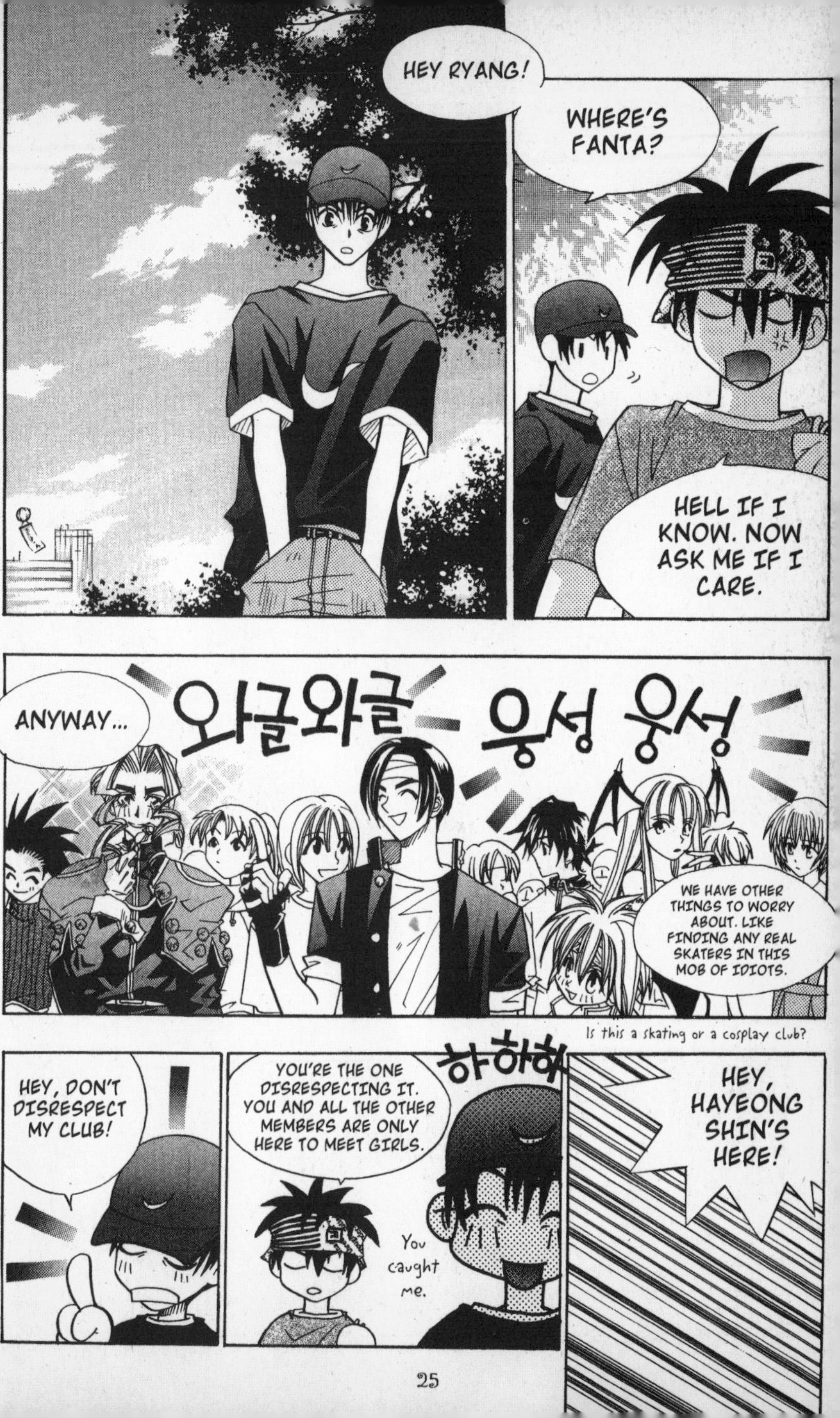
HEY RYANG!
WHERE'S FANTA?
HELL IF I KNOW. NOW ASK ME IF I CARE.
ANYWAY...
와글와글
웅성 웅성
WE HAVE OTHER THINGS TO WORRY ABOUT. LIKE FINDING ANY REAL SKATERS IN THIS MOB OF IDIOTS.
Is this a skating or a cosplay club?
HEY, DON'T DISRESPECT MY CLUB!
YOU'RE THE ONE DISRESPECTING IT. YOU AND ALL THE OTHER MEMBERS ARE ONLY HERE TO MEET GIRLS.
하하하
You caught me.
HEY, HAYEONG SHIN'S HERE!

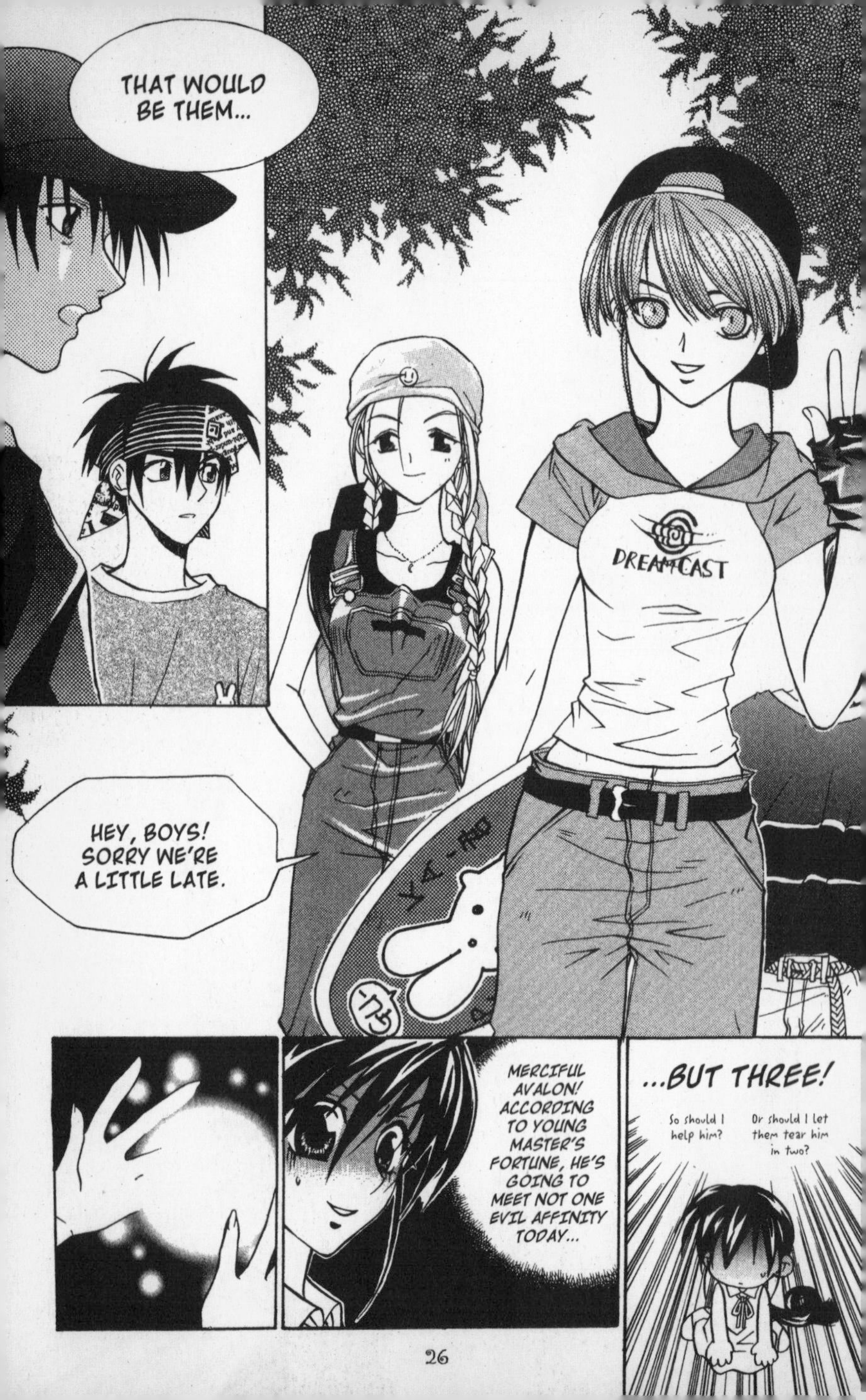
THAT WOULD BE THEM...
HEY, BOYS! SORRY WE'RE A LITTLE LATE.
DREAMCAST
MERCIFUL AVALON! ACCORDING TO YOUNG MASTER'S FORTUNE, HE'S GOING TO MEET NOT ONE EVIL AFFINITY TODAY...
...BUT THREE!
So should I help him?
Or should I let them tear him in two?

Episode 18 The Calm Before the Storm ①

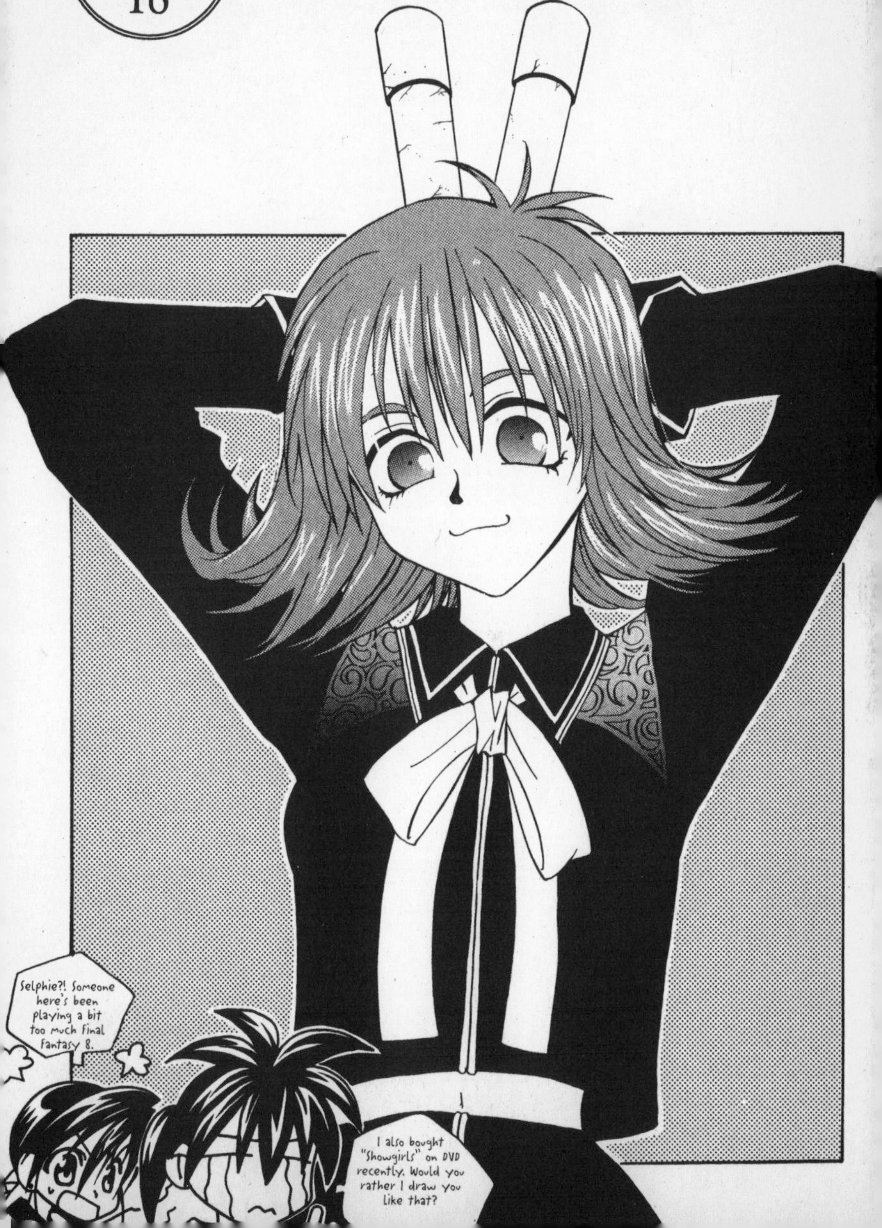
Selphie?! Someone here's been playing a bit too much Final Fantasy 8.
I also bought "Showgirls" on DVD recently. Would you rather I draw you like that?

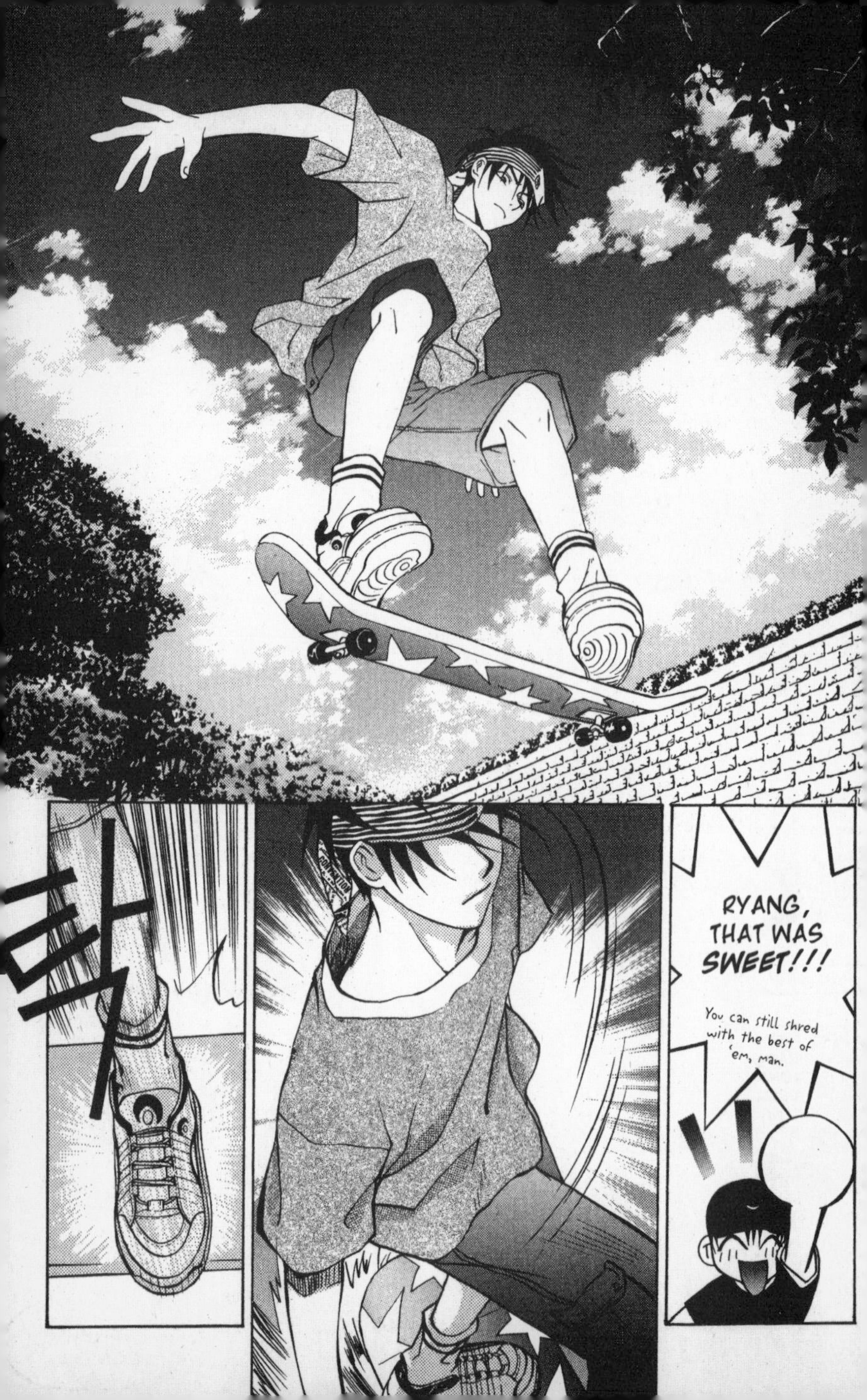
RYANG, THAT WAS SWEET!!!
You can still shred with the best of 'em, man.

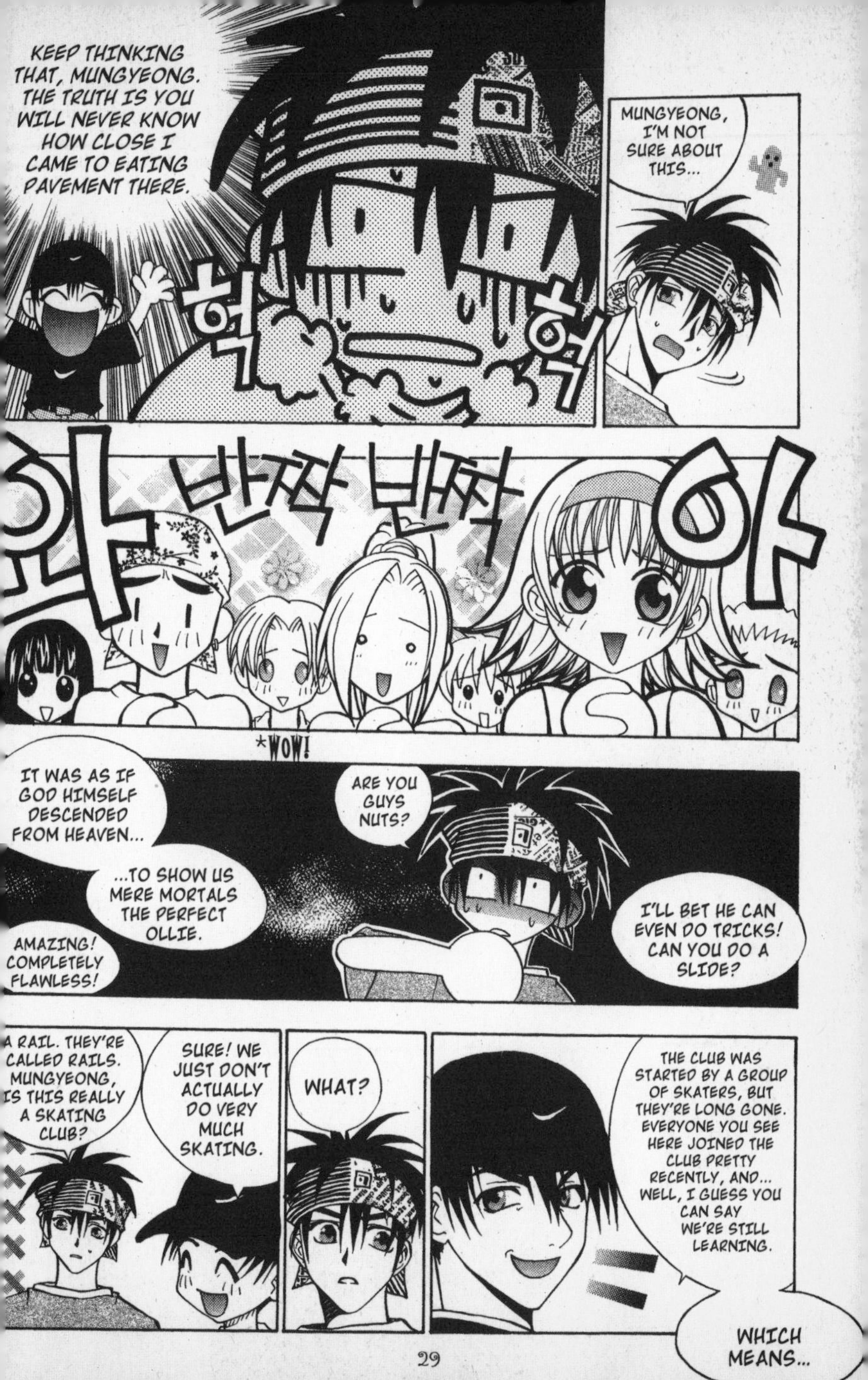
KEEP THINKING THAT, MUNGYEONG. THE TRUTH IS YOU WILL NEVER KNOW HOW CLOSE I CAME TO EATING PAVEMENT THERE.
헉
헉
MUNGYEONG, I'M NOT SURE ABOUT THIS...
와
반짝 반짝
아
*WOW!
IT WAS AS IF GOD HIMSELF DESCENDED FROM HEAVEN...
...TO SHOW US MERE MORTALS THE PERFECT OLLIE.
AMAZING! COMPLETELY FLAWLESS!
ARE YOU GUYS NUTS?
I'LL BET HE CAN EVEN DO TRICKS! CAN YOU DO A SLIDE?
A RAIL. THEY'RE CALLED RAILS. MUNGYEONG, IS THIS REALLY A SKATING CLUB?
SURE! WE JUST DON'T ACTUALLY DO VERY MUCH SKATING.
WHAT?
THE CLUB WAS STARTED BY A GROUP OF SKATERS, BUT THEY'RE LONG GONE. EVERYONE YOU SEE HERE JOINED THE CLUB PRETTY RECENTLY, AND... WELL, I GUESS YOU CAN SAY WE'RE STILL LEARNING.
WHICH MEANS...

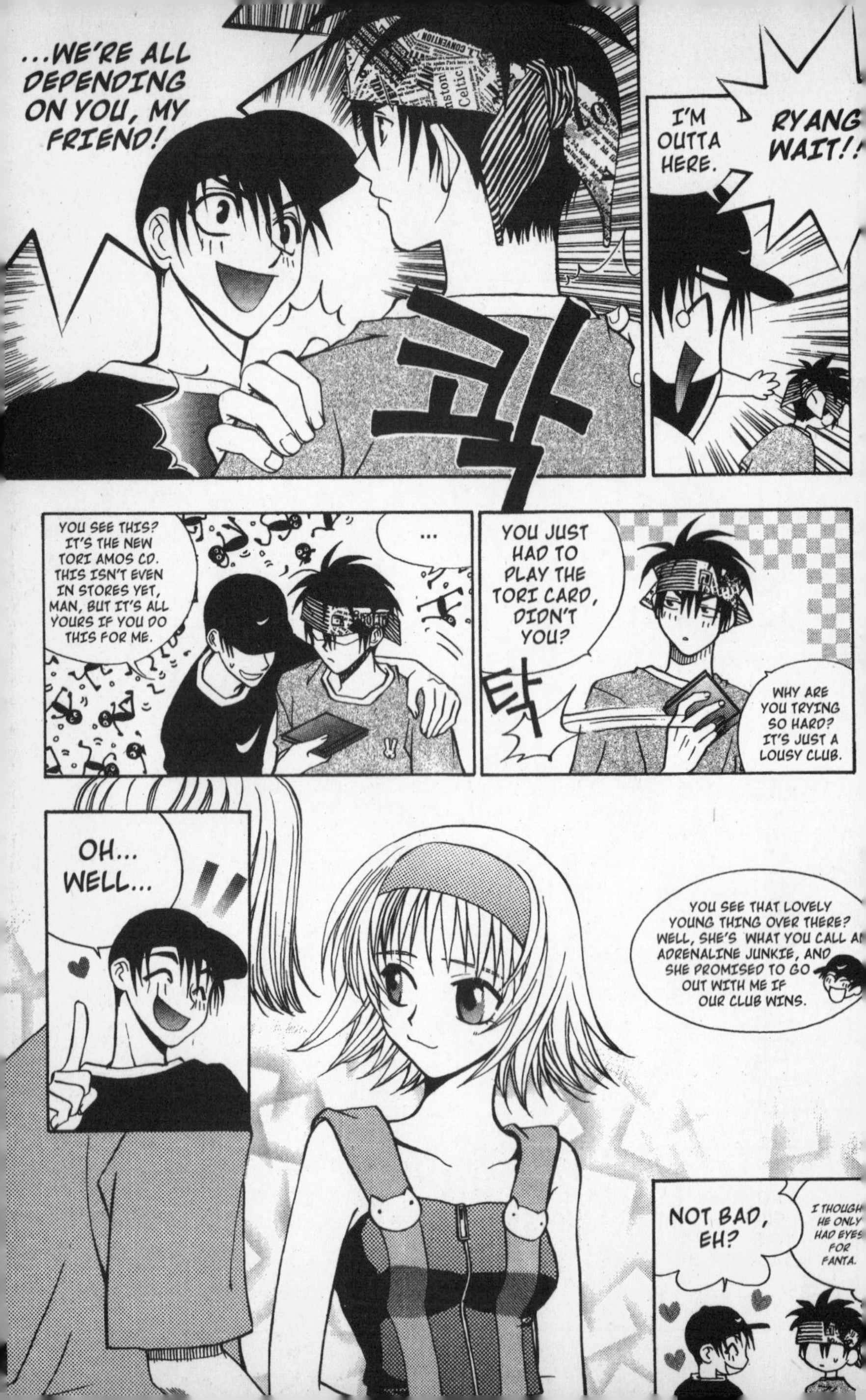
...WE'RE ALL DEPENDING ON YOU, MY FRIEND!
콱
I'M OUTTA HERE.
RYANG WAIT!!
YOU SEE THIS? IT'S THE NEW TORI AMOS CD. THIS ISN'T EVEN IN STORES YET, MAN, BUT IT'S ALL YOURS IF YOU DO THIS FOR ME.
...
YOU JUST HAD TO PLAY THE TORI CARD, DIDN'T YOU?
탁
WHY ARE YOU TRYING SO HARD? IT'S JUST A LOUSY CLUB.
OH... WELL...
YOU SEE THAT LOVELY YOUNG THING OVER THERE? WELL, SHE'S WHAT YOU CALL A ADRENALINE JUNKIE, AND SHE PROMISED TO GO OUT WITH ME IF OUR CLUB WINS.
NOT BAD, EH?
I THOUGH HE ONLY HAD EYES FOR FANTA.

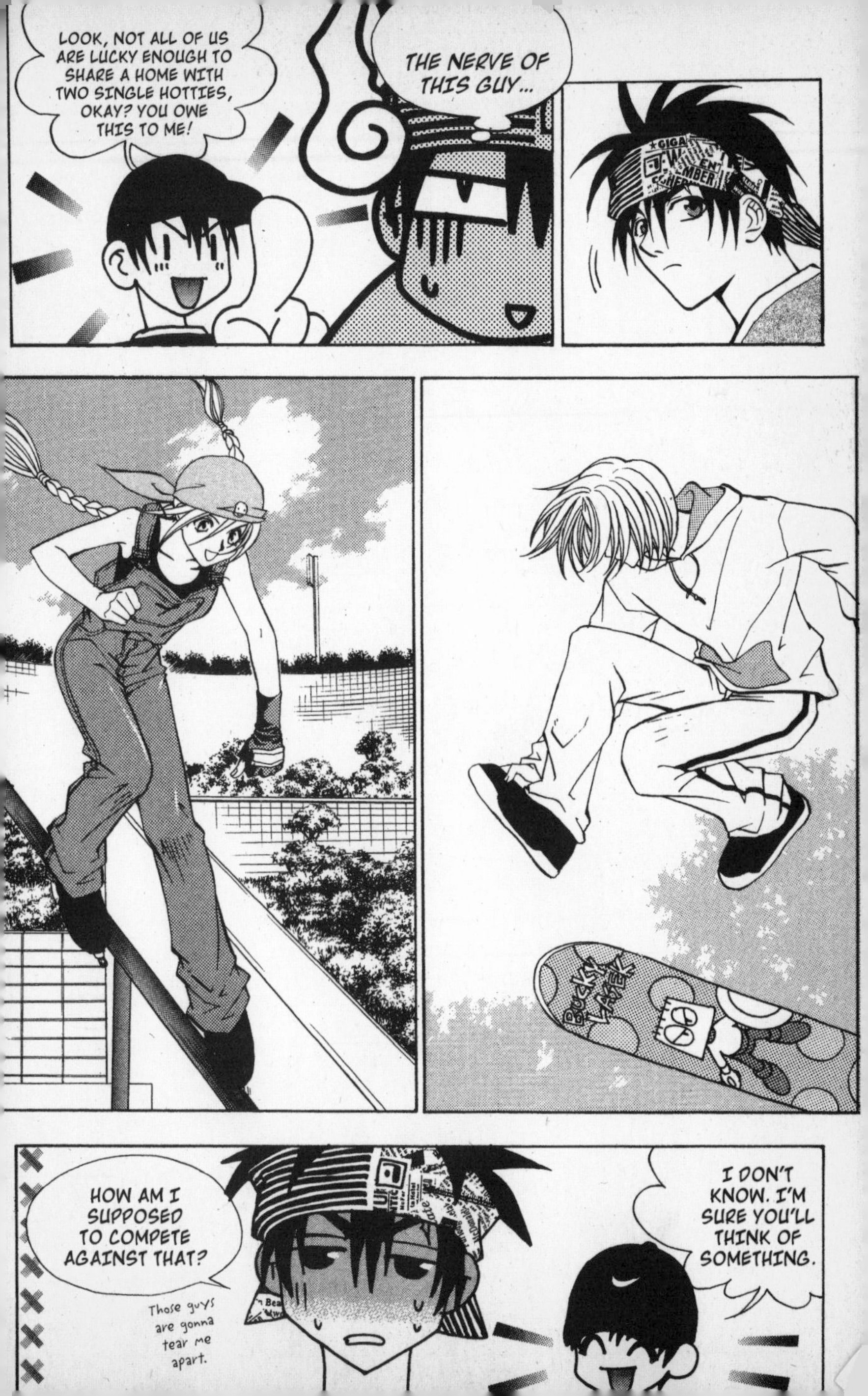
LOOK, NOT ALL OF US ARE LUCKY ENOUGH TO SHARE A HOME WITH TWO SINGLE HOTTIES, OKAY? YOU OWE THIS TO ME!
THE NERVE OF THIS GUY...
HOW AM I SUPPOSED TO COMPETE AGAINST THAT?
Those guys are gonna tear me apart.
I DON'T KNOW. I'M SURE YOU'LL THINK OF SOMETHING.

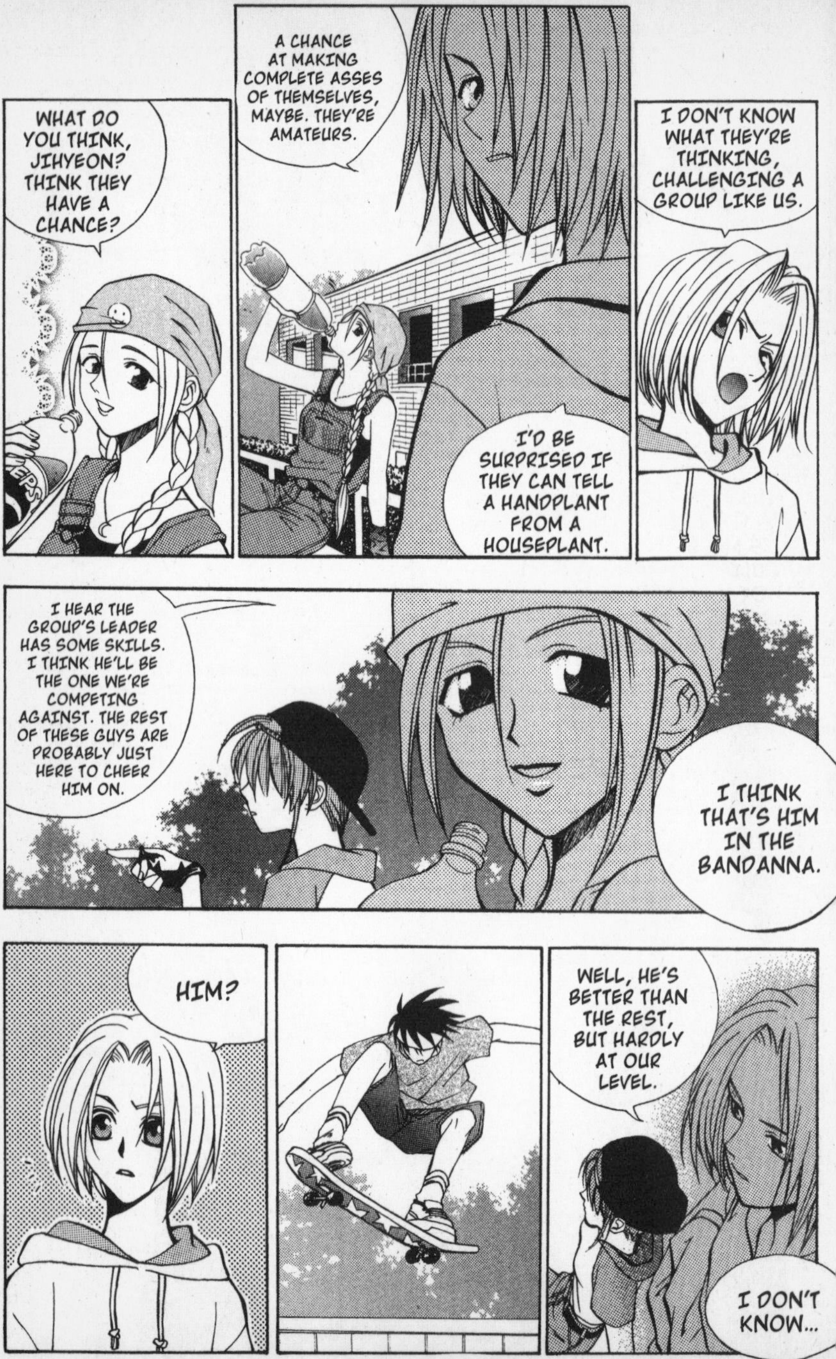
WHAT DO YOU THINK, JIHYEON? THINK THEY HAVE A CHANCE?
A CHANCE AT MAKING COMPLETE ASSES OF THEMSELVES, MAYBE. THEY'RE AMATEURS.
I'D BE SURPRISED IF THEY CAN TELL A HANDPLANT FROM A HOUSEPLANT.
I DON'T KNOW WHAT THEY'RE THINKING, CHALLENGING A GROUP LIKE US.
I HEAR THE GROUP'S LEADER HAS SOME SKILLS. I THINK HE'LL BE THE ONE WE'RE COMPETING AGAINST. THE REST OF THESE GUYS ARE PROBABLY JUST HERE TO CHEER HIM ON.
I THINK THAT'S HIM IN THE BANDANNA.
HIM?
WELL, HE'S BETTER THAN THE REST, BUT HARDLY AT OUR LEVEL.
I DON'T KNOW...

Ryang is the ollie king. Too bad he can't do much else.

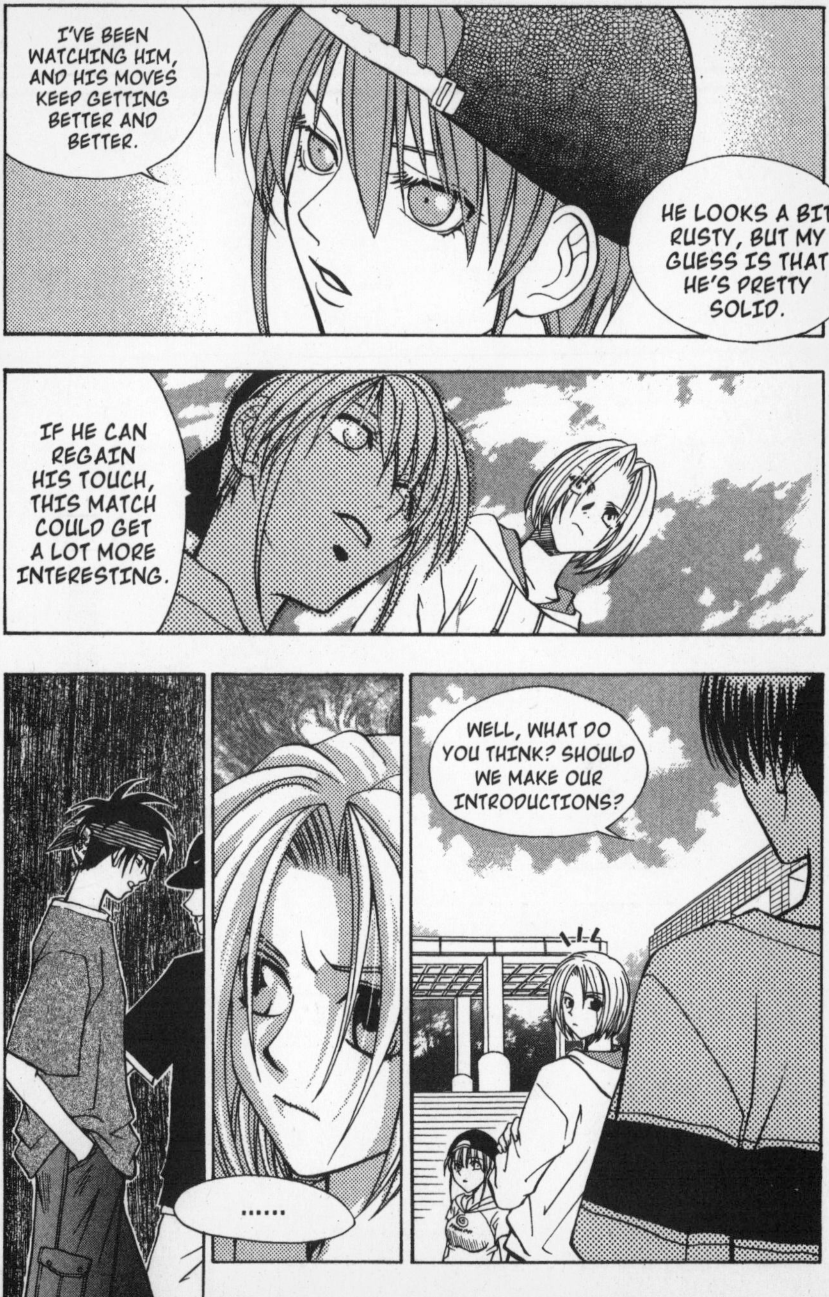

I'VE BEEN WATCHING HIM, AND HIS MOVES KEEP GETTING BETTER AND BETTER.
HE LOOKS A BIT RUSTY, BUT MY GUESS IS THAT HE'S PRETTY SOLID.
IF HE CAN REGAIN HIS TOUCH, THIS MATCH COULD GET A LOT MORE INTERESTING.
......
WELL, WHAT DO YOU THINK? SHOULD WE MAKE OUR INTRODUCTIONS?

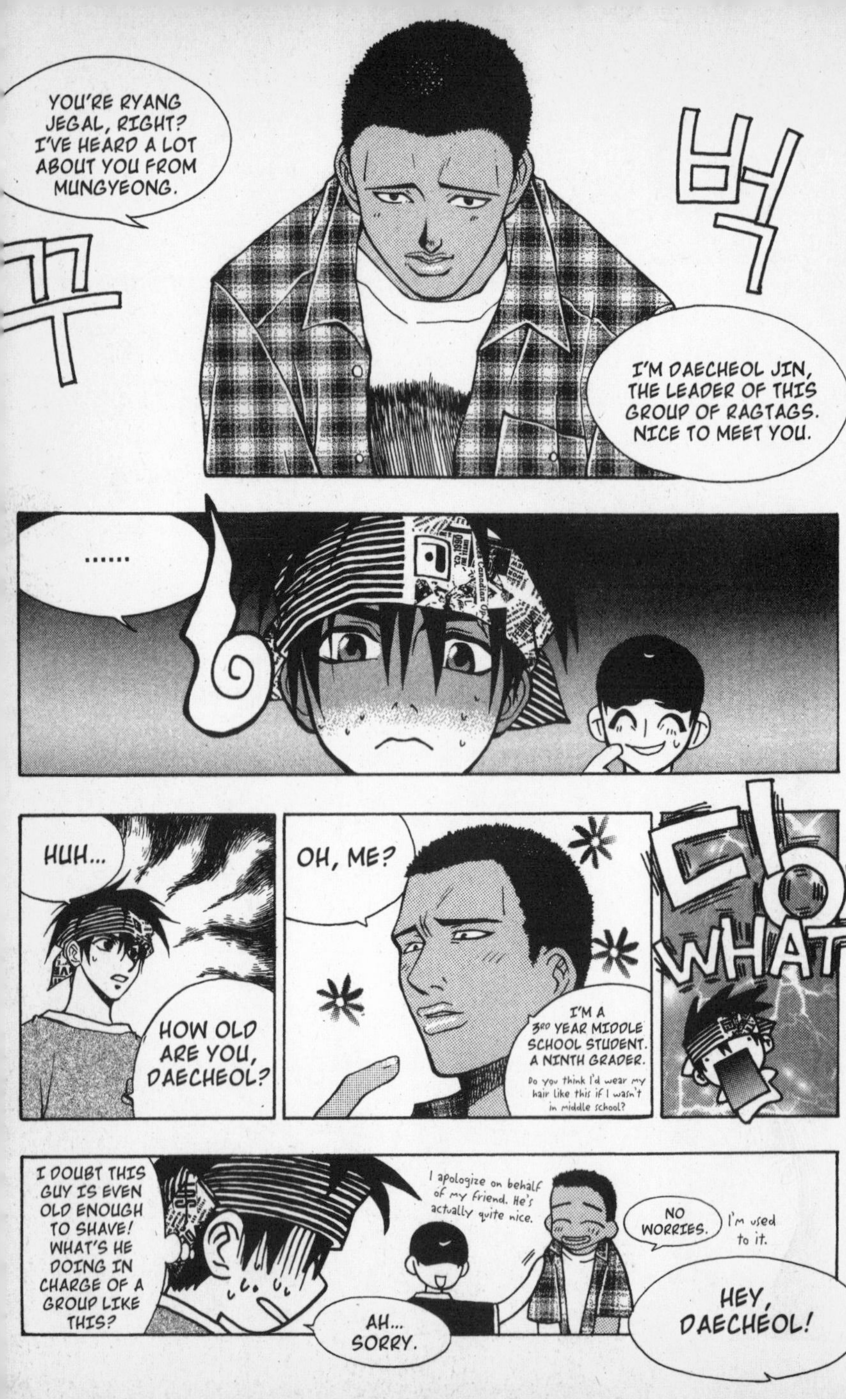
YOU'RE RYANG JEGAL, RIGHT? I'VE HEARD A LOT ABOUT YOU FROM MUNGYEONG.
꾸
벅
I'M DAECHEOL JIN, THE LEADER OF THIS GROUP OF RAGTAGS. NICE TO MEET YOU.
......
HUH...
HOW OLD ARE YOU, DAECHEOL?
OH, ME?
I'M A 3RD YEAR MIDDLE SCHOOL STUDENT. A NINTH GRADER.
Do you think I'd wear my hair like this if I wasn't in middle school?
WHAT
I DOUBT THIS GUY IS EVEN OLD ENOUGH TO SHAVE! WHAT'S HE DOING IN CHARGE OF A GROUP LIKE THIS?
HEY, DAECHEOL!
AH... SORRY.
I apologize on behalf of my friend. He's actually quite nice.
NO WORRIES.
I'm used to it.

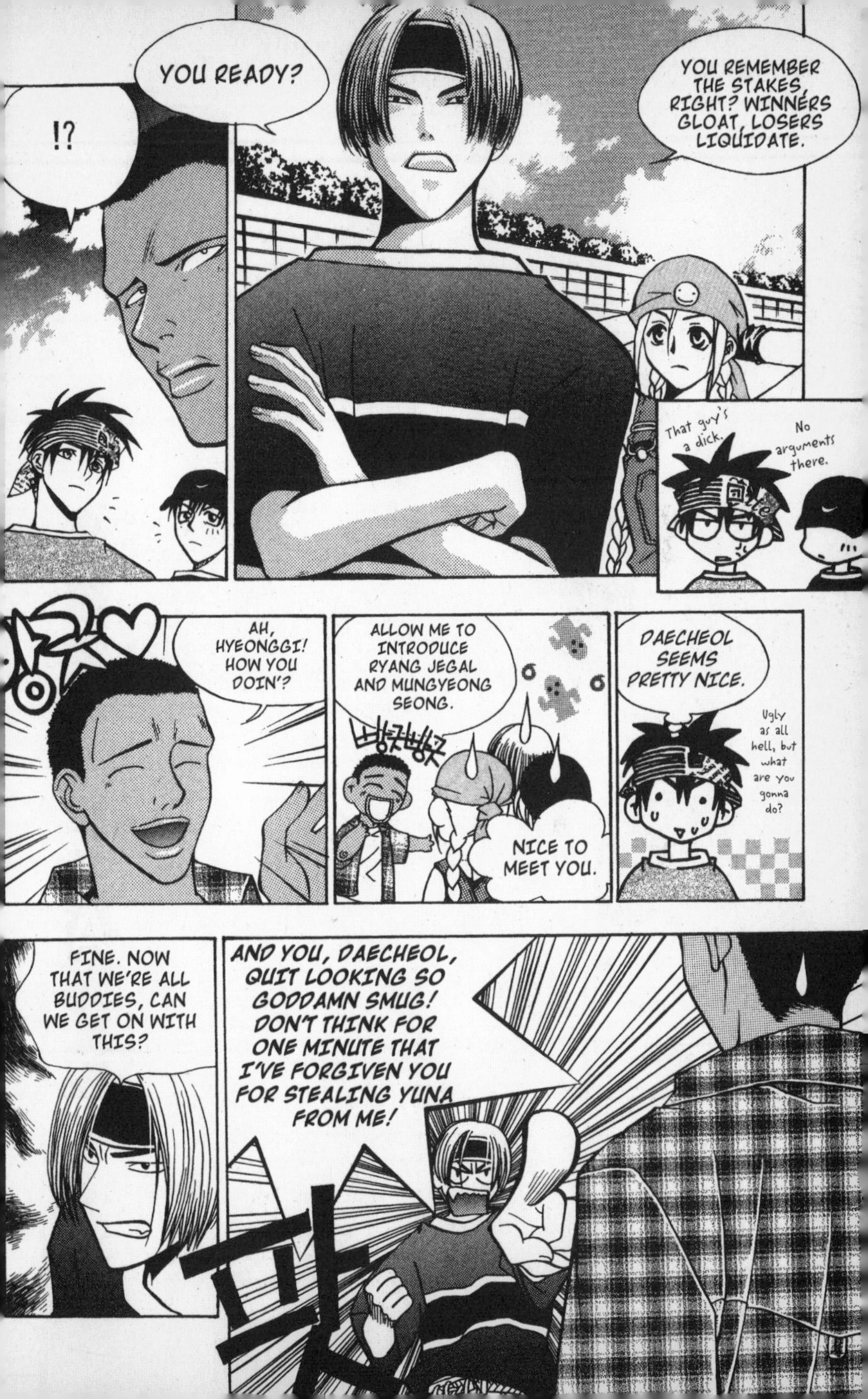
!?
YOU READY?
YOU REMEMBER THE STAKES, RIGHT? WINNERS GLOAT, LOSERS LIQUIDATE.
That guy's a dick.
No arguments there.
AH, HYEONGGI! HOW YOU DOIN'?
ALLOW ME TO INTRODUCE RYANG JEGAL AND MUNGYEONG SEONG.
NICE TO MEET YOU.
DAECHEOL SEEMS PRETTY NICE.
Ugly as all hell, but what are you gonna do?
FINE. NOW THAT WE'RE ALL BUDDIES, CAN WE GET ON WITH THIS?
AND YOU, DAECHEOL, QUIT LOOKING SO GODDAMN SMUG! DON'T THINK FOR ONE MINUTE THAT I'VE FORGIVEN YOU FOR STEALING YUNA FROM ME!

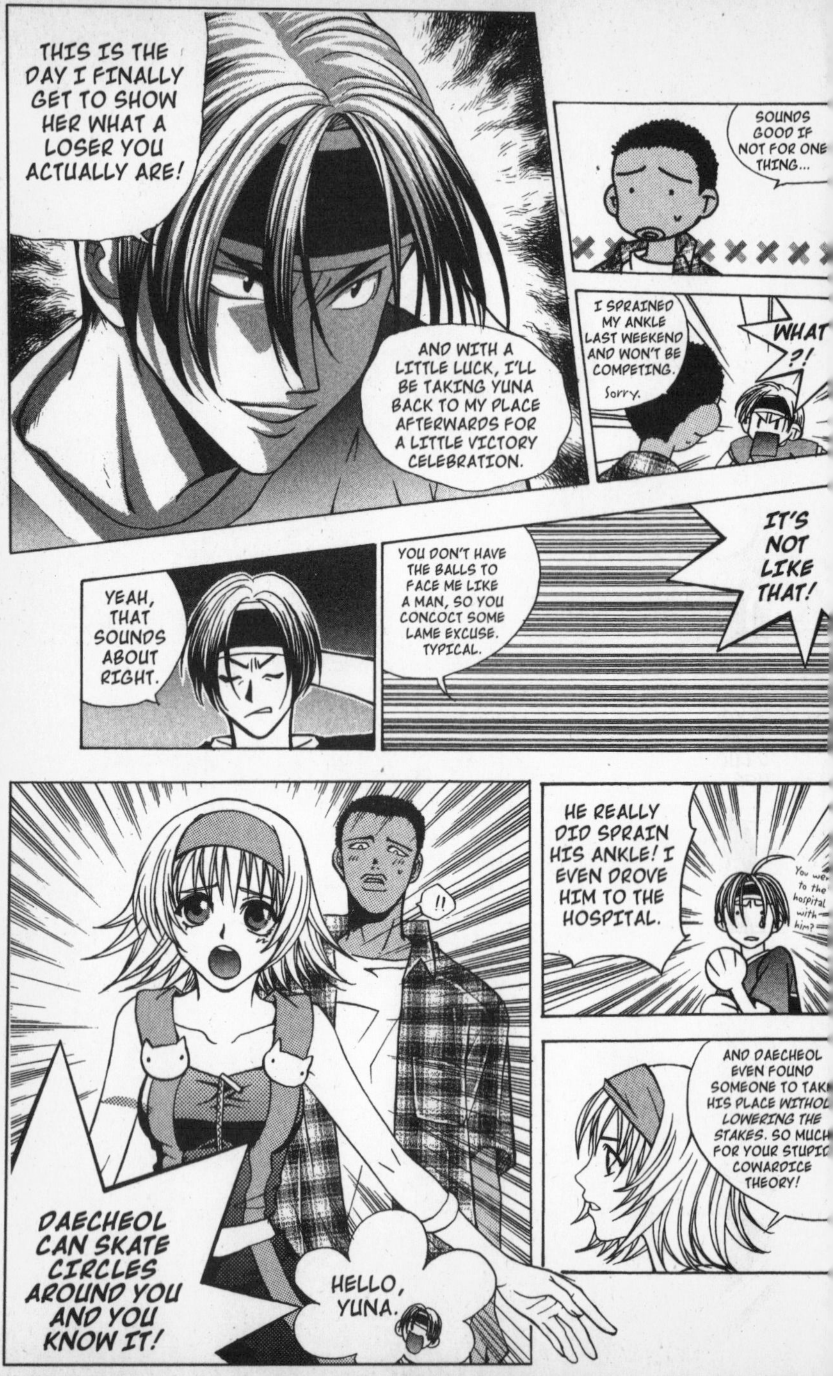
THIS IS THE DAY I FINALLY GET TO SHOW HER WHAT A LOSER YOU ACTUALLY ARE!
AND WITH A LITTLE LUCK, I'LL BE TAKING YUNA BACK TO MY PLACE AFTERWARDS FOR A LITTLE VICTORY CELEBRATION.
SOUNDS GOOD IF NOT FOR ONE THING...
I SPRAINED MY ANKLE LAST WEEKEND AND WON'T BE COMPETING.
Sorry.
WHAT?!
YEAH, THAT SOUNDS ABOUT RIGHT.
YOU DON'T HAVE THE BALLS TO FACE ME LIKE A MAN, SO YOU CONCOCT SOME LAME EXCUSE. TYPICAL.
IT'S NOT LIKE THAT!
!!
DAECHEOL CAN SKATE CIRCLES AROUND YOU AND YOU KNOW IT!
HELLO, YUNA.
HE REALLY DID SPRAIN HIS ANKLE! I EVEN DROVE HIM TO THE HOSPITAL.
You wer to the hospital with him?
AND DAECHEOL EVEN FOUND SOMEONE TO TAK HIS PLACE WITHOU LOWERING THE STAKES. SO MUCH FOR YOUR STUPID COWARDICE THEORY!

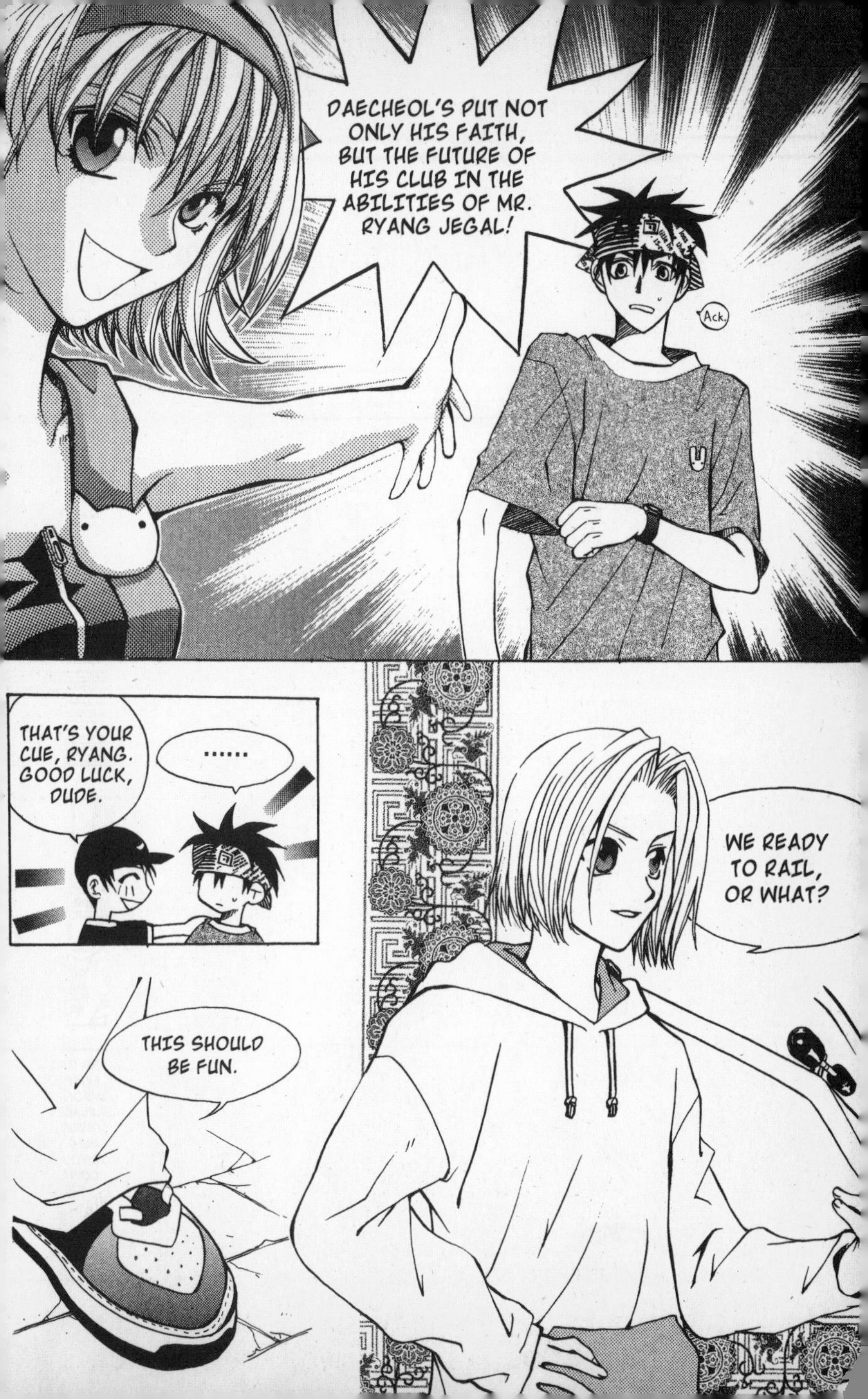
DAECHEOL'S PUT NOT ONLY HIS FAITH, BUT THE FUTURE OF HIS CLUB IN THE ABILITIES OF MR. RYANG JEGAL!
Ack.
THAT'S YOUR CUE, RYANG. GOOD LUCK, DUDE.
......
THIS SHOULD BE FUN.
WE READY TO RAIL, OR WHAT?

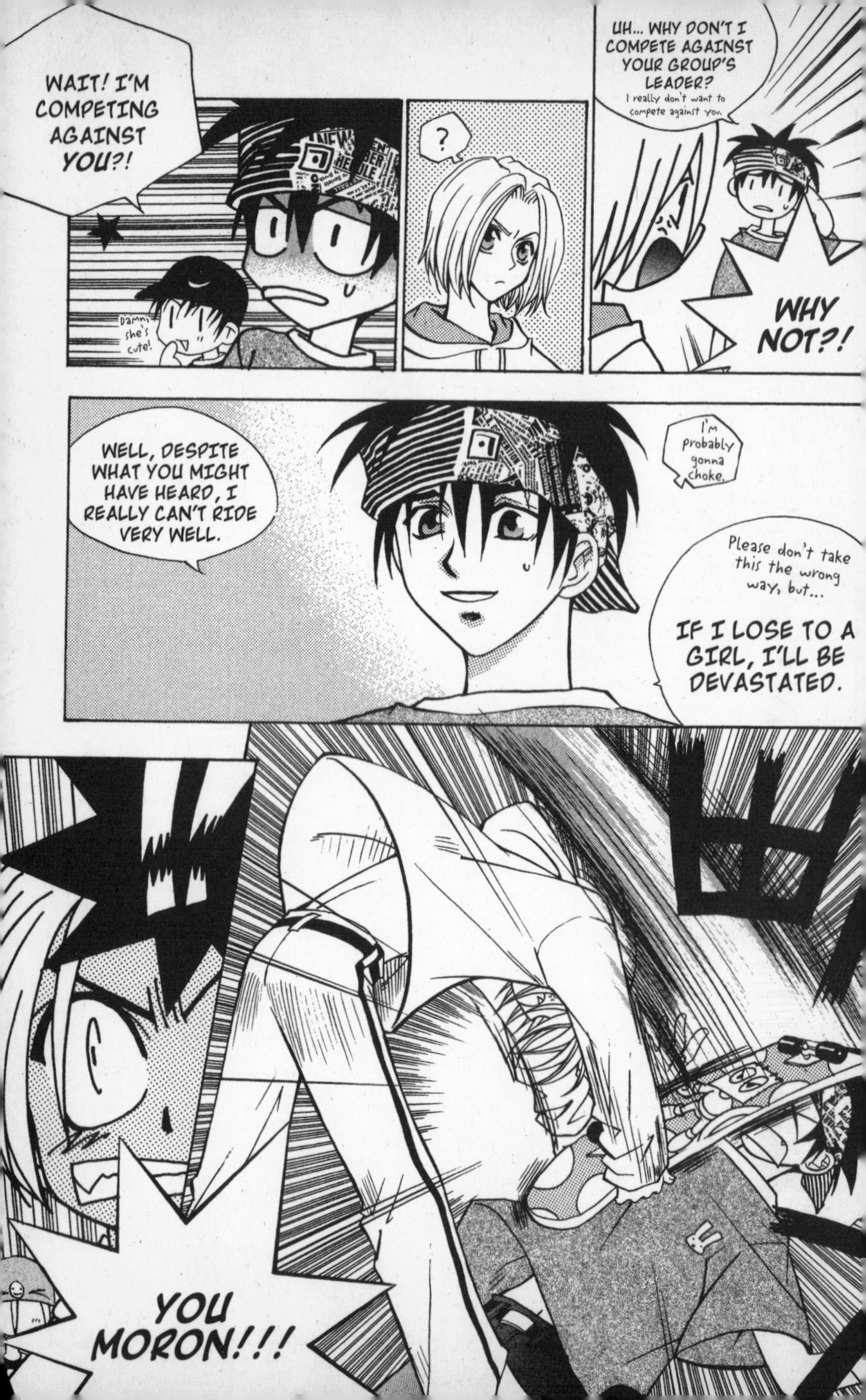
WAIT! I'M COMPETING AGAINST YOU?!
Damn she's cute!
?
UH... WHY DON'T I COMPETE AGAINST YOUR GROUP'S LEADER?
I really don't want to compete against you.
WHY NOT?!
WELL, DESPITE WHAT YOU MIGHT HAVE HEARD, I REALLY CAN'T RIDE VERY WELL.
I'm probably gonna choke.
Please don't take this the wrong way, but...
IF I LOSE TO A GIRL, I'LL BE DEVASTATED.
YOU MORON!!!

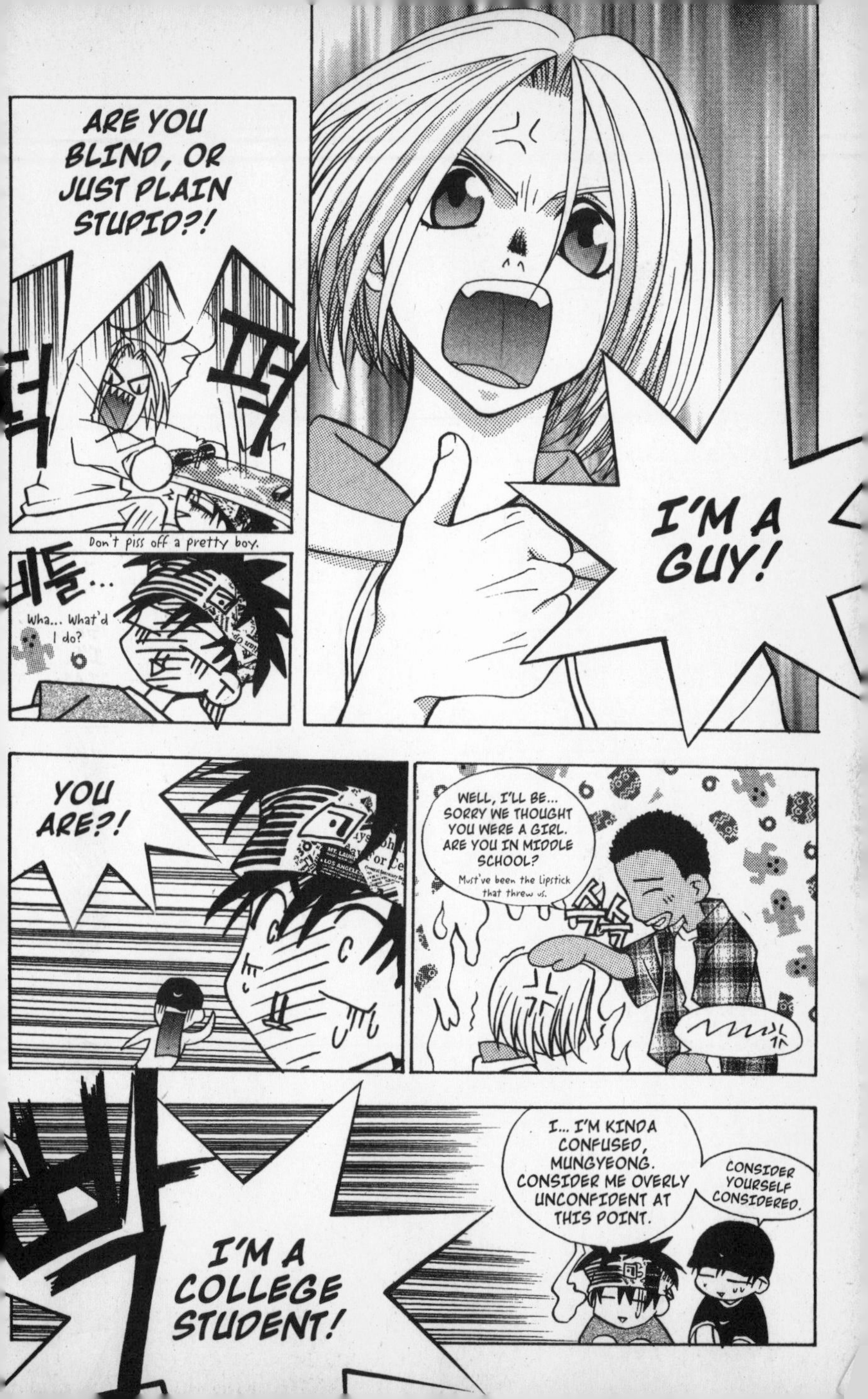
ARE YOU BLIND, OR JUST PLAIN STUPID?!
Don't piss off a pretty boy.
Wha... What'd I do?
I'M A GUY!
YOU ARE?!
WELL, I'LL BE... SORRY WE THOUGHT YOU WERE A GIRL. ARE YOU IN MIDDLE SCHOOL?
Must've been the lipstick that threw us.
I'M A COLLEGE STUDENT!
I... I'M KINDA CONFUSED, MUNGYEONG. CONSIDER ME OVERLY UNCONFIDENT AT THIS POINT.
CONSIDER YOURSELF CONSIDERED.

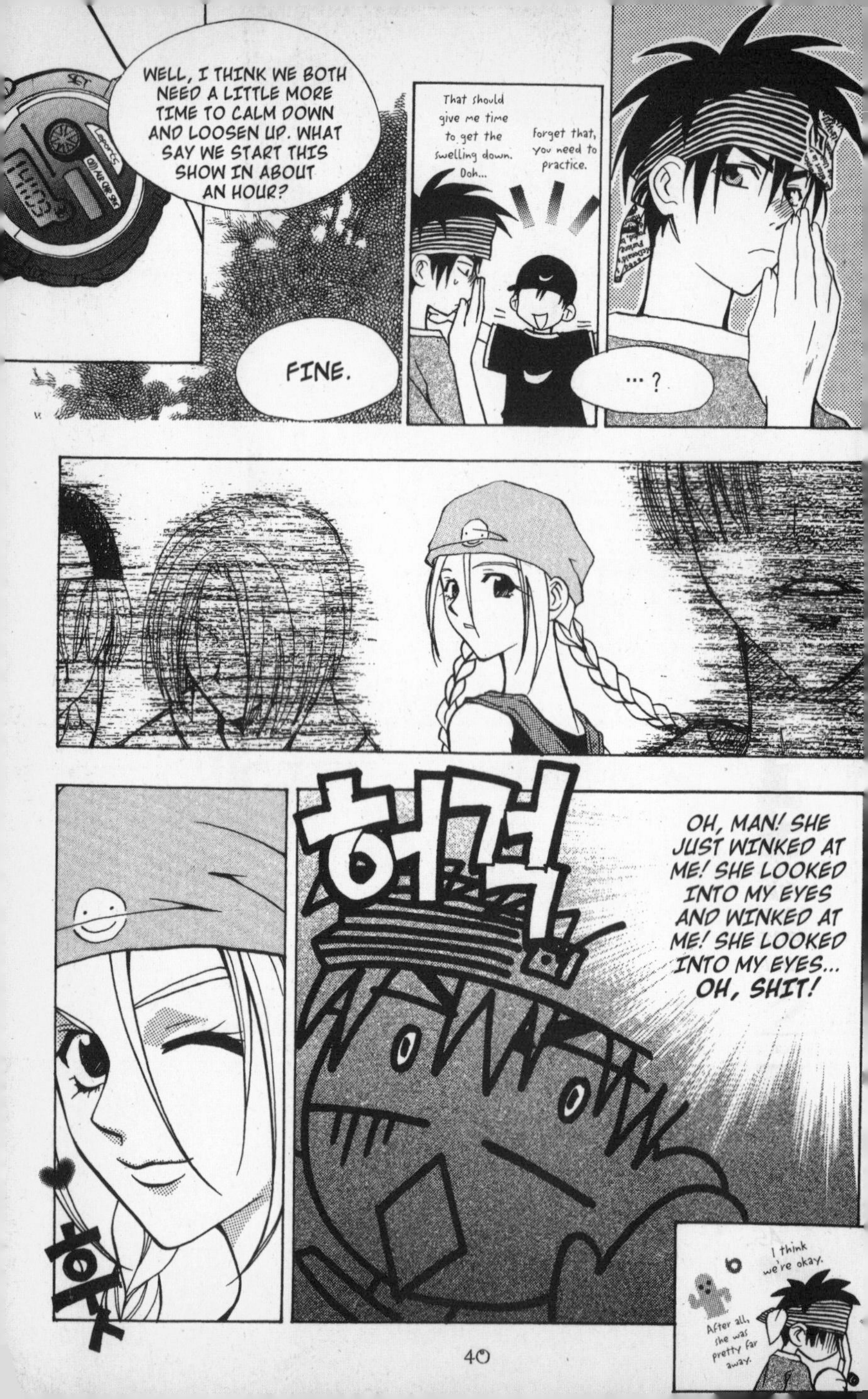
WELL, I THINK WE BOTH NEED A LITTLE MORE TIME TO CALM DOWN AND LOOSEN UP. WHAT SAY WE START THIS SHOW IN ABOUT AN HOUR?
FINE.
That should give me time to get the swelling down. Ooh...
Forget that, you need to practice.
...?
허걱!
OH, MAN! SHE JUST WINKED AT ME! SHE LOOKED INTO MY EYES AND WINKED AT ME! SHE LOOKED INTO MY EYES... OH, SHIT!
I think we're okay.
After all, she was pretty far away.

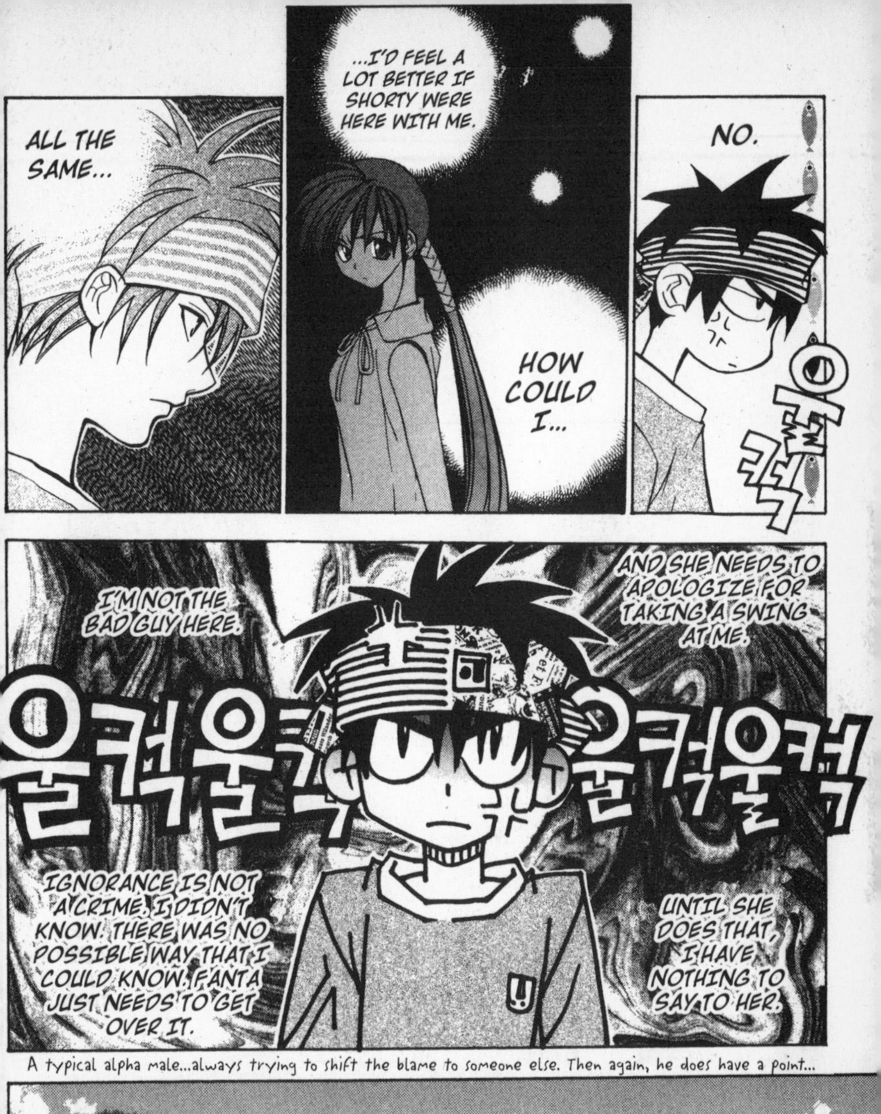
ALL THE SAME...
...I'D FEEL A LOT BETTER IF SHORTY WERE HERE WITH ME.
HOW COULD I...
NO.
울컥
I'M NOT THE BAD GUY HERE.
AND SHE NEEDS TO APOLOGIZE FOR TAKING A SWING AT ME.
울컥울컥 울컥울컥
IGNORANCE IS NOT A CRIME. I DIDN'T KNOW. THERE WAS NO POSSIBLE WAY THAT I COULD KNOW. FANTA JUST NEEDS TO GET OVER IT.
UNTIL SHE DOES THAT, I HAVE NOTHING TO SAY TO HER.

A typical alpha male...always trying to shift the blame to someone else. Then again, he does have a point...

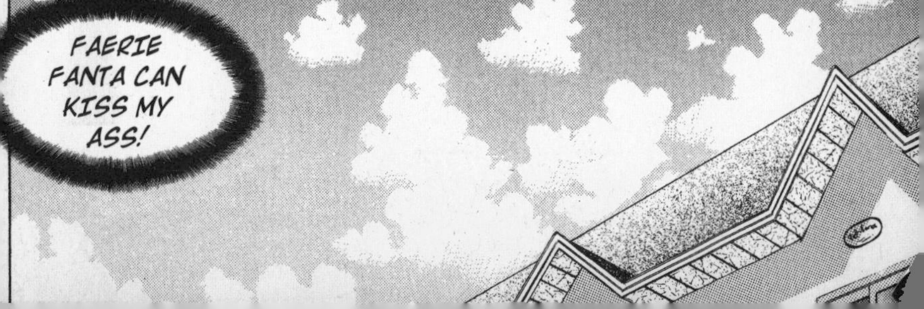
FAERIE FANTA CAN KISS MY ASS!

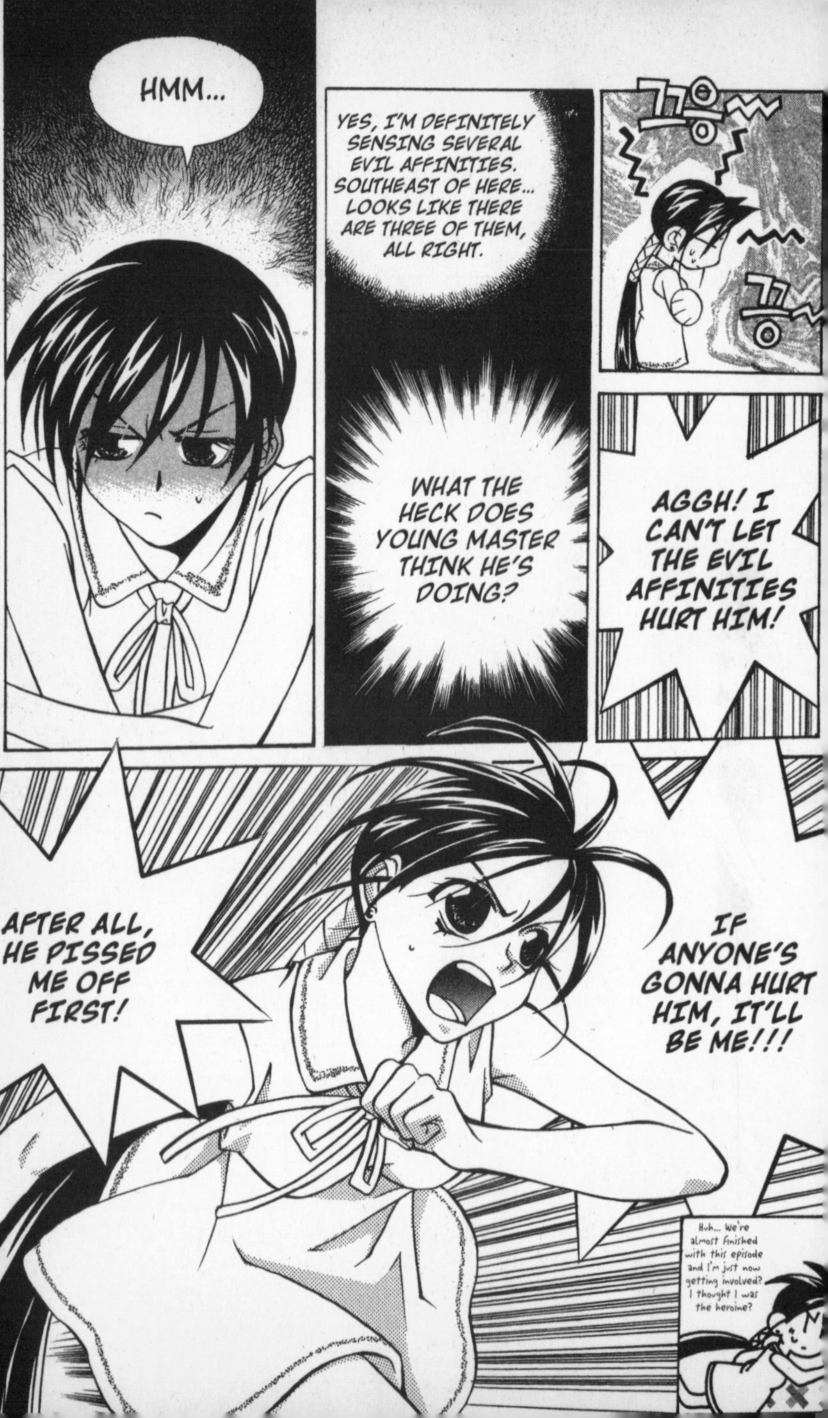
HMM...
YES, I'M DEFINITELY SENSING SEVERAL EVIL AFFINITIES. SOUTHEAST OF HERE... LOOKS LIKE THERE ARE THREE OF THEM, ALL RIGHT.
WHAT THE HECK DOES YOUNG MASTER THINK HE'S DOING?
끄응
끄응
AGGH! I CAN'T LET THE EVIL AFFINITIES HURT HIM!
AFTER ALL, HE PISSED ME OFF FIRST!
IF ANYONE'S GONNA HURT HIM, IT'LL BE ME!!!
Huh... We're almost finished with this episode and I'm just now getting involved? I thought I was the heroine?

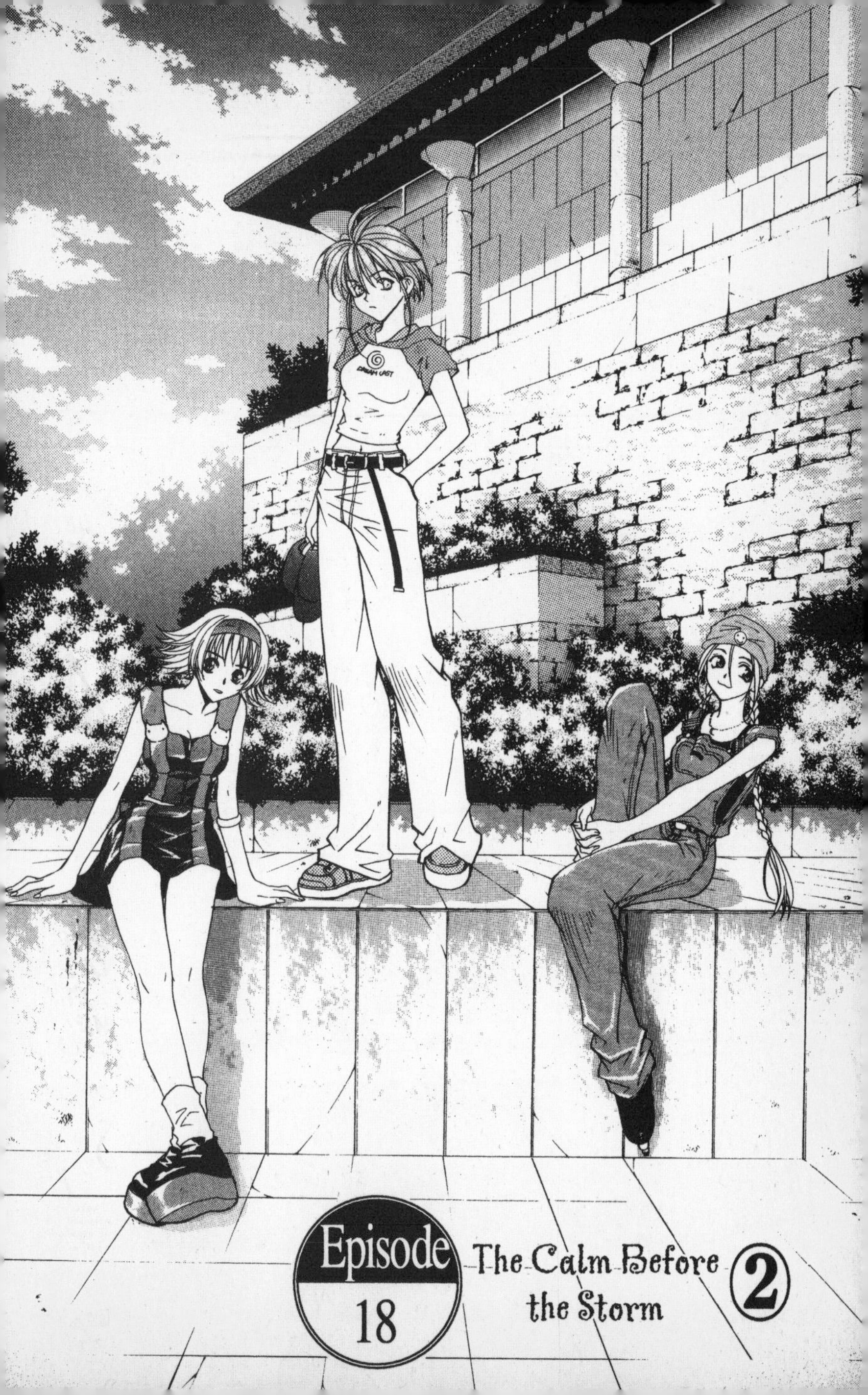
Episode 18
The Calm Before the Storm 2

About Skateboarding

Ooh... How did all this get started? I initially said that Ryang was a skater, but I forgot that I don't really know much about them. Actually, the whole reason behind having him ride a skateboard was to make sure people didn't think all he did was sit around and watch TV (and torment poor Fanta).

I was at a comic show earlier and someone who was actually in a skating club came by my booth. I was completely frozen. All he said was: "Draw it well for us." Of course, I want to draw it well. I'm doing my best. And I wanted to skip over the terms and just go about it. (It's not like I know and I don't really have anyone to look it over, so I was a bit nervous and embarrassed.) I'll use this space to lay out the skateboarding terms. I'm just copying someone else's terms. Just gloss over it, thinking something like, "Mmm... so an 'ollie' is a jump." I don't want to be wrong, but I'm not confident about any of this. Please go easy on me. Now that I think about it, I should have grabbed the person that came by the show and asked him to show me some examples, look over my work, and give me some technical details. Exactly how does a board spin when doing a flip? Huh? You think it would have been thick-skinned of me? Kyah!

Some common skateboarding terms...

Ollie: It's a trick where you jump with the board. I hear it's mandatory for learning how to flip.
Flip: A trick where you flip the board as you do an ollie. (It's so amazing.)
Rail: A trick where you slide along the board on things like, well, rails. The rail that Ryang is performing in this episode is a board slide which is supposedly the easiest of them.
Grind: Like a rail, but instead of sliding on the board you slide on the trucks, which connect the wheels to the board. What you see Jihyeon do in this episode is called a tail grind...I think. (Huh? It's not? Maybe it's a nose grind. I'm blabbering.)

Haha... I'm at such a skill level where I'd tell someone they're good at riding a skateboard if they were able to push off without falling off the board. And with this, I'm trying to re-create expert skateboarders, so the chance of me embarrassing myself is quite high. There are many amazing tricks, but I just wrote down the ones that show up in this volume. Well then...

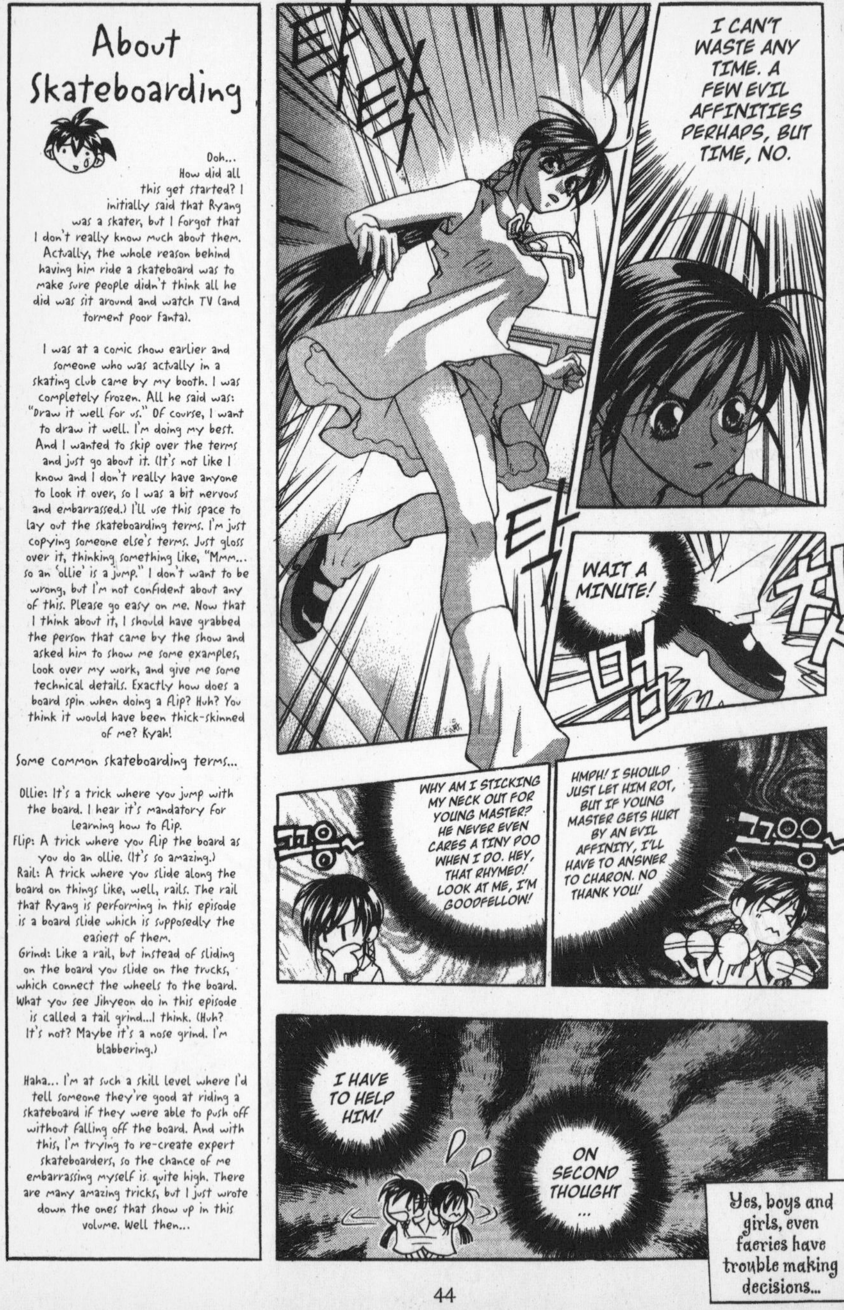
I CAN'T WASTE ANY TIME. A FEW EVIL AFFINITIES PERHAPS, BUT TIME, NO.
WAIT A MINUTE!
WHY AM I STICKING MY NECK OUT FOR YOUNG MASTER? HE NEVER EVEN CARES A TINY POO WHEN I DO. HEY, THAT RHYMED! LOOK AT ME, I'M GOODFELLOW!
HMPH! I SHOULD JUST LET HIM ROT, BUT IF YOUNG MASTER GETS HURT BY AN EVIL AFFINITY, I'LL HAVE TO ANSWER TO CHARON. NO THANK YOU!
I HAVE TO HELP HIM!
ON SECOND THOUGHT ...
Yes, boys and girls, even faeries have trouble making decisions...

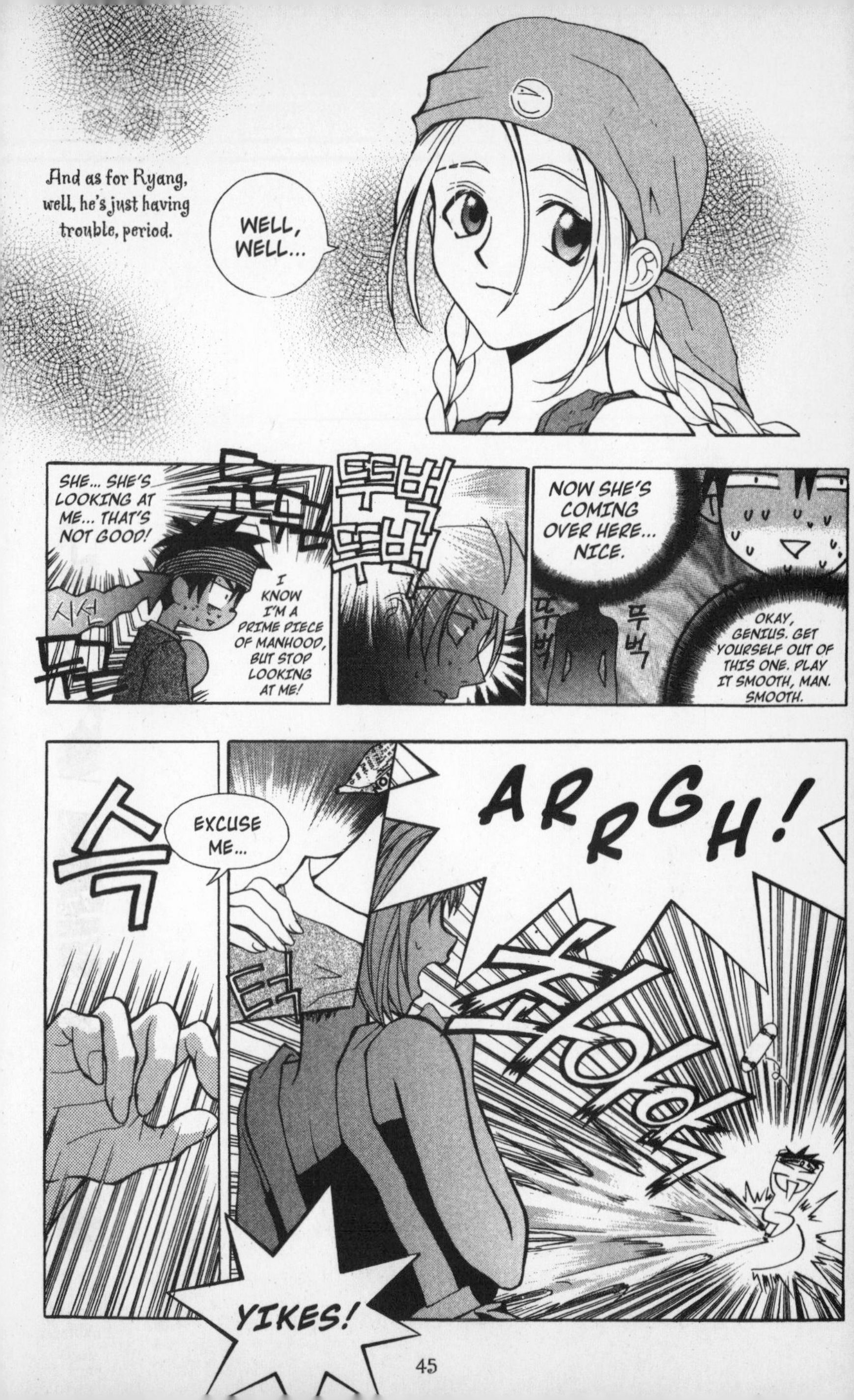

And as for Ryang, well, he's just having trouble, period.
WELL, WELL...
SHE... SHE'S LOOKING AT ME... THAT'S NOT GOOD!
시선
I KNOW I'M A PRIME PIECE OF MANHOOD, BUT STOP LOOKING AT ME!
뚜벅 뚜벅
NOW SHE'S COMING OVER HERE... NICE.
OKAY, GENIUS. GET YOURSELF OUT OF THIS ONE. PLAY IT SMOOTH, MAN. SMOOTH.
EXCUSE ME...
ARRGH!
YIKES!

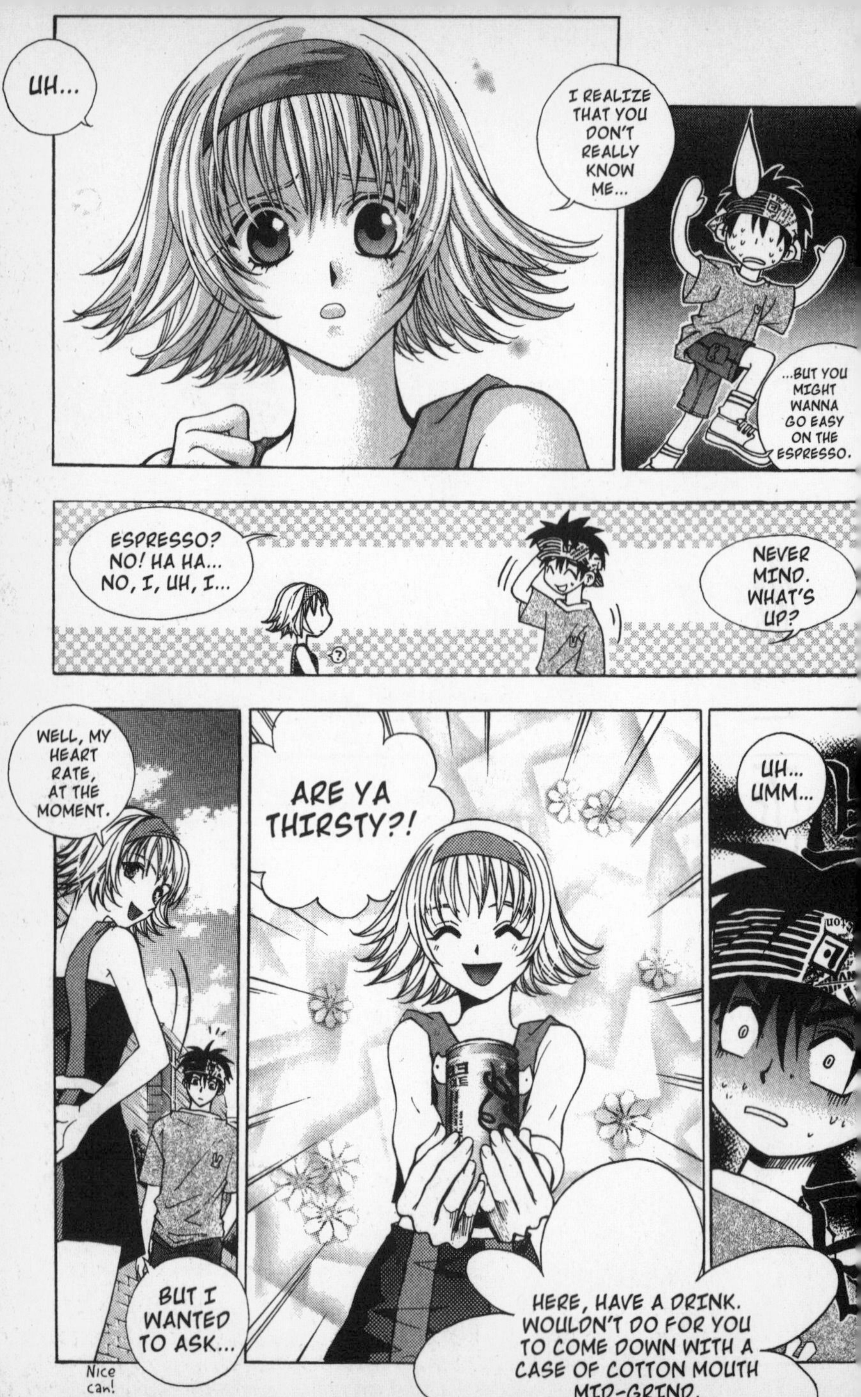
UH...
I REALIZE THAT YOU DON'T REALLY KNOW ME...
...BUT YOU MIGHT WANNA GO EASY ON THE ESPRESSO.
ESPRESSO? NO! HA HA... NO, I, UH, I...
?
NEVER MIND. WHAT'S UP?
WELL, MY HEART RATE, AT THE MOMENT.
BUT I WANTED TO ASK...
Nice can!
ARE YA THIRSTY?!
HERE, HAVE A DRINK. WOULDN'T DO FOR YOU TO COME DOWN WITH A CASE OF COTTON MOUTH MID-GRIND.
UH... UMM...

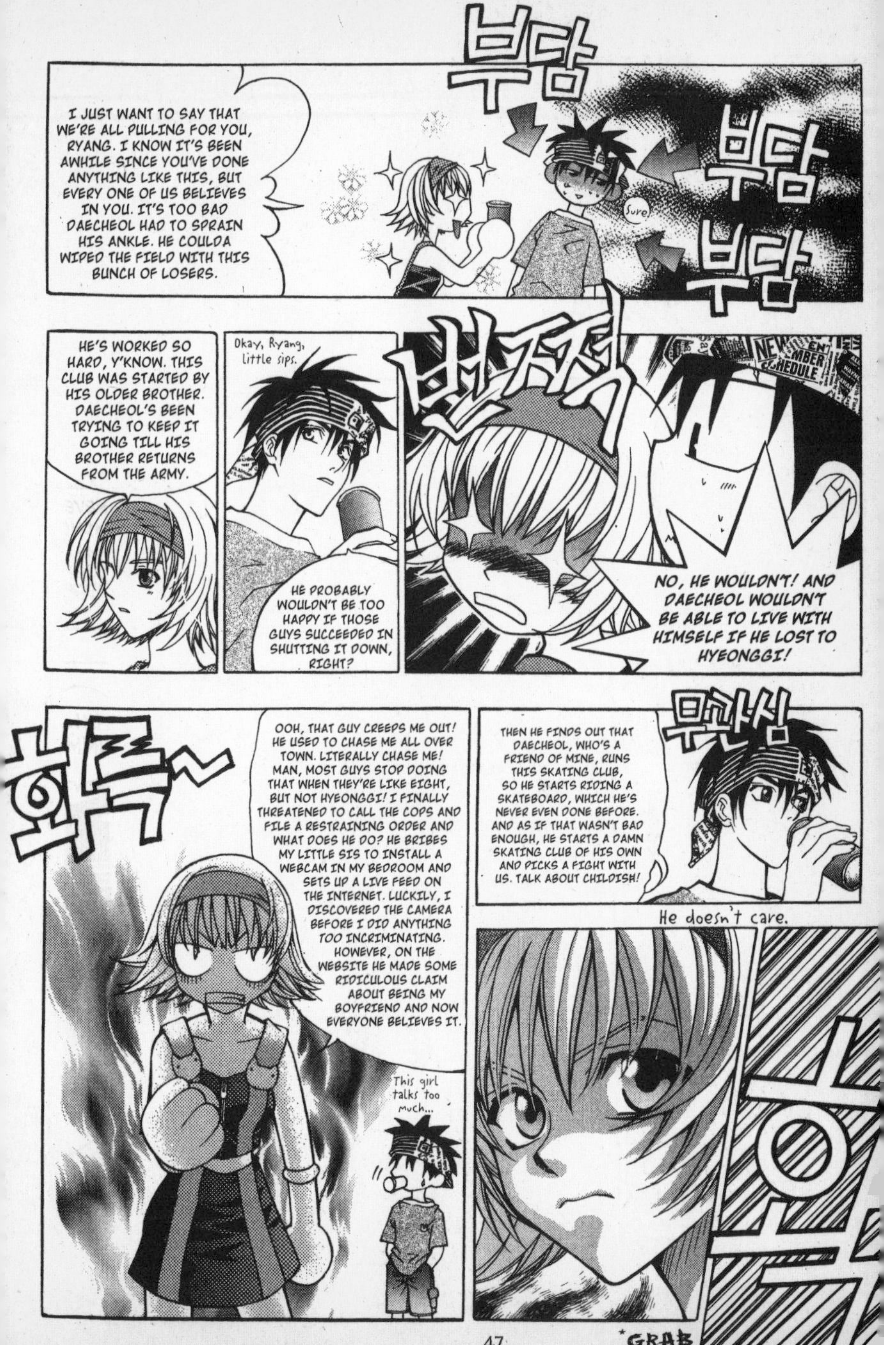
부담
I JUST WANT TO SAY THAT WE'RE ALL PULLING FOR YOU, RYANG. I KNOW IT'S BEEN AWHILE SINCE YOU'VE DONE ANYTHING LIKE THIS, BUT EVERY ONE OF US BELIEVES IN YOU. IT'S TOO BAD DAECHEOL HAD TO SPRAIN HIS ANKLE. HE COULDA WIPED THE FIELD WITH THIS BUNCH OF LOSERS.
Sure.
부담
부담
HE'S WORKED SO HARD, Y'KNOW. THIS CLUB WAS STARTED BY HIS OLDER BROTHER. DAECHEOL'S BEEN TRYING TO KEEP IT GOING TILL HIS BROTHER RETURNS FROM THE ARMY.
Okay, Ryang, little sips.
HE PROBABLY WOULDN'T BE TOO HAPPY IF THOSE GUYS SUCCEEDED IN SHUTTING IT DOWN, RIGHT?
번쩍
NO, HE WOULDN'T! AND DAECHEOL WOULDN'T BE ABLE TO LIVE WITH HIMSELF IF HE LOST TO HYEONGGI!
OOH, THAT GUY CREEPS ME OUT! HE USED TO CHASE ME ALL OVER TOWN. LITERALLY CHASE ME! MAN, MOST GUYS STOP DOING THAT WHEN THEY'RE LIKE EIGHT, BUT NOT HYEONGGI! I FINALLY THREATENED TO CALL THE COPS AND FILE A RESTRAINING ORDER AND WHAT DOES HE DO? HE BRIBES MY LITTLE SIS TO INSTALL A WEBCAM IN MY BEDROOM AND SETS UP A LIVE FEED ON THE INTERNET. LUCKILY, I DISCOVERED THE CAMERA BEFORE I DID ANYTHING TOO INCRIMINATING. HOWEVER, ON THE WEBSITE HE MADE SOME RIDICULOUS CLAIM ABOUT BEING MY BOYFRIEND AND NOW EVERYONE BELIEVES IT.
This girl talks too much...
THEN HE FINDS OUT THAT DAECHEOL, WHO'S A FRIEND OF MINE, RUNS THIS SKATING CLUB, SO HE STARTS RIDING A SKATEBOARD, WHICH HE'S NEVER EVEN DONE BEFORE. AND AS IF THAT WASN'T BAD ENOUGH, HE STARTS A DAMN SKATING CLUB OF HIS OWN AND PICKS A FIGHT WITH US. TALK ABOUT CHILDISH!
무관심
He doesn't care.
*GRAB

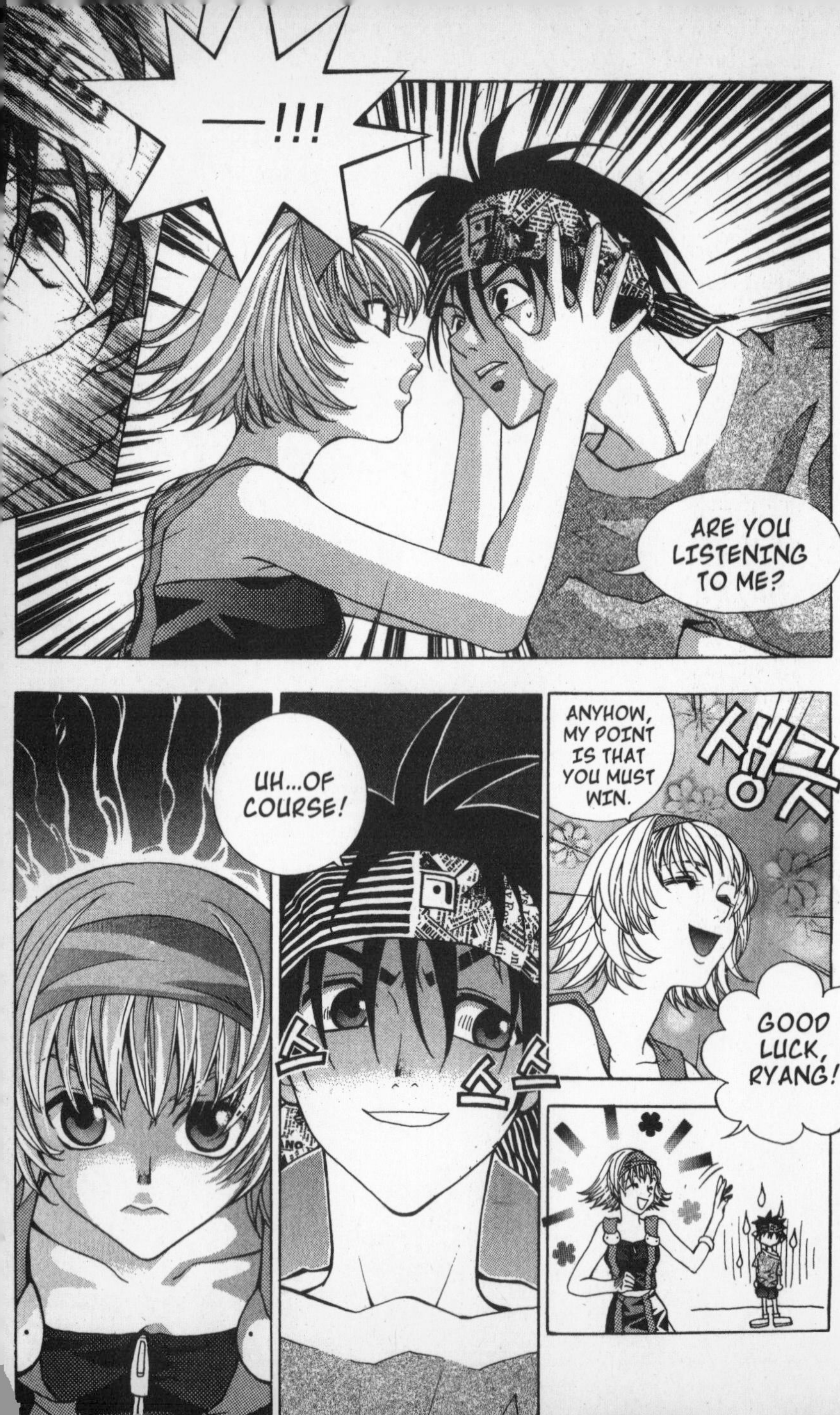
—!!!
ARE YOU LISTENING TO ME?
UH...OF COURSE!
ANYHOW, MY POINT IS THAT YOU MUST WIN.
생긋
GOOD LUCK, RYANG! ♡

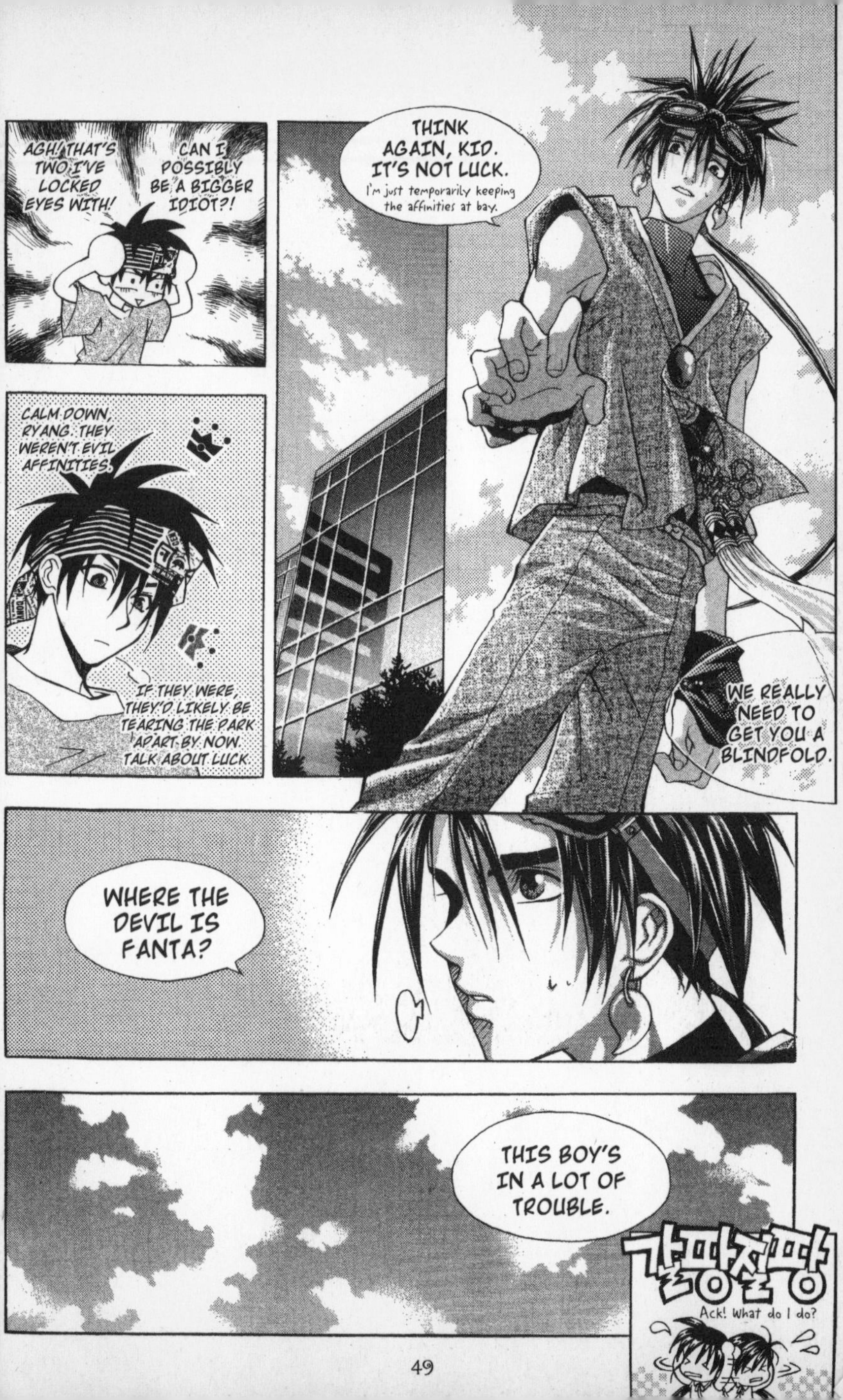
AGH! THAT'S TWO I'VE LOCKED EYES WITH!
CAN I POSSIBLY BE A BIGGER IDIOT?!
CALM DOWN, RYANG. THEY WEREN'T EVIL AFFINITIES.
IF THEY WERE, THEY'D LIKELY BE TEARING THE PARK APART BY NOW. TALK ABOUT LUCK.
THINK AGAIN, KID. IT'S NOT LUCK.
I'm just temporarily keeping the affinities at bay.
WE REALLY NEED TO GET YOU A BLINDFOLD.
WHERE THE DEVIL IS FANTA?
THIS BOY'S IN A LOT OF TROUBLE.
갈팡질팡
Ack! What do I do?

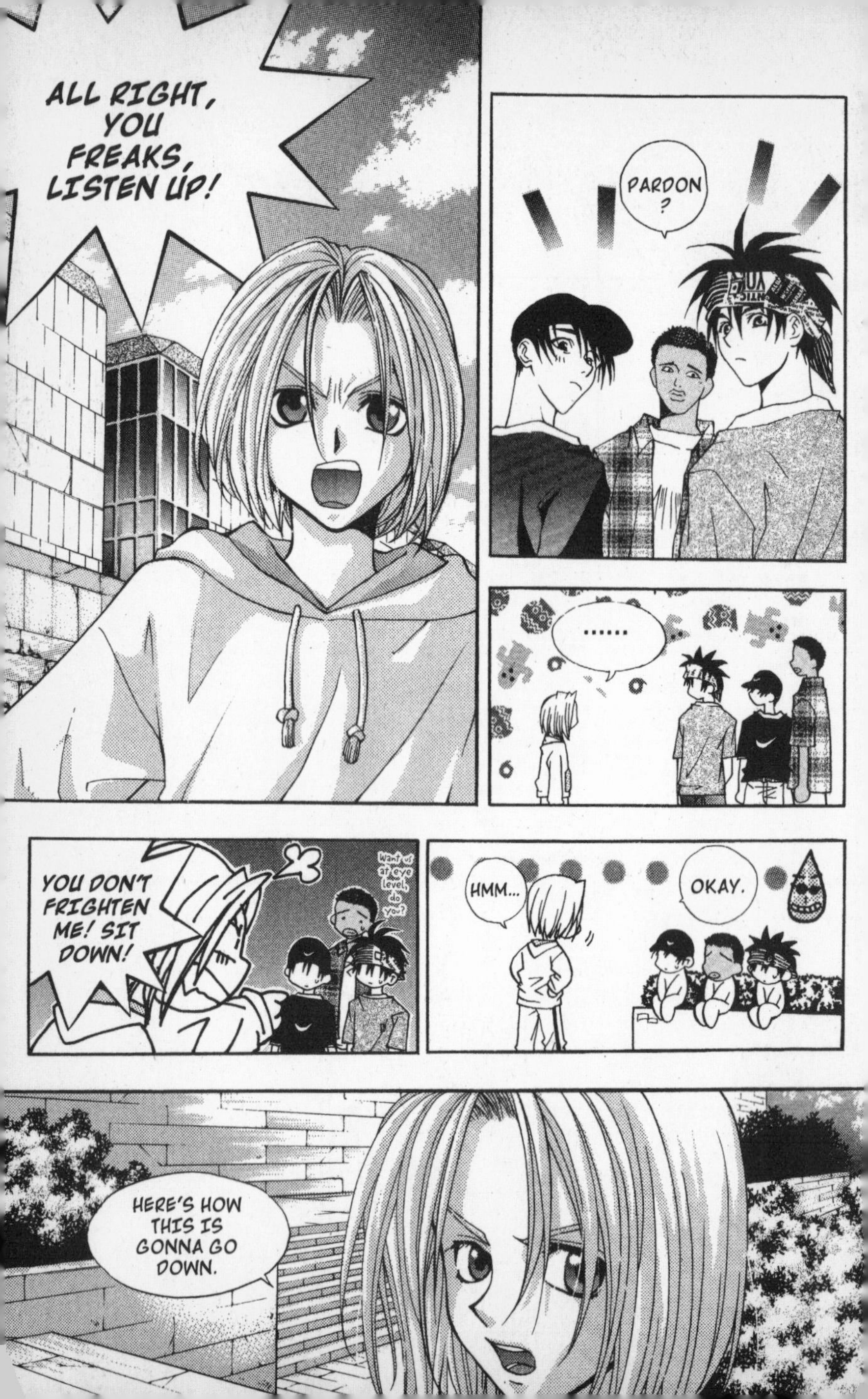

ALL RIGHT, YOU FREAKS, LISTEN UP!
PARDON?
......
YOU DON'T FRIGHTEN ME! SIT DOWN!
Want us at eye level, do you?
HMM...
OKAY.
HERE'S HOW THIS IS GONNA GO DOWN.

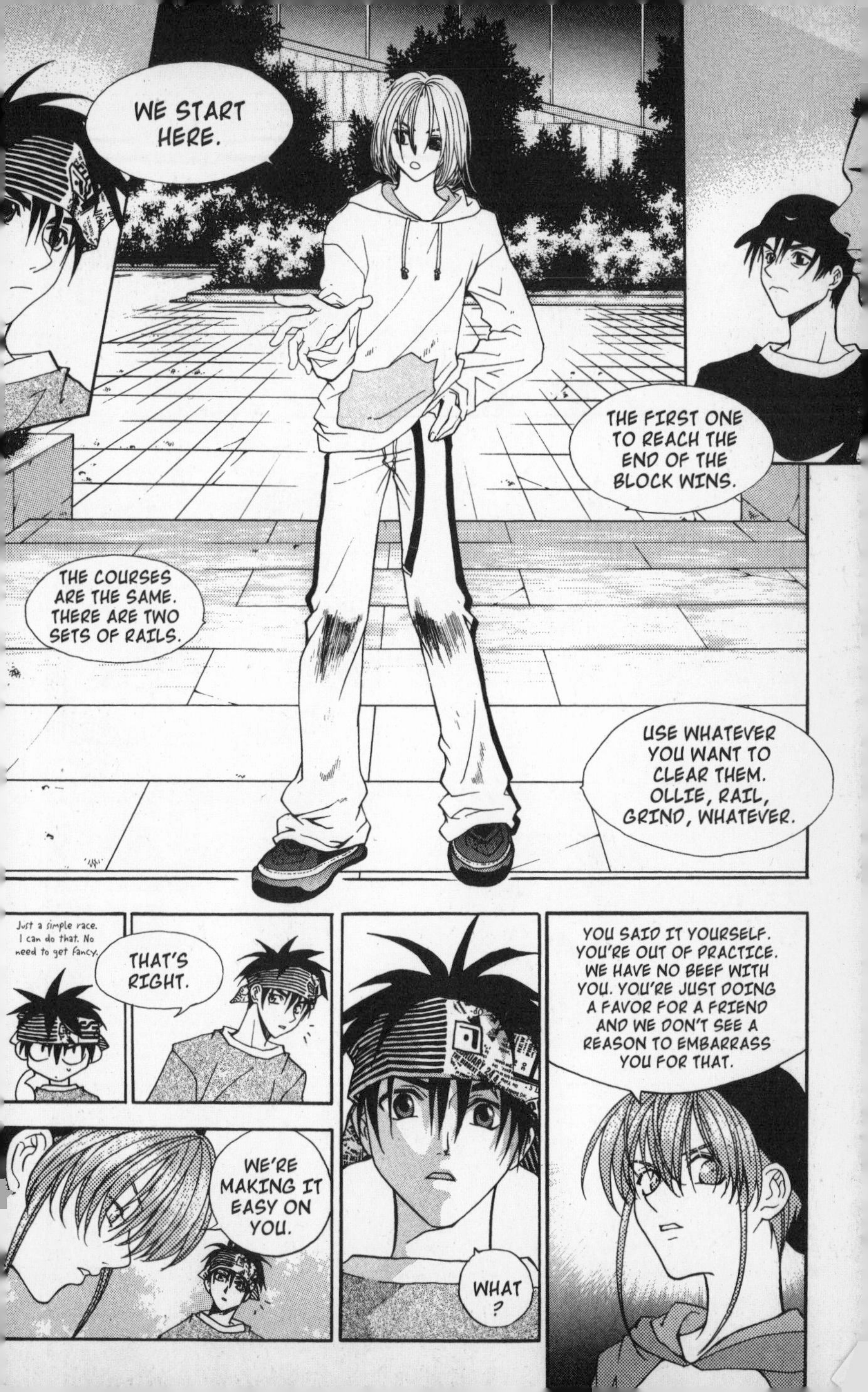
WE START HERE.
THE FIRST ONE TO REACH THE END OF THE BLOCK WINS.
THE COURSES ARE THE SAME. THERE ARE TWO SETS OF RAILS.
USE WHATEVER YOU WANT TO CLEAR THEM. OLLIE, RAIL, GRIND, WHATEVER.
Just a simple race. I can do that. No need to get fancy.
THAT'S RIGHT.
WE'RE MAKING IT EASY ON YOU.
WHAT?
YOU SAID IT YOURSELF. YOU'RE OUT OF PRACTICE. WE HAVE NO BEEF WITH YOU. YOU'RE JUST DOING A FAVOR FOR A FRIEND AND WE DON'T SEE A REASON TO EMBARRASS YOU FOR THAT.

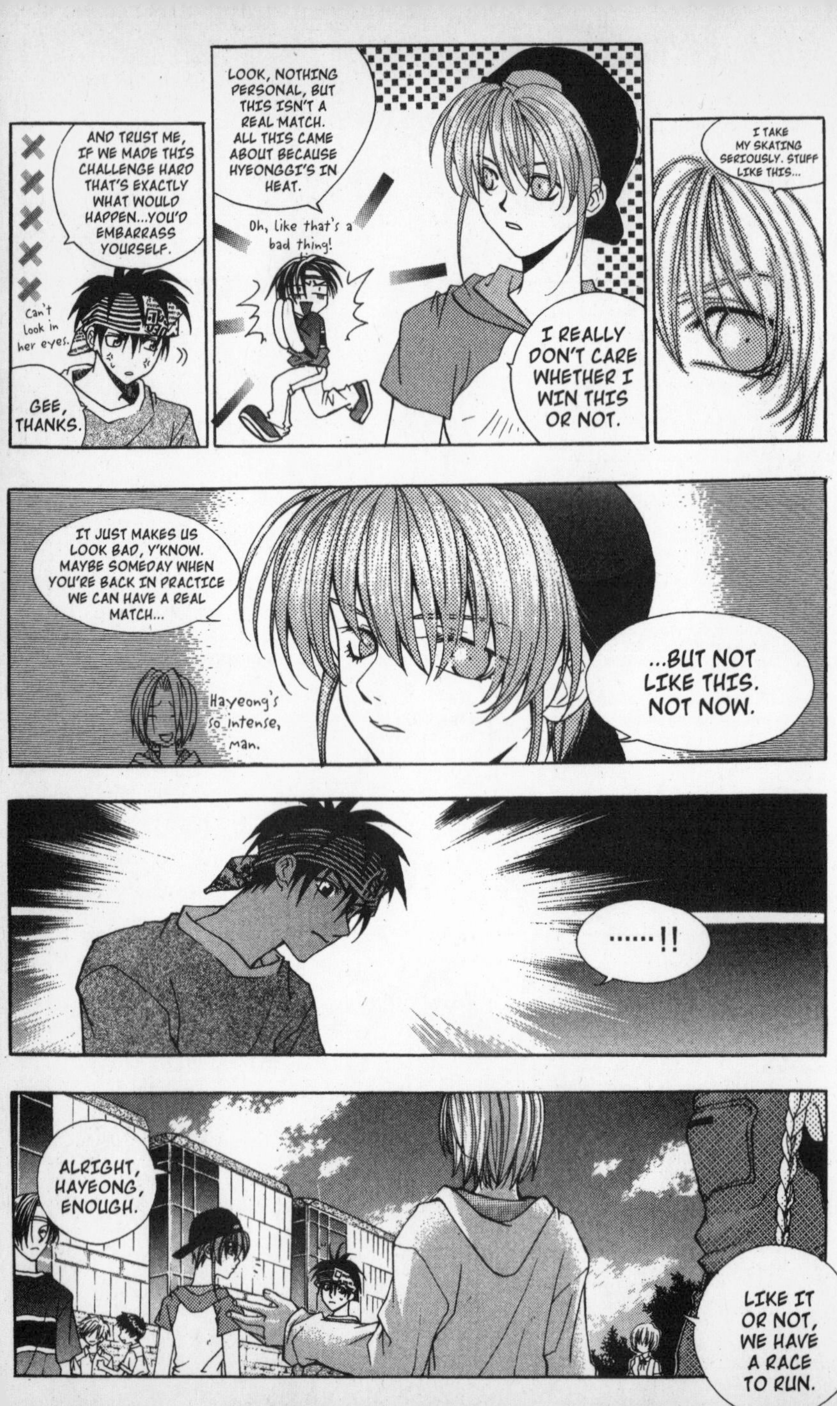
AND TRUST ME, IF WE MADE THIS CHALLENGE HARD THAT'S EXACTLY WHAT WOULD HAPPEN...YOU'D EMBARRASS YOURSELF.
Can't look in her eyes.
GEE, THANKS.
LOOK, NOTHING PERSONAL, BUT THIS ISN'T A REAL MATCH. ALL THIS CAME ABOUT BECAUSE HYEONGGI'S IN HEAT.
Oh, like that's a bad thing!
I REALLY DON'T CARE WHETHER I WIN THIS OR NOT.
I TAKE MY SKATING SERIOUSLY. STUFF LIKE THIS...
IT JUST MAKES US LOOK BAD, Y'KNOW. MAYBE SOMEDAY WHEN YOU'RE BACK IN PRACTICE WE CAN HAVE A REAL MATCH...
Hayeong's so intense, man.
...BUT NOT LIKE THIS. NOT NOW.
......!!
ALRIGHT, HAYEONG, ENOUGH.
LIKE IT OR NOT, WE HAVE A RACE TO RUN.

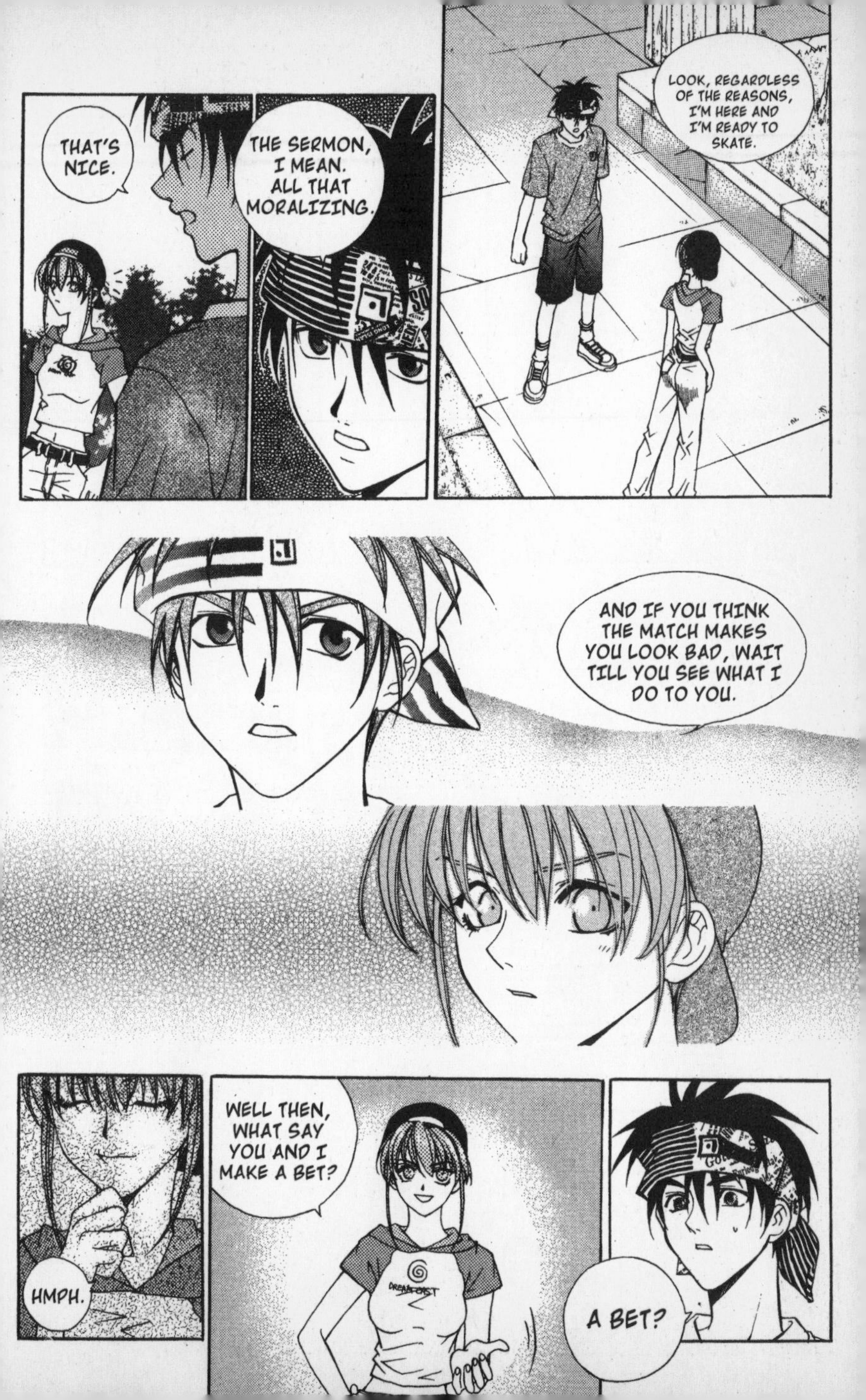
THAT'S NICE.
THE SERMON, I MEAN. ALL THAT MORALIZING.
LOOK, REGARDLESS OF THE REASONS, I'M HERE AND I'M READY TO SKATE.
AND IF YOU THINK THE MATCH MAKES YOU LOOK BAD, WAIT TILL YOU SEE WHAT I DO TO YOU.
HMPH.
WELL THEN, WHAT SAY YOU AND I MAKE A BET?
A BET?

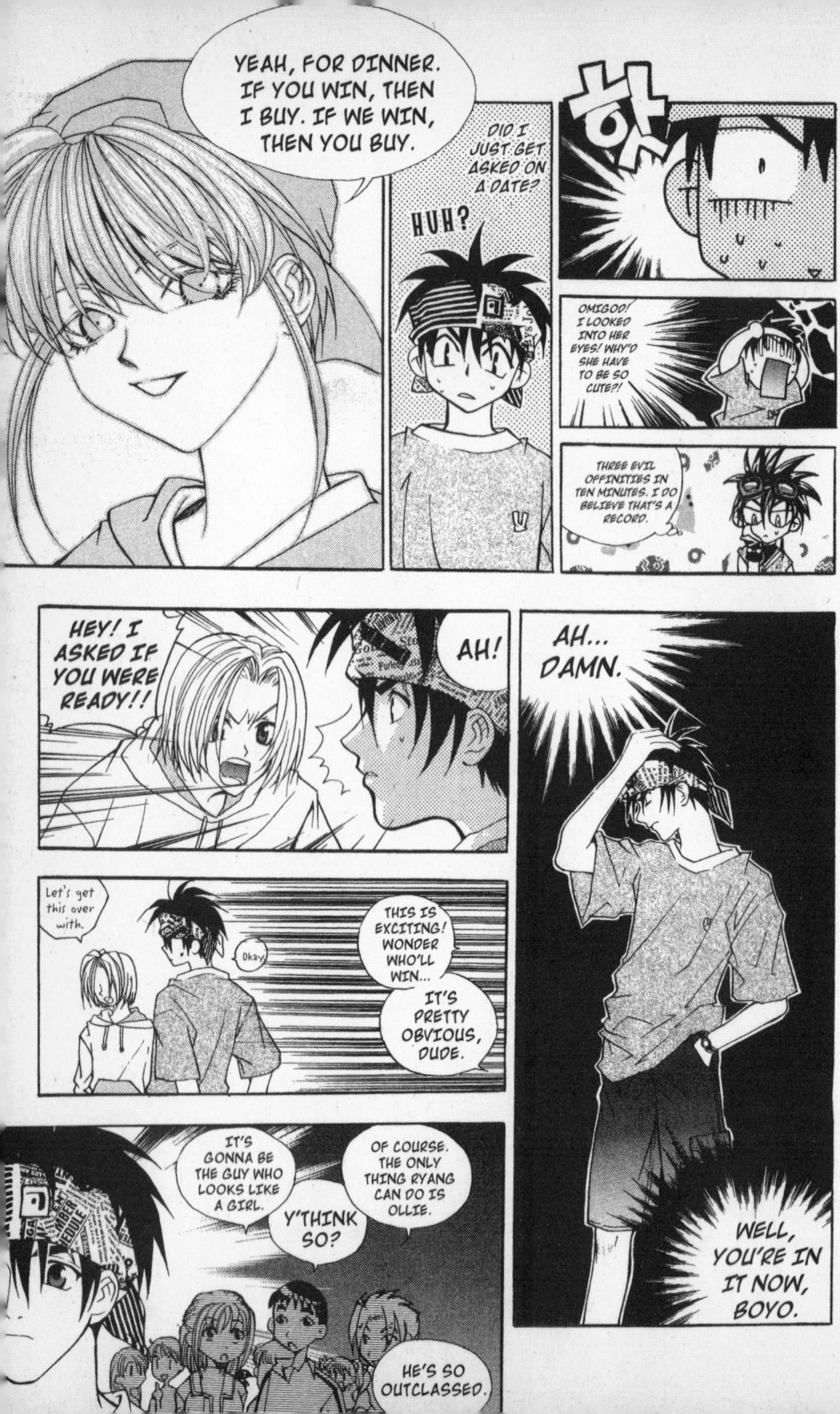
YEAH, FOR DINNER. IF YOU WIN, THEN I BUY. IF WE WIN, THEN YOU BUY.
DID I JUST GET ASKED ON A DATE?
HUH?
OMIGOD! I LOOKED INTO HER EYES! WHY'D SHE HAVE TO BE SO CUTE?!
THREE EVIL OFFINITIES IN TEN MINUTES. I DO BELIEVE THAT'S A RECORD.
HEY! I ASKED IF YOU WERE READY!!
AH!
Let's get this over with.
Okay.
THIS IS EXCITING! WONDER WHO'LL WIN...
IT'S PRETTY OBVIOUS, DUDE.
IT'S GONNA BE THE GUY WHO LOOKS LIKE A GIRL.
OF COURSE. THE ONLY THING RYANG CAN DO IS OLLIE.
Y'THINK SO?
HE'S SO OUTCLASSED.
AH... DAMN.
WELL, YOU'RE IN IT NOW, BOYO.

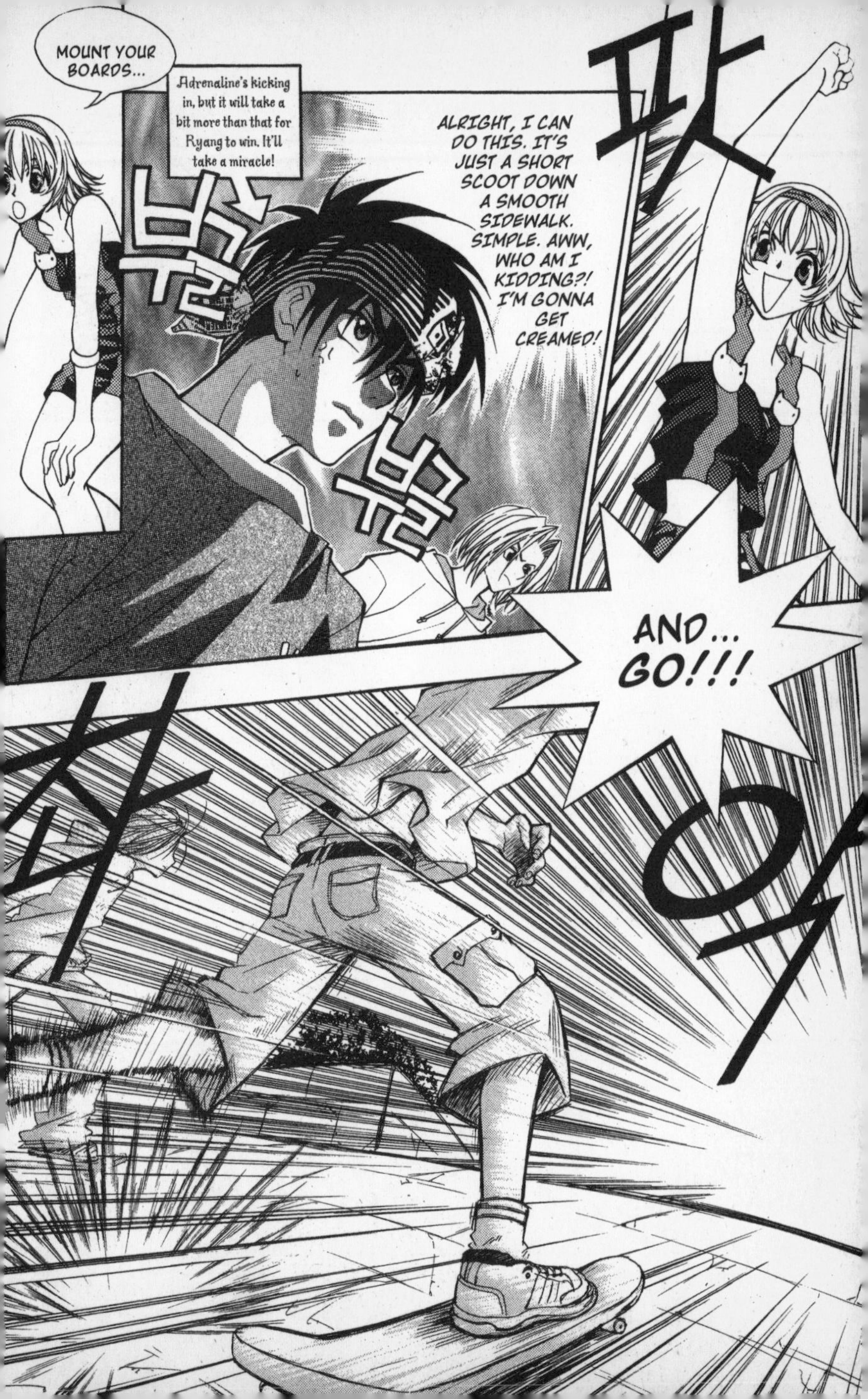
MOUNT YOUR BOARDS...
Adrenaline's kicking in, but it will take a bit more than that for Ryang to win. It'll take a miracle!
ALRIGHT, I CAN DO THIS. IT'S JUST A SHORT SCOOT DOWN A SMOOTH SIDEWALK. SIMPLE. AWW, WHO AM I KIDDING?! I'M GONNA GET CREAMED!
AND... GO!!!

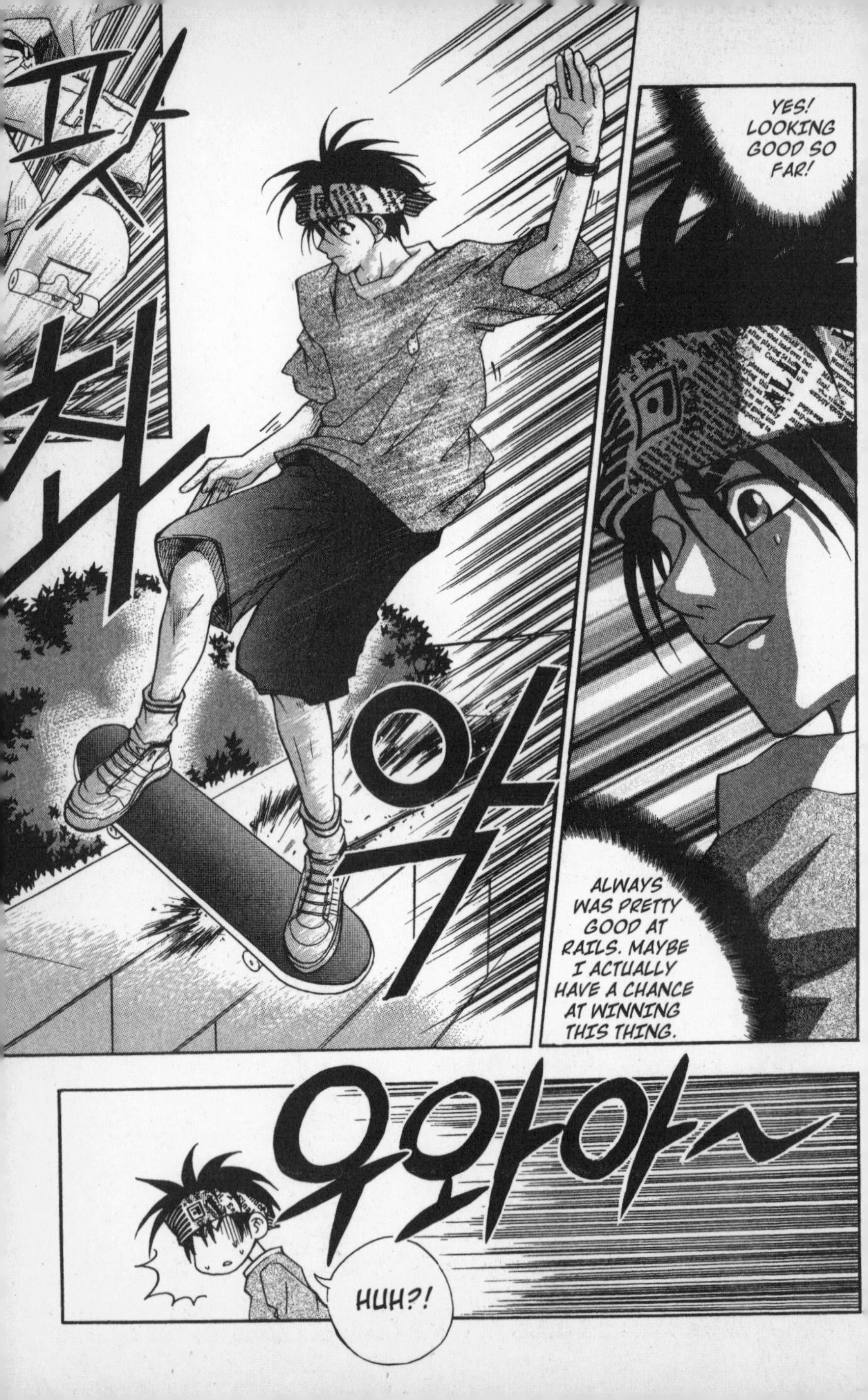
YES! LOOKING GOOD SO FAR!
ALWAYS WAS PRETTY GOOD AT RAILS. MAYBE I ACTUALLY HAVE A CHANCE AT WINNING THIS THING.
HUH?!

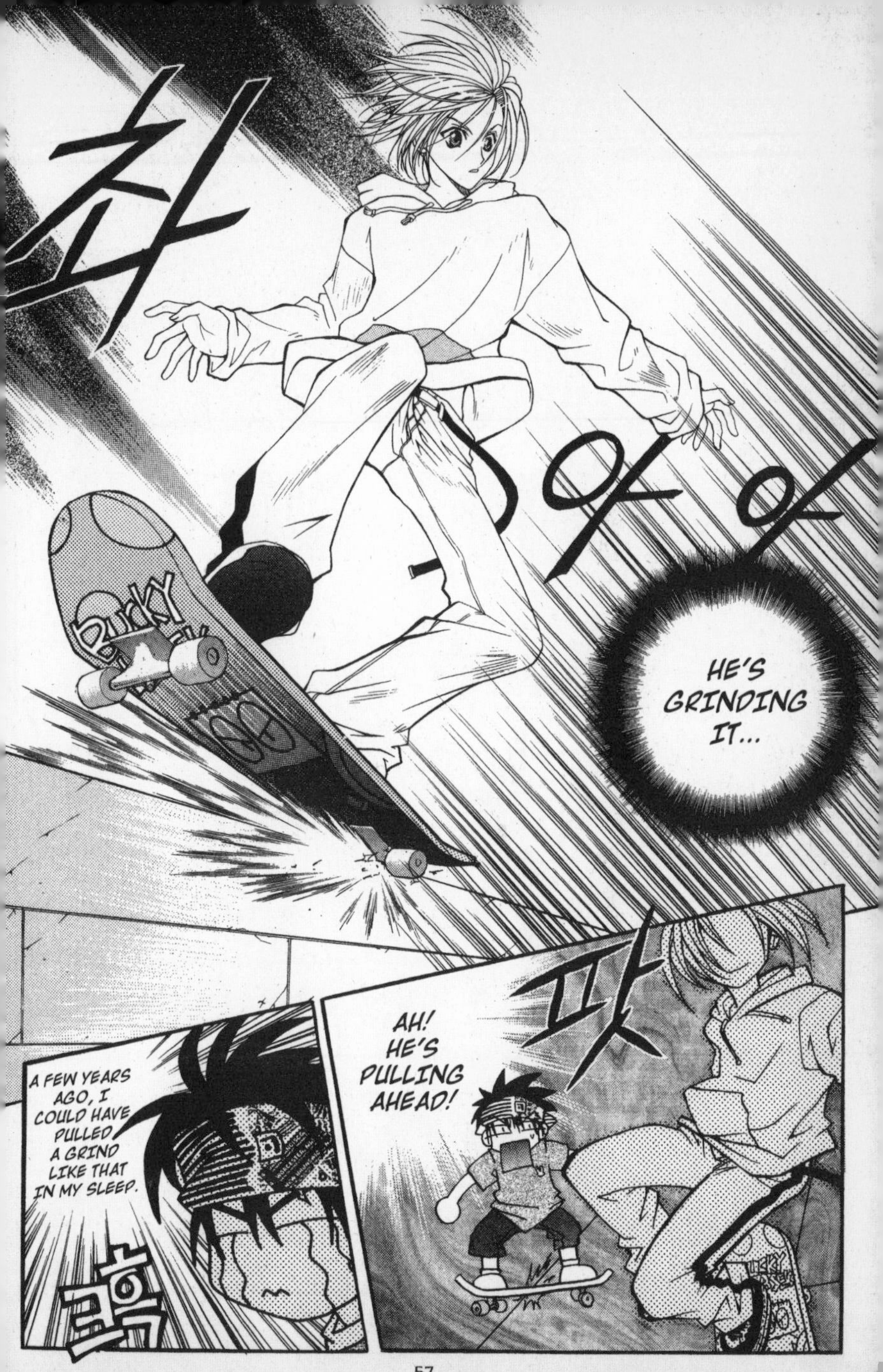
HE'S GRINDING IT...
A FEW YEARS AGO, I COULD HAVE PULLED A GRIND LIKE THAT IN MY SLEEP.
AH! HE'S PULLING AHEAD!

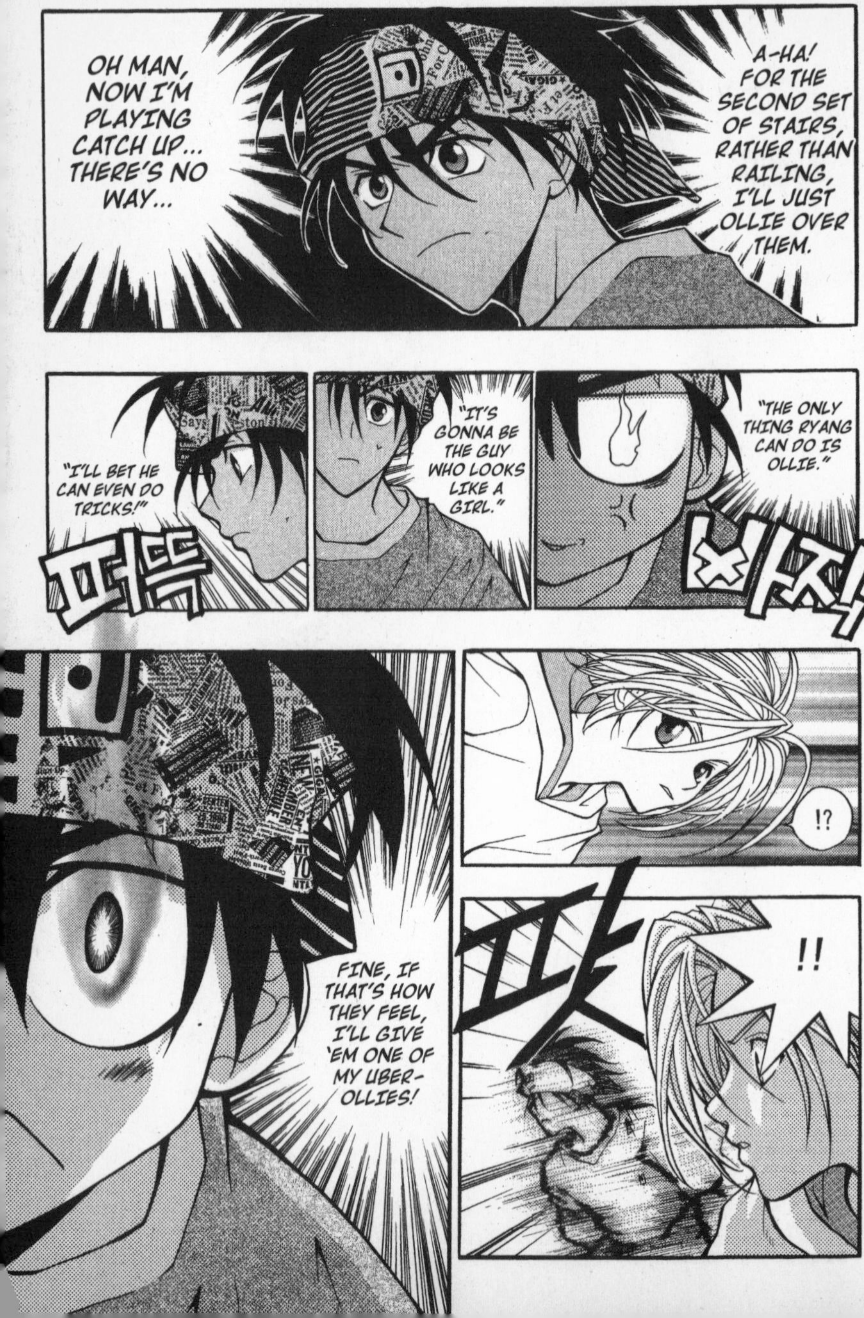
OH MAN, NOW I'M PLAYING CATCH UP... THERE'S NO WAY...
A-HA! FOR THE SECOND SET OF STAIRS, RATHER THAN RAILING, I'LL JUST OLLIE OVER THEM.
"I'LL BET HE CAN EVEN DO TRICKS!"
"IT'S GONNA BE THE GUY WHO LOOKS LIKE A GIRL."
"THE ONLY THING RYANG CAN DO IS OLLIE."
FINE, IF THAT'S HOW THEY FEEL, I'LL GIVE 'EM ONE OF MY UBER-OLLIES!
!?
!!

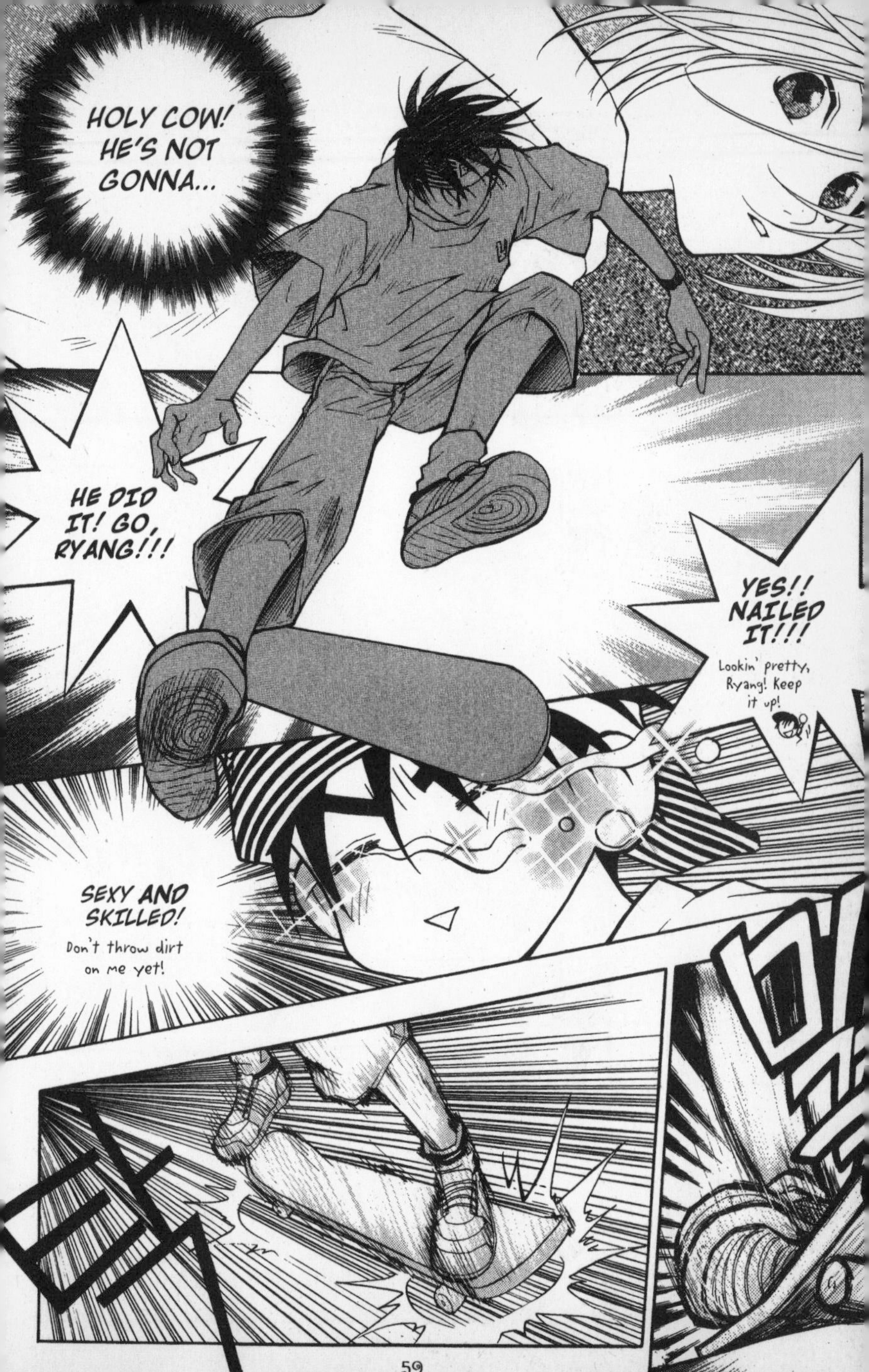
HOLY COW! HE'S NOT GONNA...
YES!! NAILED IT!!!
Lookin' pretty, Ryang! Keep it up!
HE DID IT! GO, RYANG!!!
SEXY AND SKILLED!
Don't throw dirt on me yet!

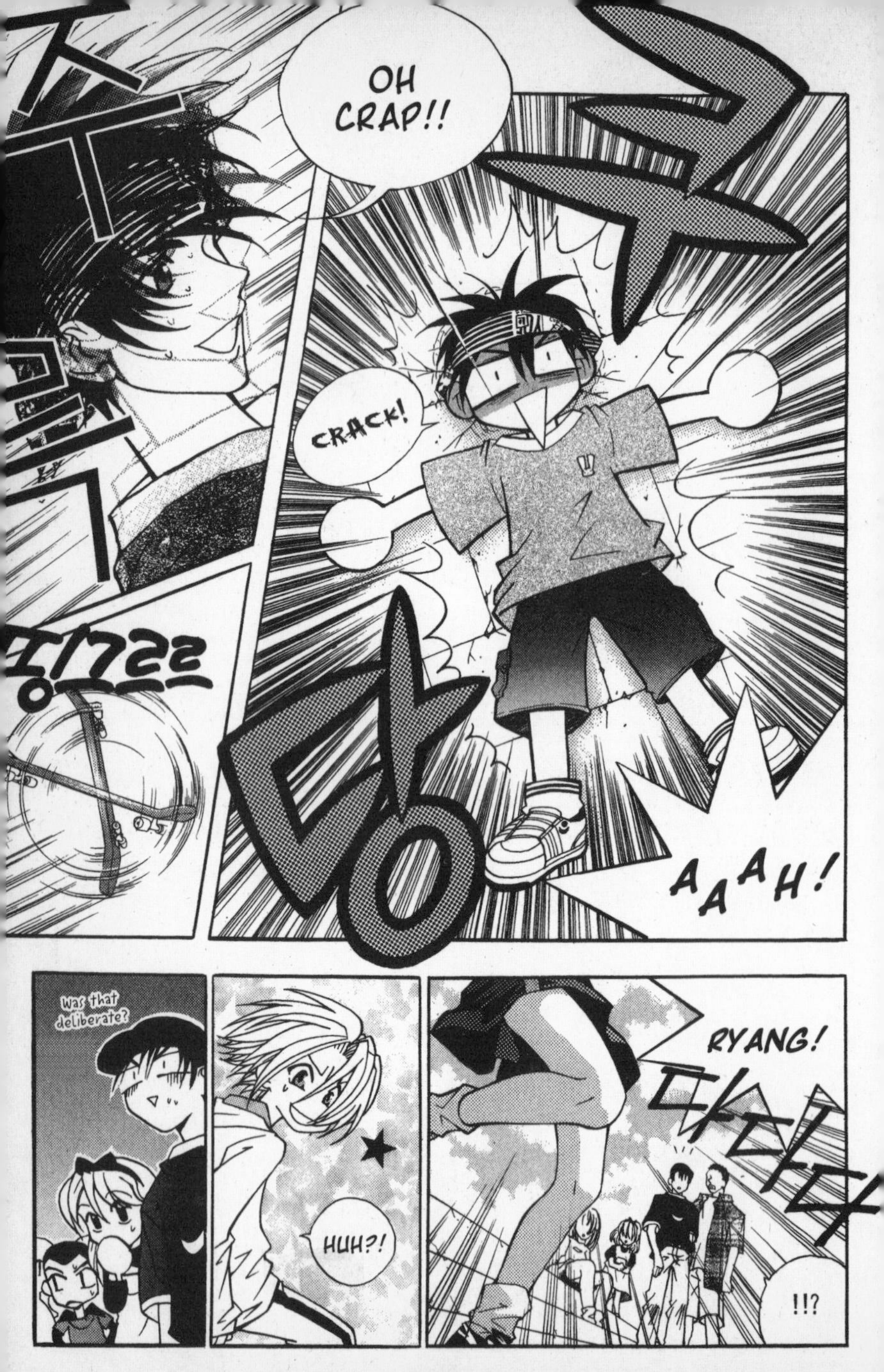
OH CRAP!!
CRACK!
AAAAH!
Was that deliberate?
HUH?!
RYANG!
!!?

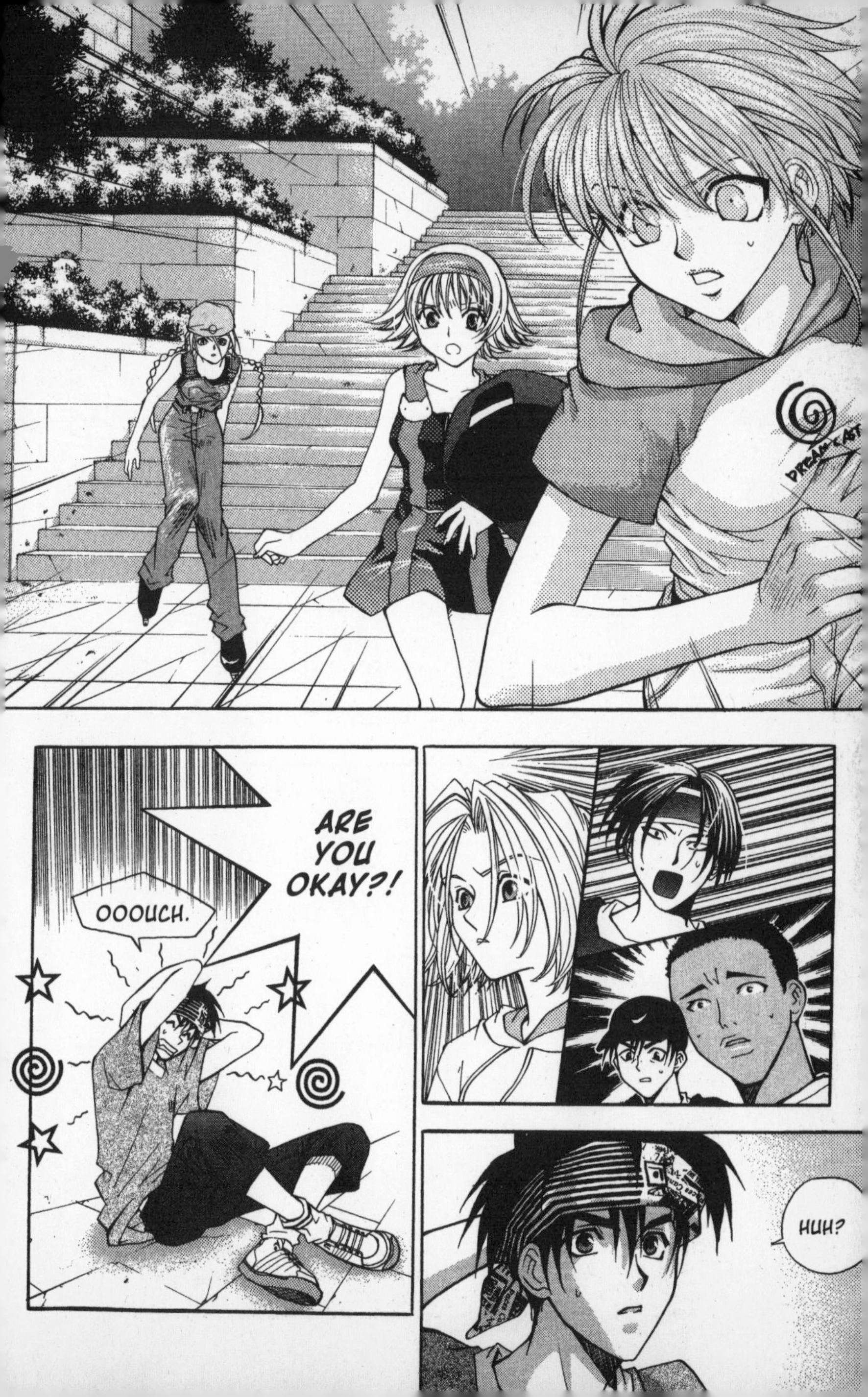
DREAM-CAST
ARE YOU OKAY?!
OOOUCH.
HUH?

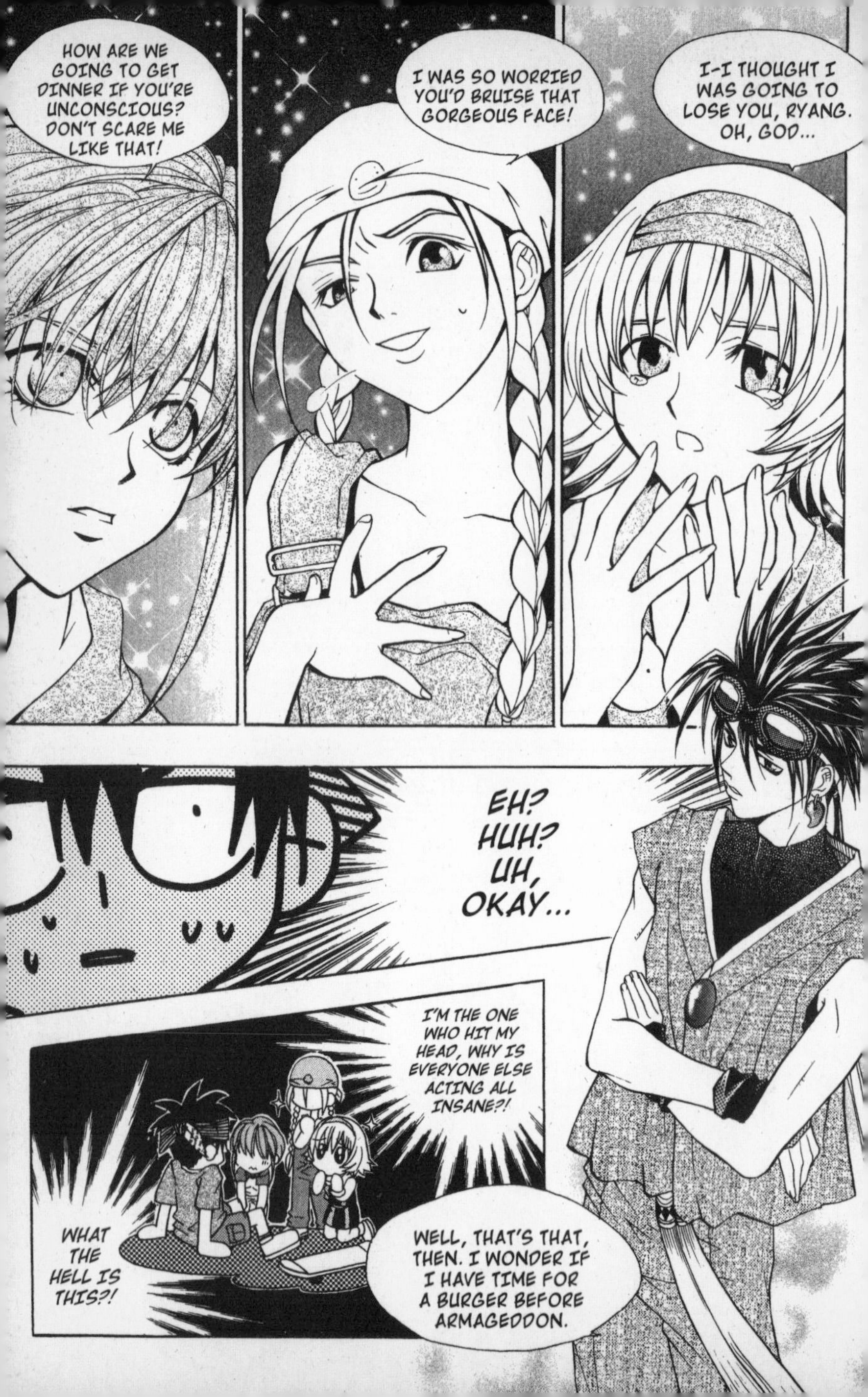
HOW ARE WE GOING TO GET DINNER IF YOU'RE UNCONSCIOUS? DON'T SCARE ME LIKE THAT!
I WAS SO WORRIED YOU'D BRUISE THAT GORGEOUS FACE!
I-I THOUGHT I WAS GOING TO LOSE YOU, RYANG. OH, GOD...
EH? HUH? UH, OKAY...
I'M THE ONE WHO HIT MY HEAD, WHY IS EVERYONE ELSE ACTING ALL INSANE?!
WHAT THE HELL IS THIS?!
WELL, THAT'S THAT, THEN. I WONDER IF I HAVE TIME FOR A BURGER BEFORE ARMAGEDDON.

Episode 19 Bring the Pain!

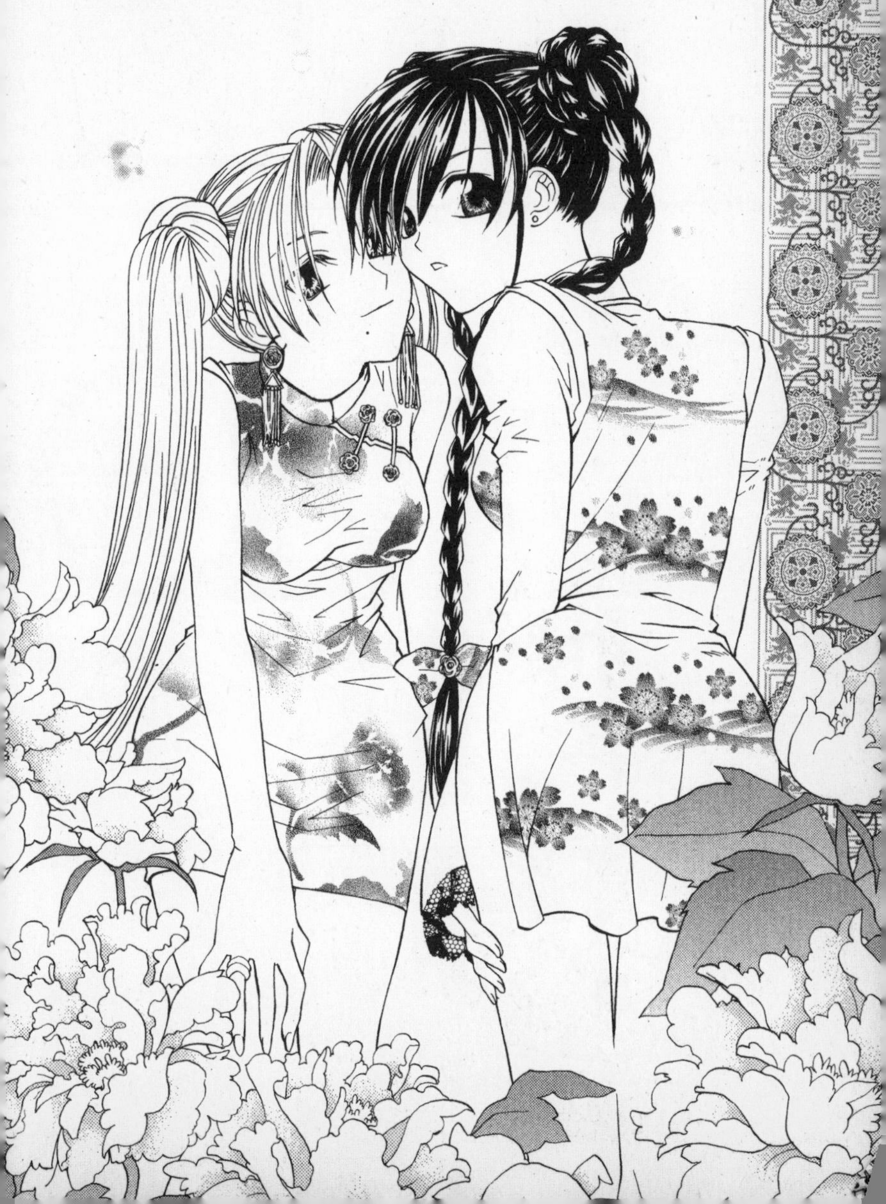

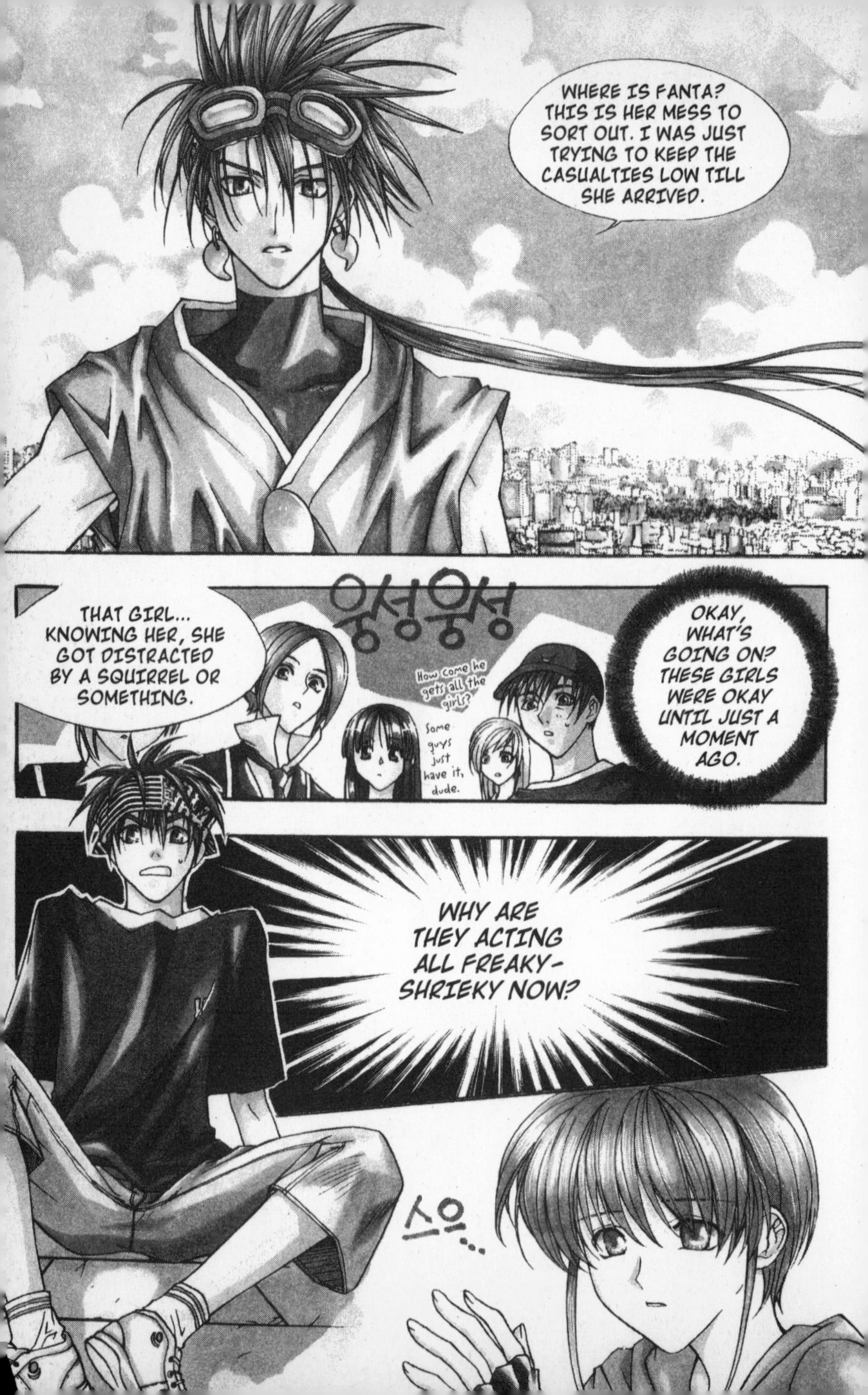
WHERE IS FANTA? THIS IS HER MESS TO SORT OUT. I WAS JUST TRYING TO KEEP THE CASUALTIES LOW TILL SHE ARRIVED.
THAT GIRL... KNOWING HER, SHE GOT DISTRACTED BY A SQUIRREL OR SOMETHING.
웅성웅성
How come he gets all the girls?
Some guys just have it, dude.
OKAY, WHAT'S GOING ON? THESE GIRLS WERE OKAY UNTIL JUST A MOMENT AGO.
WHY ARE THEY ACTING ALL FREAKY-SHRIEKY NOW?
스으...

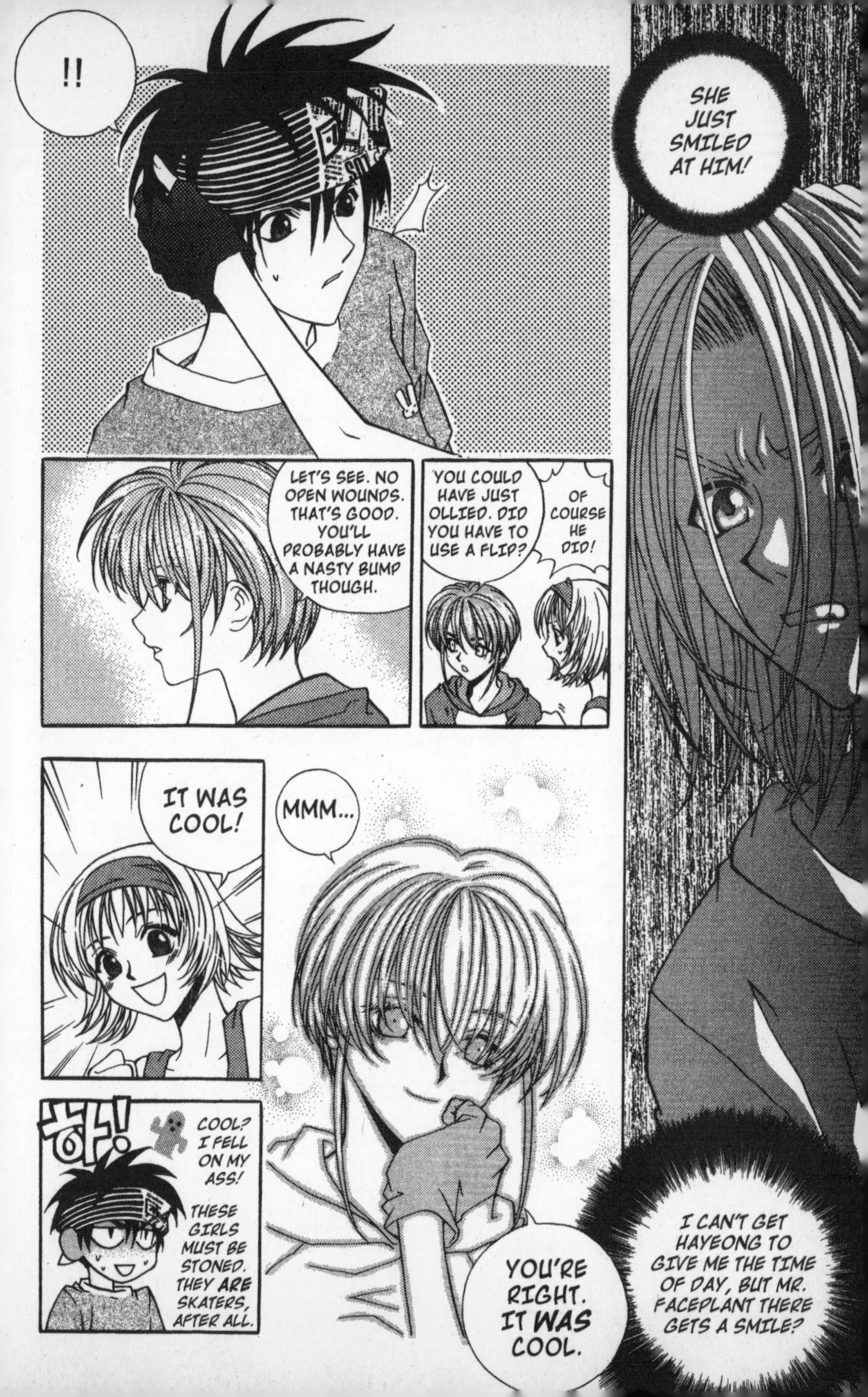
!!
LET'S SEE. NO OPEN WOUNDS. THAT'S GOOD. YOU'LL PROBABLY HAVE A NASTY BUMP THOUGH.
YOU COULD HAVE JUST OLLIED. DID YOU HAVE TO USE A FLIP?
OF COURSE HE DID!
IT WAS COOL!
MMM...
YOU'RE RIGHT. IT WAS COOL.
COOL? I FELL ON MY ASS!
THESE GIRLS MUST BE STONED. THEY ARE SKATERS, AFTER ALL.
SHE JUST SMILED AT HIM!
I CAN'T GET HAYEONG TO GIVE ME THE TIME OF DAY, BUT MR. FACEPLANT THERE GETS A SMILE?

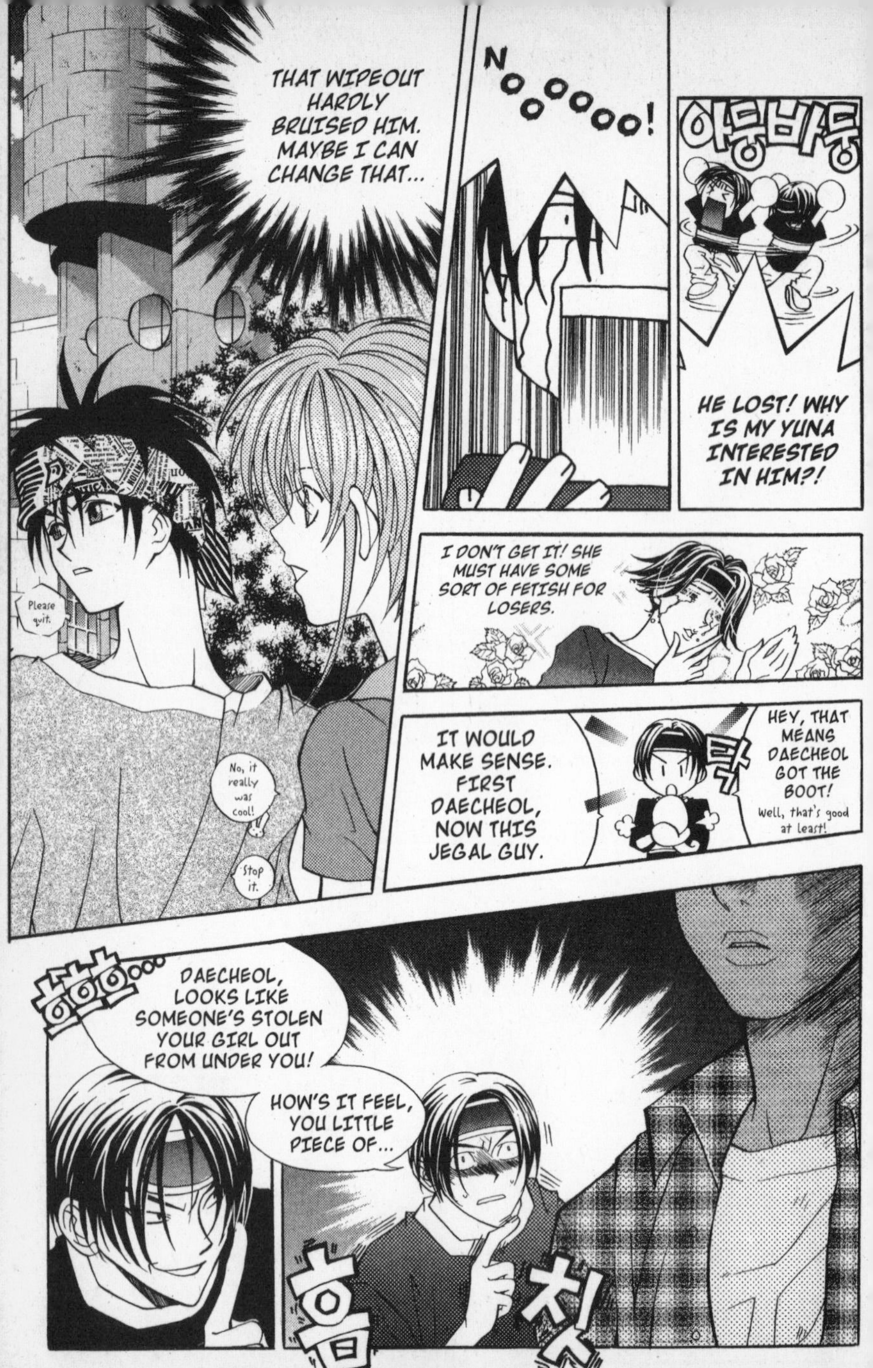
THAT WIPEOUT HARDLY BRUISED HIM. MAYBE I CAN CHANGE THAT...
Please quit.
No, it really was cool!
Stop it.
NOOOOOOO!
아둥바둥
HE LOST! WHY IS MY YUNA INTERESTED IN HIM?!
I DON'T GET IT! SHE MUST HAVE SOME SORT OF FETISH FOR LOSERS.
IT WOULD MAKE SENSE. FIRST DAECHEOL, NOW THIS JEGAL GUY.
탁
HEY, THAT MEANS DAECHEOL GOT THE BOOT!
Well, that's good at least!
흐흐흐...
DAECHEOL, LOOKS LIKE SOMEONE'S STOLEN YOUR GIRL OUT FROM UNDER YOU!
HOW'S IT FEEL, YOU LITTLE PIECE OF...
흡
칫

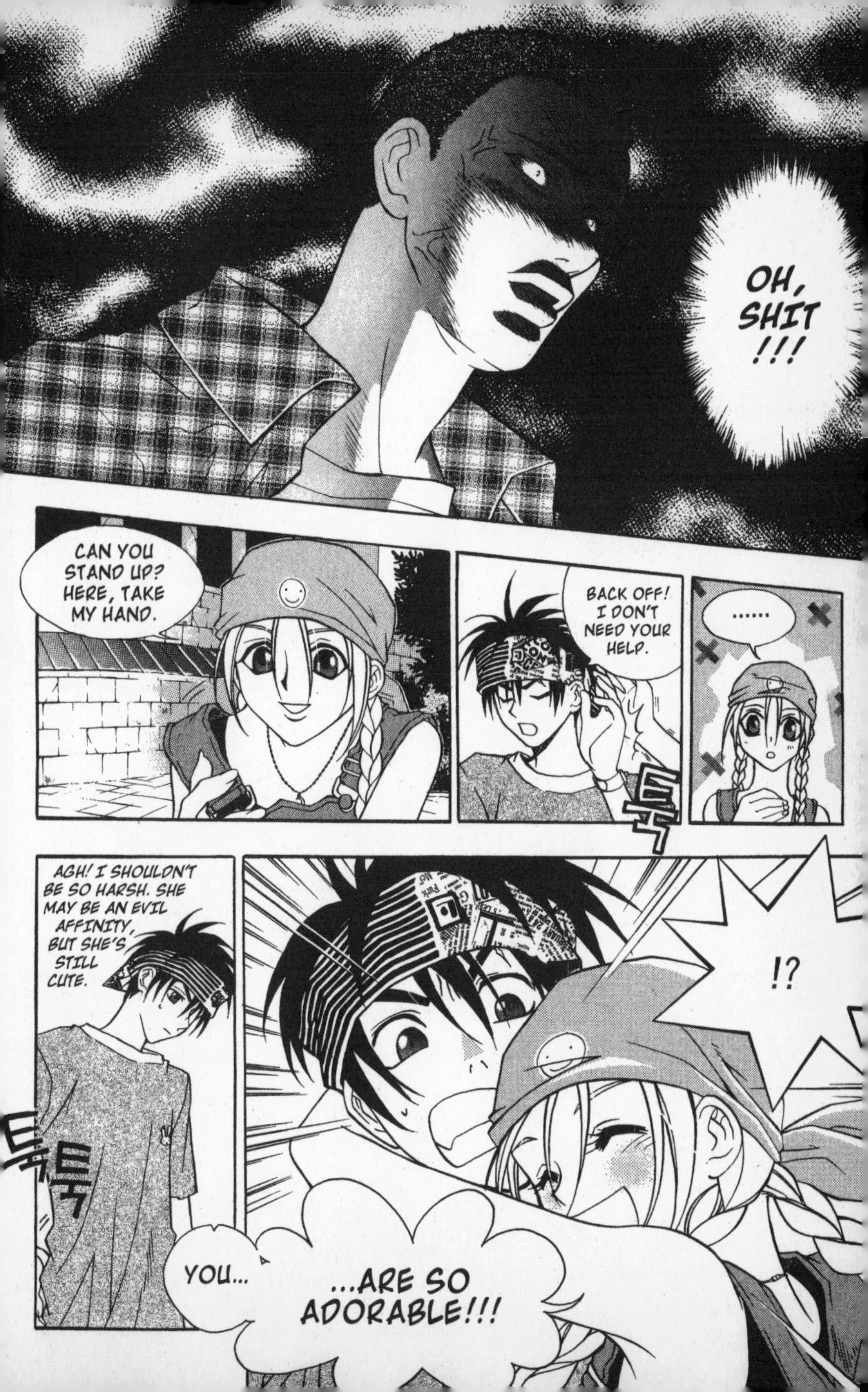
OH, SHIT !!!
CAN YOU STAND UP? HERE, TAKE MY HAND.
BACK OFF! I DON'T NEED YOUR HELP.
......
AGH! I SHOULDN'T BE SO HARSH. SHE MAY BE AN EVIL AFFINITY, BUT SHE'S STILL CUTE.
!?
YOU...
...ARE SO ADORABLE!!!

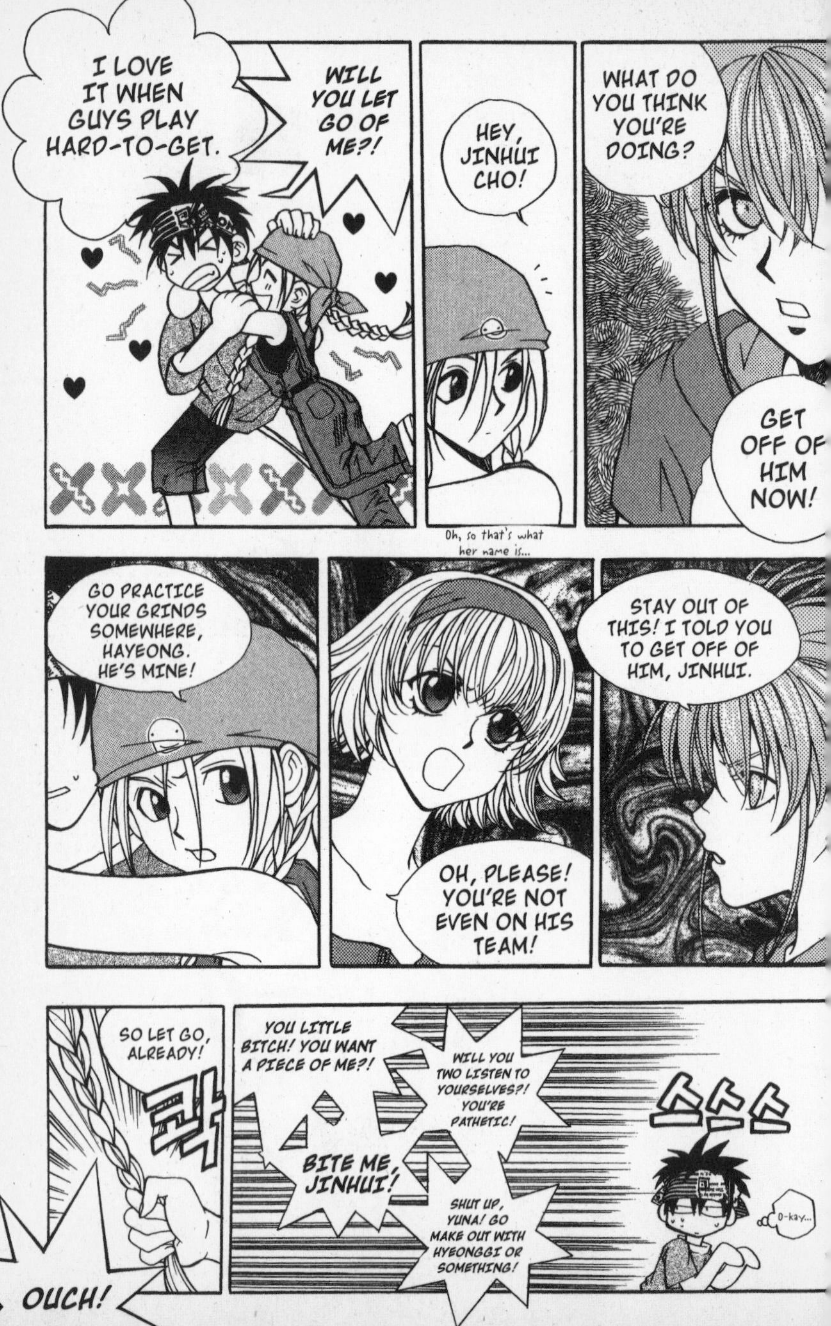
I LOVE IT WHEN GUYS PLAY HARD-TO-GET.
WILL YOU LET GO OF ME?!
HEY, JINHUI CHO!
Oh, so that's what her name is...
WHAT DO YOU THINK YOU'RE DOING?
GET OFF OF HIM NOW!
GO PRACTICE YOUR GRINDS SOMEWHERE, HAYEONG. HE'S MINE!
OH, PLEASE! YOU'RE NOT EVEN ON HIS TEAM!
STAY OUT OF THIS! I TOLD YOU TO GET OFF OF HIM, JINHUI.
SO LET GO, ALREADY!
콱
OUCH!
YOU LITTLE BITCH! YOU WANT A PIECE OF ME?!
WILL YOU TWO LISTEN TO YOURSELVES?! YOU'RE PATHETIC!
BITE ME, JINHUI!
SHUT UP, YUNA! GO MAKE OUT WITH HYEONGGI OR SOMETHING!
스스스
O-kay...

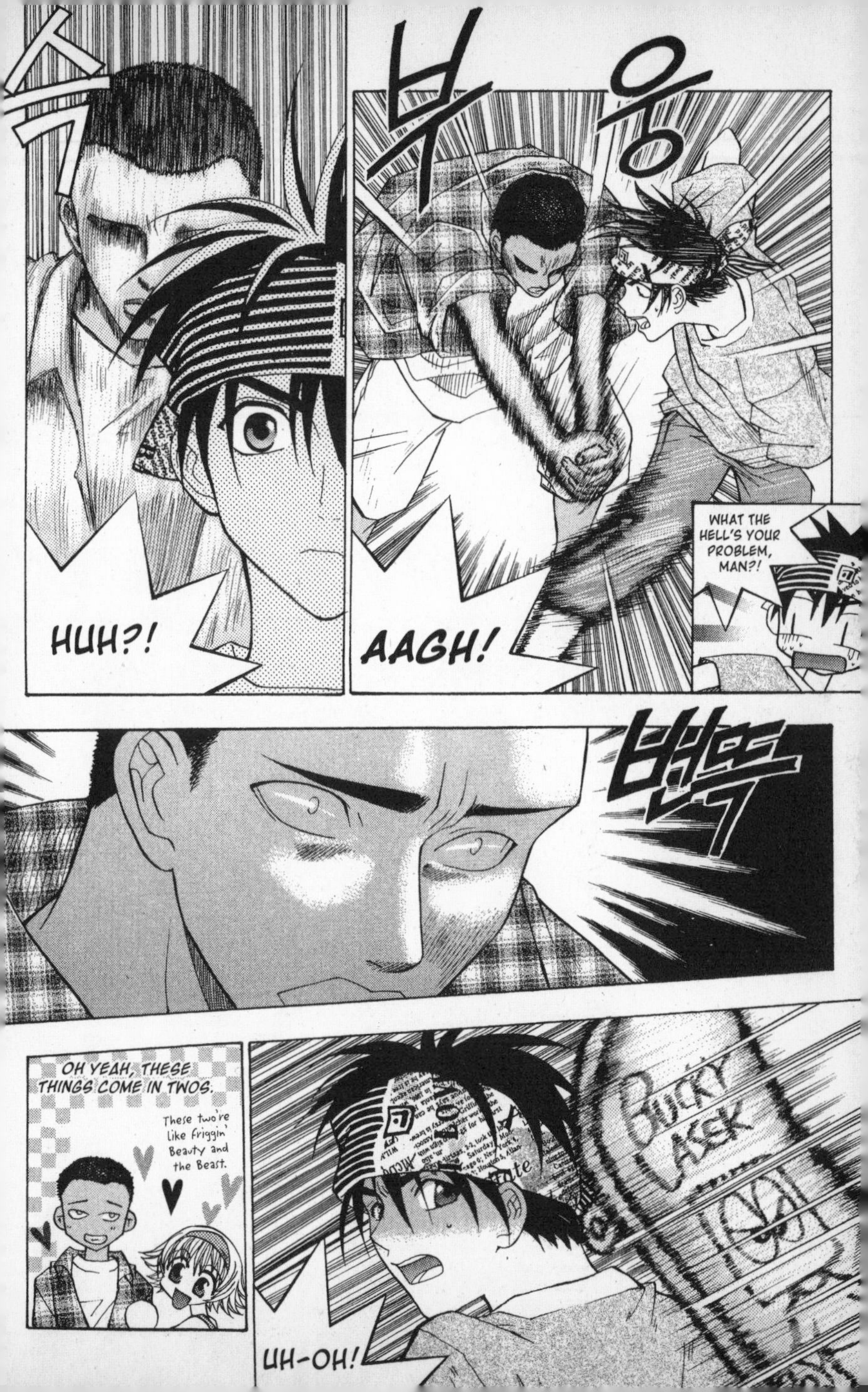
HUH?!
부웅
AAGH!
WHAT THE HELL'S YOUR PROBLEM, MAN?!
번뜩
OH YEAH, THESE THINGS COME IN TWOS.
These two're like friggin' Beauty and the Beast.
BUCKY LASEK
UH-OH!

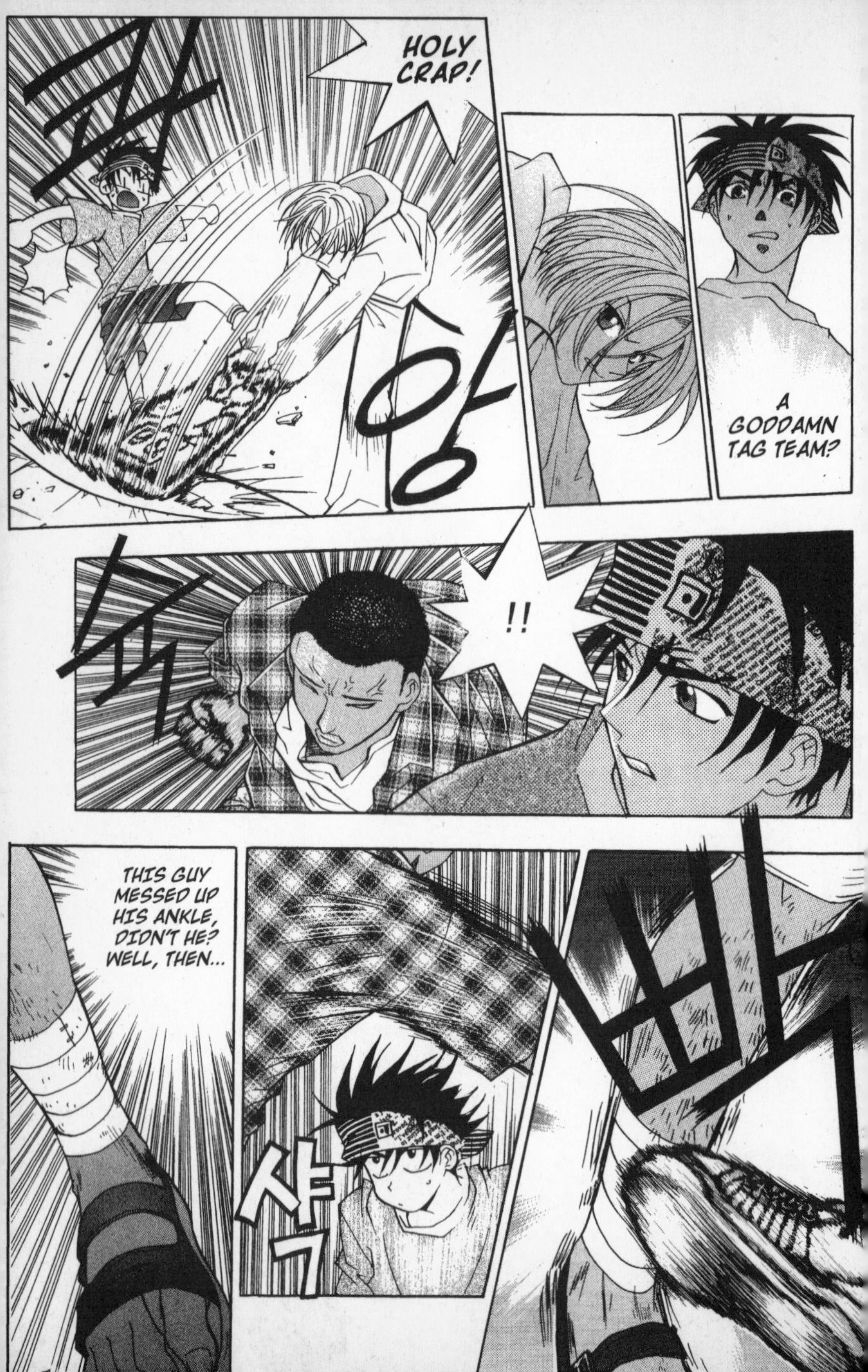
HOLY CRAP!
A GODDAMN TAG TEAM?
!!
THIS GUY MESSED UP HIS ANKLE, DIDN'T HE? WELL, THEN...

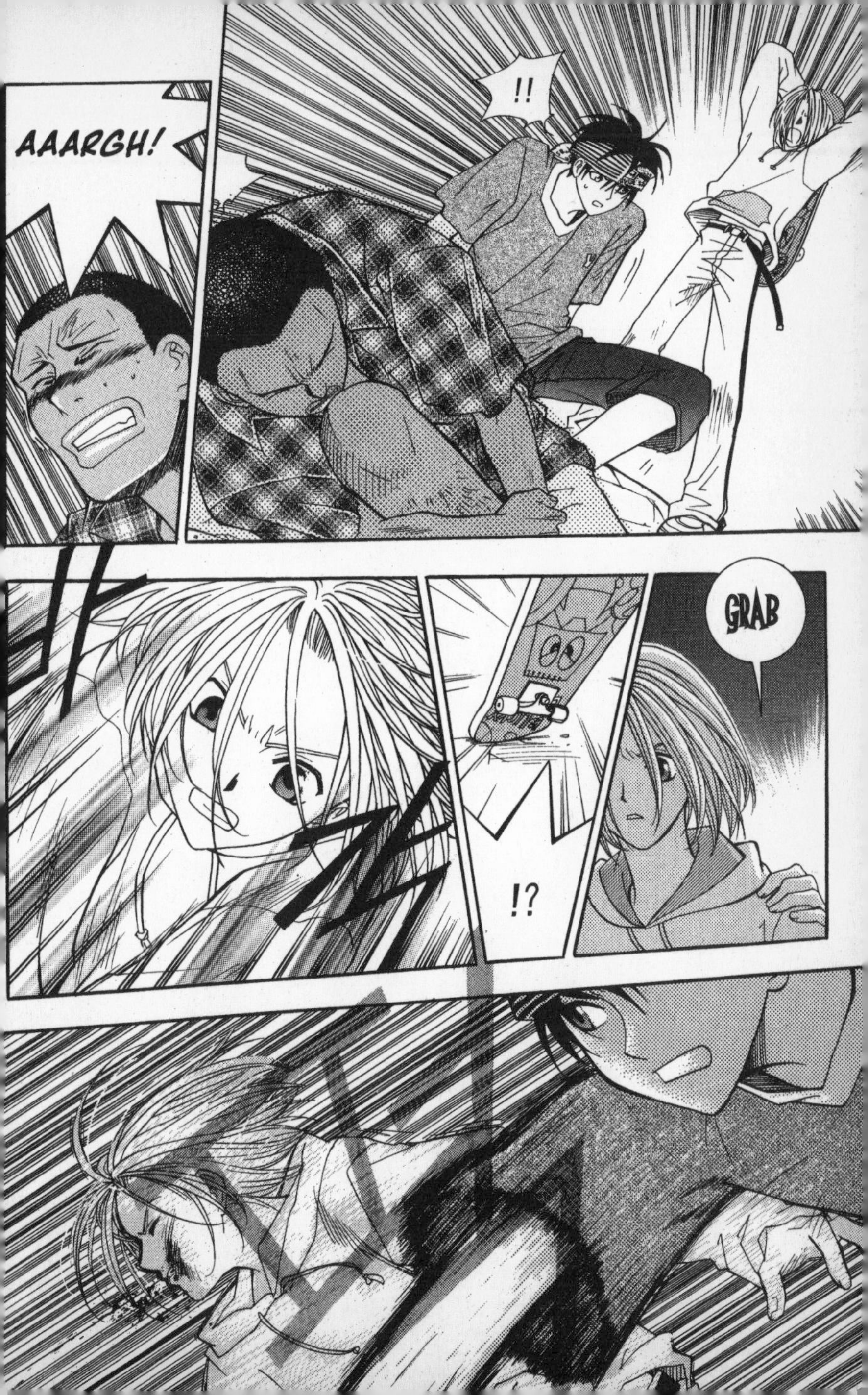
AAARGH!
!!
!?
GRAB

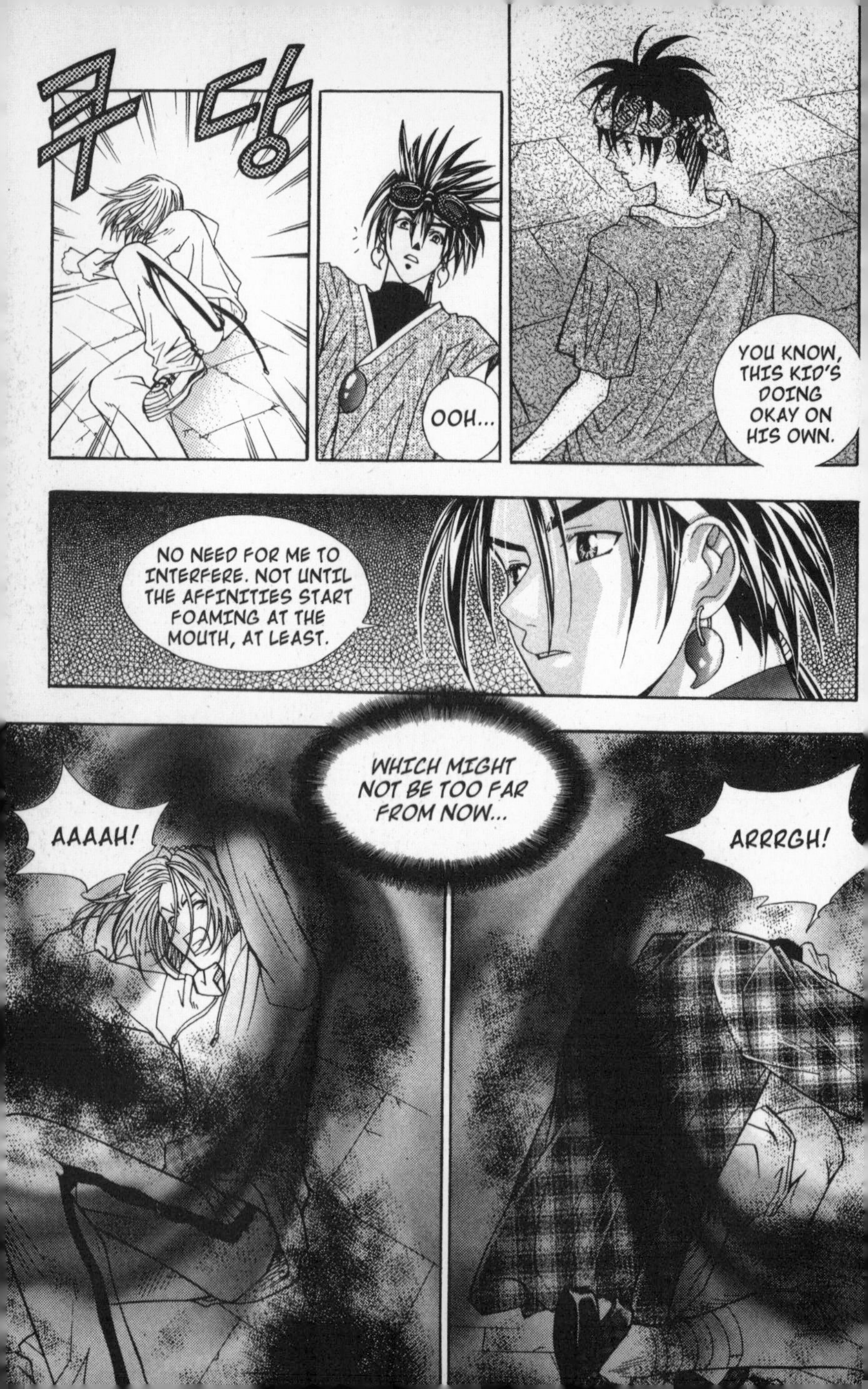
쿠당
OOH...
YOU KNOW, THIS KID'S DOING OKAY ON HIS OWN.
NO NEED FOR ME TO INTERFERE. NOT UNTIL THE AFFINITIES START FOAMING AT THE MOUTH, AT LEAST.
AAAAH!
WHICH MIGHT NOT BE TOO FAR FROM NOW...
ARRRGH!

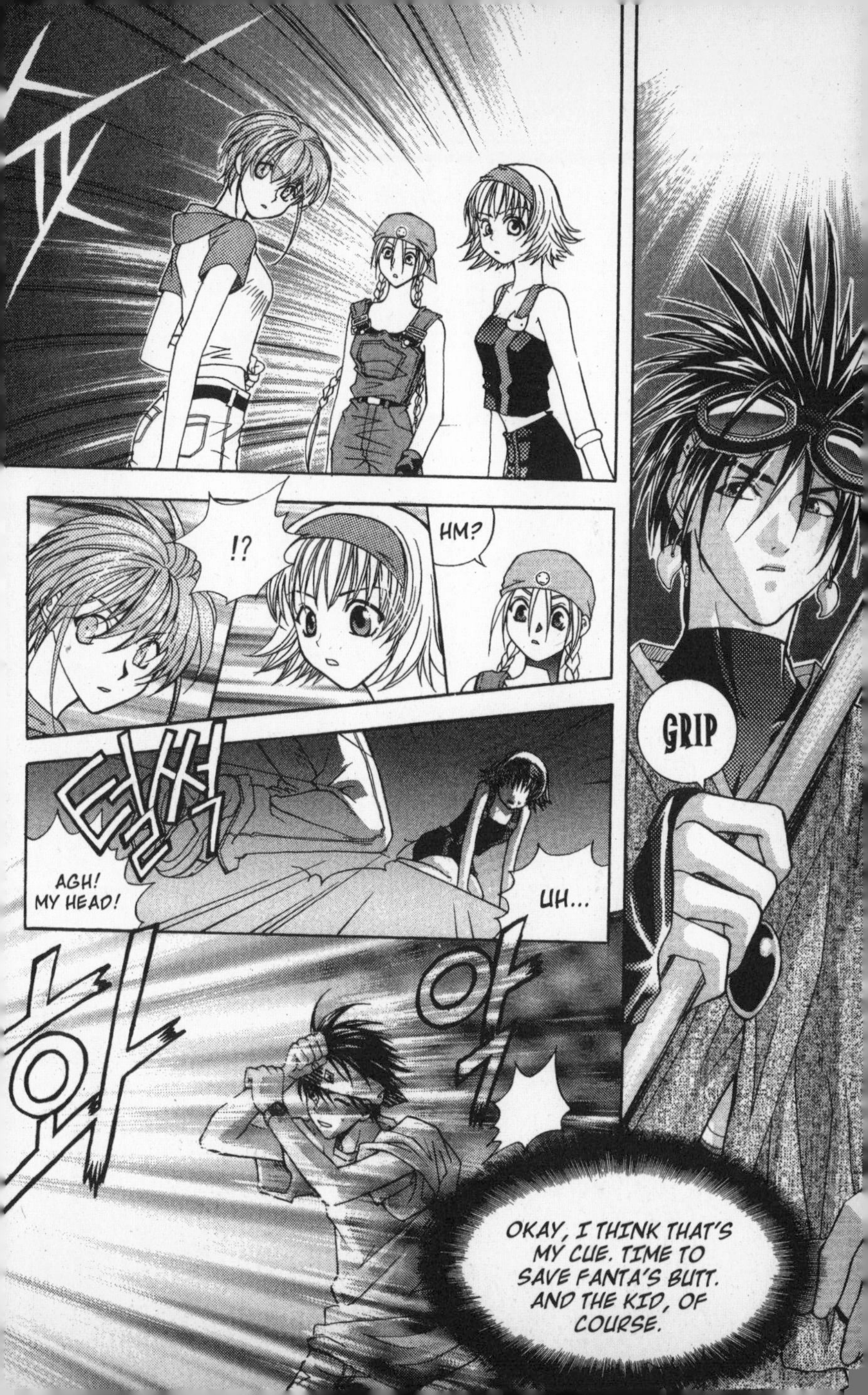
!?
HM?
AGH! MY HEAD!
UH...
GRIP
OKAY, I THINK THAT'S MY CUE. TIME TO SAVE FANTA'S BUTT. AND THE KID, OF COURSE.

IT APPEARS THESE EVIL AFFINITIES ARE ABOUT TO SHOW THEIR TRUE FACES!

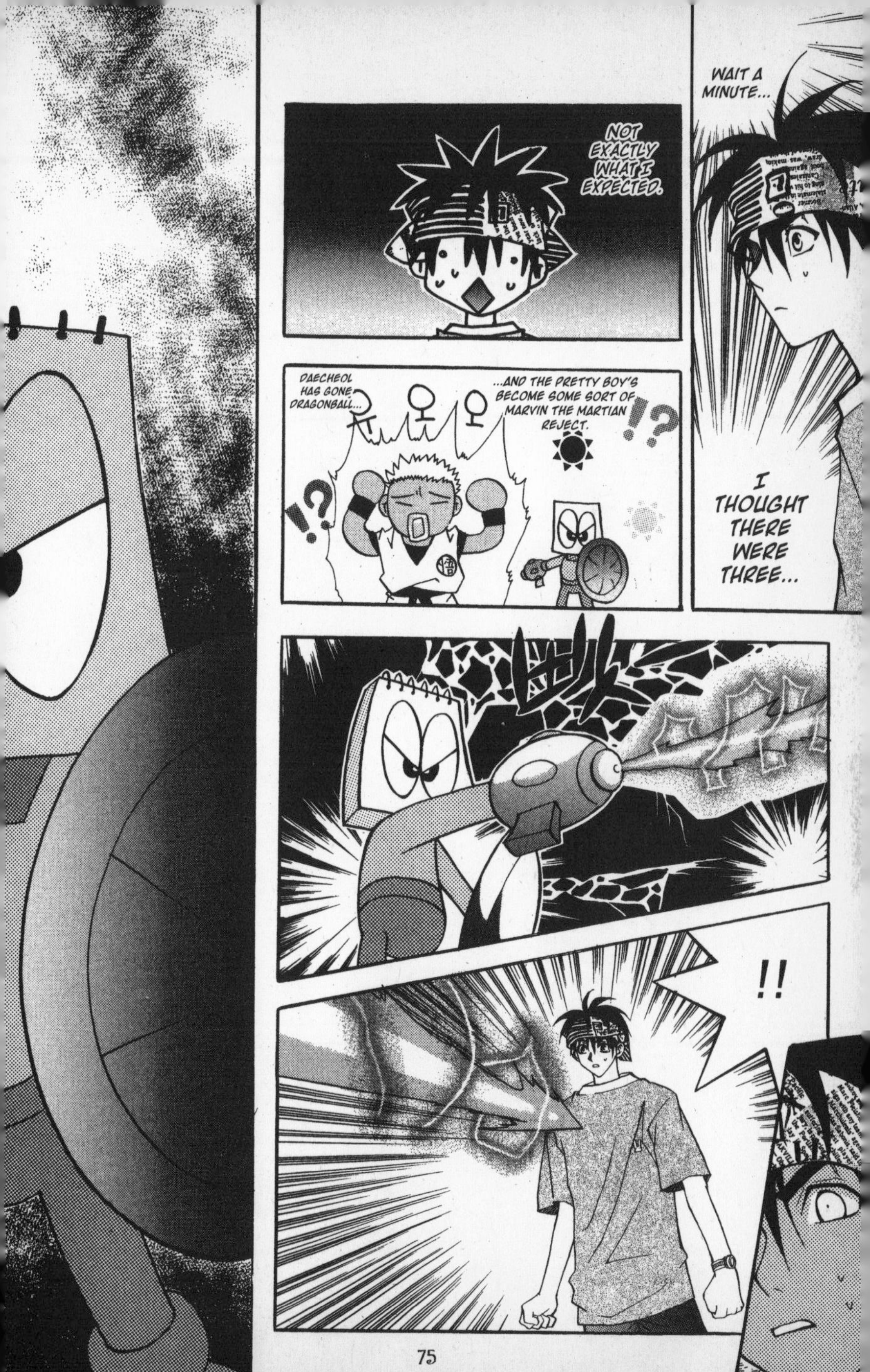
NOT EXACTLY WHAT I EXPECTED.
DAECHEOL HAS GONE DRAGONBALL...
...AND THE PRETTY BOY'S BECOME SOME SORT OF MARVIN THE MARTIAN REJECT.
!?
!?
WAIT A MINUTE...
I THOUGHT THERE WERE THREE...
!!

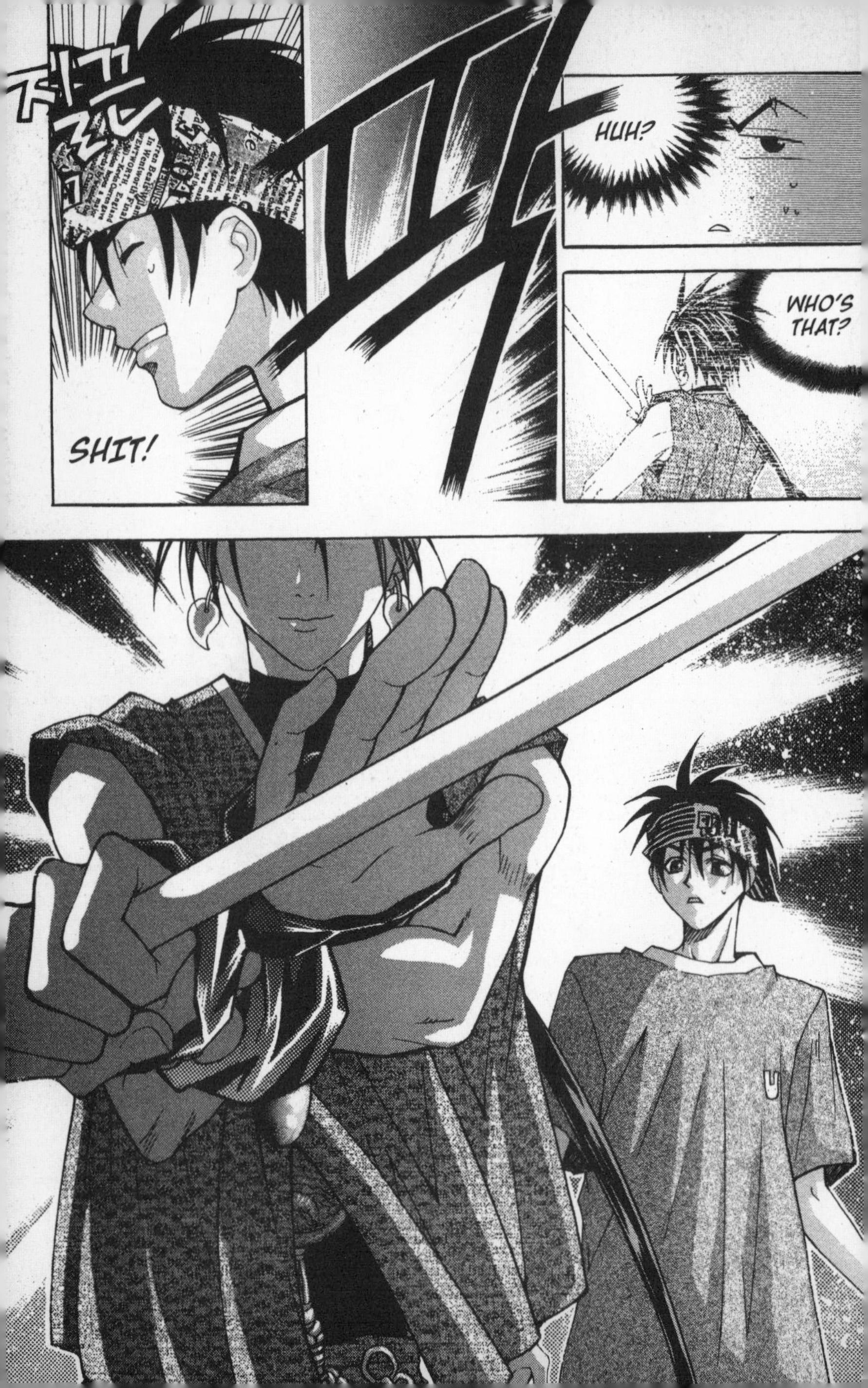
SHIT!
HUH?
WHO'S THAT?

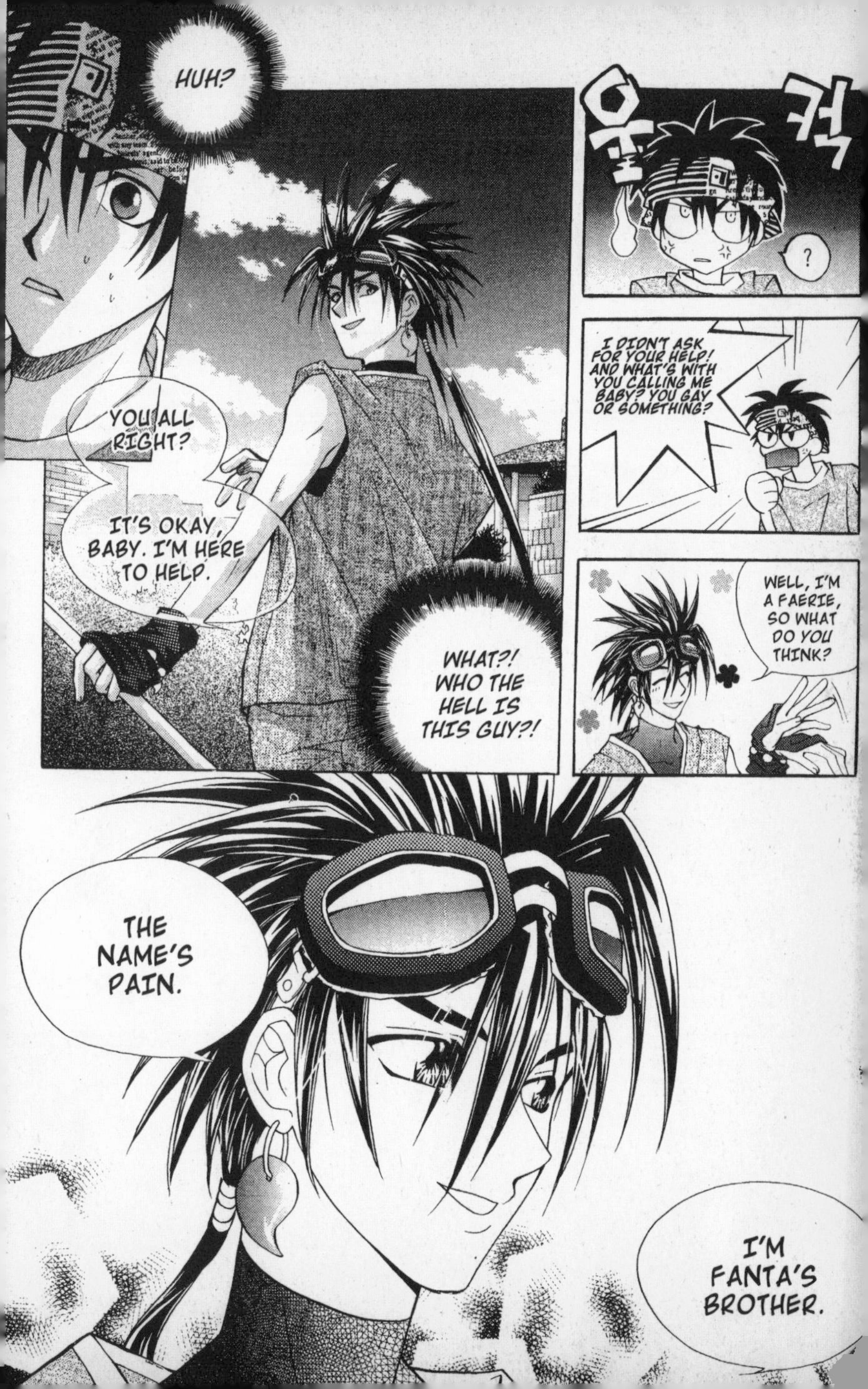
HUH?
YOU ALL RIGHT?
IT'S OKAY, BABY. I'M HERE TO HELP.
WHAT?! WHO THE HELL IS THIS GUY?!
울컥
?
I DIDN'T ASK FOR YOUR HELP! AND WHAT'S WITH YOU CALLING ME BABY? YOU GAY OR SOMETHING?
WELL, I'M A FAERIE, SO WHAT DO YOU THINK?
THE NAME'S PAIN.
I'M FANTA'S BROTHER.

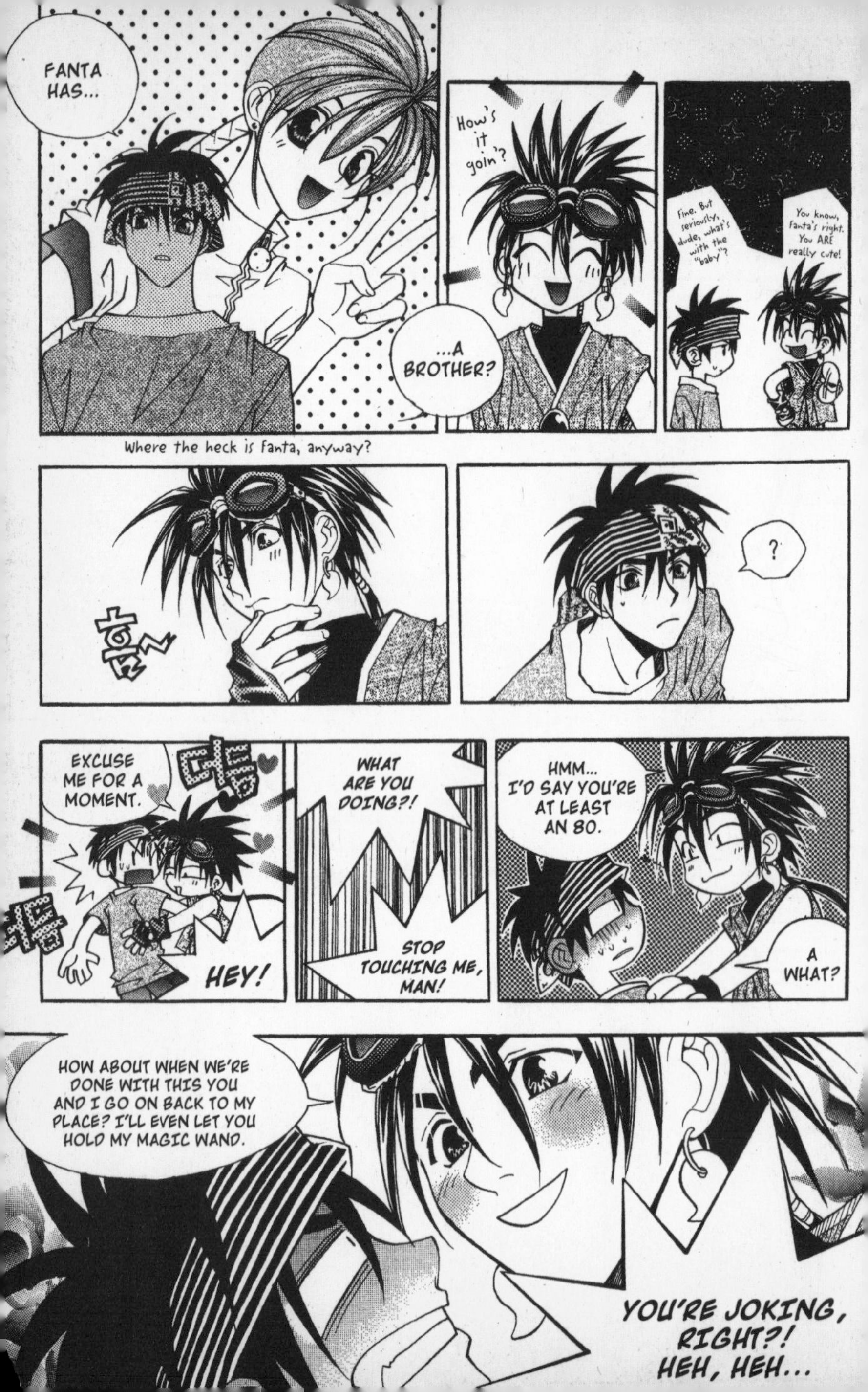
FANTA HAS...
...A BROTHER?
How's it goin'?
Fine. But seriously, dude, what's with the "baby"?
You know, Fanta's right. You ARE really cute!
Where the heck is Fanta, anyway?
?
EXCUSE ME FOR A MOMENT.
HEY!
WHAT ARE YOU DOING?!
STOP TOUCHING ME, MAN!
HMM... I'D SAY YOU'RE AT LEAST AN 80.
A WHAT?
HOW ABOUT WHEN WE'RE DONE WITH THIS YOU AND I GO ON BACK TO MY PLACE? I'LL EVEN LET YOU HOLD MY MAGIC WAND.
YOU'RE JOKING, RIGHT?! HEH, HEH...

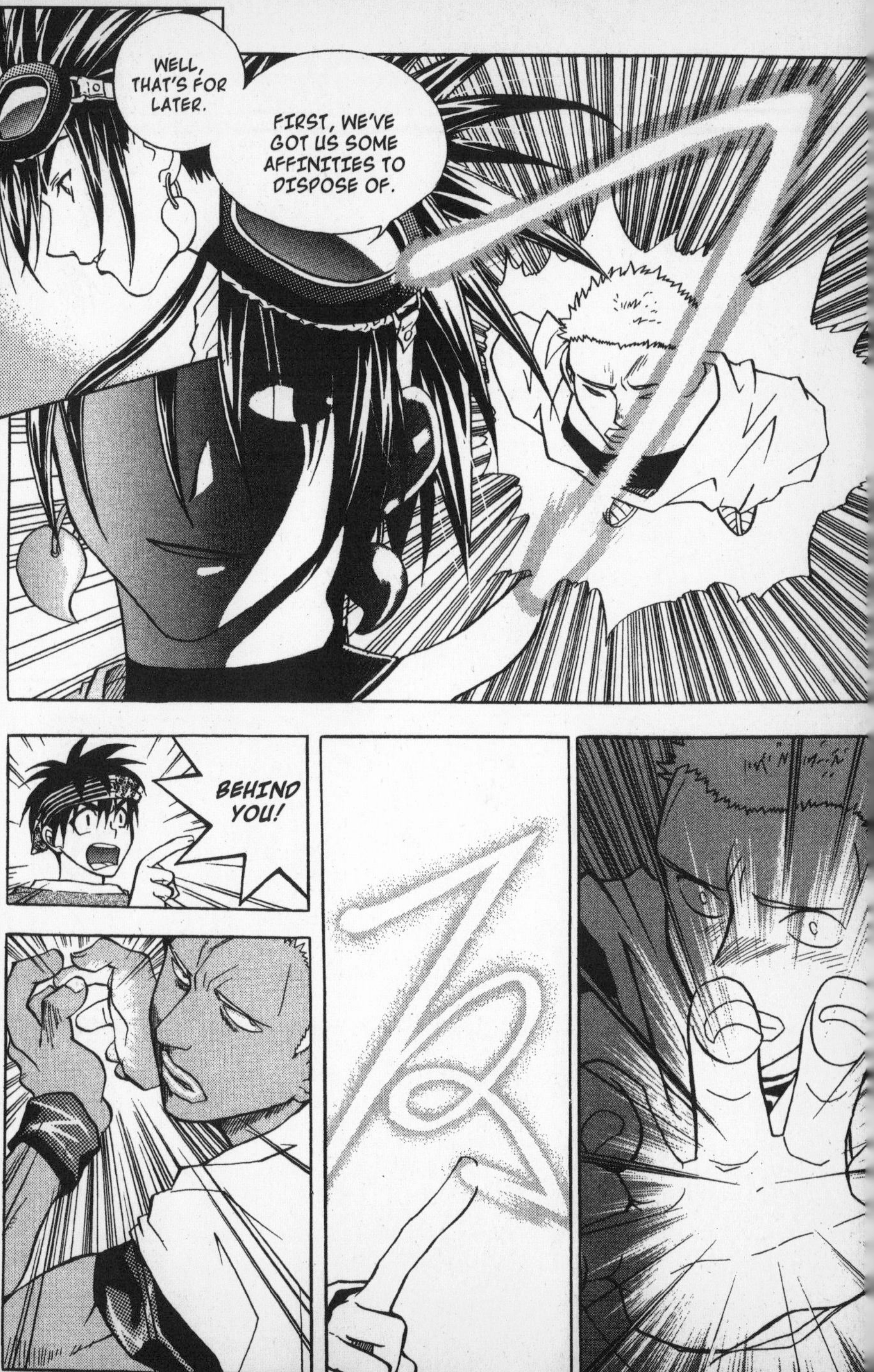
WELL, THAT'S FOR LATER.
FIRST, WE'VE GOT US SOME AFFINITIES TO DISPOSE OF.
BEHIND YOU!

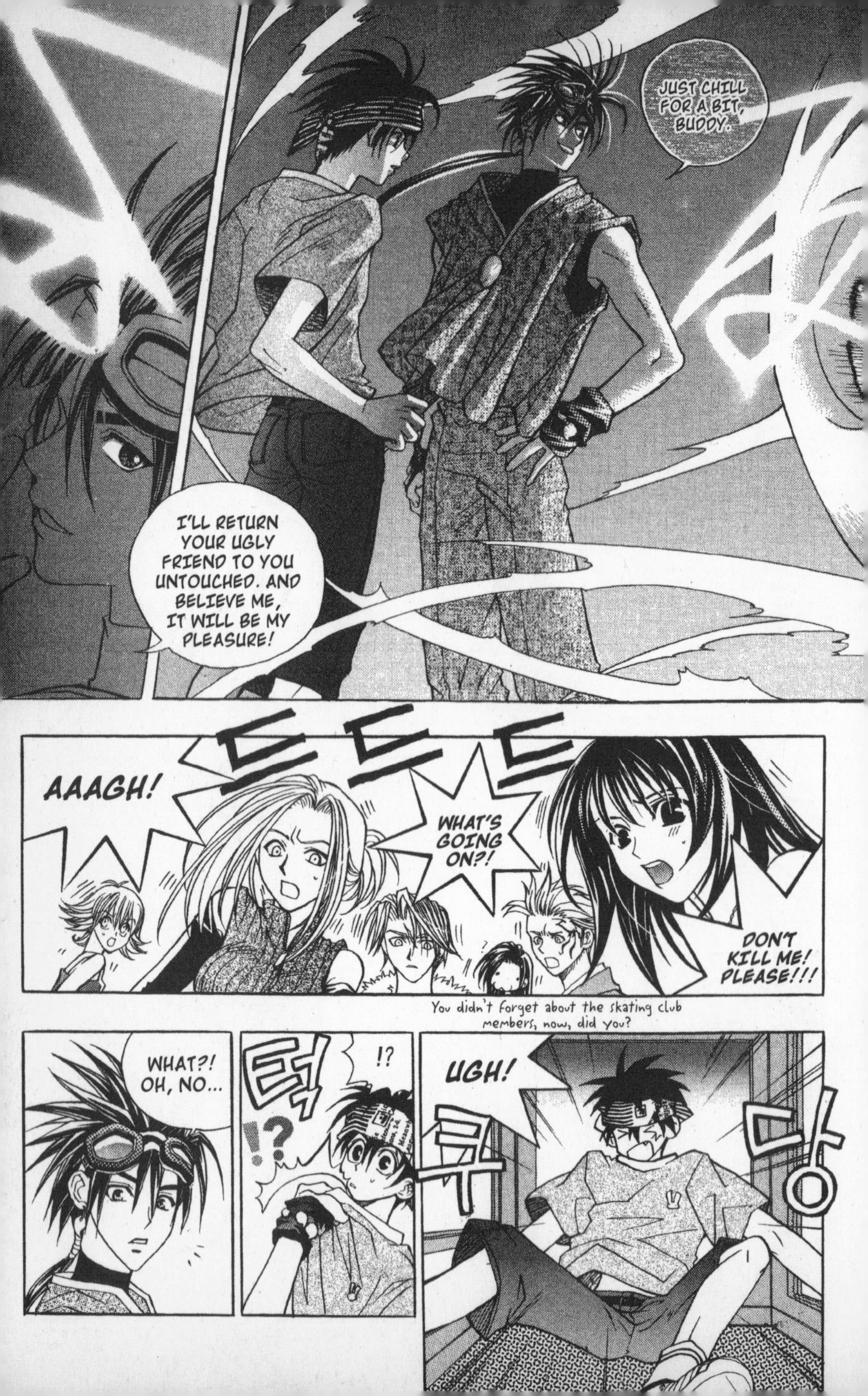
JUST CHILL FOR A BIT, BUDDY.
I'LL RETURN YOUR UGLY FRIEND TO YOU UNTOUCHED. AND BELIEVE ME, IT WILL BE MY PLEASURE!
AAAGH!
드드드
WHAT'S GOING ON?!
DON'T KILL ME! PLEASE!!!
You didn't forget about the skating club members, now, did you?
WHAT?! OH, NO...
턱
!?
!?
UGH!
쿠
당

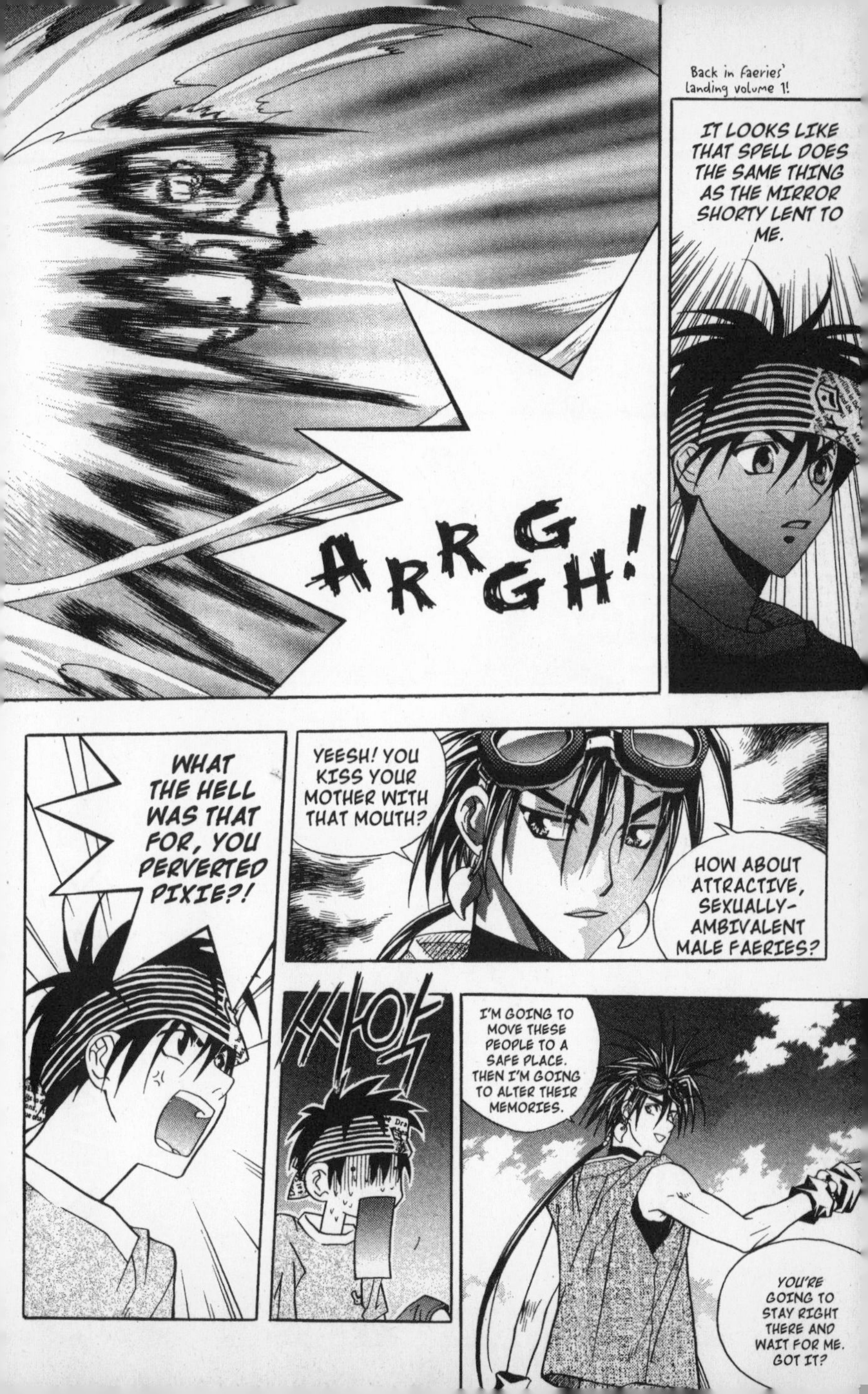
ARRGH!
Back in faeries' landing volume 1!
IT LOOKS LIKE THAT SPELL DOES THE SAME THING AS THE MIRROR SHORTY LENT TO ME.
WHAT THE HELL WAS THAT FOR, YOU PERVERTED PIXIE?!
YEESH! YOU KISS YOUR MOTHER WITH THAT MOUTH?
HOW ABOUT ATTRACTIVE, SEXUALLY-AMBIVALENT MALE FAERIES?
I'M GOING TO MOVE THESE PEOPLE TO A SAFE PLACE. THEN I'M GOING TO ALTER THEIR MEMORIES.
YOU'RE GOING TO STAY RIGHT THERE AND WAIT FOR ME. GOT IT?

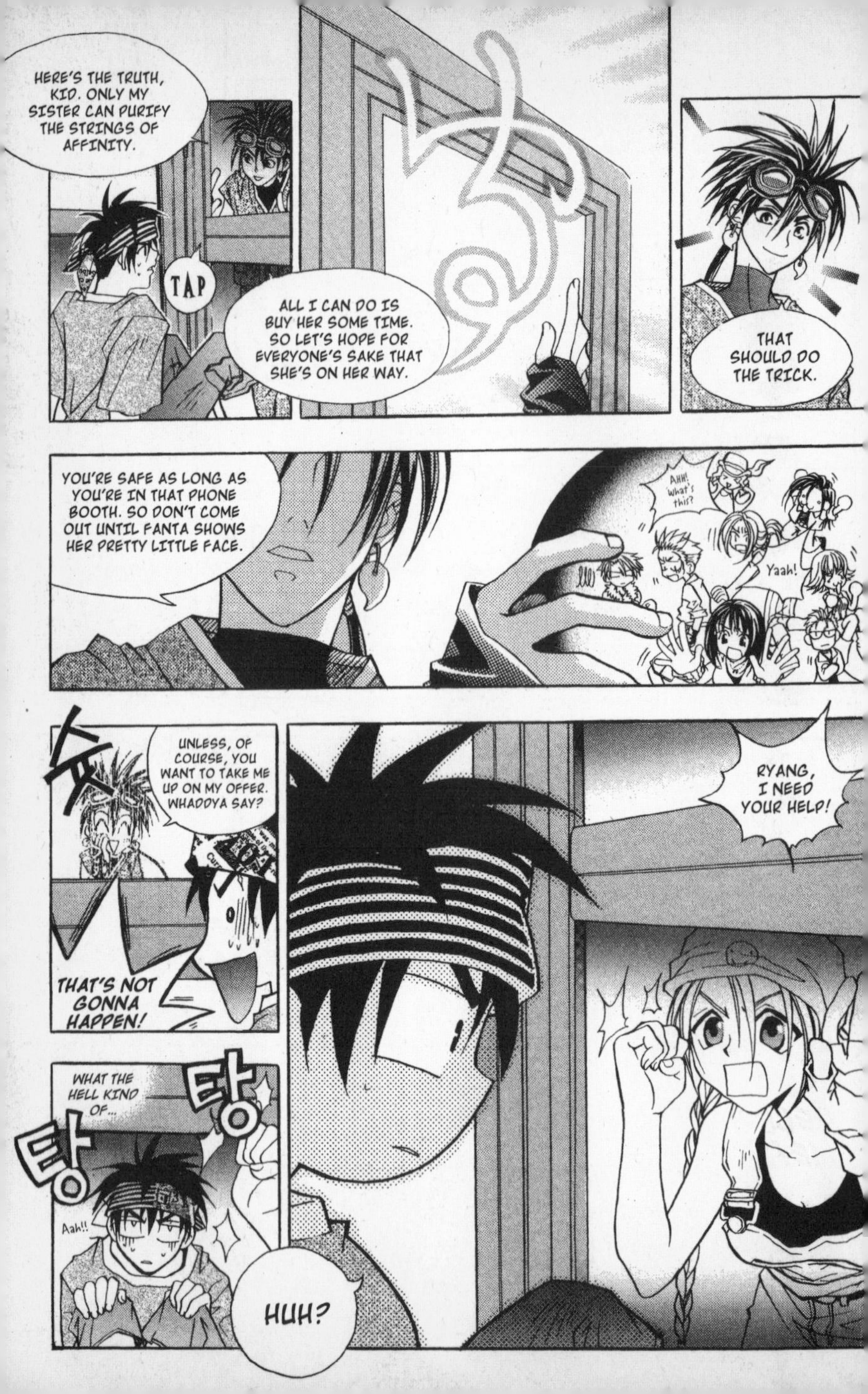
HERE'S THE TRUTH, KID. ONLY MY SISTER CAN PURIFY THE STRINGS OF AFFINITY.
TAP
ALL I CAN DO IS BUY HER SOME TIME. SO LET'S HOPE FOR EVERYONE'S SAKE THAT SHE'S ON HER WAY.
THAT SHOULD DO THE TRICK.
YOU'RE SAFE AS LONG AS YOU'RE IN THAT PHONE BOOTH. SO DON'T COME OUT UNTIL FANTA SHOWS HER PRETTY LITTLE FACE.
AHH! What's this?
Yaah!
UNLESS, OF COURSE, YOU WANT TO TAKE ME UP ON MY OFFER. WHADDYA SAY?
THAT'S NOT GONNA HAPPEN!
WHAT THE HELL KIND OF...
탕
탕
Aah!!
RYANG, I NEED YOUR HELP!
HUH?

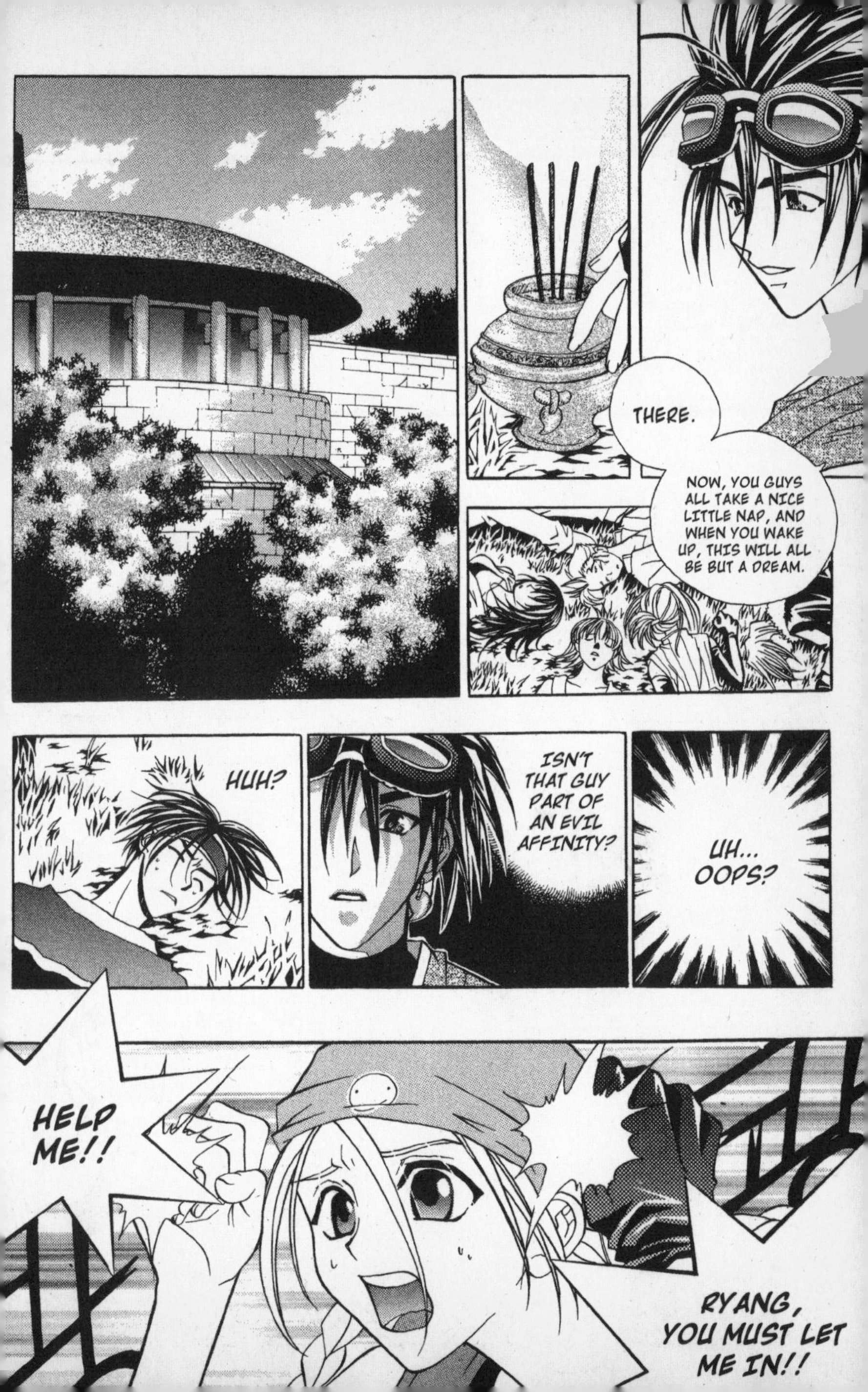
THERE.
NOW, YOU GUYS ALL TAKE A NICE LITTLE NAP, AND WHEN YOU WAKE UP, THIS WILL ALL BE BUT A DREAM.
HUH?
ISN'T THAT GUY PART OF AN EVIL AFFINITY?
UH... OOPS?
HELP ME!!
RYANG, YOU MUST LET ME IN!!

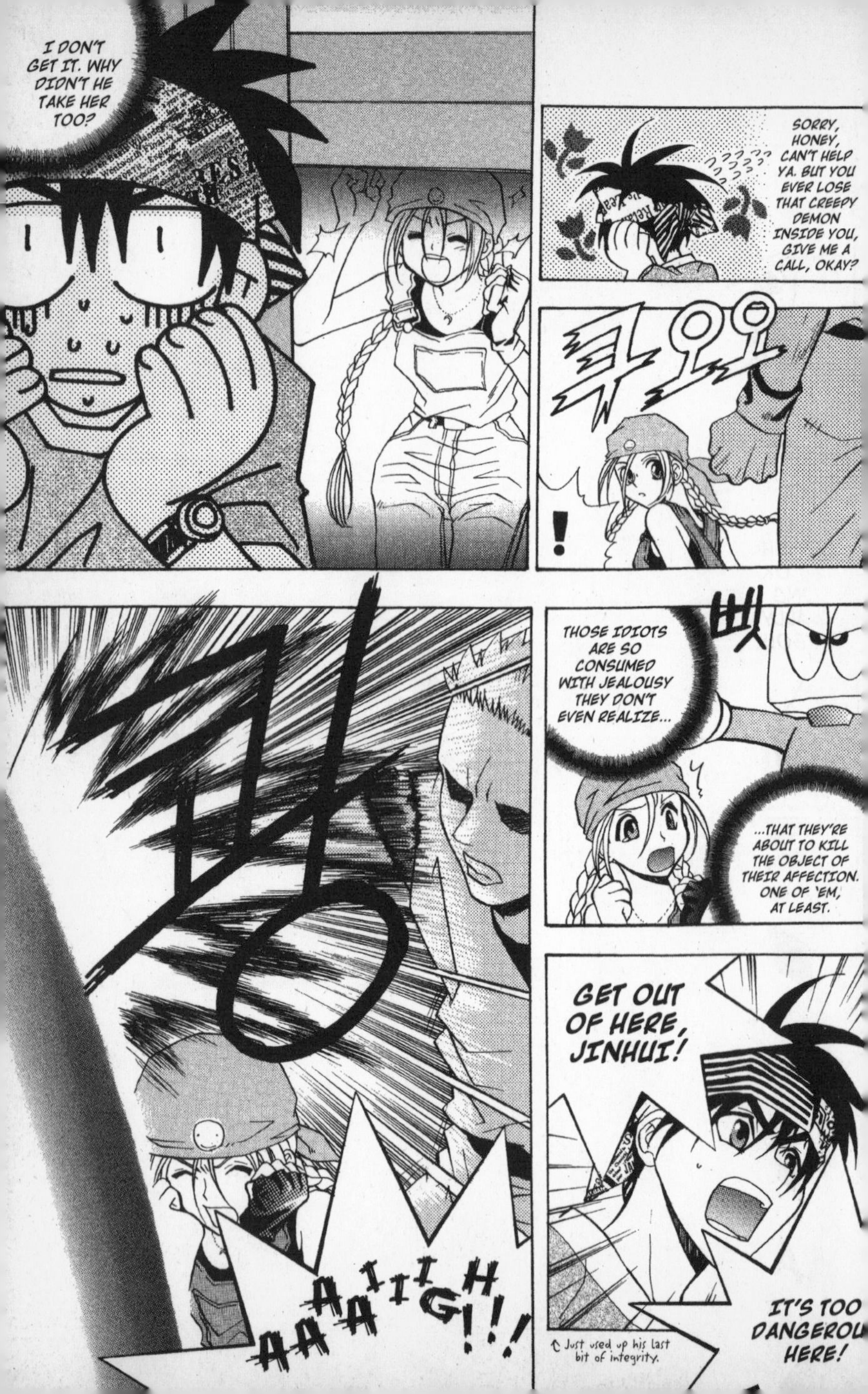
I DON'T GET IT. WHY DIDN'T HE TAKE HER TOO?
SORRY, HONEY, CAN'T HELP YA. BUT YOU EVER LOSE THAT CREEPY DEMON INSIDE YOU, GIVE ME A CALL, OKAY?
!
AAAIIIGH!!!
THOSE IDIOTS ARE SO CONSUMED WITH JEALOUSY THEY DON'T EVEN REALIZE...
...THAT THEY'RE ABOUT TO KILL THE OBJECT OF THEIR AFFECTION. ONE OF 'EM, AT LEAST.
GET OUT OF HERE, JINHUI!
IT'S TOO DANGEROU HERE!
Just used up his last bit of integrity.

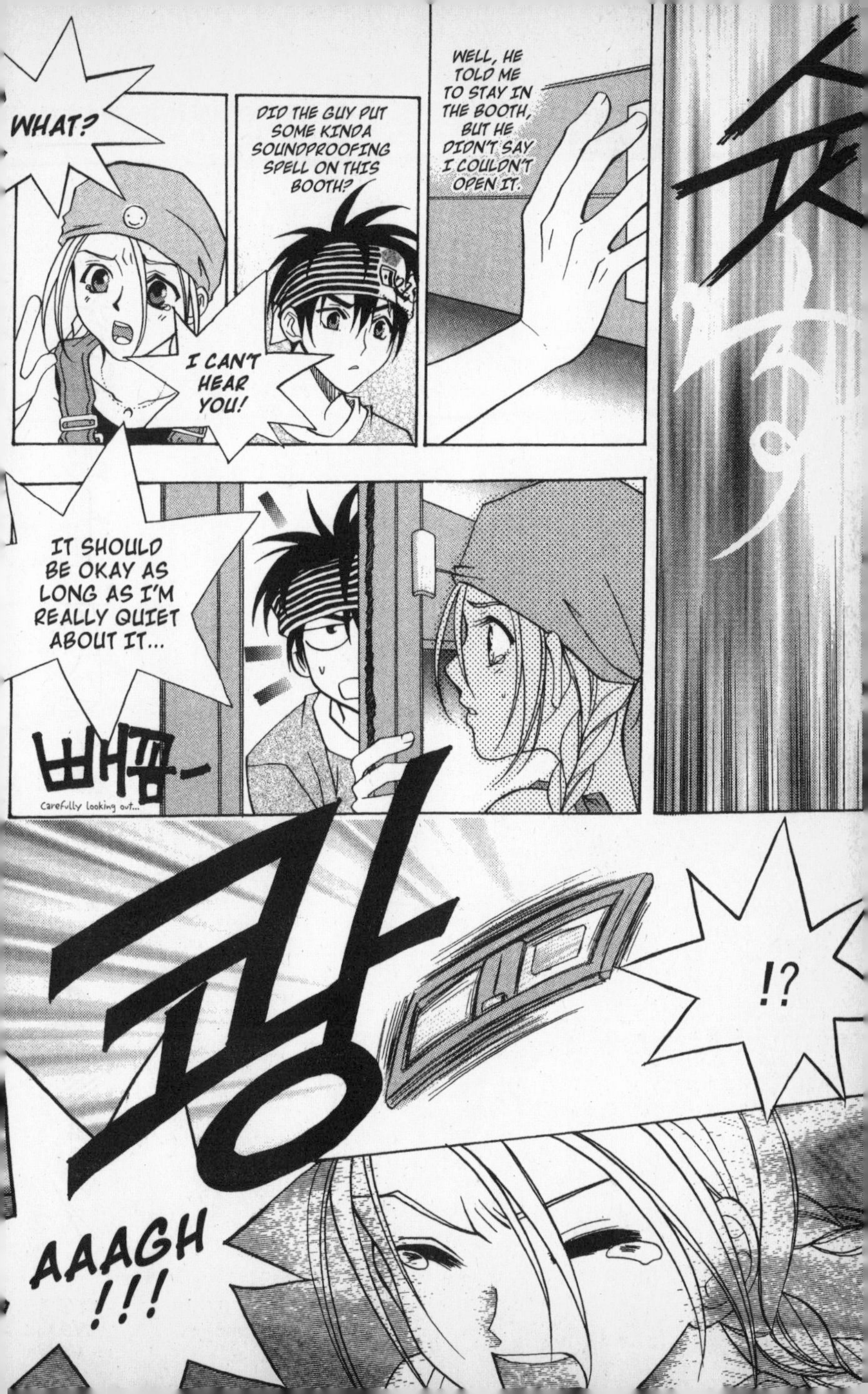
WHAT?
DID THE GUY PUT SOME KINDA SOUNDPROOFING SPELL ON THIS BOOTH?
I CAN'T HEAR YOU!
WELL, HE TOLD ME TO STAY IN THE BOOTH, BUT HE DIDN'T SAY I COULDN'T OPEN IT.
IT SHOULD BE OKAY AS LONG AS I'M REALLY QUIET ABOUT IT...
빼꼼-
Carefully looking out...
!?
AAAGH !!!

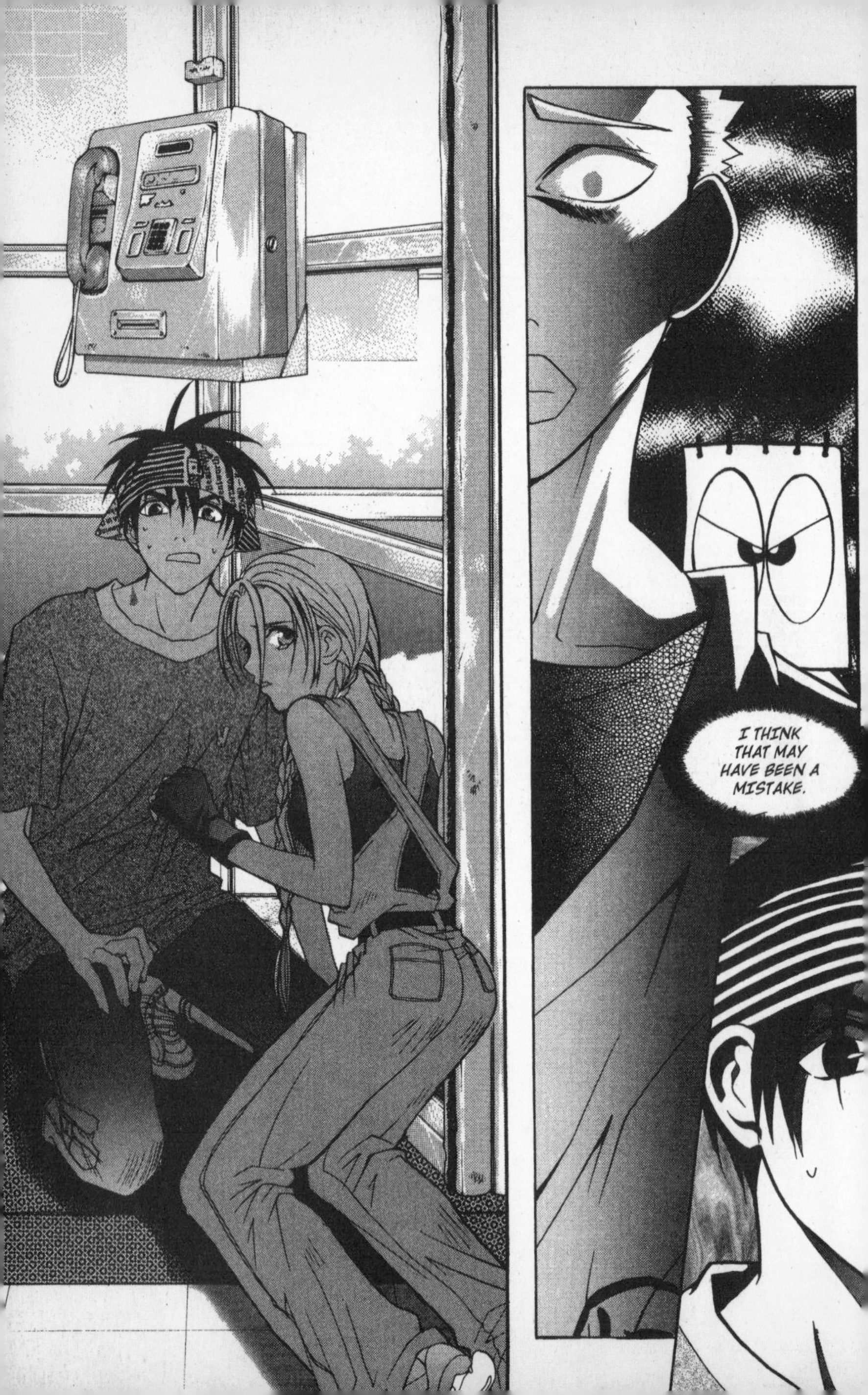
I THINK THAT MAY HAVE BEEN A MISTAKE.

Episode 20
Excaliboard

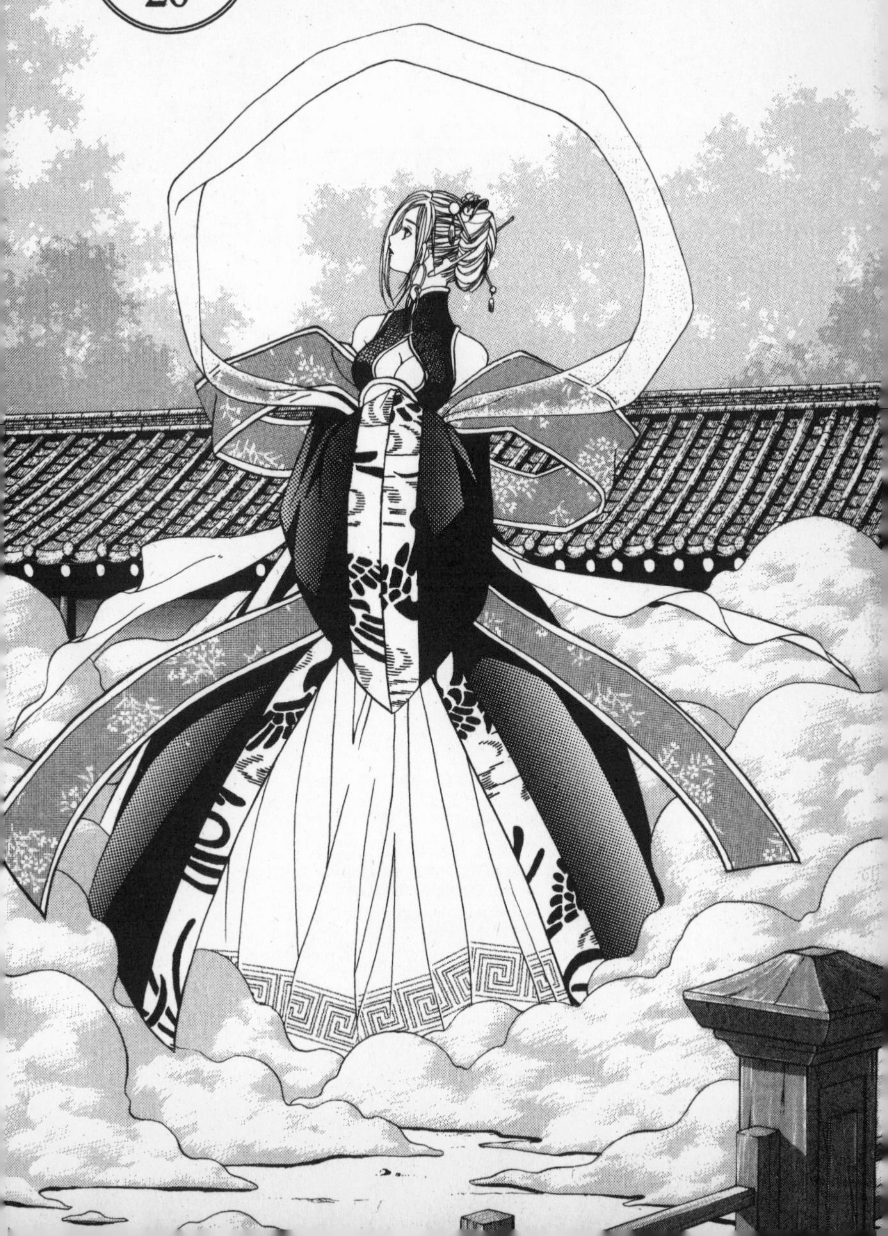

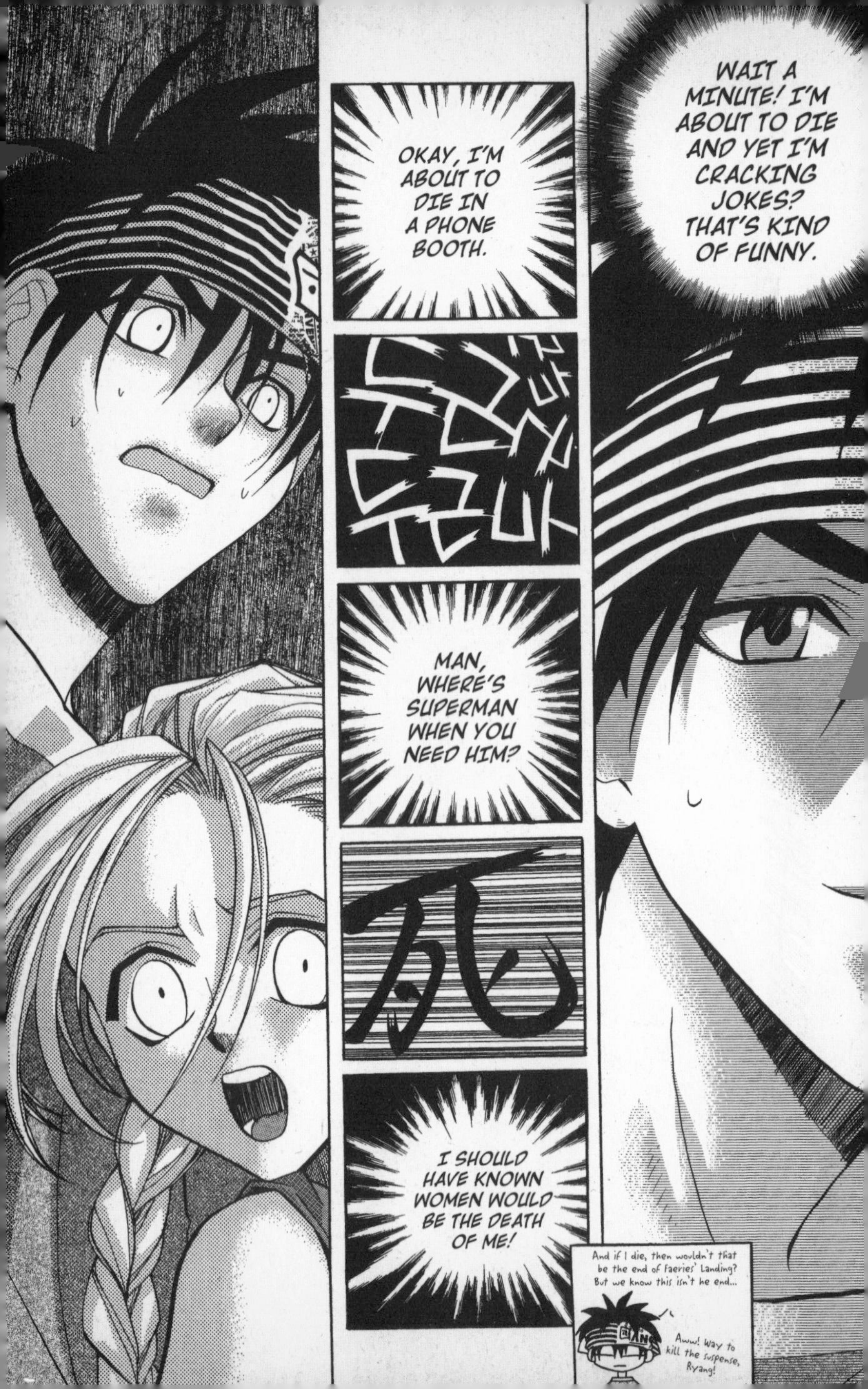
OKAY, I'M ABOUT TO DIE IN A PHONE BOOTH.
MAN, WHERE'S SUPERMAN WHEN YOU NEED HIM?
I SHOULD HAVE KNOWN WOMEN WOULD BE THE DEATH OF ME!
WAIT A MINUTE! I'M ABOUT TO DIE AND YET I'M CRACKING JOKES? THAT'S KIND OF FUNNY.
And if I die, then wouldn't that be the end of Faeries' Landing? But we know this isn't he end...
Aww! Way to kill the suspense, Ryang!

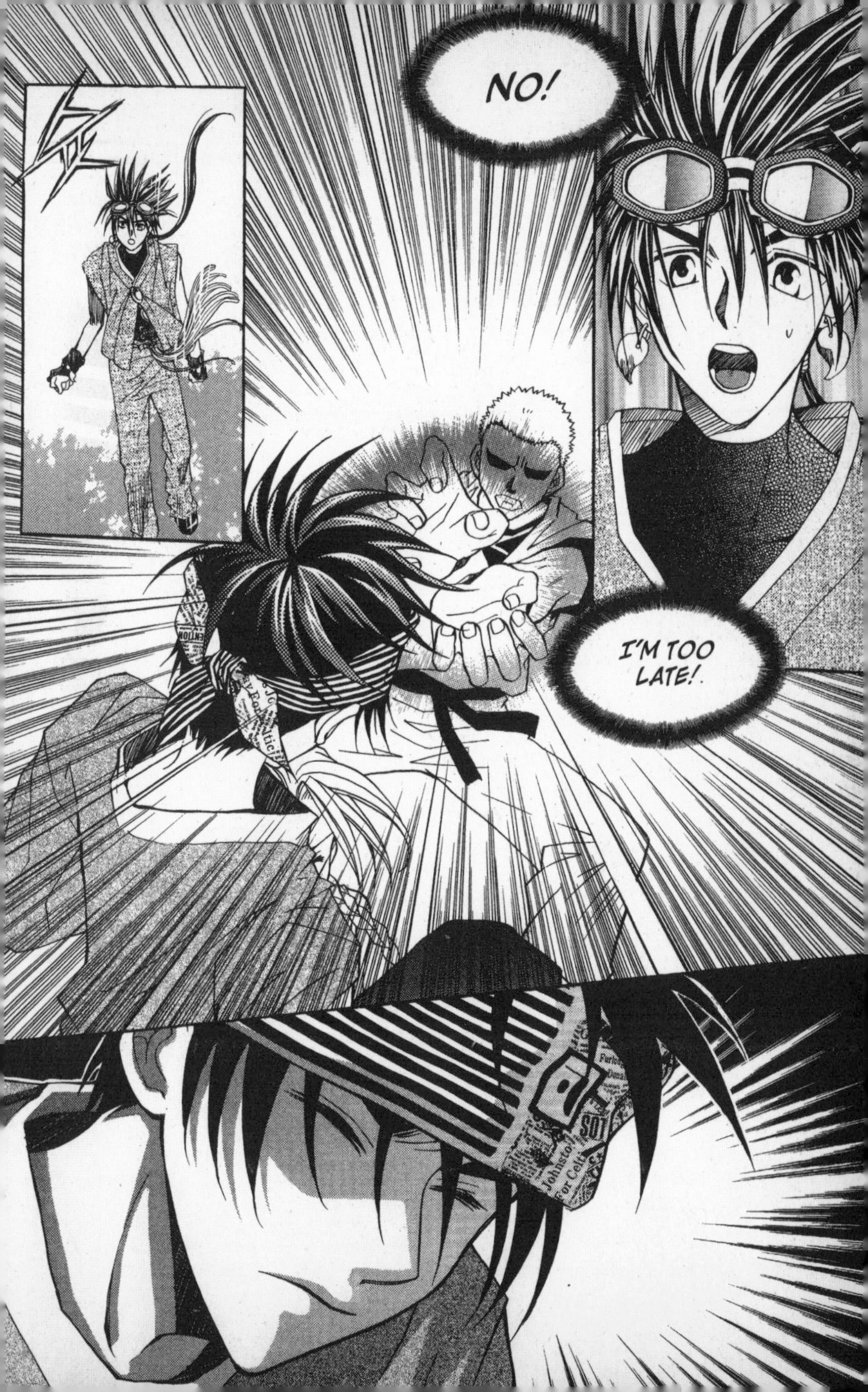
NO!
I'M TOO LATE!

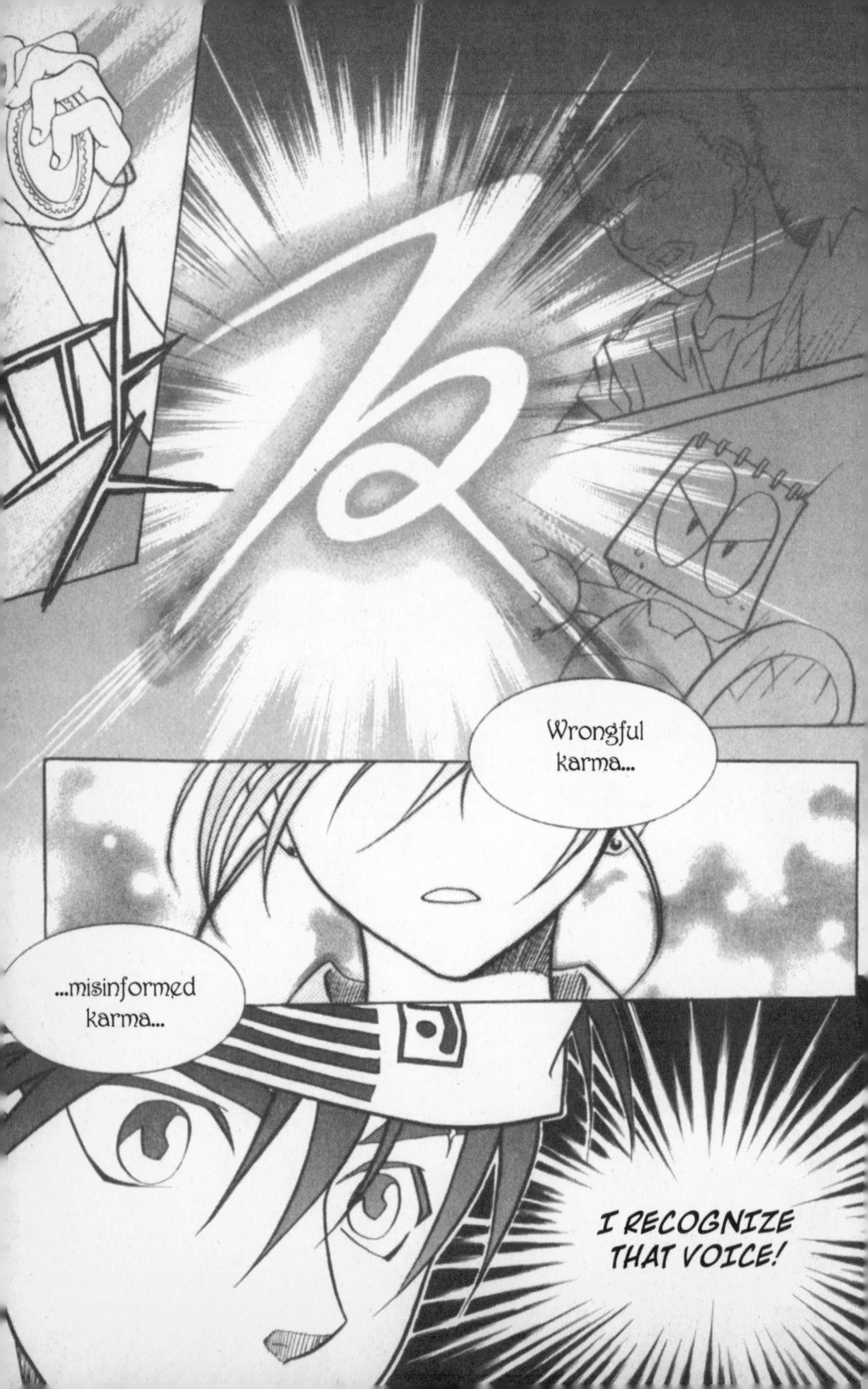
Wrongful karma...
...misinformed karma...
I RECOGNIZE THAT VOICE!

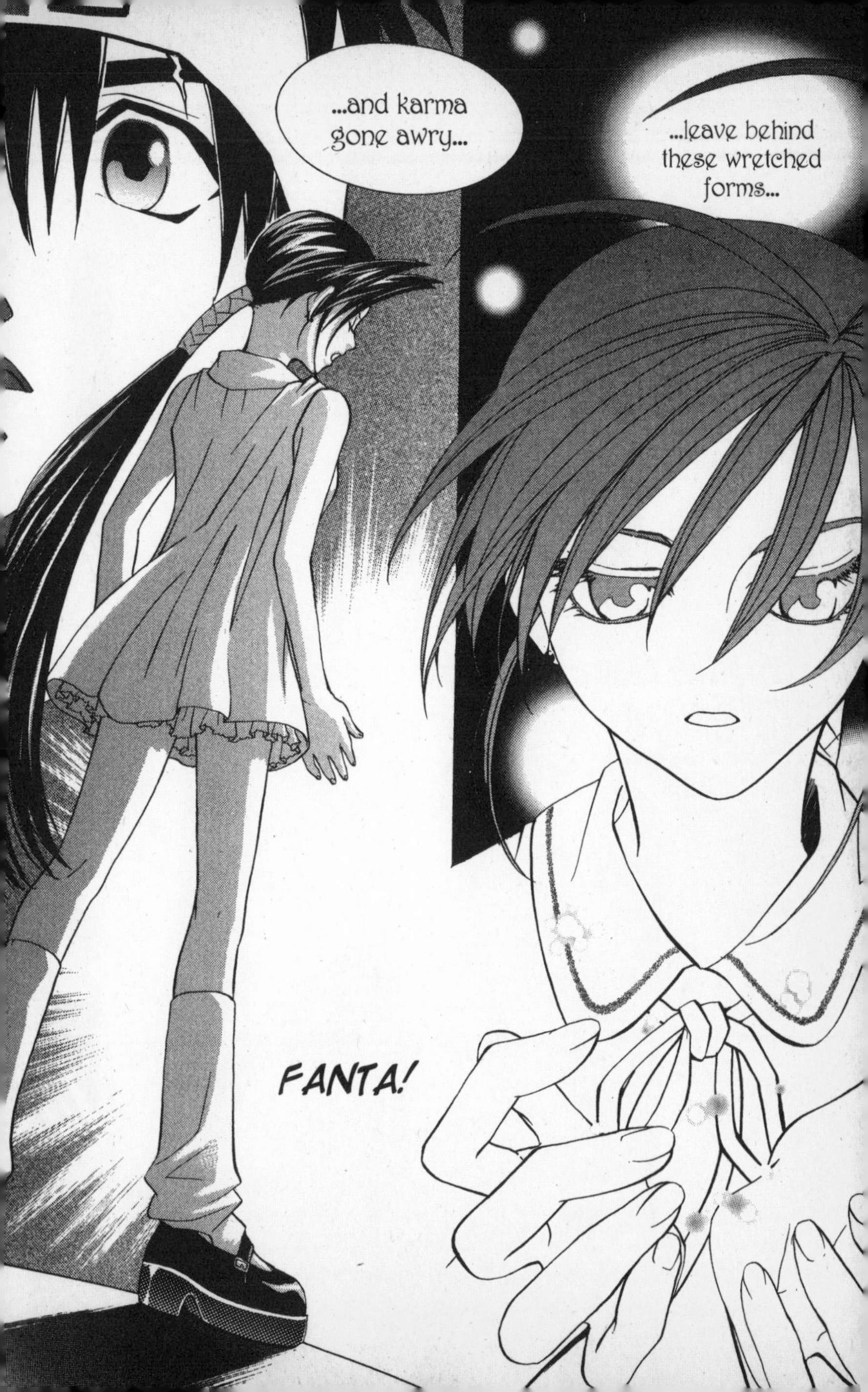
...and karma gone awry...
FANTA!
...leave behind these wretched forms...

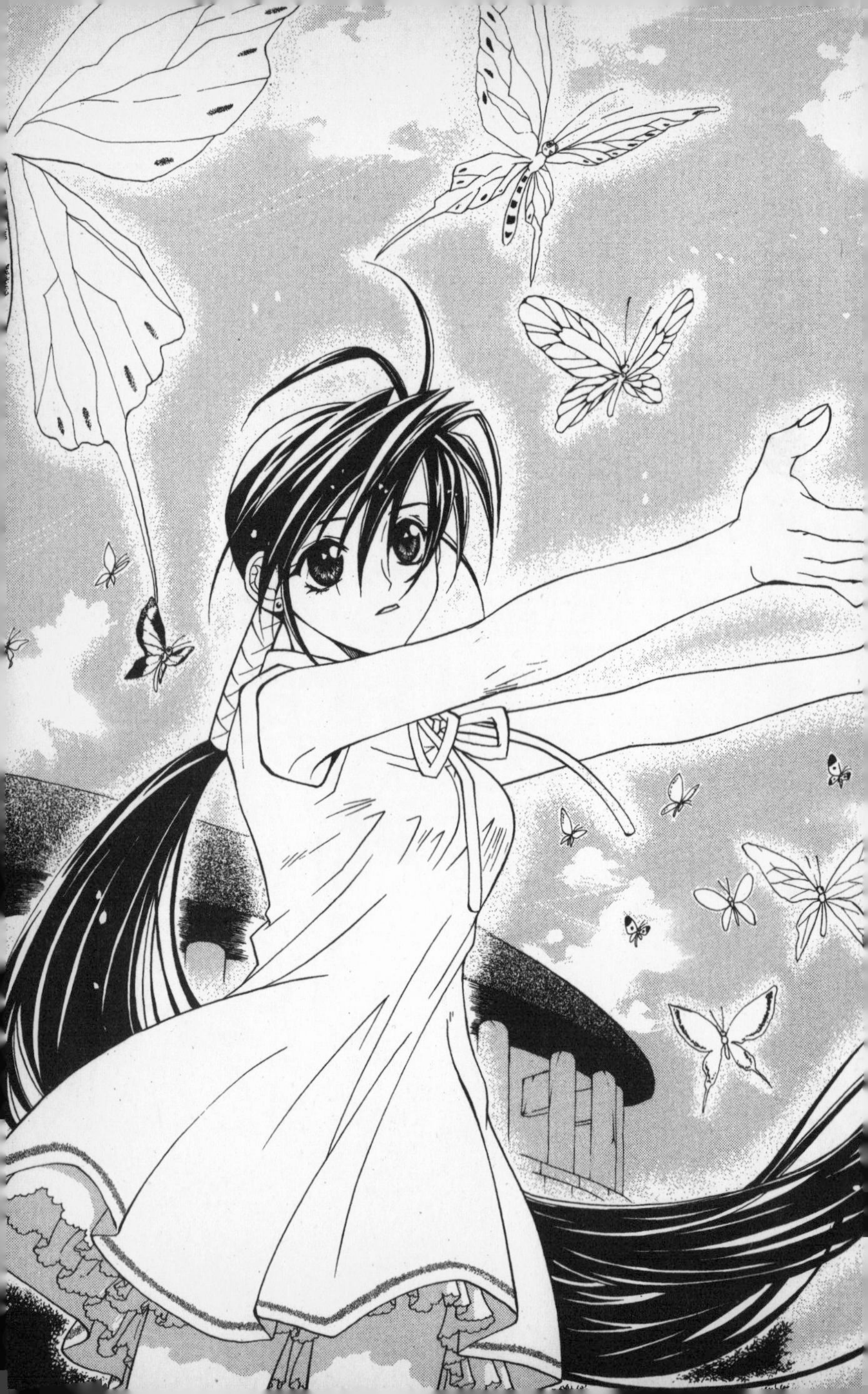

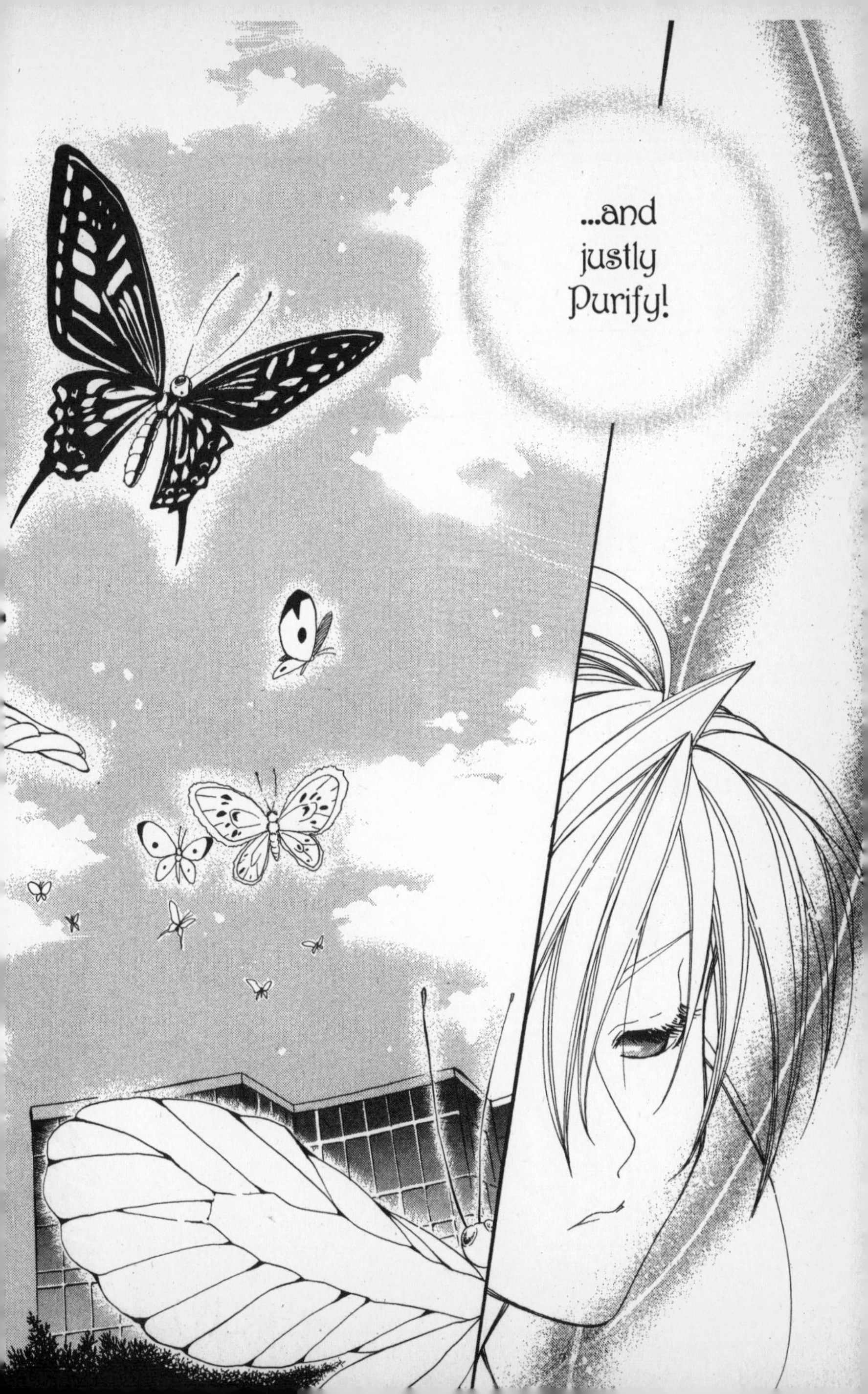
...and justly Purify!

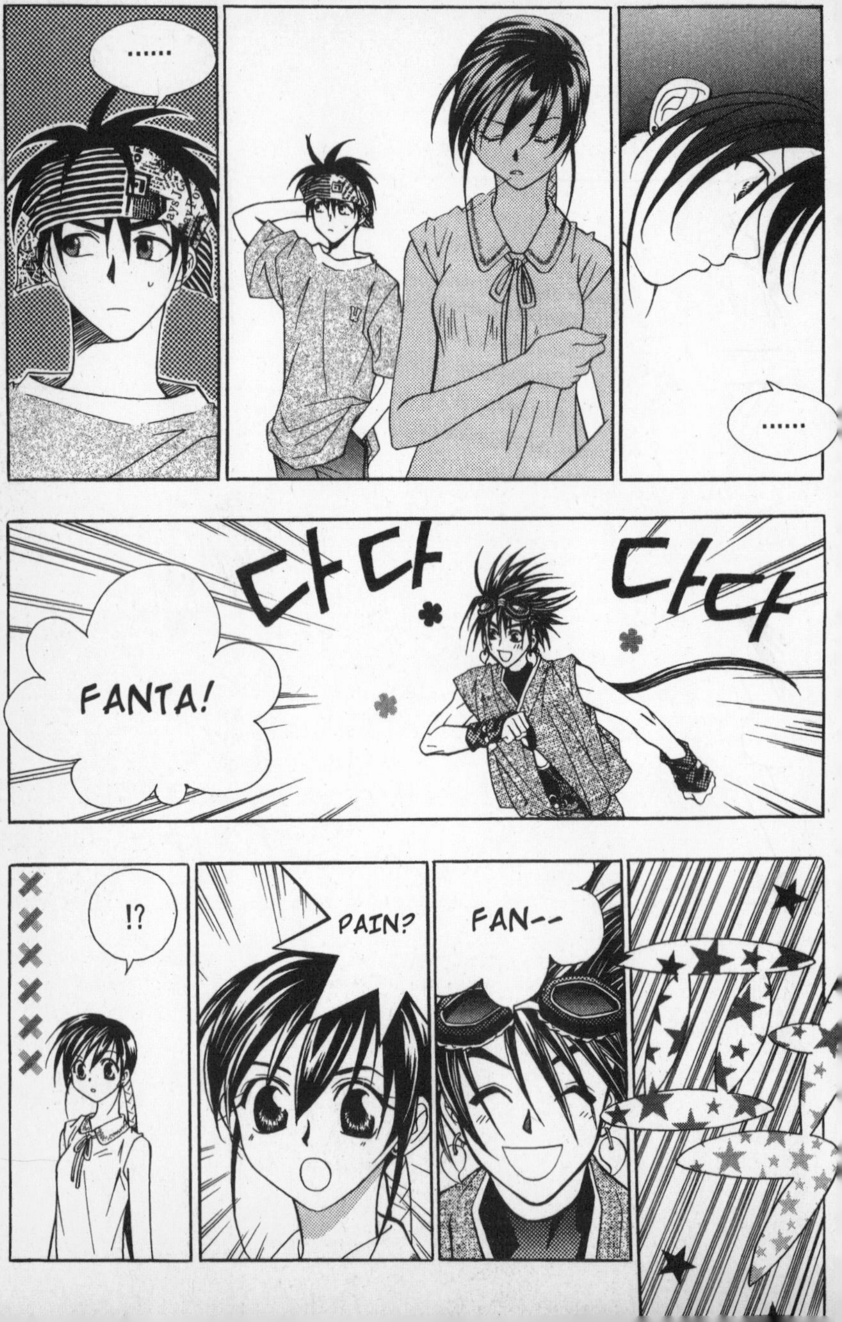
......
......
다다
다다
FANTA!
!?
PAIN?
FAN--

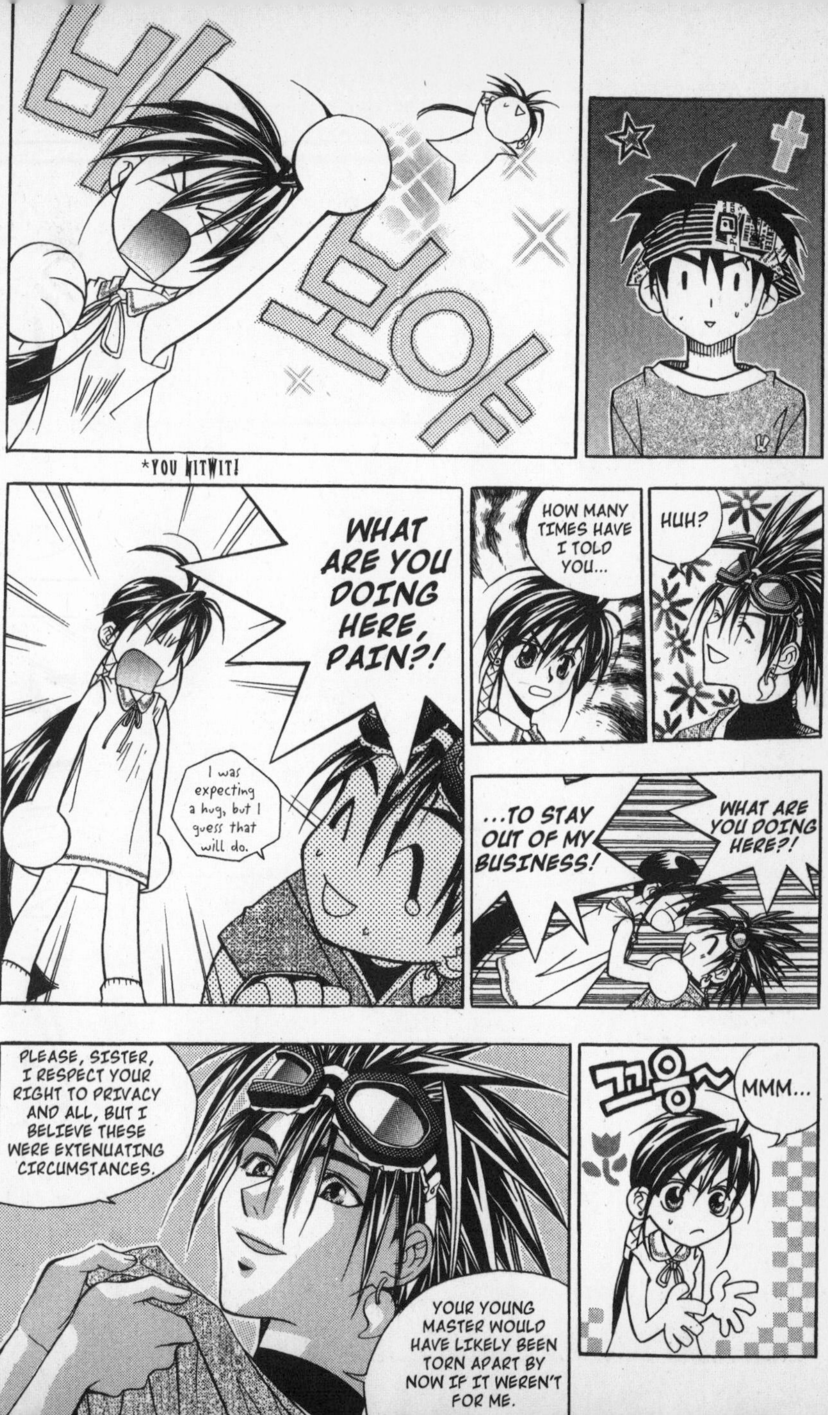
바보야
*YOU NITWIT!
WHAT ARE YOU DOING HERE, PAIN?!
I was expecting a hug, but I guess that will do.
HOW MANY TIMES HAVE I TOLD YOU...
HUH?
...TO STAY OUT OF MY BUSINESS!
WHAT ARE YOU DOING HERE?!
PLEASE, SISTER, I RESPECT YOUR RIGHT TO PRIVACY AND ALL, BUT I BELIEVE THESE WERE EXTENUATING CIRCUMSTANCES.
YOUR YOUNG MASTER WOULD HAVE LIKELY BEEN TORN APART BY NOW IF IT WEREN'T FOR ME.
끄응~
MMM...

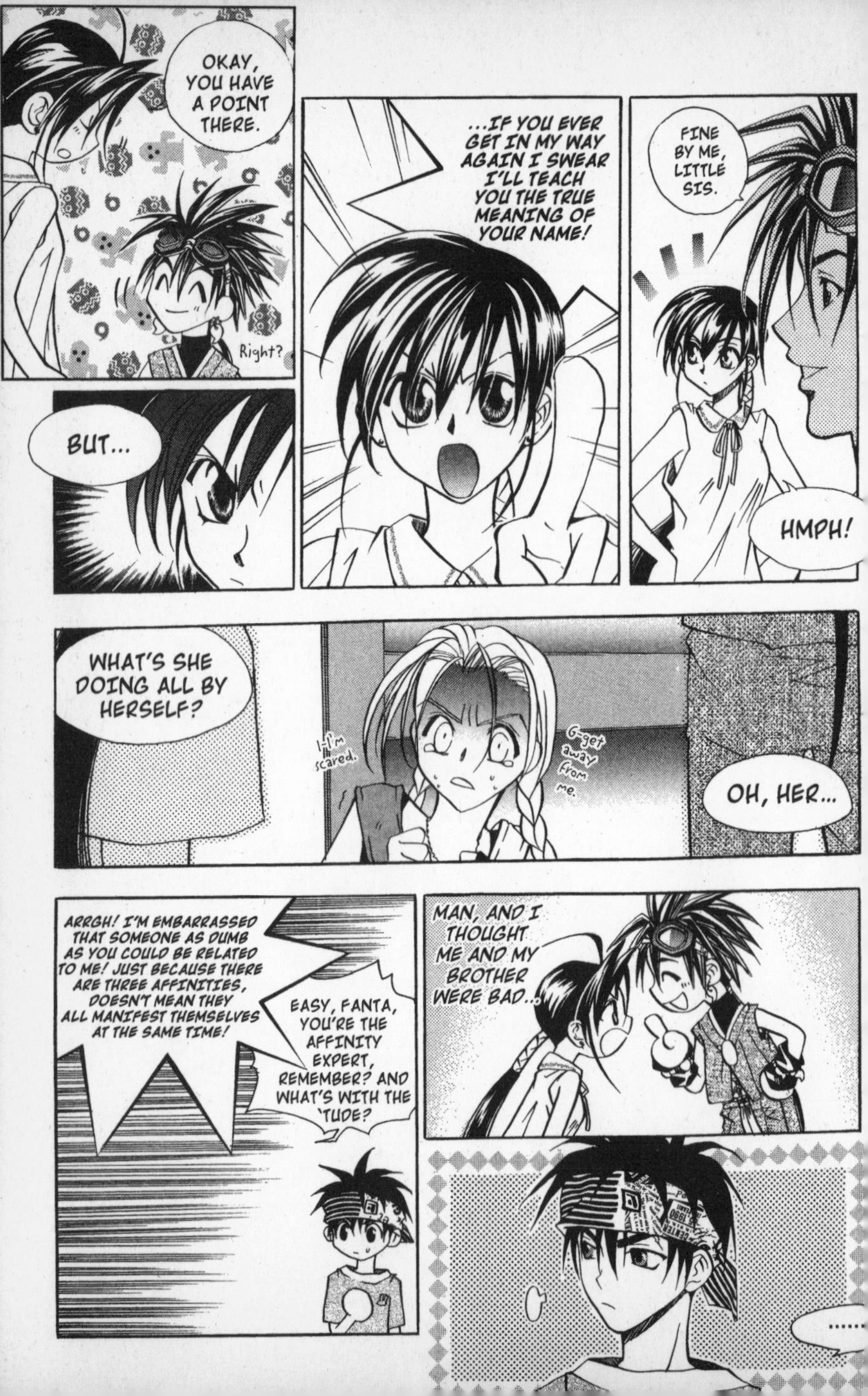
OKAY, YOU HAVE A POINT THERE.
Right?
...IF YOU EVER GET IN MY WAY AGAIN I SWEAR I'LL TEACH YOU THE TRUE MEANING OF YOUR NAME!
FINE BY ME, LITTLE SIS.
BUT...
HMPH!
WHAT'S SHE DOING ALL BY HERSELF?
I-I'm scared.
G-get away from me.
OH, HER...
ARRGH! I'M EMBARRASSED THAT SOMEONE AS DUMB AS YOU COULD BE RELATED TO ME! JUST BECAUSE THERE ARE THREE AFFINITIES, DOESN'T MEAN THEY ALL MANIFEST THEMSELVES AT THE SAME TIME!
EASY, FANTA, YOU'RE THE AFFINITY EXPERT, REMEMBER? AND WHAT'S WITH THE 'TUDE?
MAN, AND I THOUGHT ME AND MY BROTHER WERE BAD...
......

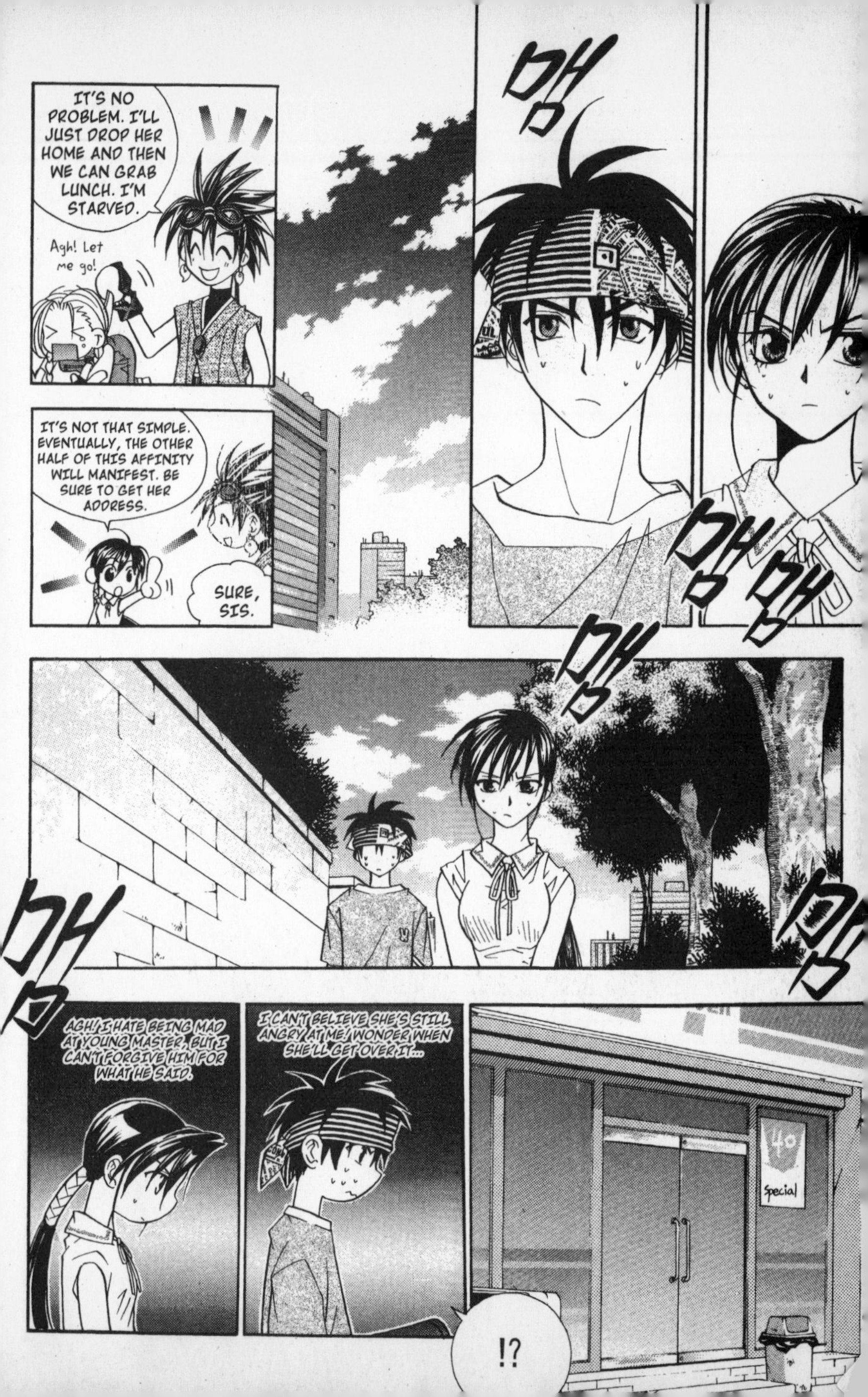
IT'S NO PROBLEM. I'LL JUST DROP HER HOME AND THEN WE CAN GRAB LUNCH. I'M STARVED.
Agh! Let me go!
IT'S NOT THAT SIMPLE. EVENTUALLY, THE OTHER HALF OF THIS AFFINITY WILL MANIFEST. BE SURE TO GET HER ADDRESS.
SURE, SIS.
멍
멍
멍
멍
멍
멍
AGH! I HATE BEING MAD AT YOUNG MASTER, BUT I CAN'T FORGIVE HIM FOR WHAT HE SAID.
I CAN'T BELIEVE SHE'S STILL ANGRY AT ME. WONDER WHEN SHE'LL GET OVER IT...
40
Special
!?

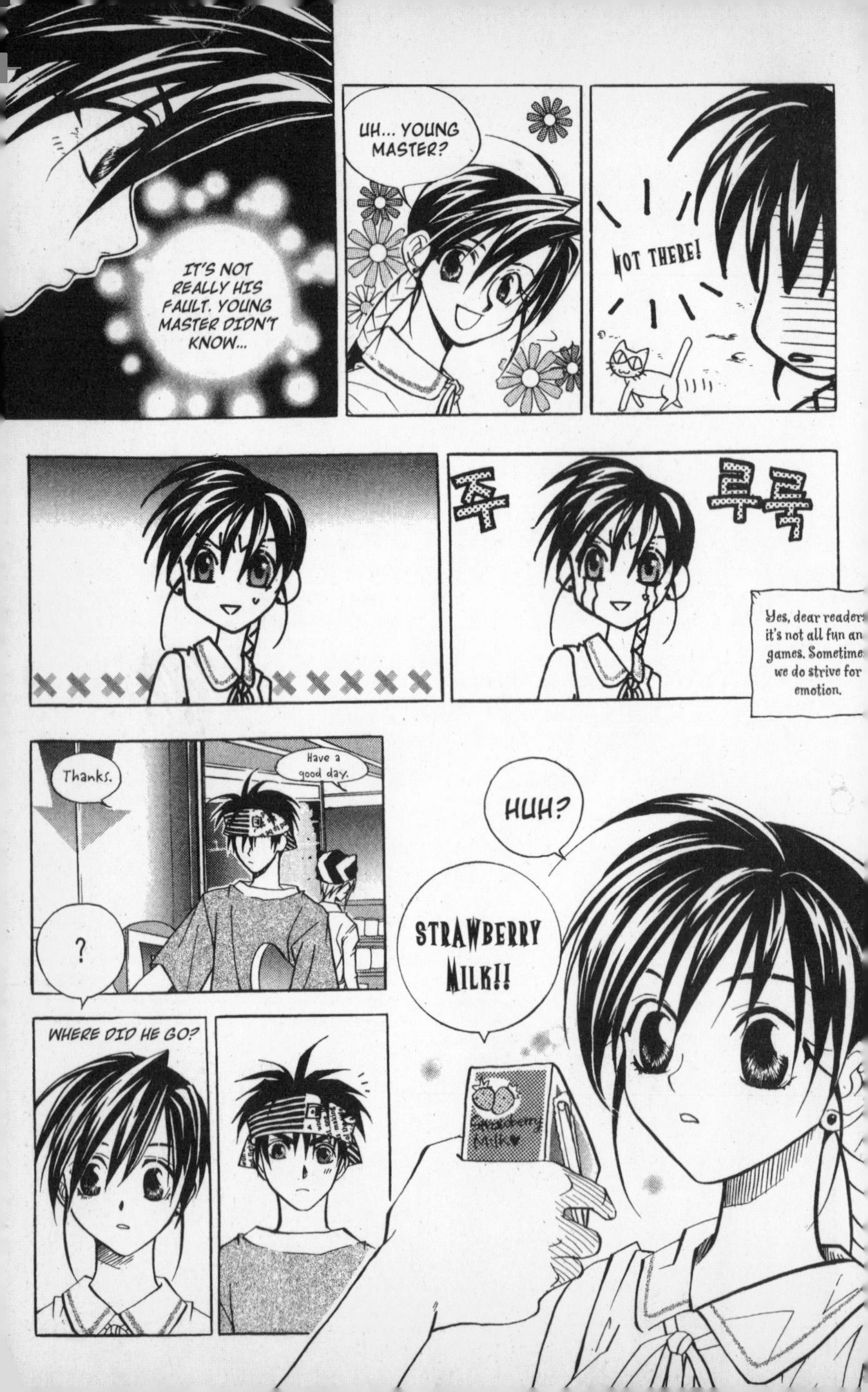
IT'S NOT REALLY HIS FAULT. YOUNG MASTER DIDN'T KNOW...
UH... YOUNG MASTER?
NOT THERE!
주
르륵
Yes, dear reader: it's not all fun and games. Sometimes we do strive for emotion.
Thanks.
Have a good day.
?
WHERE DID HE GO?
HUH?
STRAWBERRY MILK!!
Strawberry milk♥

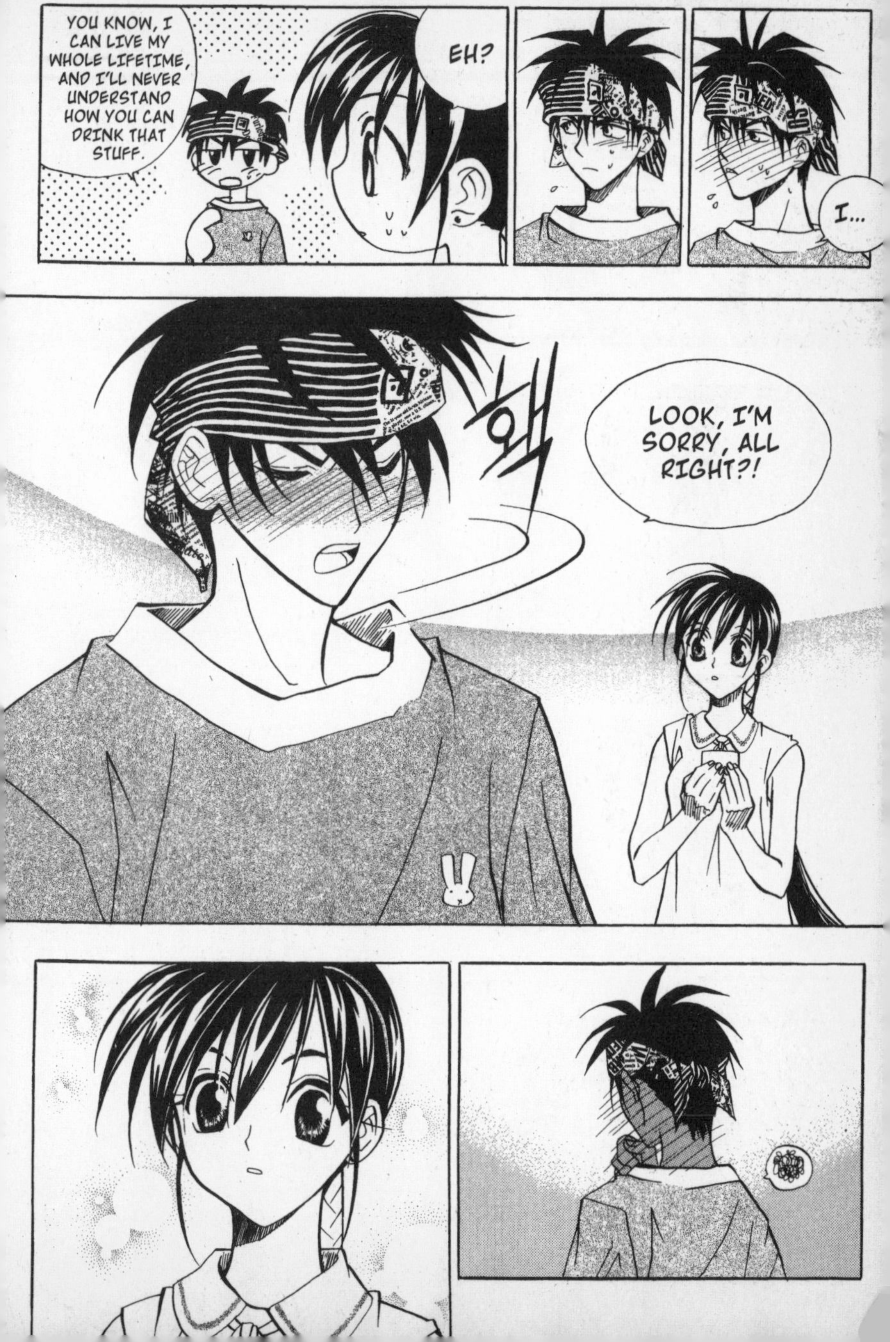
YOU KNOW, I CAN LIVE MY WHOLE LIFETIME, AND I'LL NEVER UNDERSTAND HOW YOU CAN DRINK THAT STUFF.
EH?
I...
확
LOOK, I'M SORRY, ALL RIGHT?!

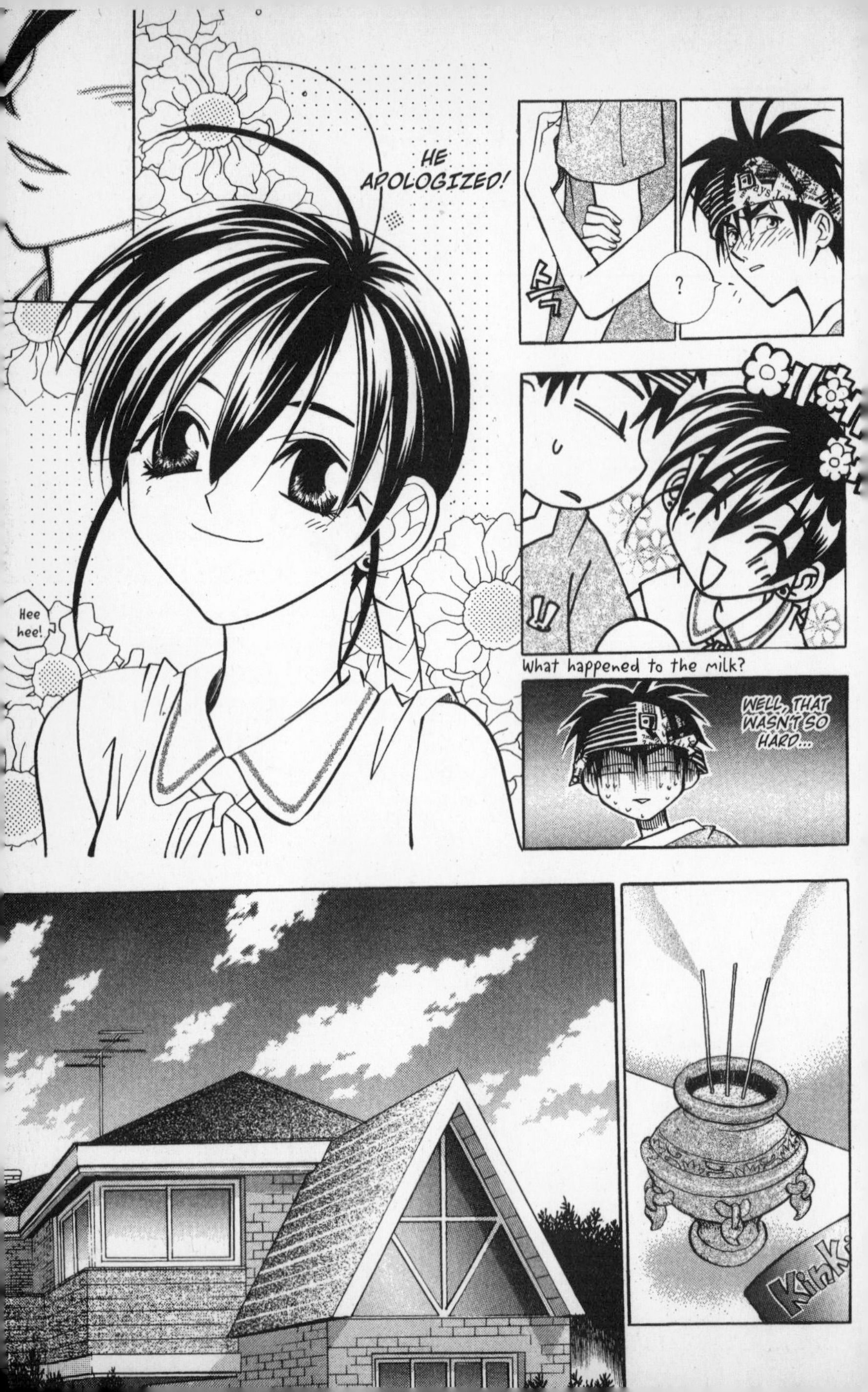
HE APOLOGIZED!
Hee hee!
?
What happened to the milk?
WELL, THAT WASN'T SO HARD...

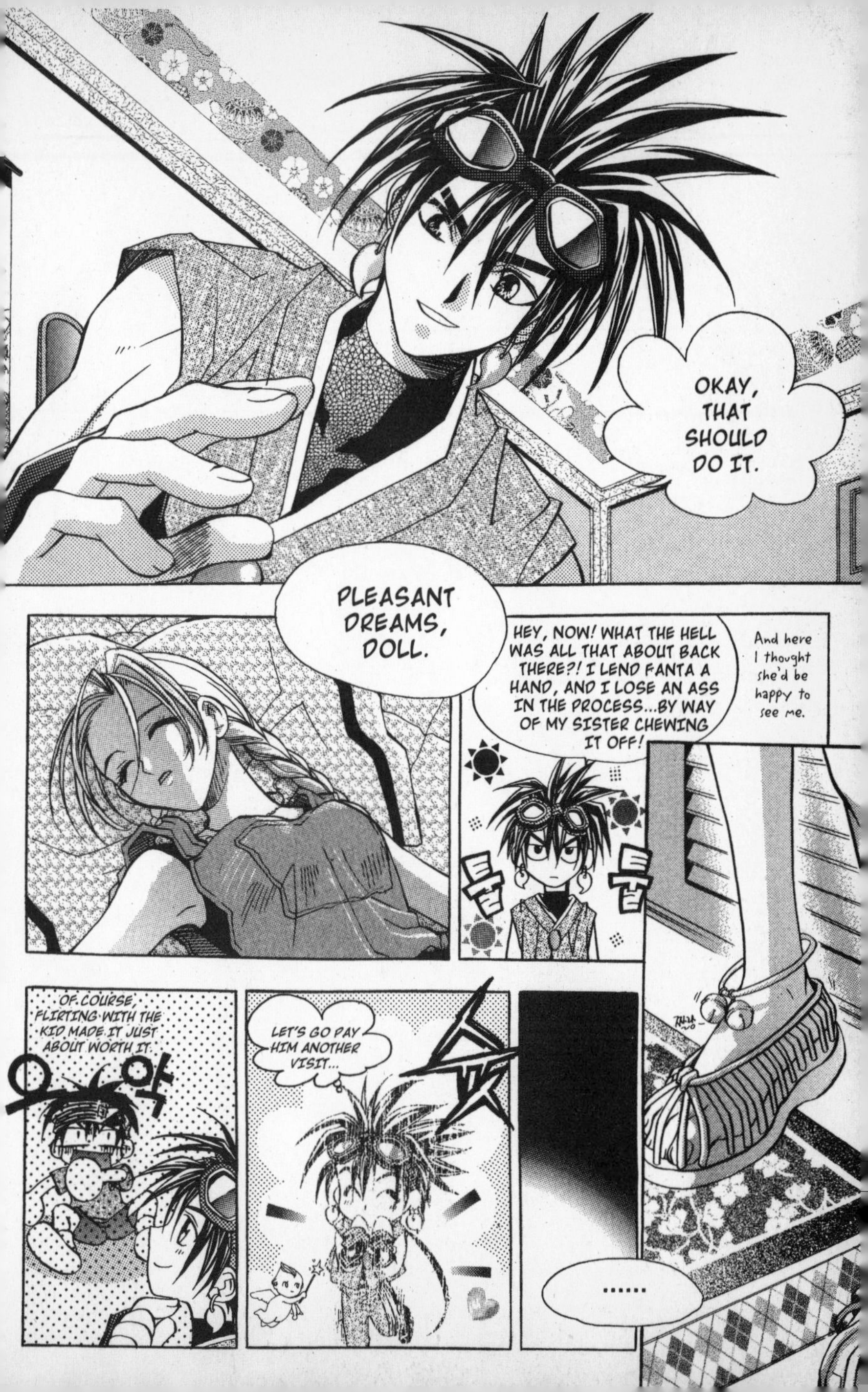
OKAY, THAT SHOULD DO IT.
PLEASANT DREAMS, DOLL.
HEY, NOW! WHAT THE HELL WAS ALL THAT ABOUT BACK THERE?! I LEND FANTA A HAND, AND I LOSE AN ASS IN THE PROCESS...BY WAY OF MY SISTER CHEWING IT OFF!
And here I thought she'd be happy to see me.
OF COURSE, FLIRTING WITH THE KID MADE IT JUST ABOUT WORTH IT.
LET'S GO PAY HIM ANOTHER VISIT...
......

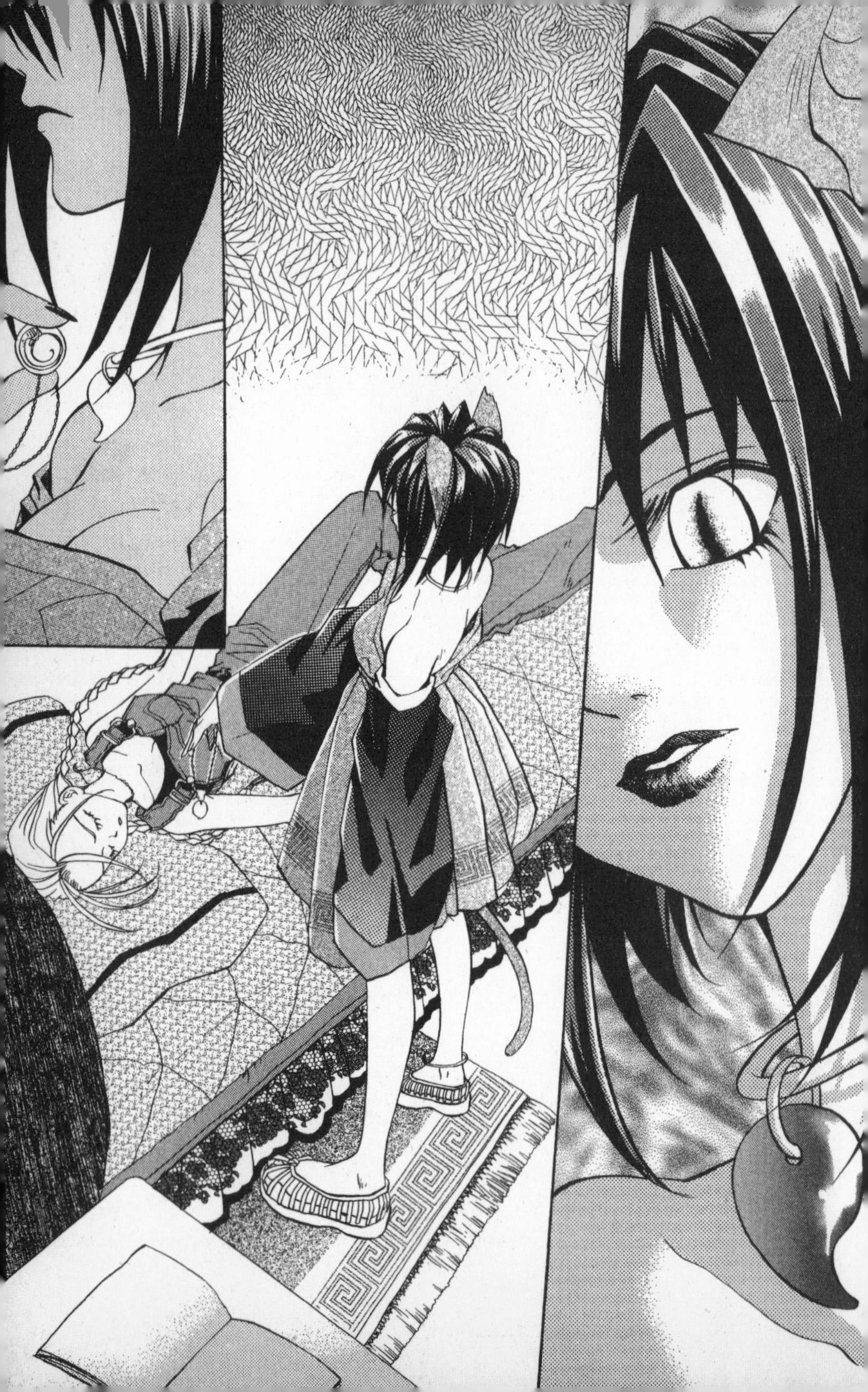

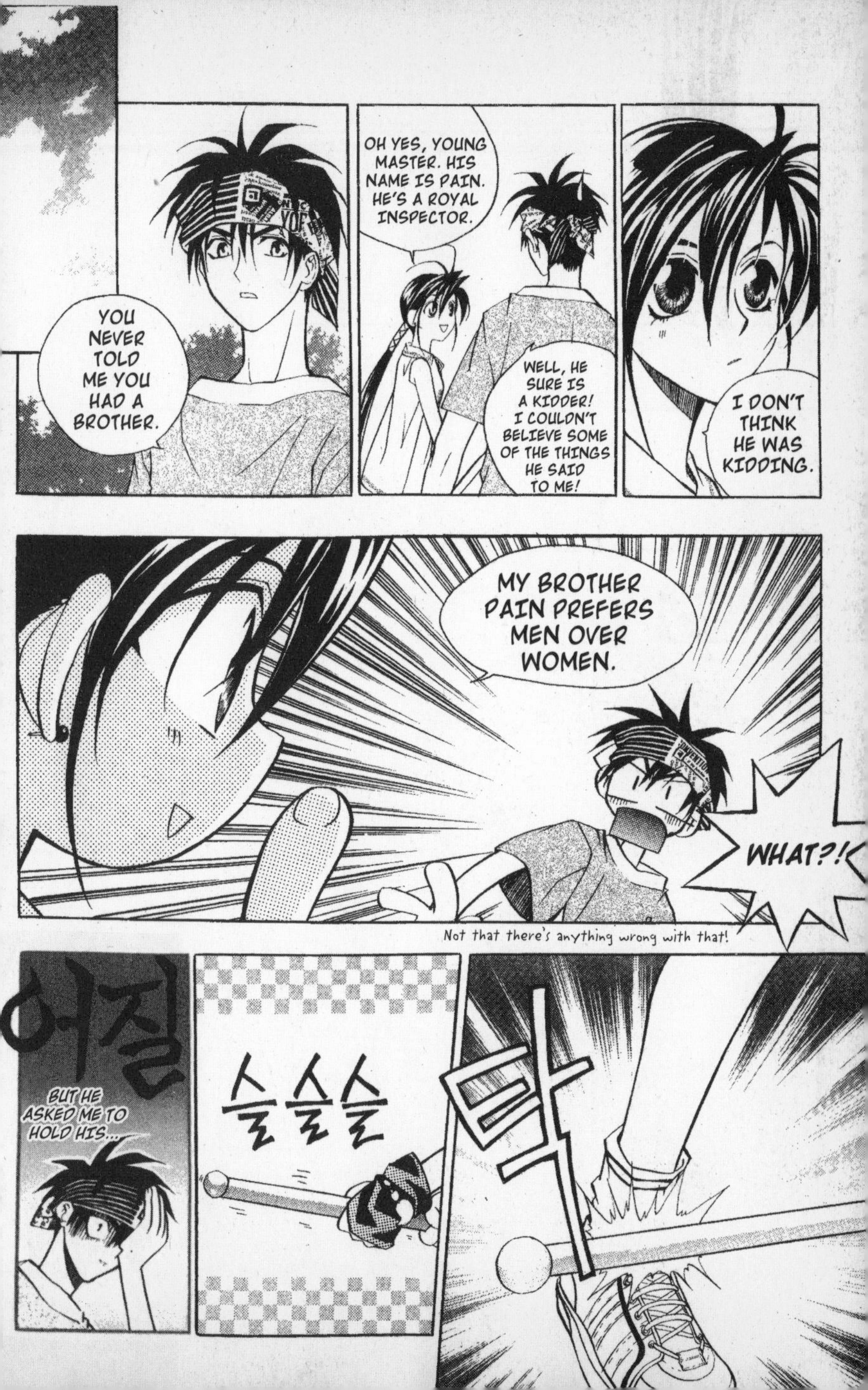
YOU NEVER TOLD ME YOU HAD A BROTHER.
OH YES, YOUNG MASTER. HIS NAME IS PAIN. HE'S A ROYAL INSPECTOR.
WELL, HE SURE IS A KIDDER! I COULDN'T BELIEVE SOME OF THE THINGS HE SAID TO ME!
I DON'T THINK HE WAS KIDDING.
MY BROTHER PAIN PREFERS MEN OVER WOMEN.
WHAT?!
Not that there's anything wrong with that!
어질
BUT HE ASKED ME TO HOLD HIS...
슬슬슬

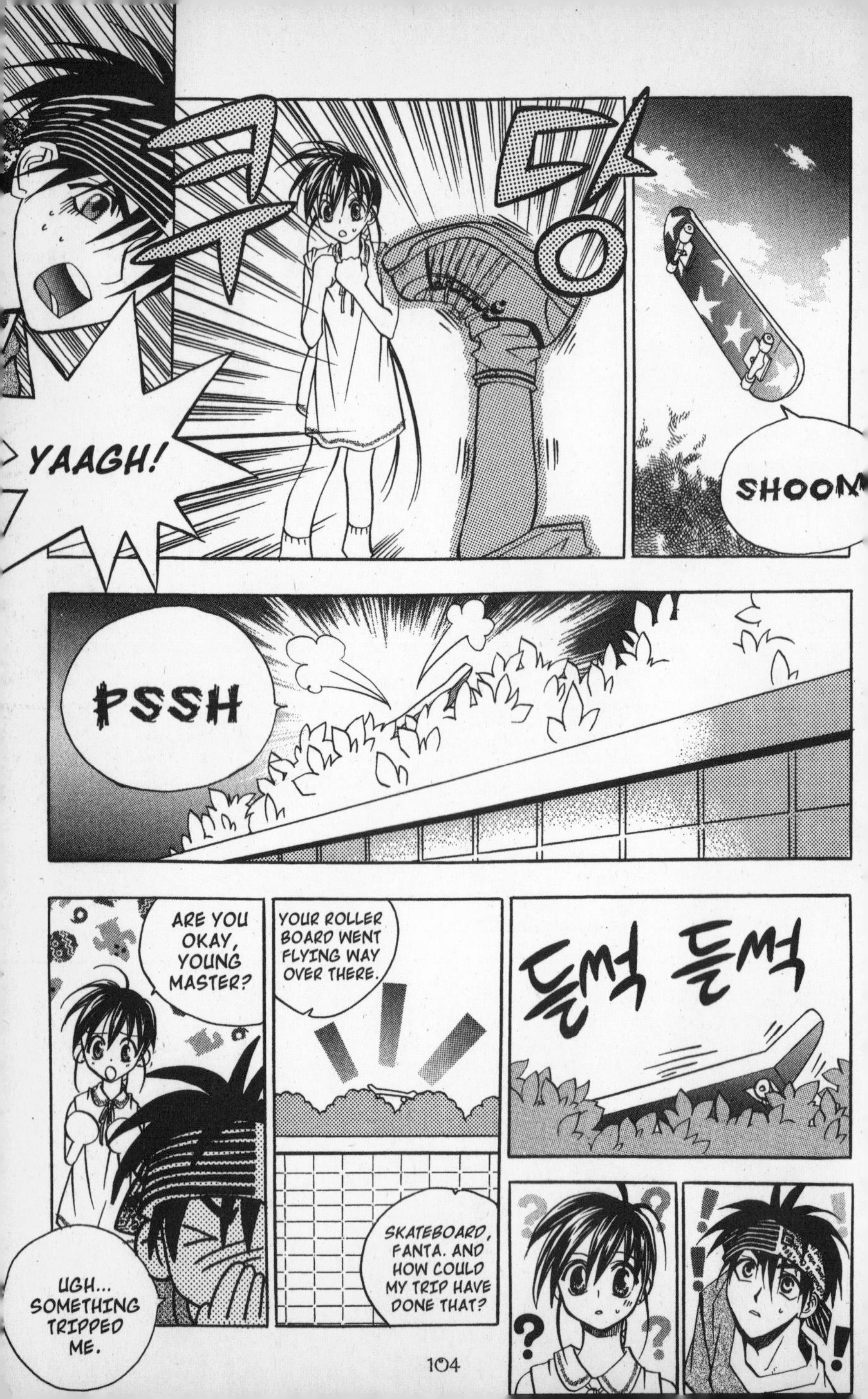
콰당
YAAGH!
SHOOM
PSSH
ARE YOU OKAY, YOUNG MASTER?
UGH... SOMETHING TRIPPED ME.
YOUR ROLLER BOARD WENT FLYING WAY OVER THERE.
SKATEBOARD, FANTA. AND HOW COULD MY TRIP HAVE DONE THAT?
들썩 들썩

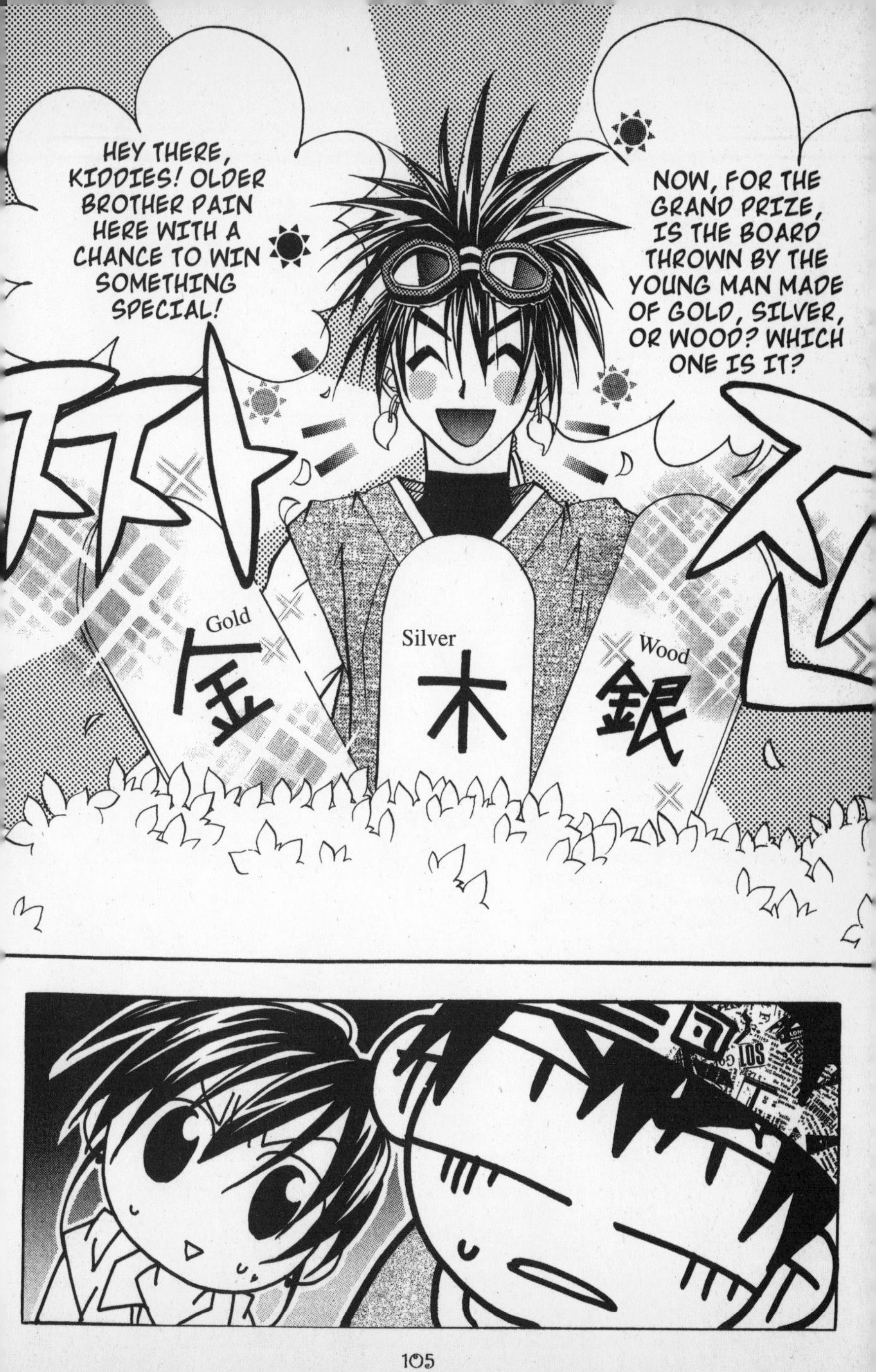
HEY THERE, KIDDIES! OLDER BROTHER PAIN HERE WITH A CHANCE TO WIN SOMETHING SPECIAL!
NOW, FOR THE GRAND PRIZE, IS THE BOARD THROWN BY THE YOUNG MAN MADE OF GOLD, SILVER, OR WOOD? WHICH ONE IS IT?
Gold
金
Silver
木
Wood
銀

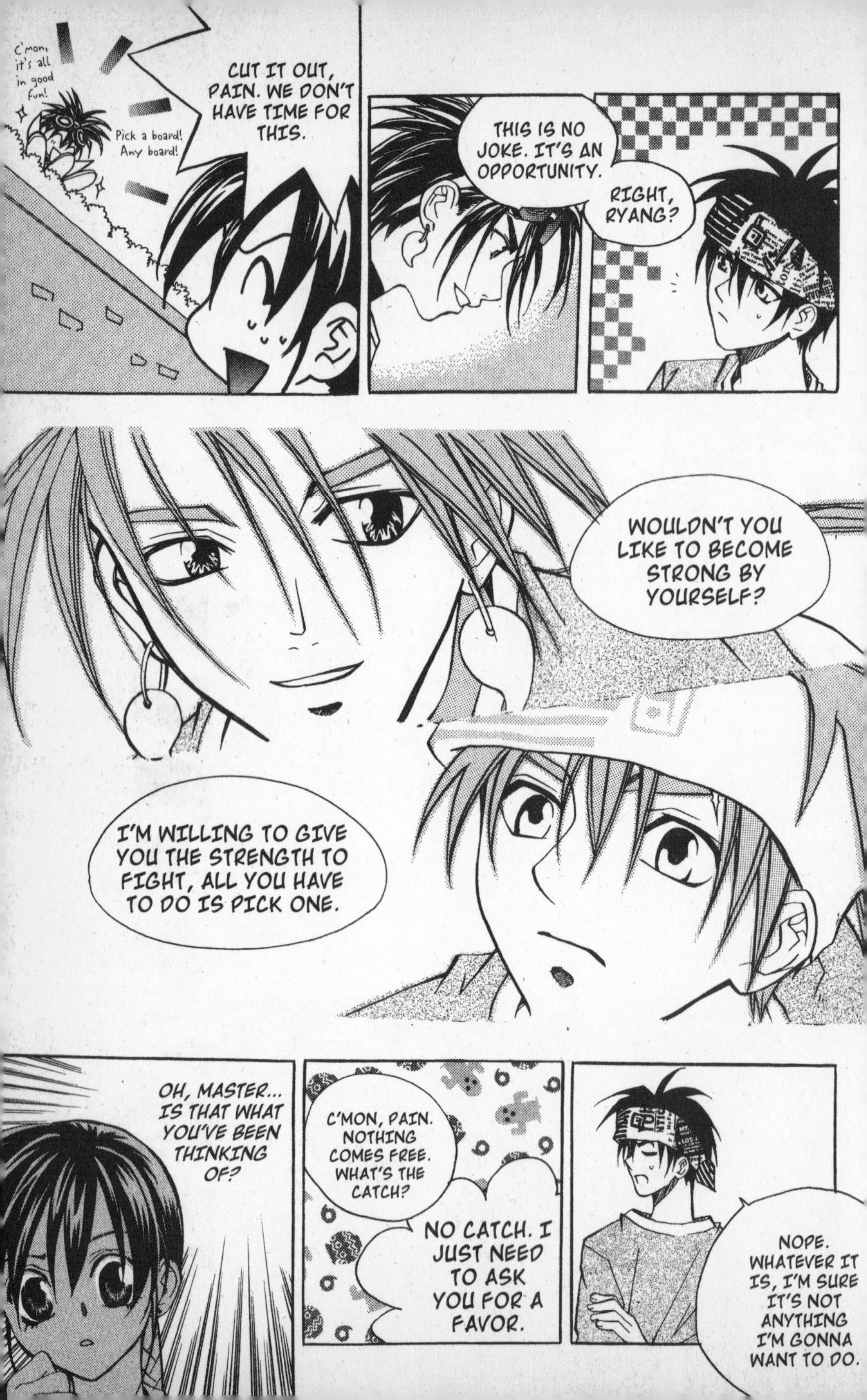
C'mon, it's all in good fun!
Pick a board! Any board!
CUT IT OUT, PAIN. WE DON'T HAVE TIME FOR THIS.
THIS IS NO JOKE. IT'S AN OPPORTUNITY.
RIGHT, RYANG?
WOULDN'T YOU LIKE TO BECOME STRONG BY YOURSELF?
I'M WILLING TO GIVE YOU THE STRENGTH TO FIGHT, ALL YOU HAVE TO DO IS PICK ONE.
OH, MASTER... IS THAT WHAT YOU'VE BEEN THINKING OF?
C'MON, PAIN. NOTHING COMES FREE. WHAT'S THE CATCH?
NO CATCH. I JUST NEED TO ASK YOU FOR A FAVOR.
NOPE. WHATEVER IT IS, I'M SURE IT'S NOT ANYTHING I'M GONNA WANT TO DO.

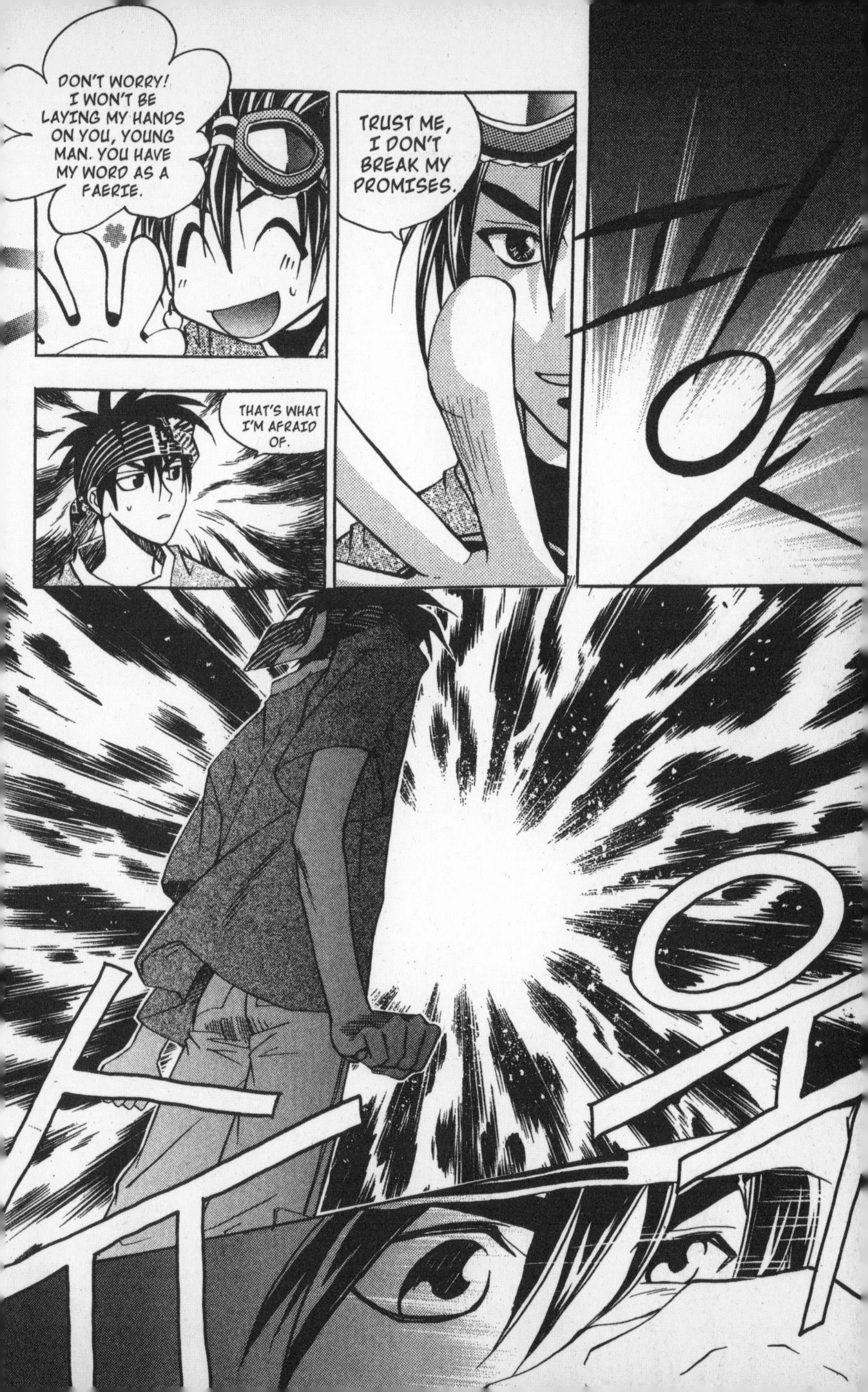

DON'T WORRY! I WON'T BE LAYING MY HANDS ON YOU, YOUNG MAN. YOU HAVE MY WORD AS A FAERIE.
TRUST ME, I DON'T BREAK MY PROMISES.
THAT'S WHAT I'M AFRAID OF.

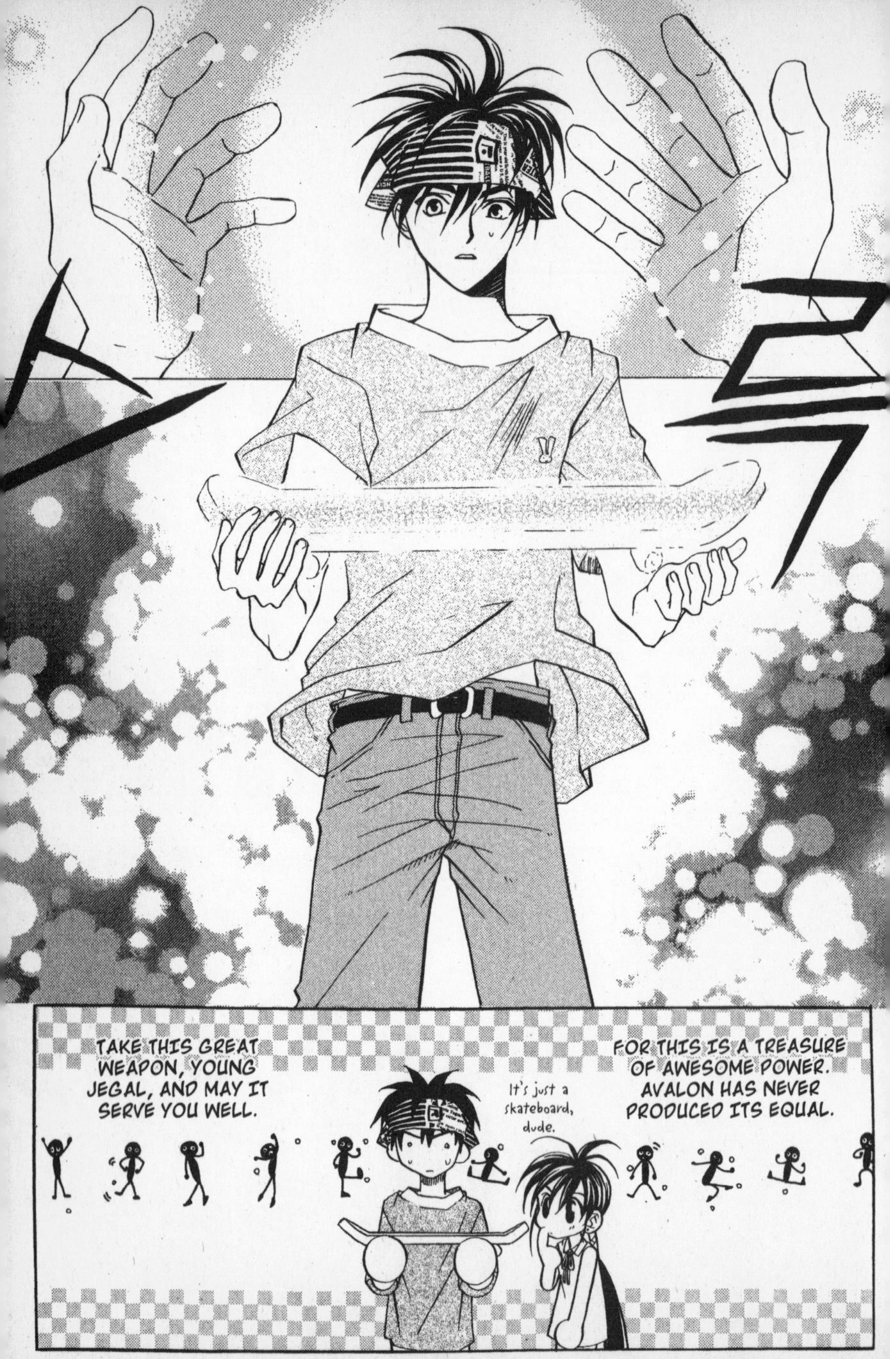
TAKE THIS GREAT WEAPON, YOUNG JEGAL, AND MAY IT SERVE YOU WELL.
It's just a skateboard, dude.
FOR THIS IS A TREASURE OF AWESOME POWER. AVALON HAS NEVER PRODUCED ITS EQUAL.

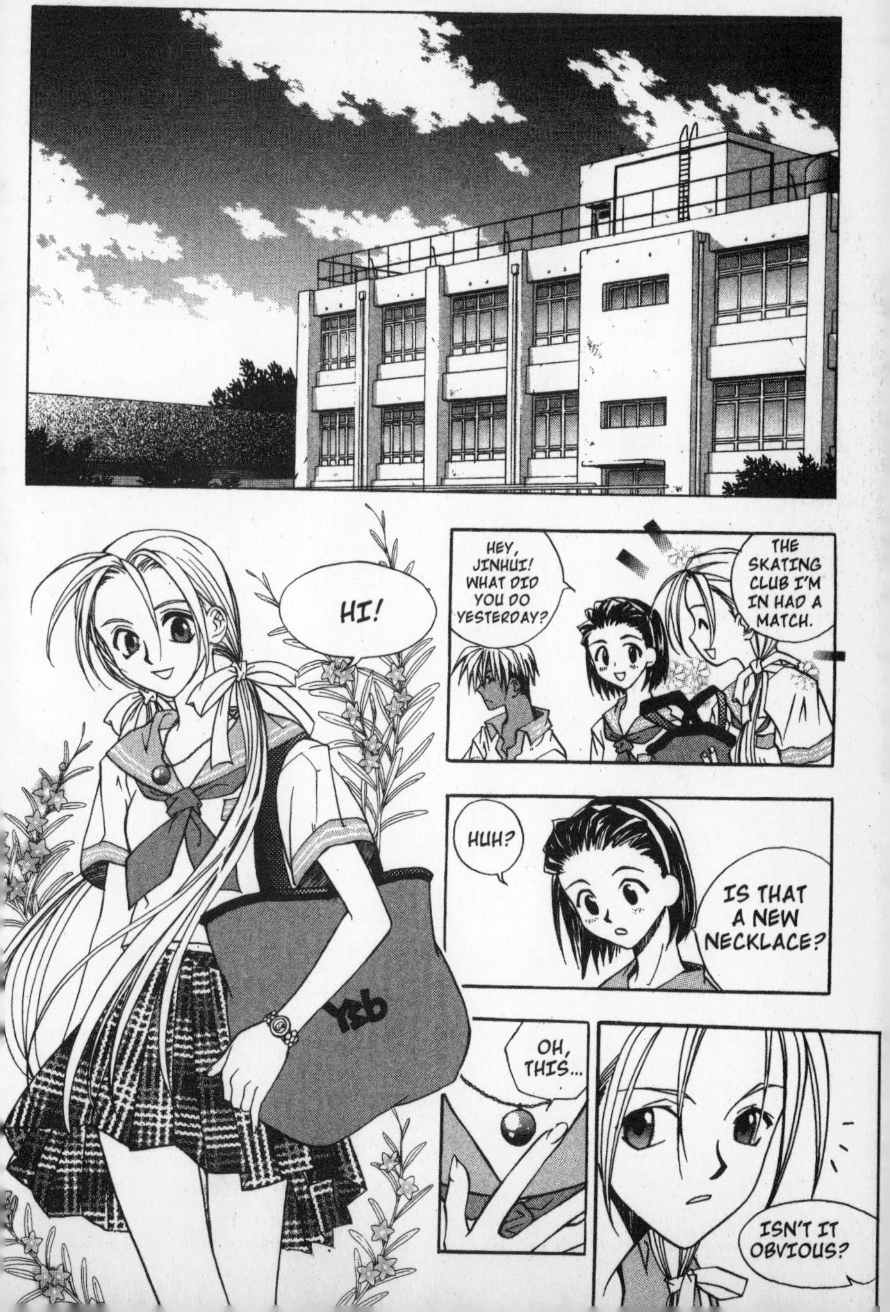
HI!
HEY, JINHUI! WHAT DID YOU DO YESTERDAY?
THE SKATING CLUB I'M IN HAD A MATCH.
HUH?
IS THAT A NEW NECKLACE?
OH, THIS...
ISN'T IT OBVIOUS?

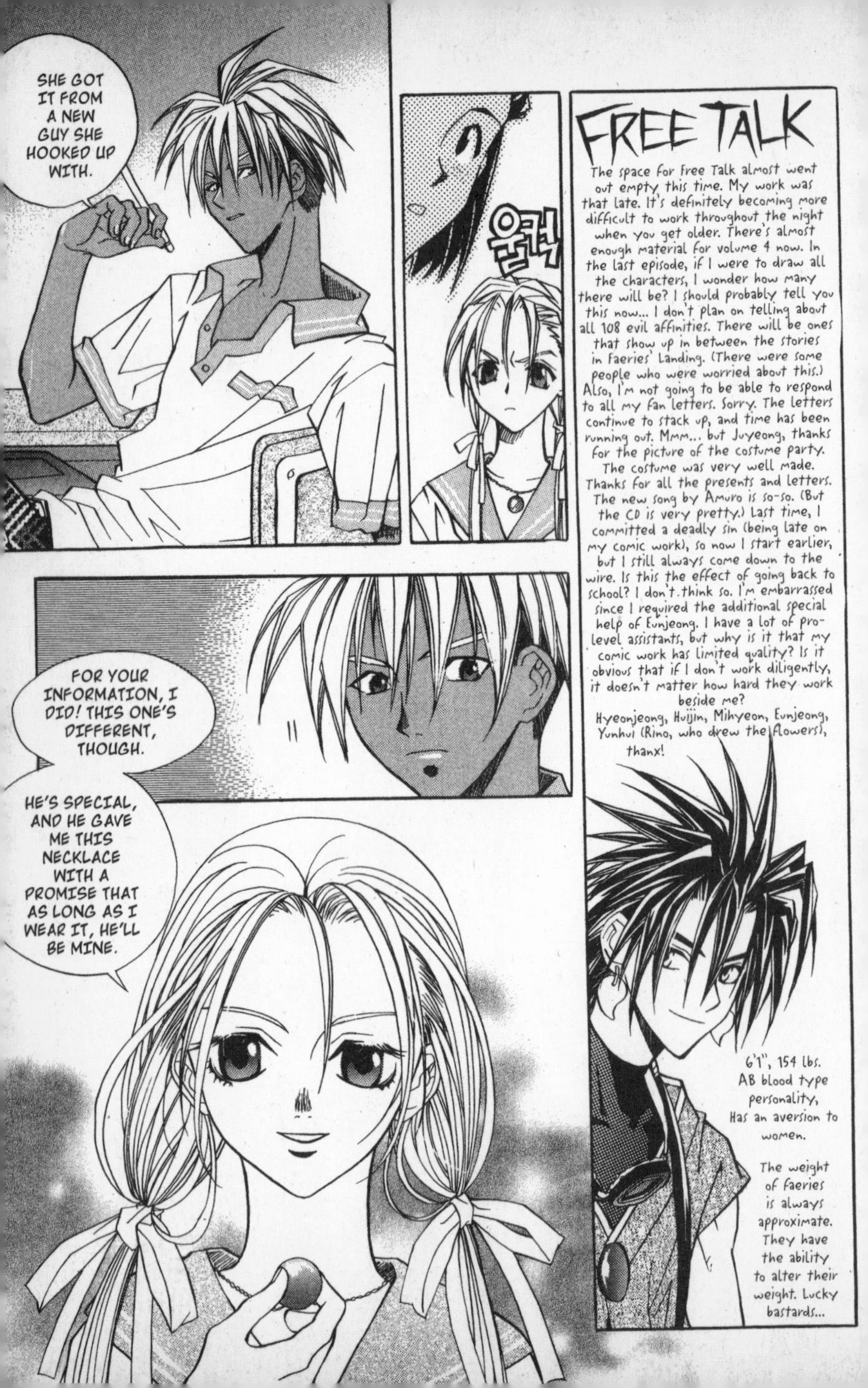
SHE GOT IT FROM A NEW GUY SHE HOOKED UP WITH.
울컥
FOR YOUR INFORMATION, I DID! THIS ONE'S DIFFERENT, THOUGH.
HE'S SPECIAL, AND HE GAVE ME THIS NECKLACE WITH A PROMISE THAT AS LONG AS I WEAR IT, HE'LL BE MINE.

FREE TALK

The space for Free Talk almost went out empty this time. My work was that late. It's definitely becoming more difficult to work throughout the night when you get older. There's almost enough material for volume 4 now. In the last episode, if I were to draw all the characters, I wonder how many there will be? I should probably tell you this now... I don't plan on telling about all 108 evil affinities. There will be ones that show up in between the stories in Faeries' Landing. (There were some people who were worried about this.) Also, I'm not going to be able to respond to all my fan letters. Sorry. The letters continue to stack up, and time has been running out. Mmm... but Juyeong, thanks for the picture of the costume party. The costume was very well made. Thanks for all the presents and letters. The new song by Amuro is so-so. (But the CD is very pretty.) Last time, I committed a deadly sin (being late on my comic work), so now I start earlier, but I still always come down to the wire. Is this the effect of going back to school? I don't think so. I'm embarrassed since I required the additional special help of Eunjeong. I have a lot of pro-level assistants, but why is it that my comic work has limited quality? Is it obvious that if I don't work diligently, it doesn't matter how hard they work beside me?

Hyeonjeong, Huijin, Mihyeon, Eunjeong, Yunhui (Rino, who drew the flowers), thanx!

6'1", 154 lbs.
AB blood type personality,
Has an aversion to women.

The weight of faeries is always approximate. They have the ability to alter their weight. Lucky bastards...

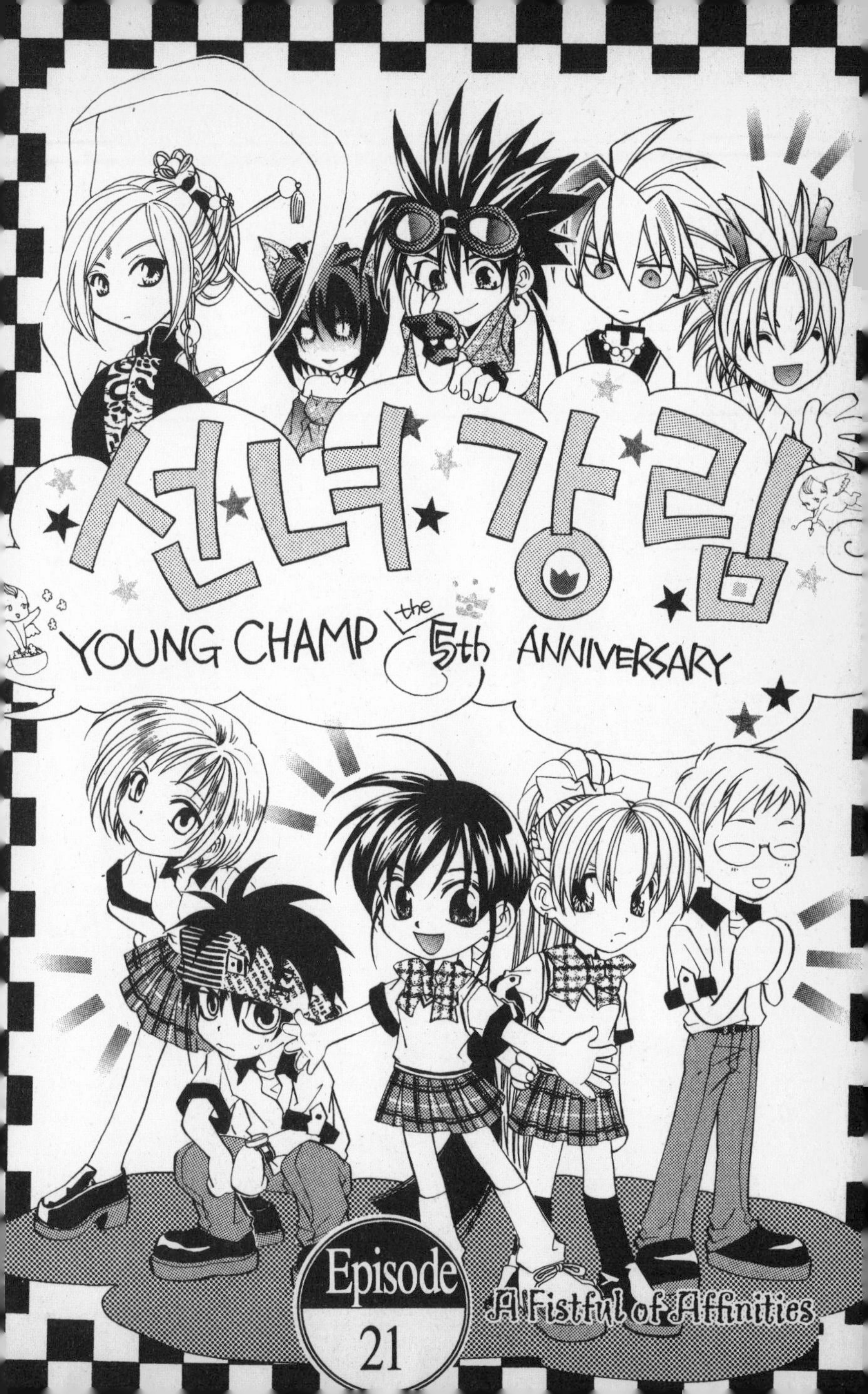
선녀강림
YOUNG CHAMP the 5th ANNIVERSARY
Episode 21
A Fistful of Affinities

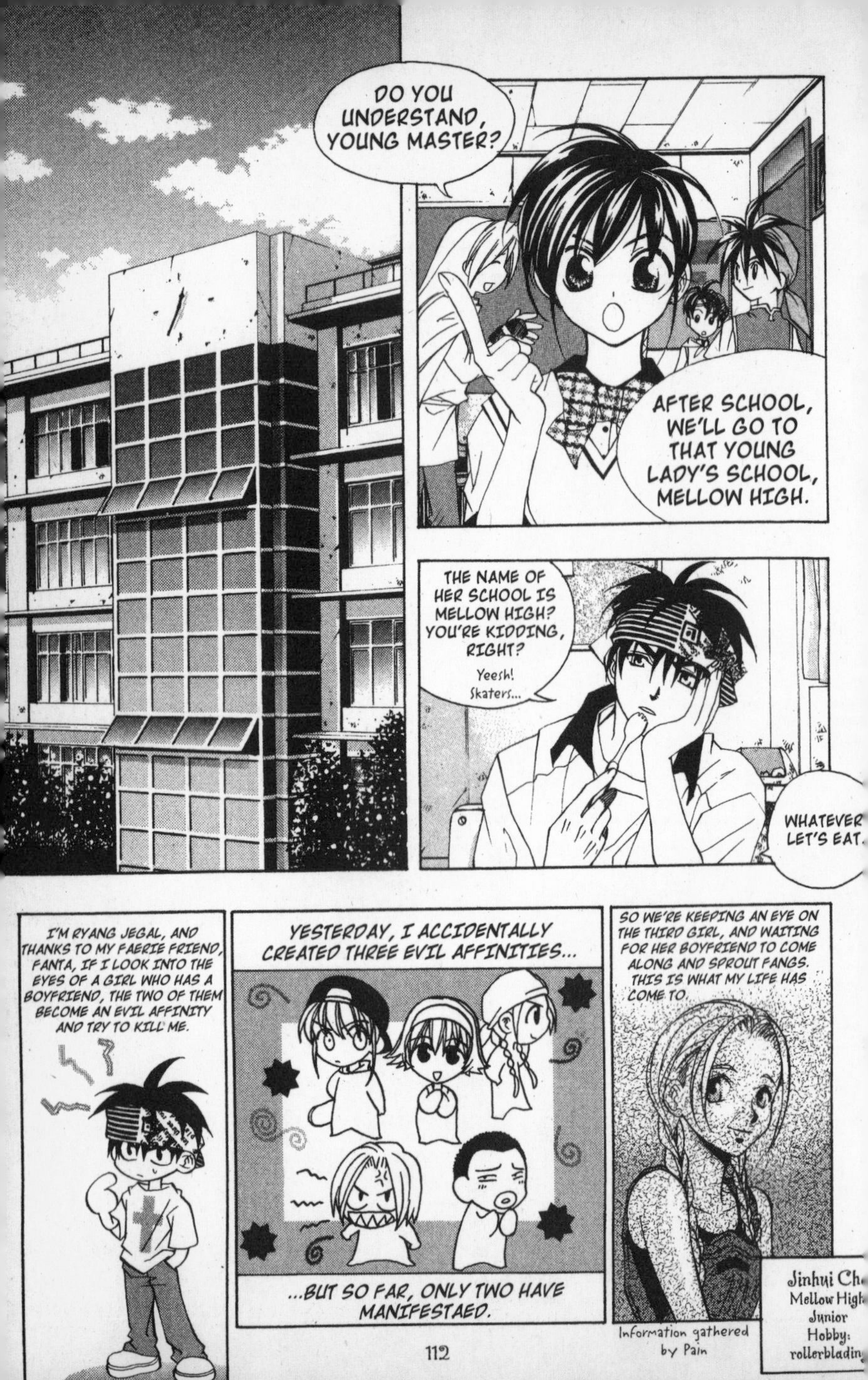

DO YOU UNDERSTAND, YOUNG MASTER?
AFTER SCHOOL, WE'LL GO TO THAT YOUNG LADY'S SCHOOL, MELLOW HIGH.
THE NAME OF HER SCHOOL IS MELLOW HIGH? YOU'RE KIDDING, RIGHT?
Yeesh! Skaters...
WHATEVER LET'S EAT.
I'M RYANG JEGAL, AND THANKS TO MY FAERIE FRIEND, FANTA, IF I LOOK INTO THE EYES OF A GIRL WHO HAS A BOYFRIEND, THE TWO OF THEM BECOME AN EVIL AFFINITY AND TRY TO KILL ME.
YESTERDAY, I ACCIDENTALLY CREATED THREE EVIL AFFINITIES...
...BUT SO FAR, ONLY TWO HAVE MANIFESTAED.
SO WE'RE KEEPING AN EYE ON THE THIRD GIRL, AND WAITING FOR HER BOYFRIEND TO COME ALONG AND SPROUT FANGS. THIS IS WHAT MY LIFE HAS COME TO.
Jinhui Ch
Mellow High
Junior
Hobby: rollerbladin
Information gathered by Pain

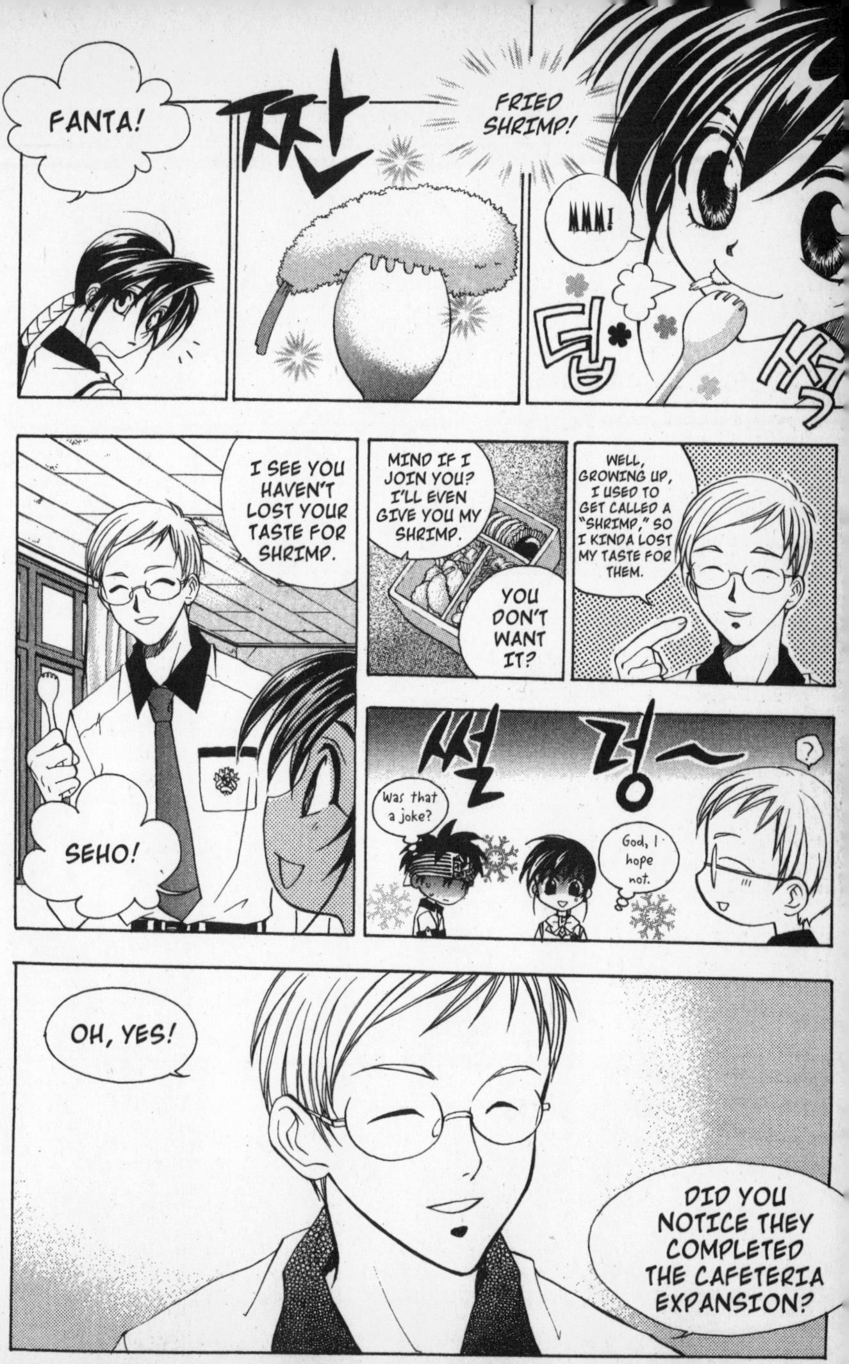
FANTA!
짠
FRIED SHRIMP!
MMM!
덥
I SEE YOU HAVEN'T LOST YOUR TASTE FOR SHRIMP.
SEHO!
MIND IF I JOIN YOU? I'LL EVEN GIVE YOU MY SHRIMP.
YOU DON'T WANT IT?
WELL, GROWING UP, I USED TO GET CALLED A "SHRIMP," SO I KINDA LOST MY TASTE FOR THEM.
썰렁~
?
Was that a joke?
God, I hope not.
OH, YES!
DID YOU NOTICE THEY COMPLETED THE CAFETERIA EXPANSION?

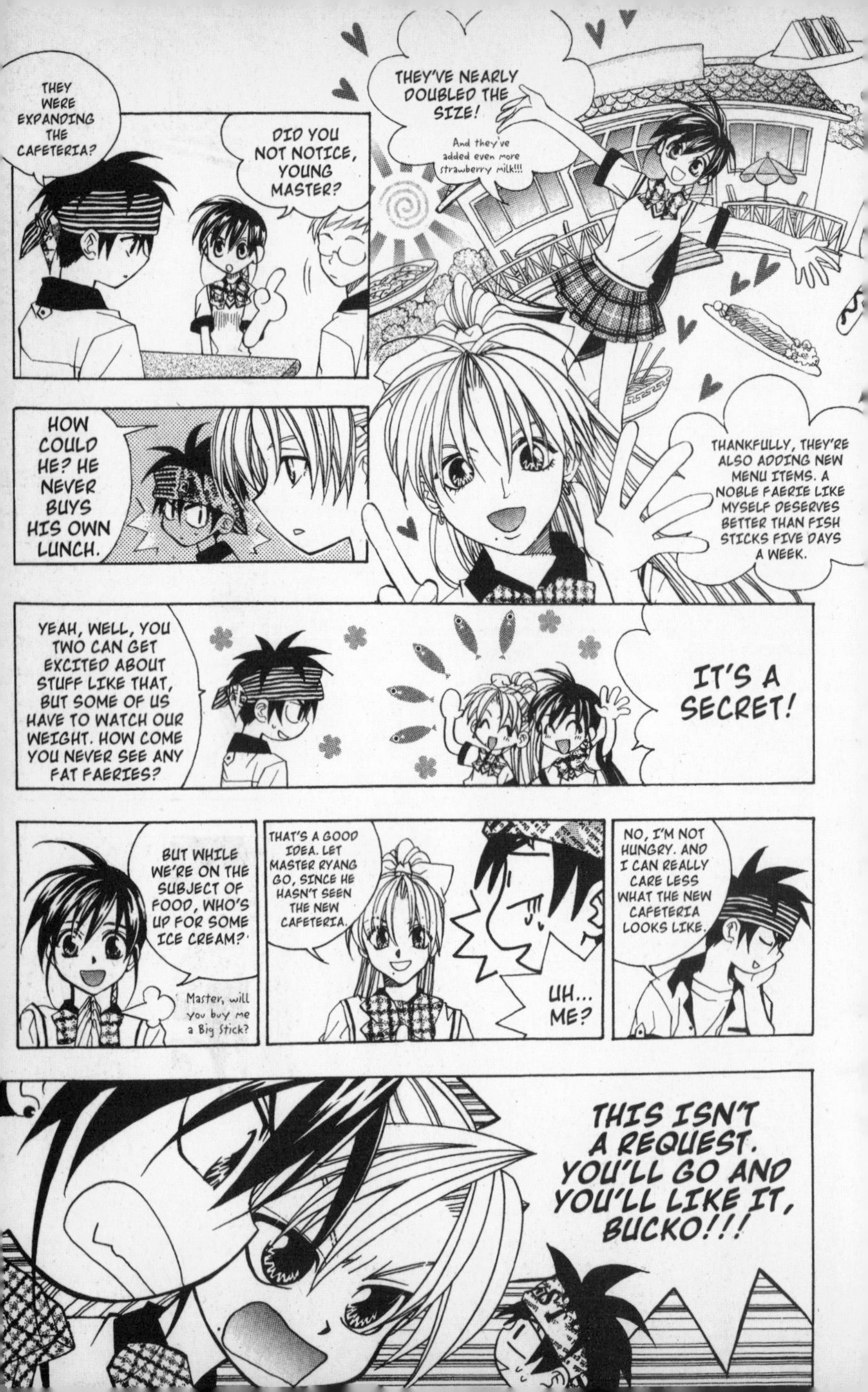
THEY WERE EXPANDING THE CAFETERIA?
DID YOU NOT NOTICE, YOUNG MASTER?
THEY'VE NEARLY DOUBLED THE SIZE!
And they've added even more strawberry milk!!!
HOW COULD HE? HE NEVER BUYS HIS OWN LUNCH.
THANKFULLY, THEY'RE ALSO ADDING NEW MENU ITEMS. A NOBLE FAERIE LIKE MYSELF DESERVES BETTER THAN FISH STICKS FIVE DAYS A WEEK.
YEAH, WELL, YOU TWO CAN GET EXCITED ABOUT STUFF LIKE THAT, BUT SOME OF US HAVE TO WATCH OUR WEIGHT. HOW COME YOU NEVER SEE ANY FAT FAERIES?
IT'S A SECRET!
BUT WHILE WE'RE ON THE SUBJECT OF FOOD, WHO'S UP FOR SOME ICE CREAM?
Master, will you buy me a Big Stick?
THAT'S A GOOD IDEA. LET MASTER RYANG GO, SINCE HE HASN'T SEEN THE NEW CAFETERIA.
UH... ME?
NO, I'M NOT HUNGRY. AND I CAN REALLY CARE LESS WHAT THE NEW CAFETERIA LOOKS LIKE.
THIS ISN'T A REQUEST. YOU'LL GO AND YOU'LL LIKE IT, BUCKO!!!

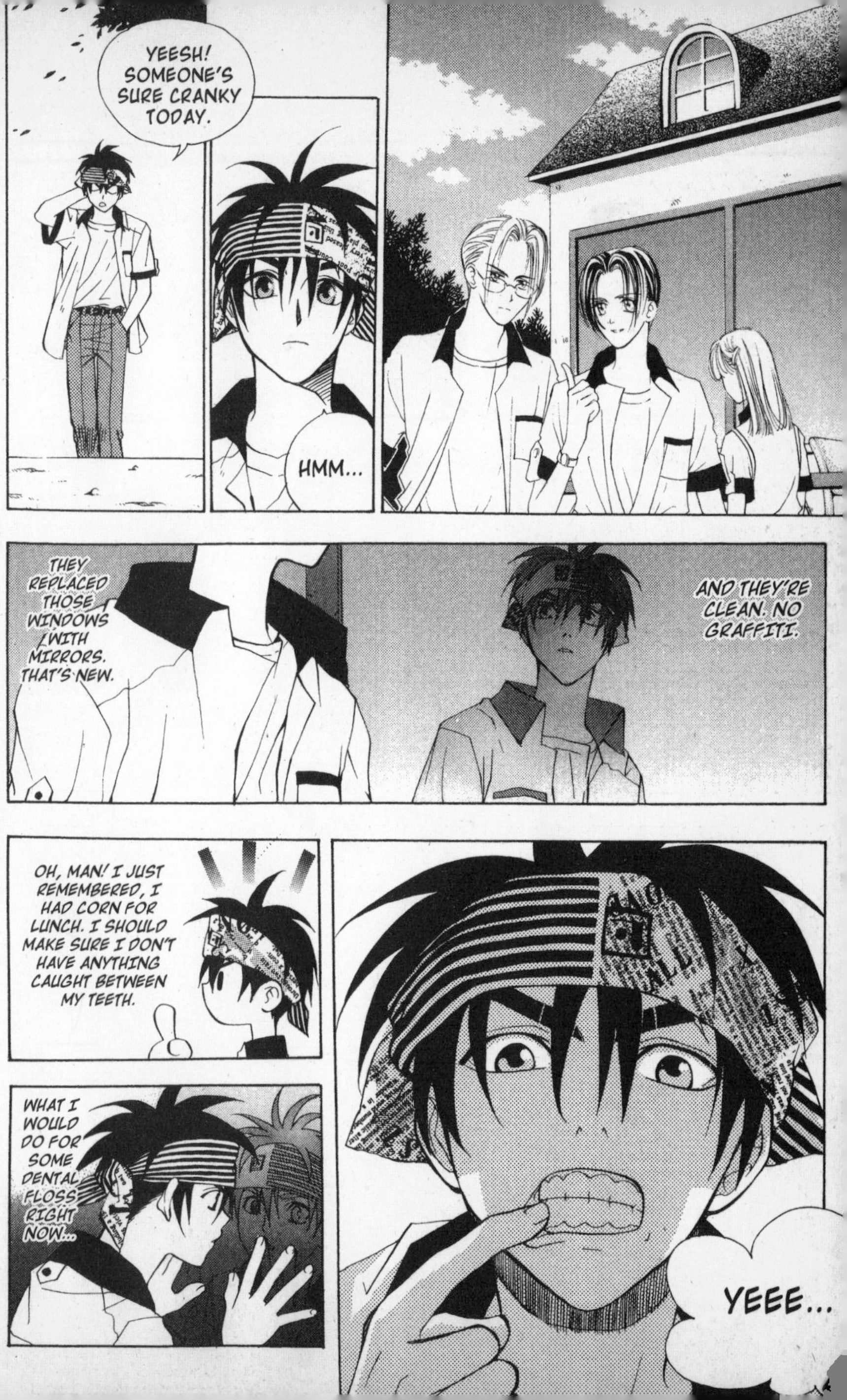
YEESH! SOMEONE'S SURE CRANKY TODAY.
HMM...
THEY REPLACED THOSE WINDOWS WITH MIRRORS. THAT'S NEW.
AND THEY'RE CLEAN. NO GRAFFITI.
OH, MAN! I JUST REMEMBERED, I HAD CORN FOR LUNCH. I SHOULD MAKE SURE I DON'T HAVE ANYTHING CAUGHT BETWEEN MY TEETH.
WHAT I WOULD DO FOR SOME DENTAL FLOSS RIGHT NOW...
YEEE...

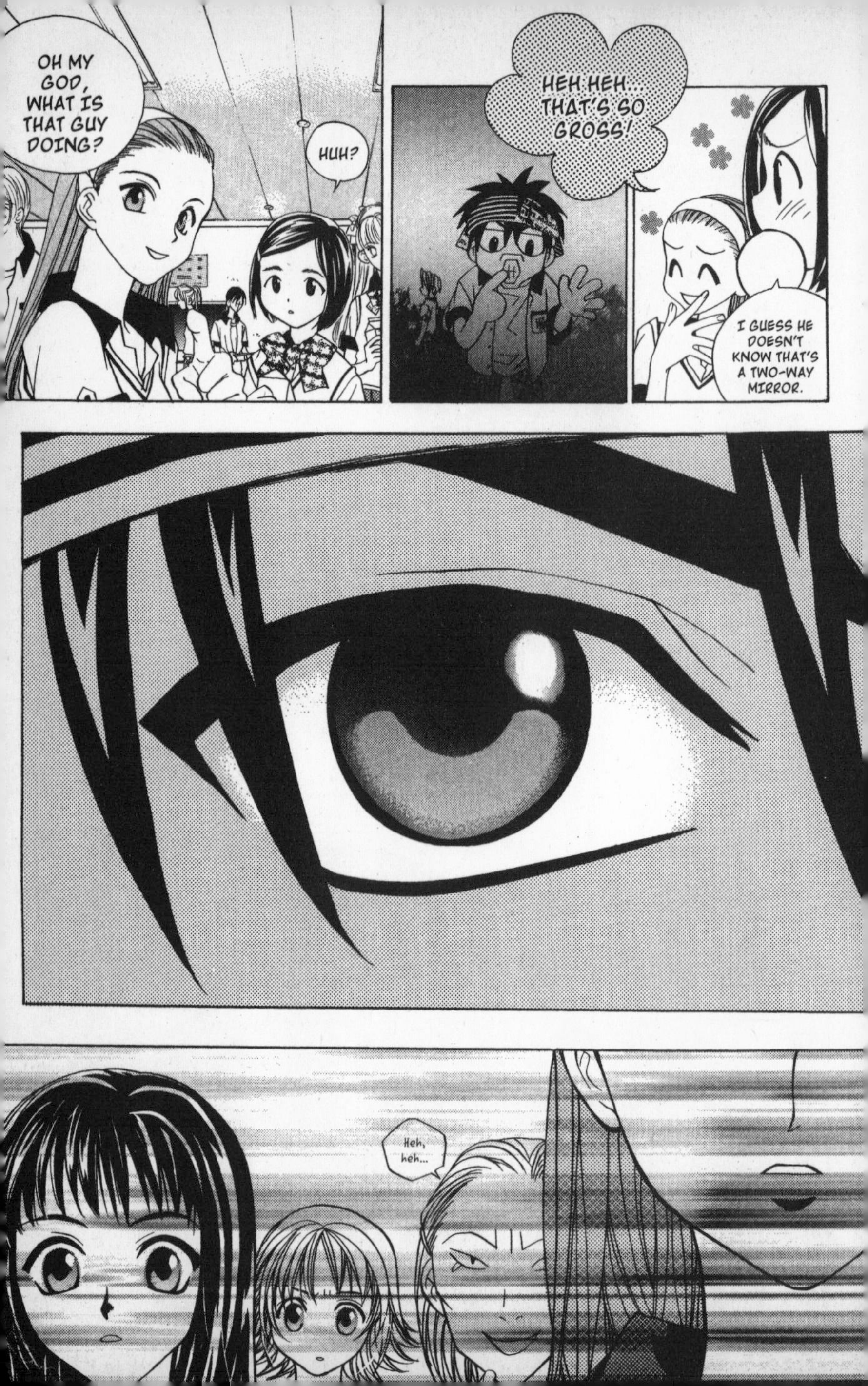
OH MY GOD, WHAT IS THAT GUY DOING?
HUH?
HEH HEH... THAT'S SO GROSS!
I GUESS HE DOESN'T KNOW THAT'S A TWO-WAY MIRROR.
Heh, heh...

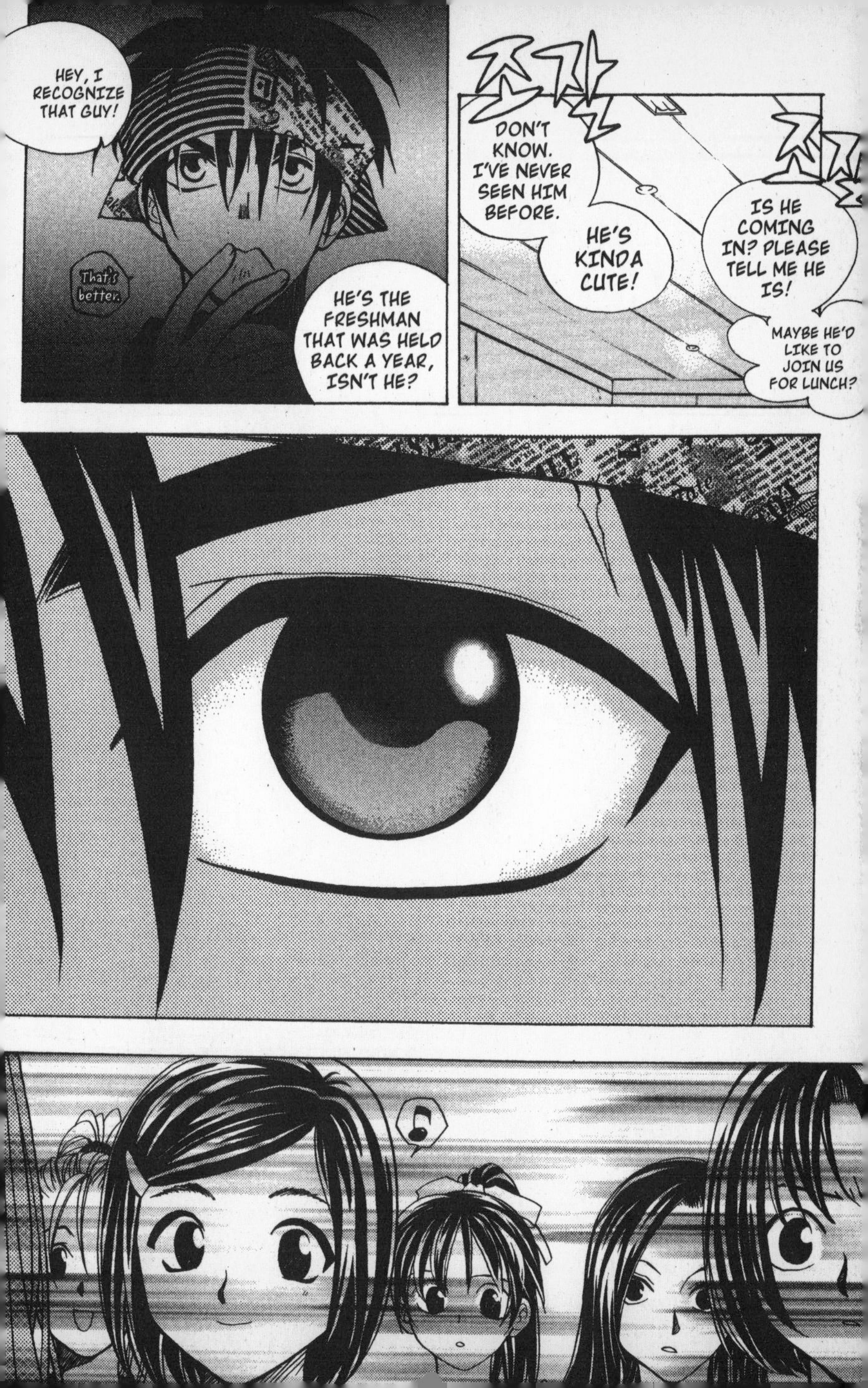
HEY, I RECOGNIZE THAT GUY!
That's better.
HE'S THE FRESHMAN THAT WAS HELD BACK A YEAR, ISN'T HE?
DON'T KNOW. I'VE NEVER SEEN HIM BEFORE.
HE'S KINDA CUTE!
IS HE COMING IN? PLEASE TELL ME HE IS!
MAYBE HE'D LIKE TO JOIN US FOR LUNCH?

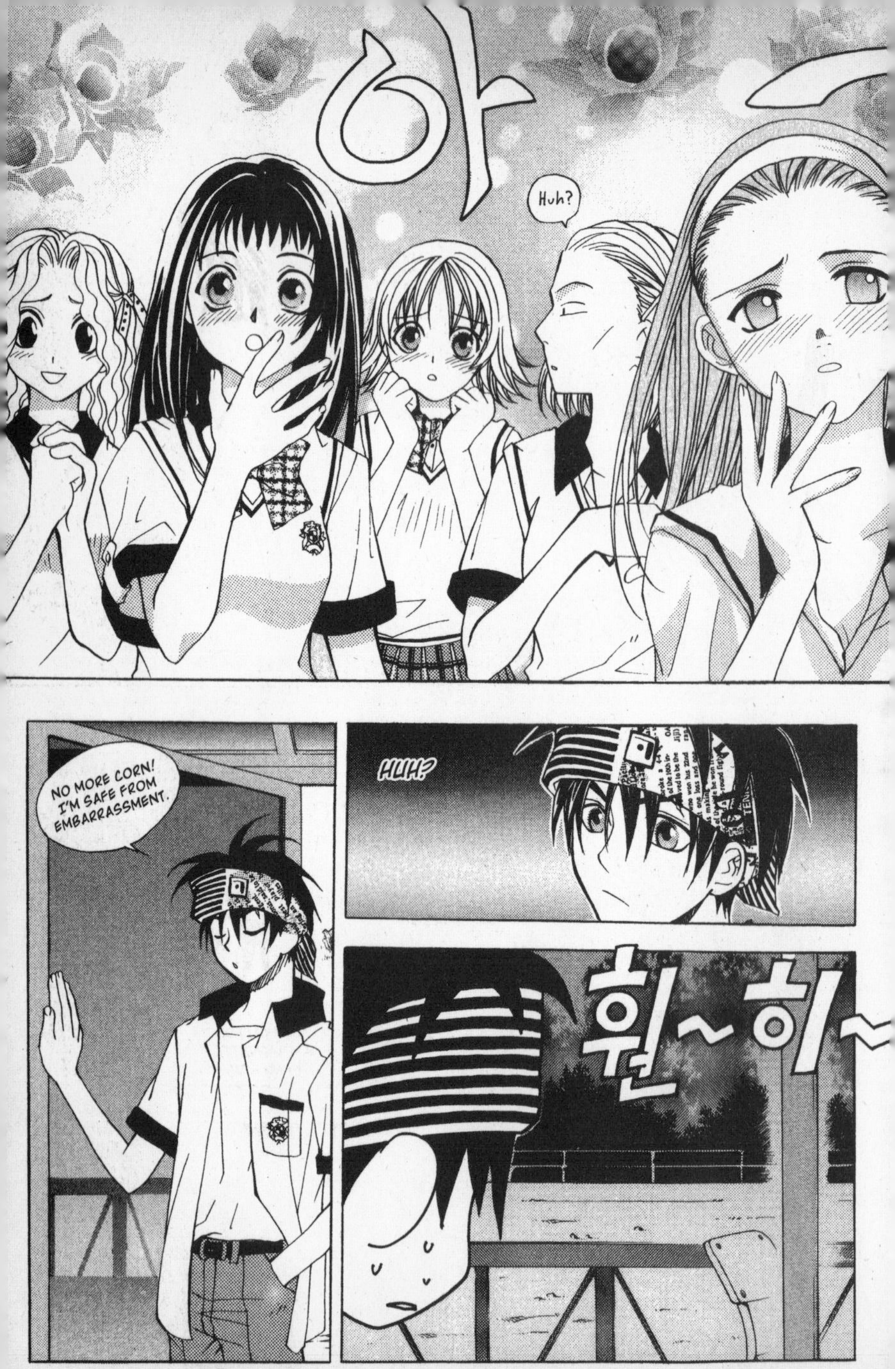
아~
Huh?
NO MORE CORN! I'M SAFE FROM EMBARRASSMENT.
HUH?
휜~히~

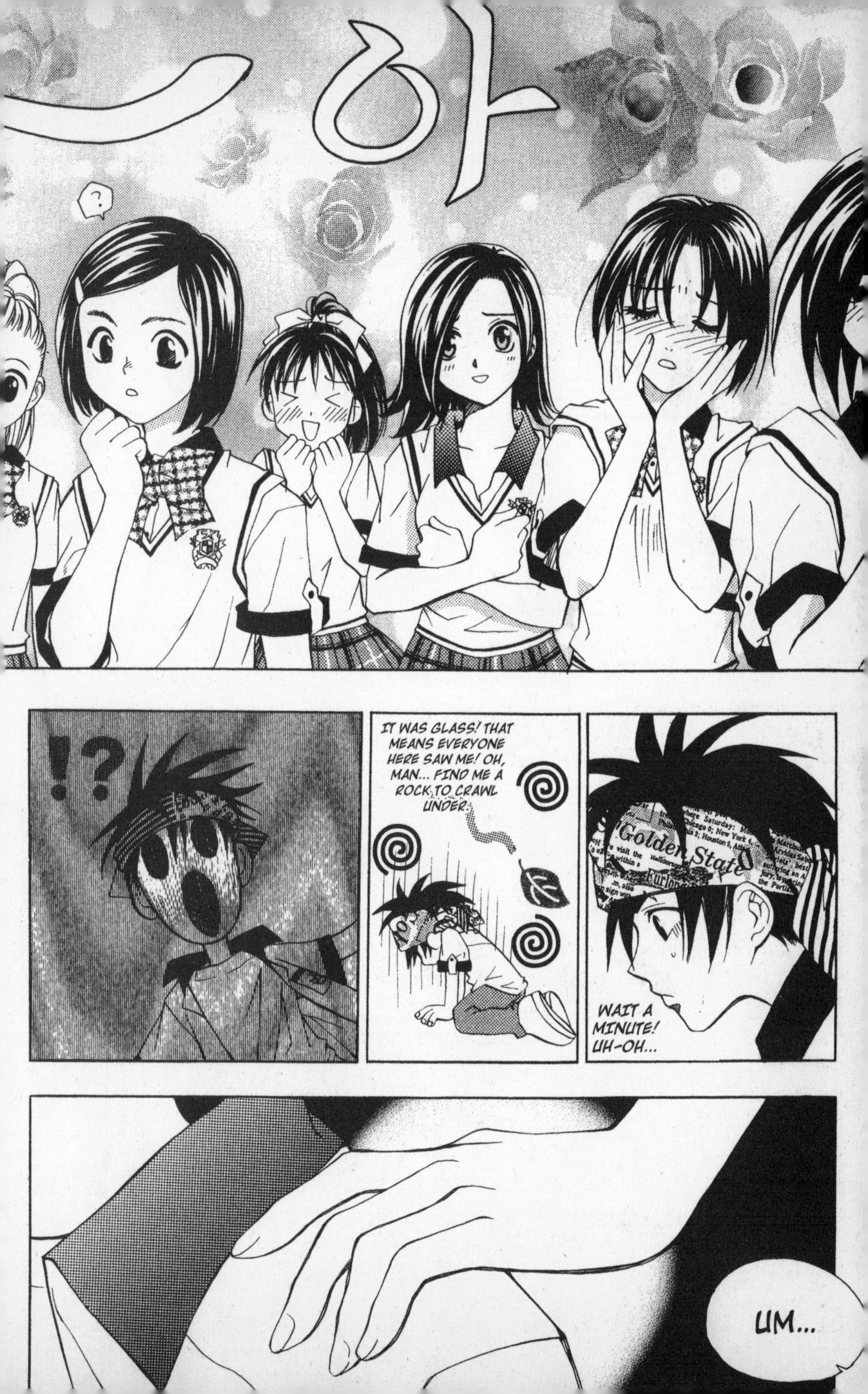

ー아
?
!?
IT WAS GLASS! THAT MEANS EVERYONE HERE SAW ME! OH, MAN... FIND ME A ROCK TO CRAWL UNDER.
WAIT A MINUTE! UH-OH...
UM...

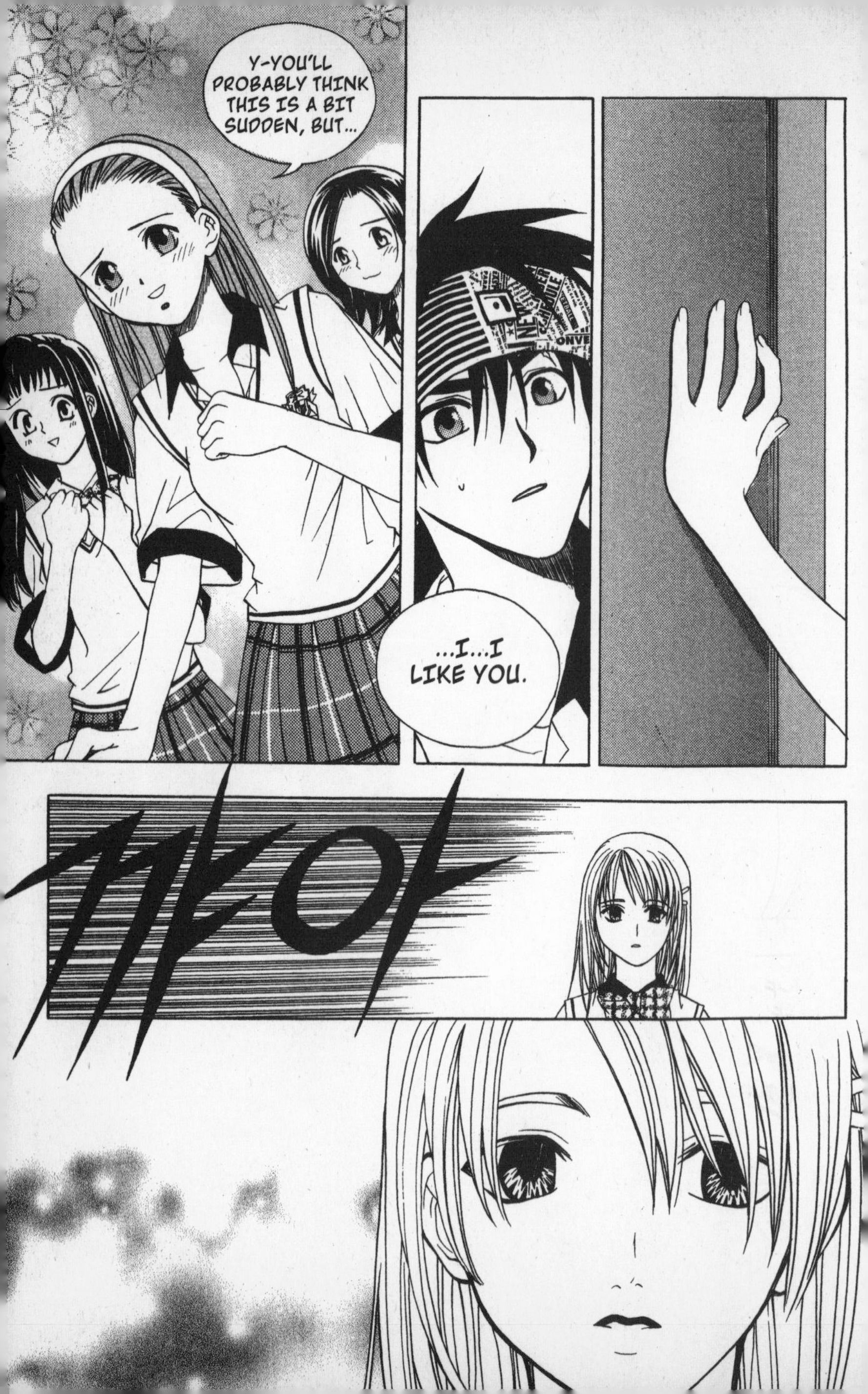
Y-YOU'LL PROBABLY THINK THIS IS A BIT SUDDEN, BUT...
...I...I LIKE YOU.

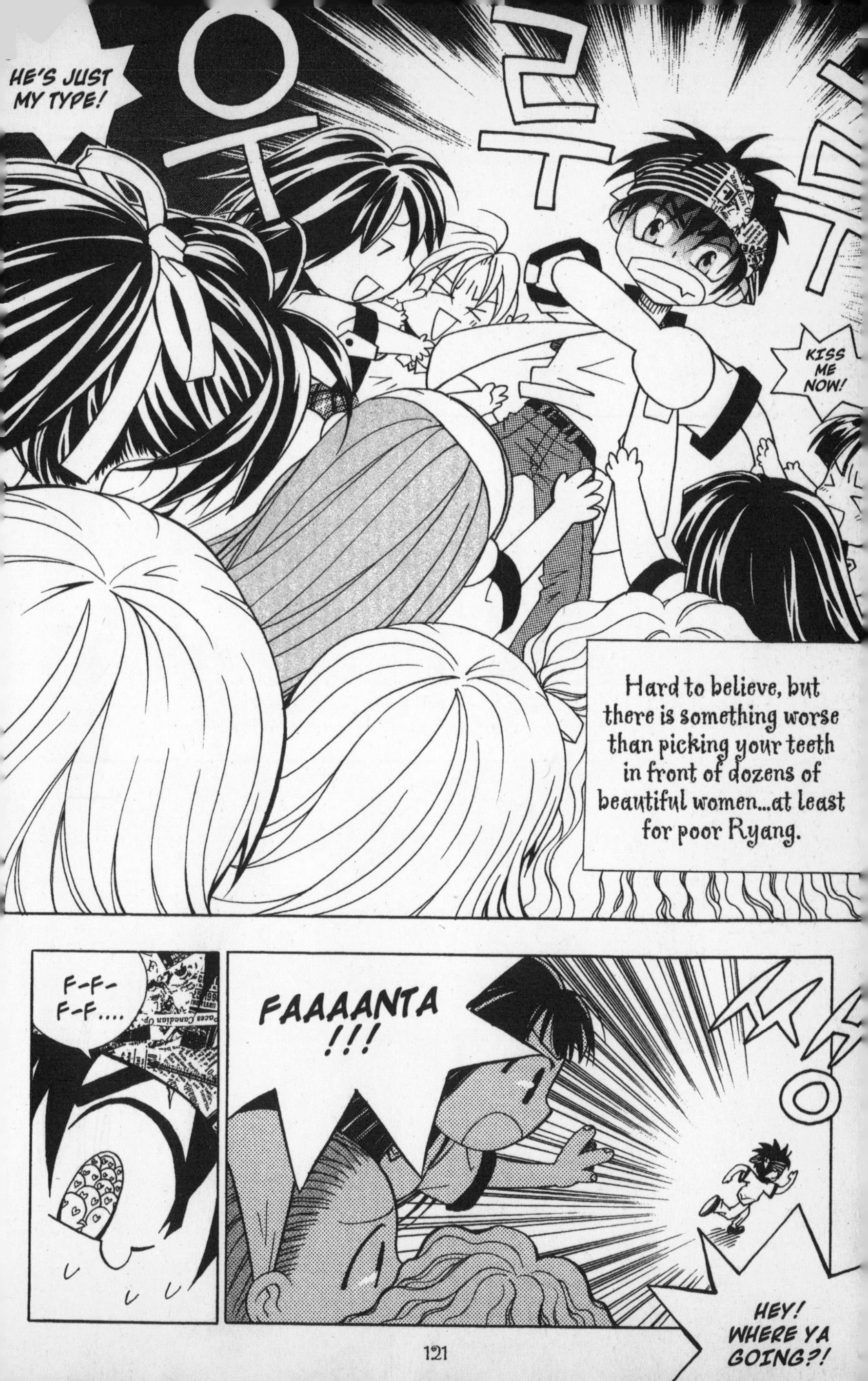
HE'S JUST MY TYPE!
KISS ME NOW!
Hard to believe, but there is something worse than picking your teeth in front of dozens of beautiful women...at least for poor Ryang.
F-F-F-F....
FAAAANTA !!!
HEY! WHERE YA GOING?!

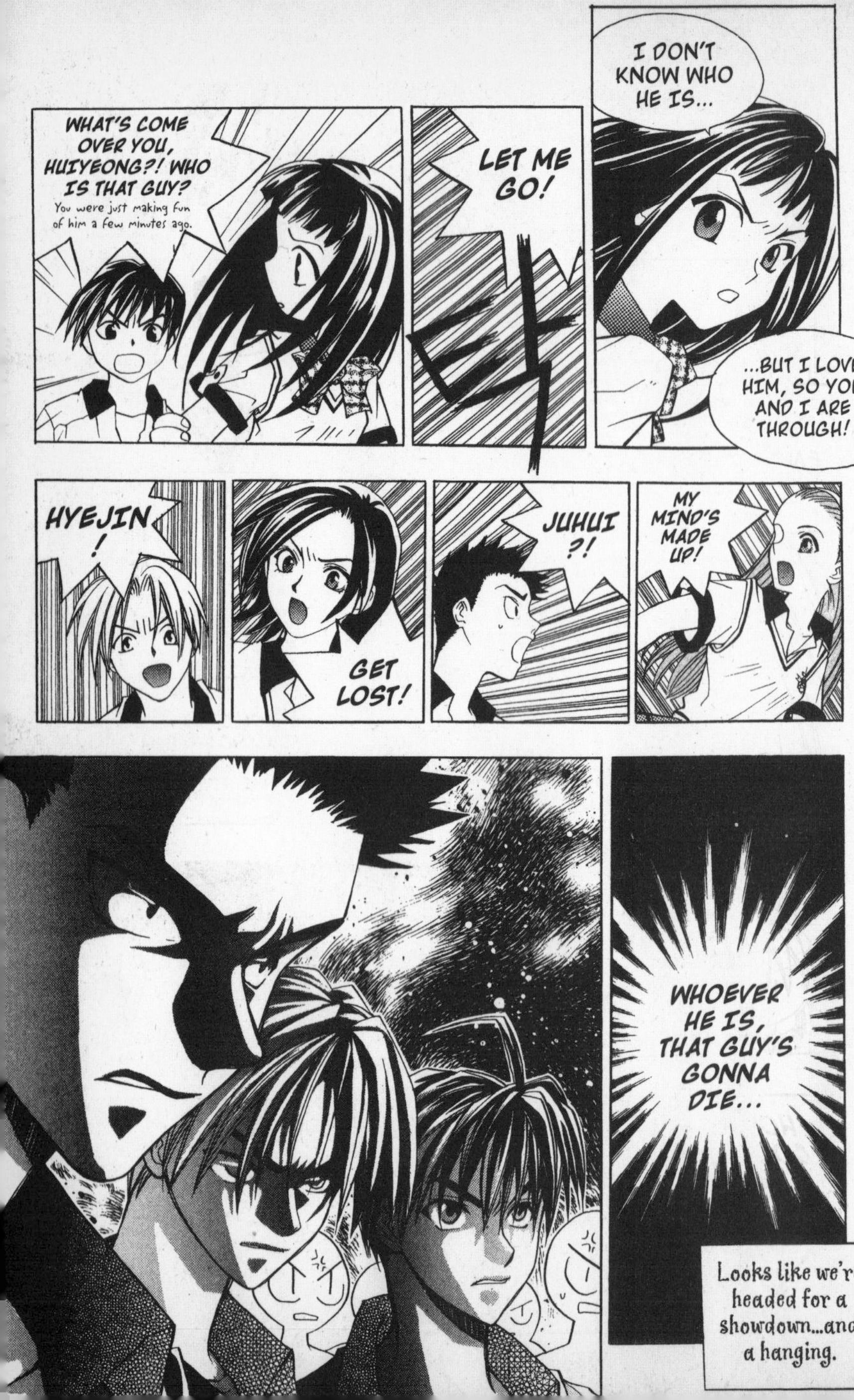
WHAT'S COME OVER YOU, HUIYEONG?! WHO IS THAT GUY?
You were just making fun of him a few minutes ago.
LET ME GO!
I DON'T KNOW WHO HE IS...
...BUT I LOVE HIM, SO YOU AND I ARE THROUGH!
HYEJIN!
GET LOST!
JUHUI?!
MY MIND'S MADE UP!
WHOEVER HE IS, THAT GUY'S GONNA DIE...
Looks like we're headed for a showdown...and a hanging.

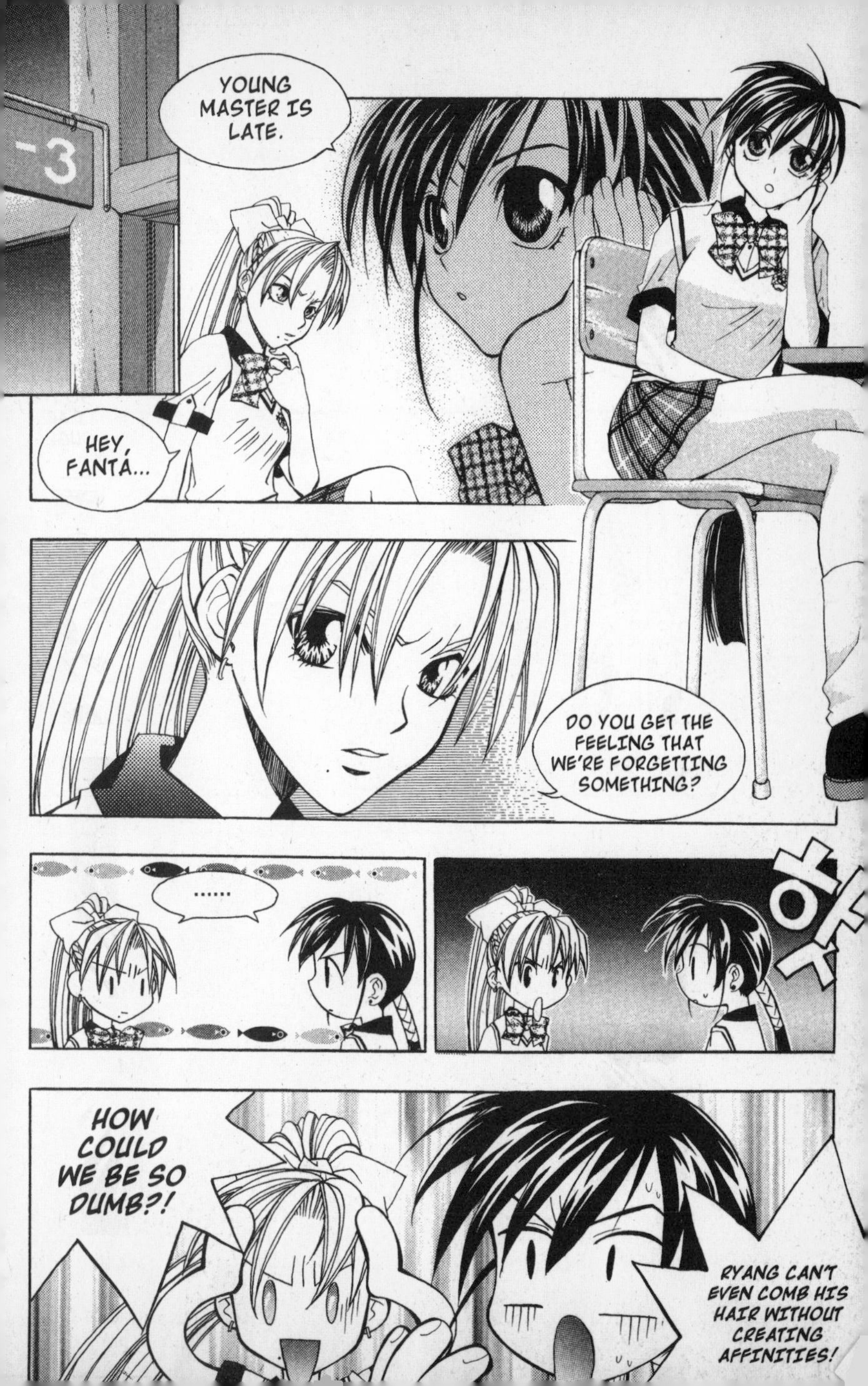
YOUNG MASTER IS LATE.
HEY, FANTÁ...
DO YOU GET THE FEELING THAT WE'RE FORGETTING SOMETHING?
......
약
HOW COULD WE BE SO DUMB?!
RYANG CAN'T EVEN COMB HIS HAIR WITHOUT CREATING AFFINITIES!

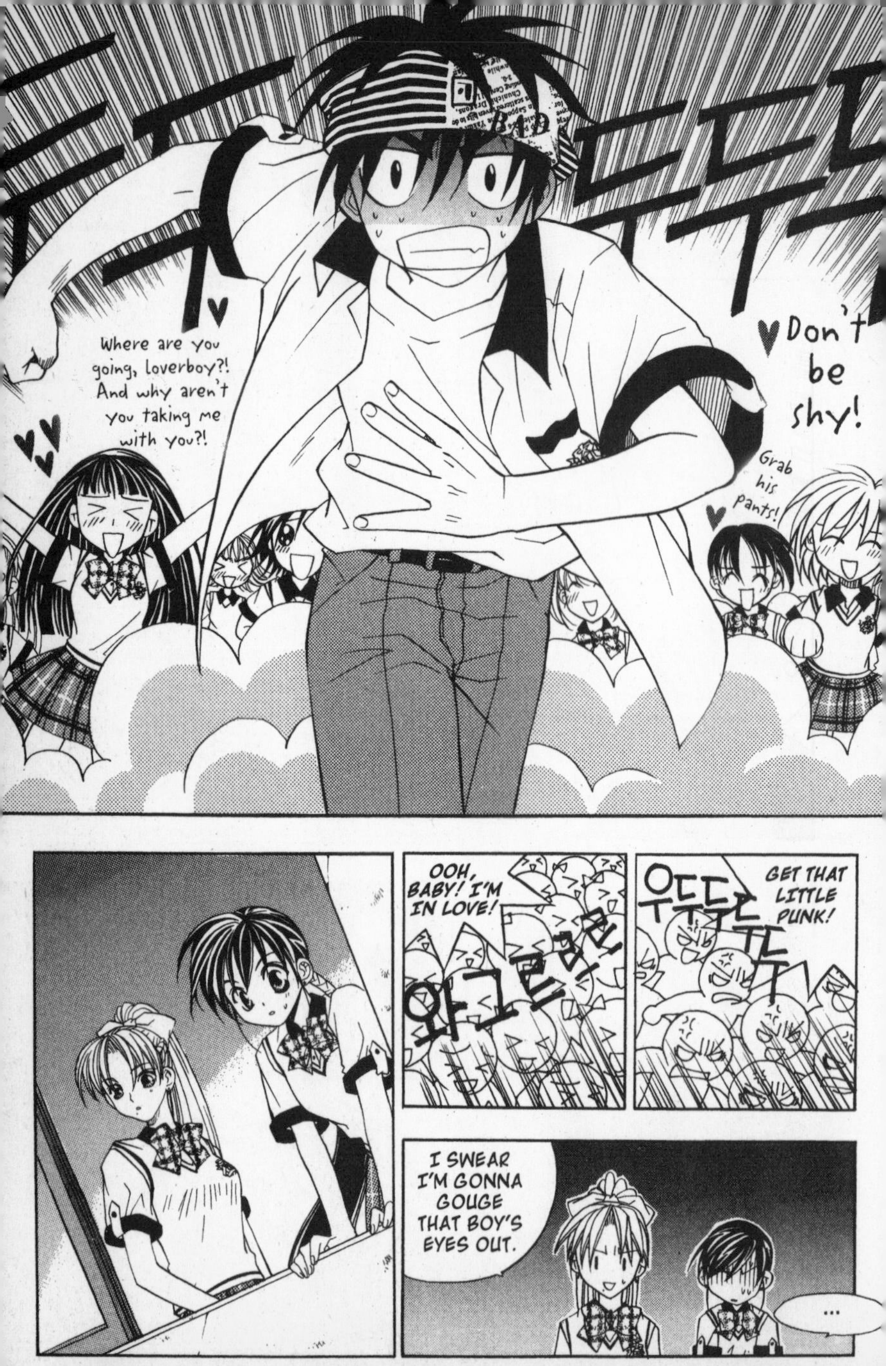
Where are you going, loverboy?! And why aren't you taking me with you?!
Don't be shy!
Grab his pants!
OOH, BABY! I'M IN LOVE!
GET THAT LITTLE PUNK!
I SWEAR I'M GONNA GOUGE THAT BOY'S EYES OUT.
...

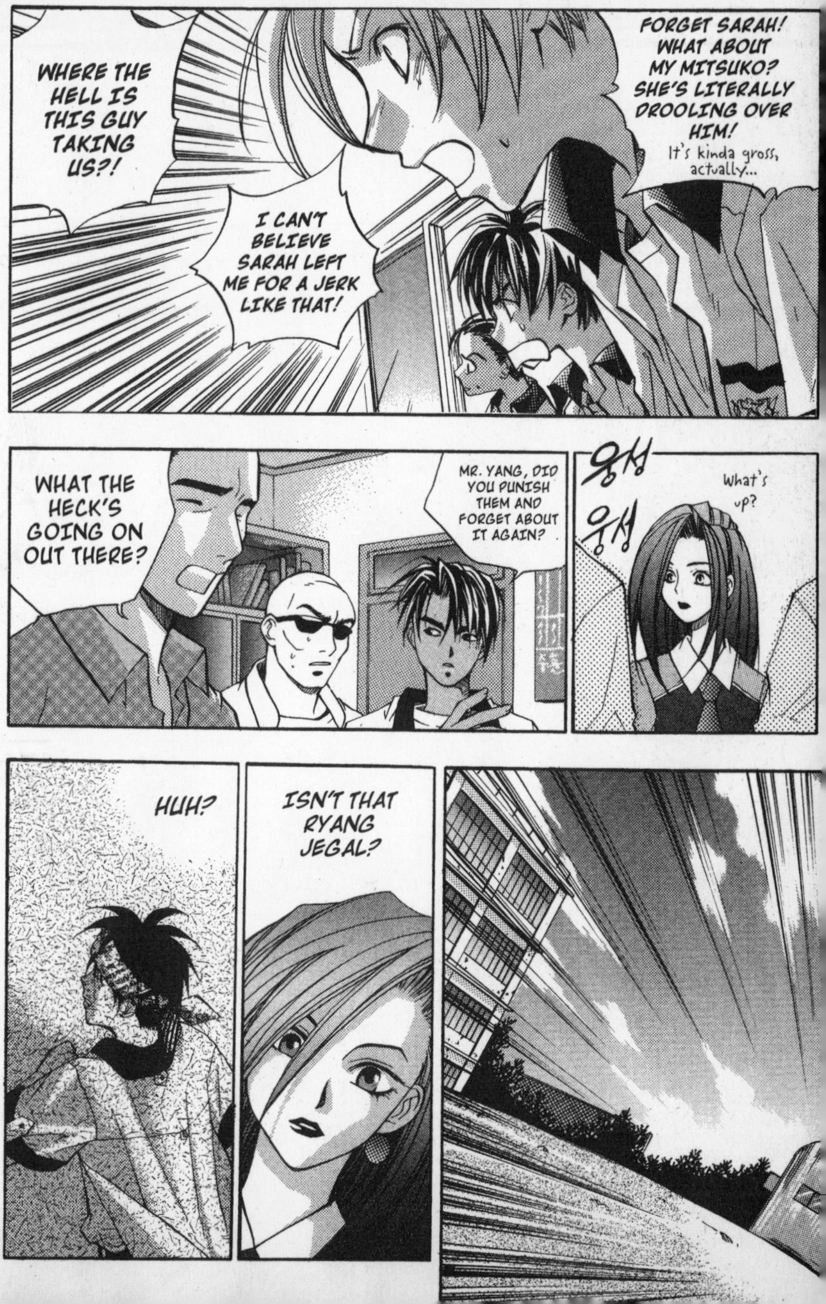
WHERE THE HELL IS THIS GUY TAKING US?!
I CAN'T BELIEVE SARAH LEFT ME FOR A JERK LIKE THAT!
FORGET SARAH! WHAT ABOUT MY MITSUKO? SHE'S LITERALLY DROOLING OVER HIM!
It's kinda gross, actually...
WHAT THE HECK'S GOING ON OUT THERE?
MR. YANG, DID YOU PUNISH THEM AND FORGET ABOUT IT AGAIN?
웅성
웅성
What's up?
HUH?
ISN'T THAT RYANG JEGAL?

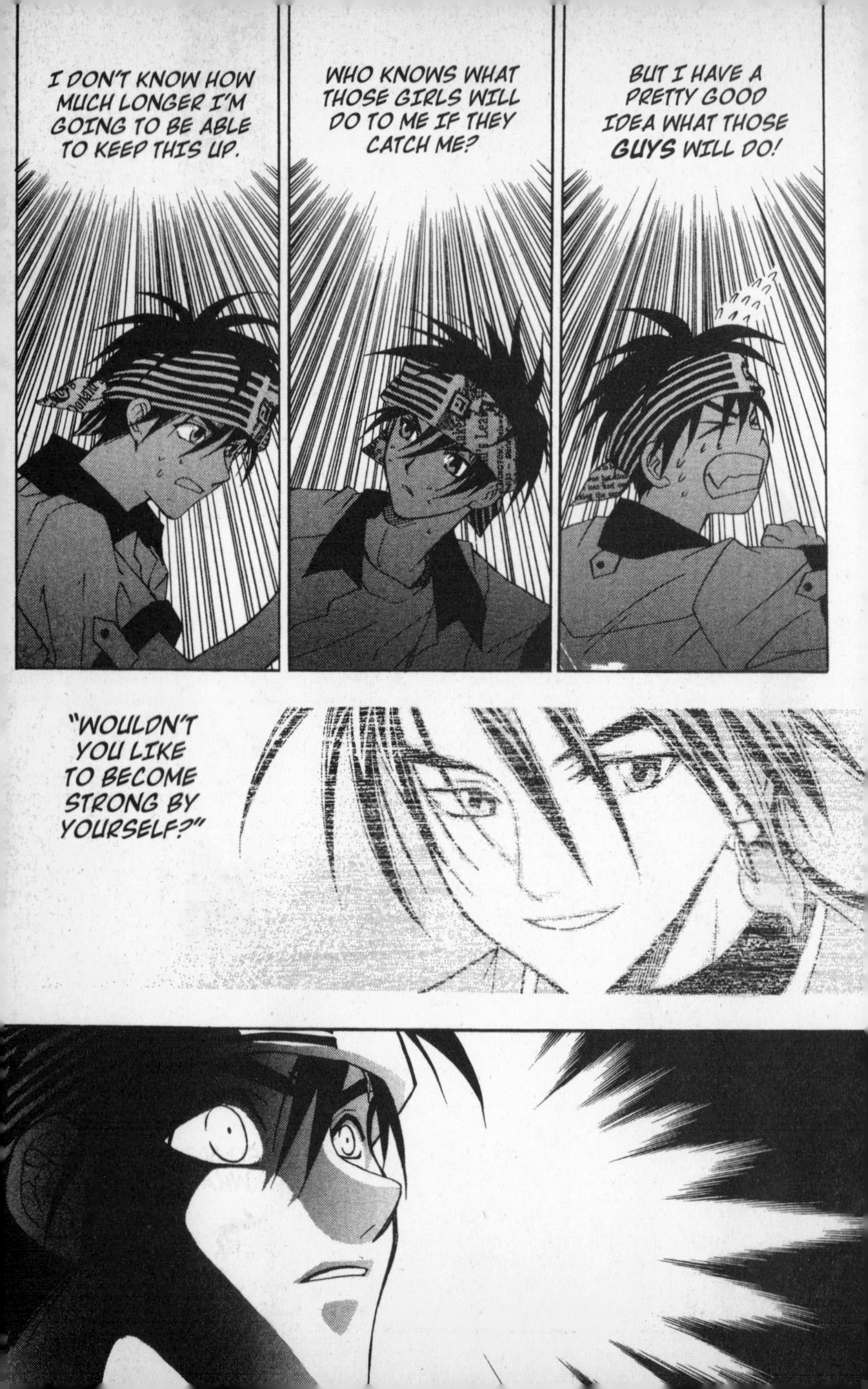
I DON'T KNOW HOW MUCH LONGER I'M GOING TO BE ABLE TO KEEP THIS UP.
WHO KNOWS WHAT THOSE GIRLS WILL DO TO ME IF THEY CATCH ME?
BUT I HAVE A PRETTY GOOD IDEA WHAT THOSE **GUYS** WILL DO!
"WOULDN'T YOU LIKE TO BECOME STRONG BY YOURSELF?"

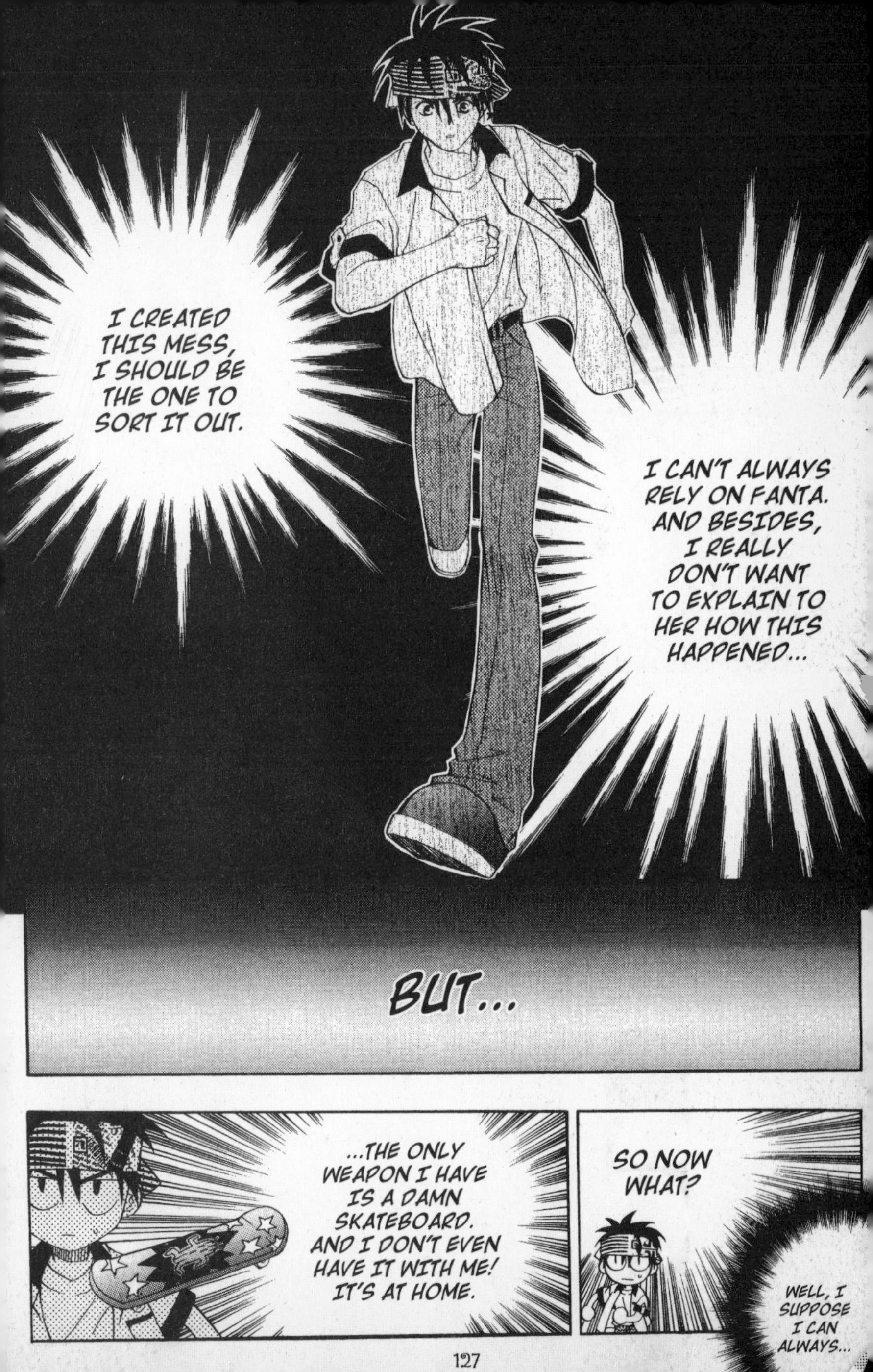
I CREATED THIS MESS, I SHOULD BE THE ONE TO SORT IT OUT.
I CAN'T ALWAYS RELY ON FANTA. AND BESIDES, I REALLY DON'T WANT TO EXPLAIN TO HER HOW THIS HAPPENED...
BUT...
...THE ONLY WEAPON I HAVE IS A DAMN SKATEBOARD. AND I DON'T EVEN HAVE IT WITH ME! IT'S AT HOME.
SO NOW WHAT?
WELL, I SUPPOSE I CAN ALWAYS...

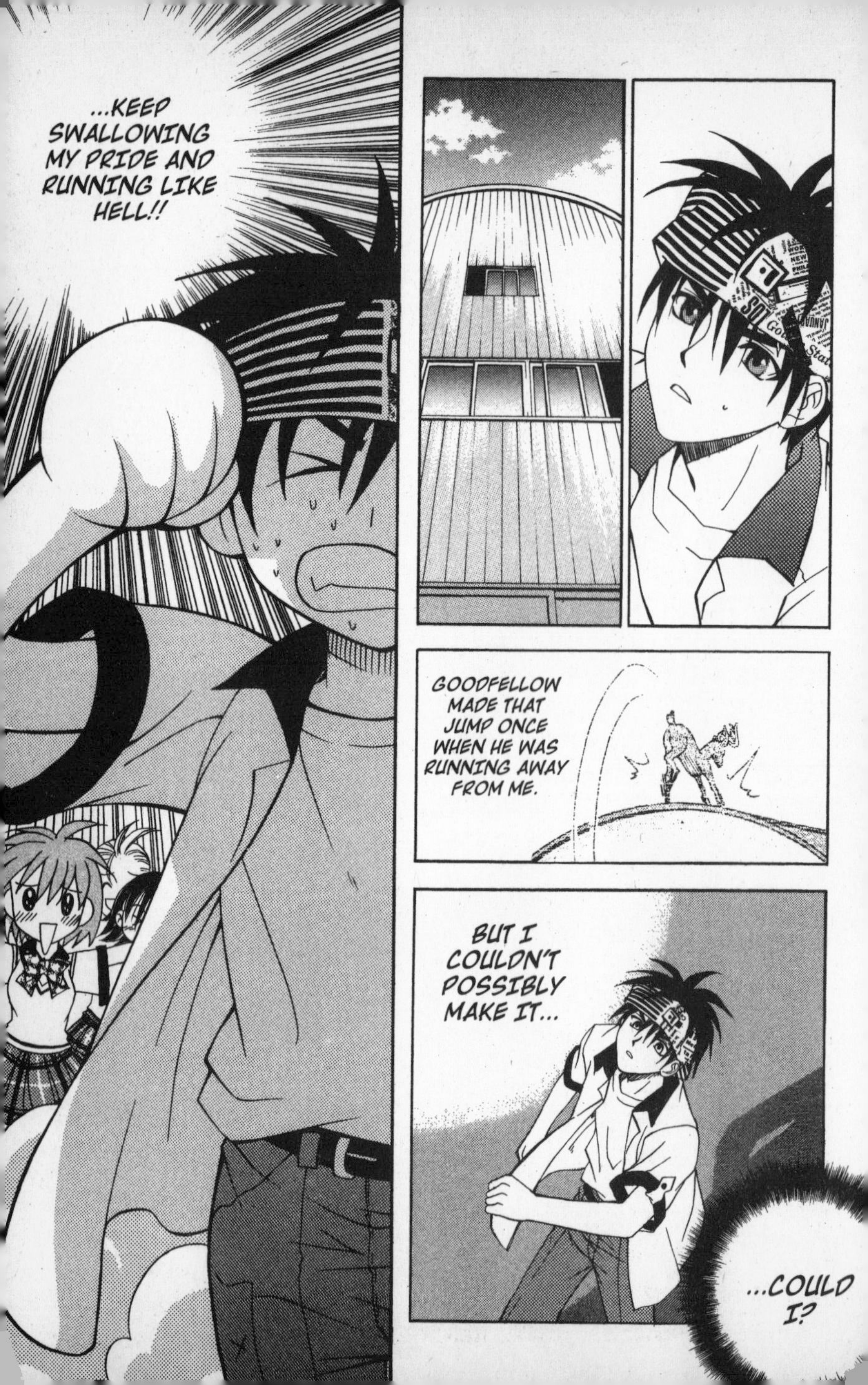
...KEEP SWALLOWING MY PRIDE AND RUNNING LIKE HELL!!
GOODFELLOW MADE THAT JUMP ONCE WHEN HE WAS RUNNING AWAY FROM ME.
BUT I COULDN'T POSSIBLY MAKE IT...
...COULD I?

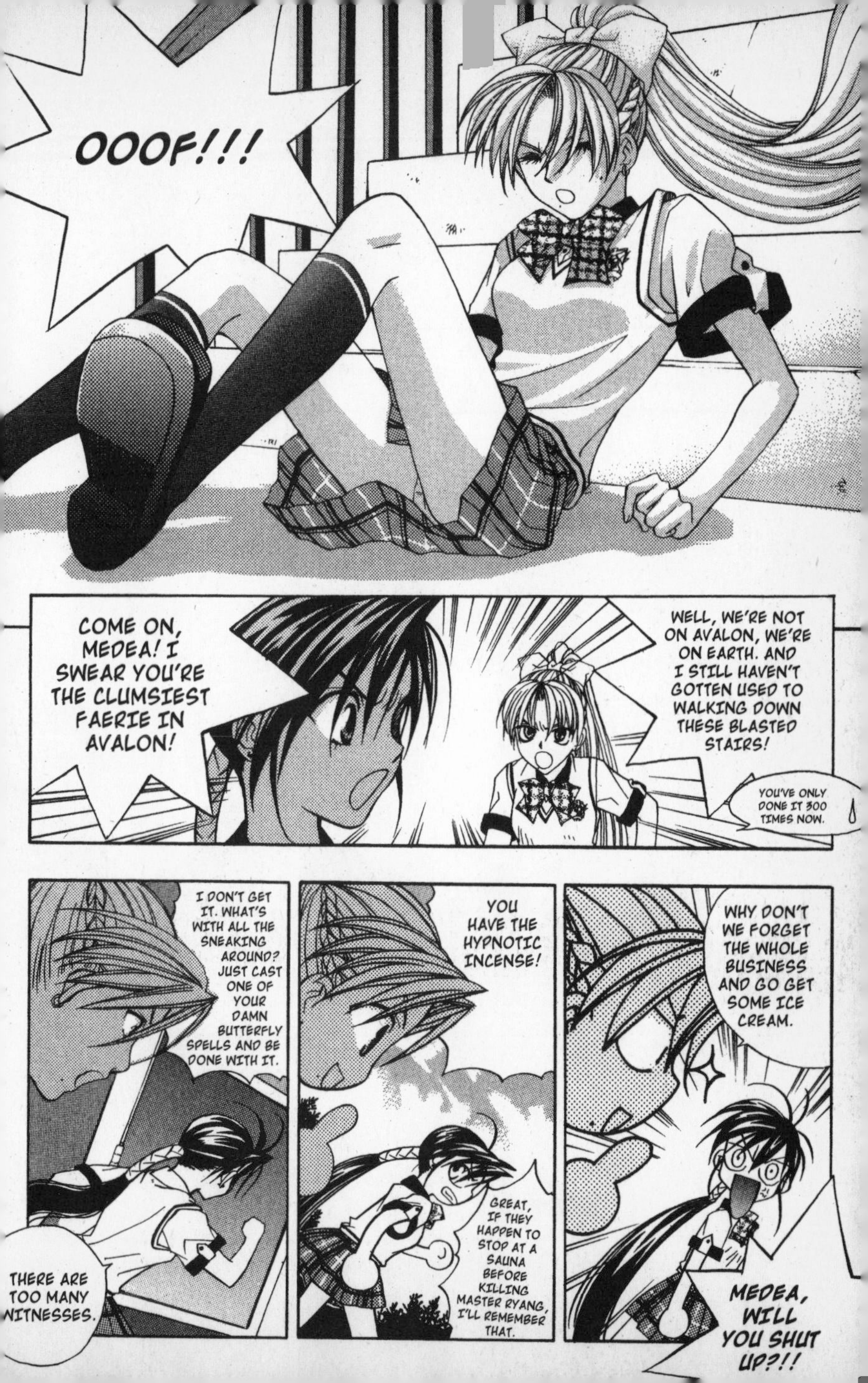
OOOF!!!
COME ON, MEDEA! I SWEAR YOU'RE THE CLUMSIEST FAERIE IN AVALON!
WELL, WE'RE NOT ON AVALON, WE'RE ON EARTH. AND I STILL HAVEN'T GOTTEN USED TO WALKING DOWN THESE BLASTED STAIRS!
YOU'VE ONLY DONE IT 300 TIMES NOW.
I DON'T GET IT. WHAT'S WITH ALL THE SNEAKING AROUND? JUST CAST ONE OF YOUR DAMN BUTTERFLY SPELLS AND BE DONE WITH IT.
THERE ARE TOO MANY WITNESSES.
YOU HAVE THE HYPNOTIC INCENSE!
GREAT, IF THEY HAPPEN TO STOP AT A SAUNA BEFORE KILLING MASTER RYANG, I'LL REMEMBER THAT.
WHY DON'T WE FORGET THE WHOLE BUSINESS AND GO GET SOME ICE CREAM.
MEDEA, WILL YOU SHUT UP?!!

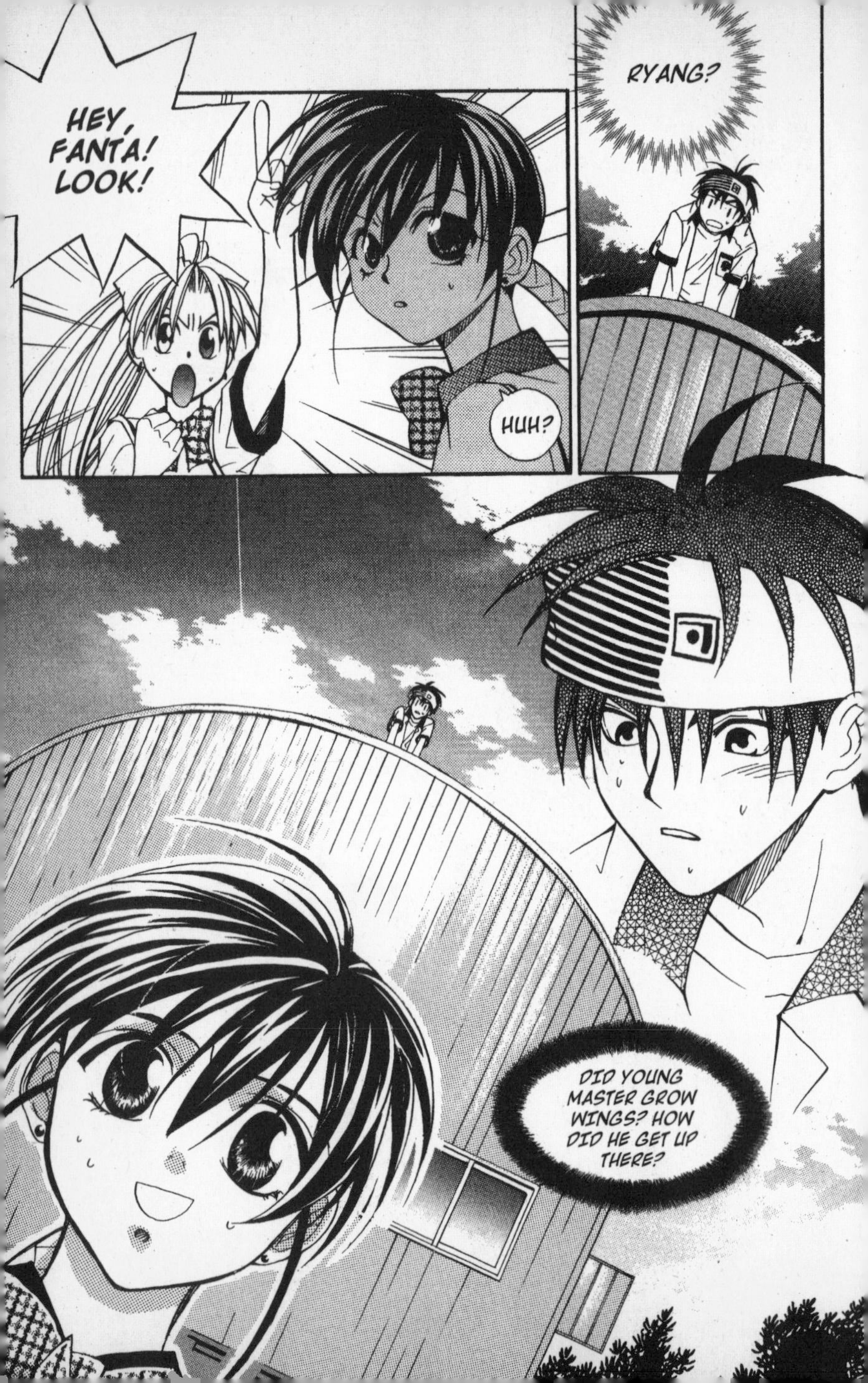
HEY, FANTA! LOOK!
HUH?
RYANG?
DID YOUNG MASTER GROW WINGS? HOW DID HE GET UP THERE?

Episode 22 It's All Part of the Show

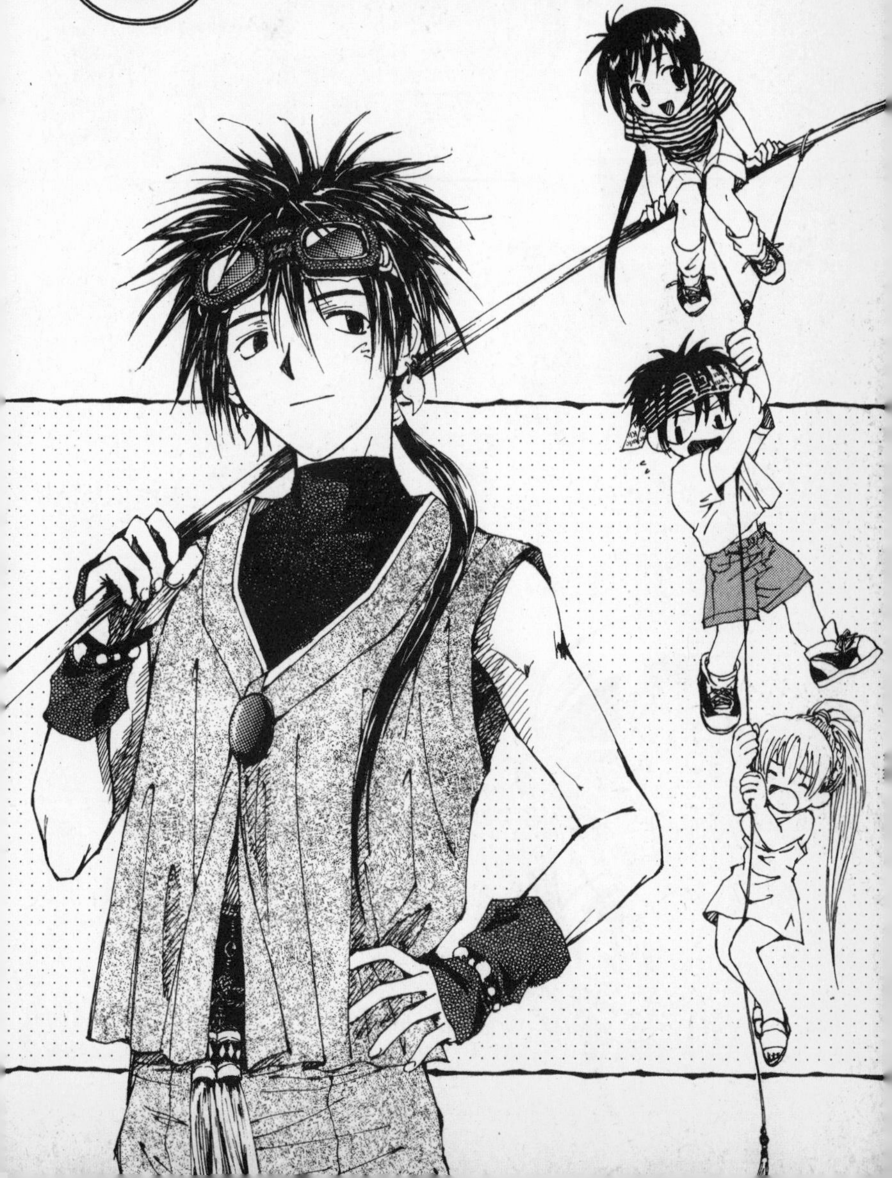

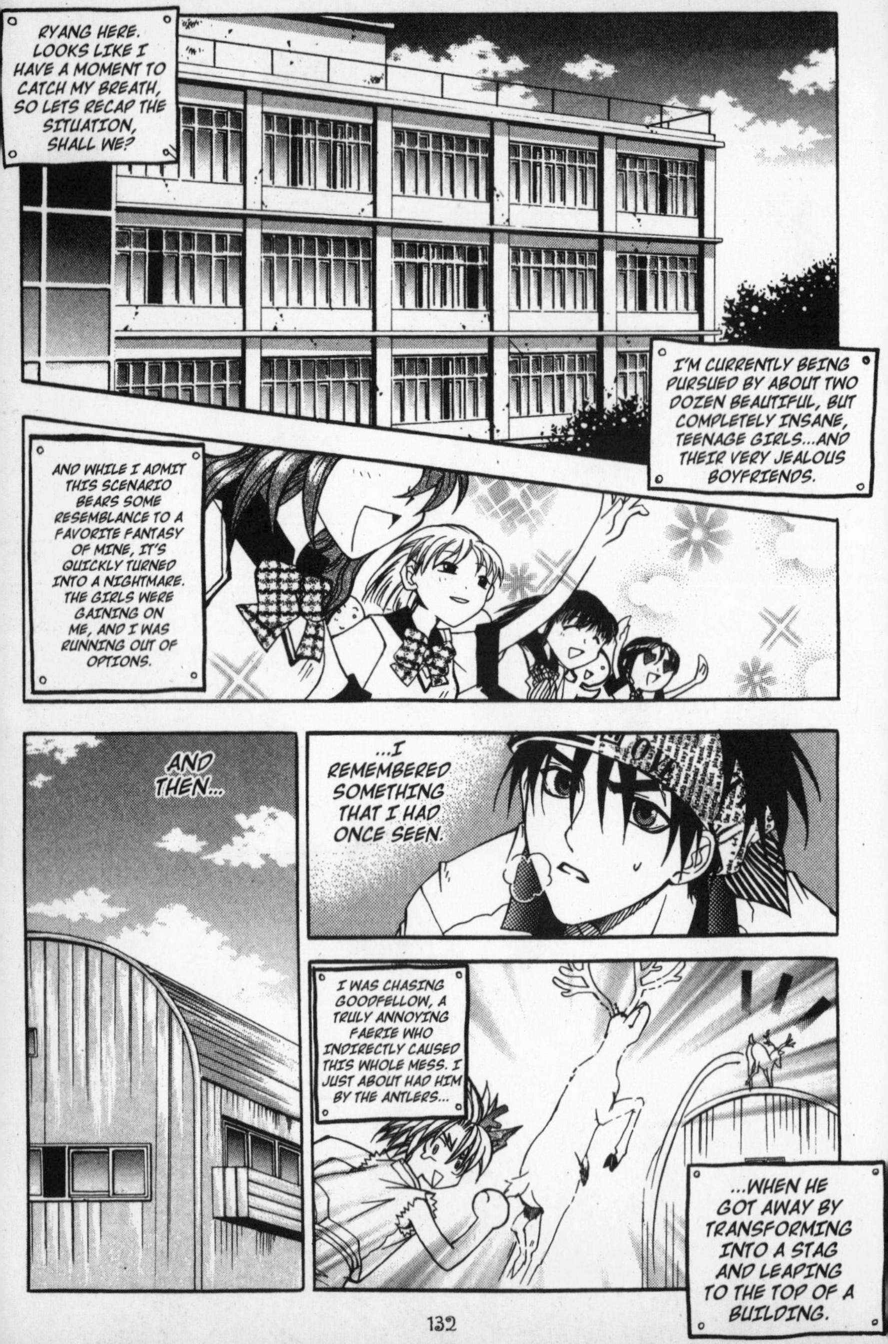
RYANG HERE. LOOKS LIKE I HAVE A MOMENT TO CATCH MY BREATH, SO LETS RECAP THE SITUATION, SHALL WE?
I'M CURRENTLY BEING PURSUED BY ABOUT TWO DOZEN BEAUTIFUL, BUT COMPLETELY INSANE, TEENAGE GIRLS...AND THEIR VERY JEALOUS BOYFRIENDS.
AND WHILE I ADMIT THIS SCENARIO BEARS SOME RESEMBLANCE TO A FAVORITE FANTASY OF MINE, IT'S QUICKLY TURNED INTO A NIGHTMARE. THE GIRLS WERE GAINING ON ME, AND I WAS RUNNING OUT OF OPTIONS.
AND THEN...
...I REMEMBERED SOMETHING THAT I HAD ONCE SEEN.
I WAS CHASING GOODFELLOW, A TRULY ANNOYING FAERIE WHO INDIRECTLY CAUSED THIS WHOLE MESS. I JUST ABOUT HAD HIM BY THE ANTLERS...
...WHEN HE GOT AWAY BY TRANSFORMING INTO A STAG AND LEAPING TO THE TOP OF A BUILDING.

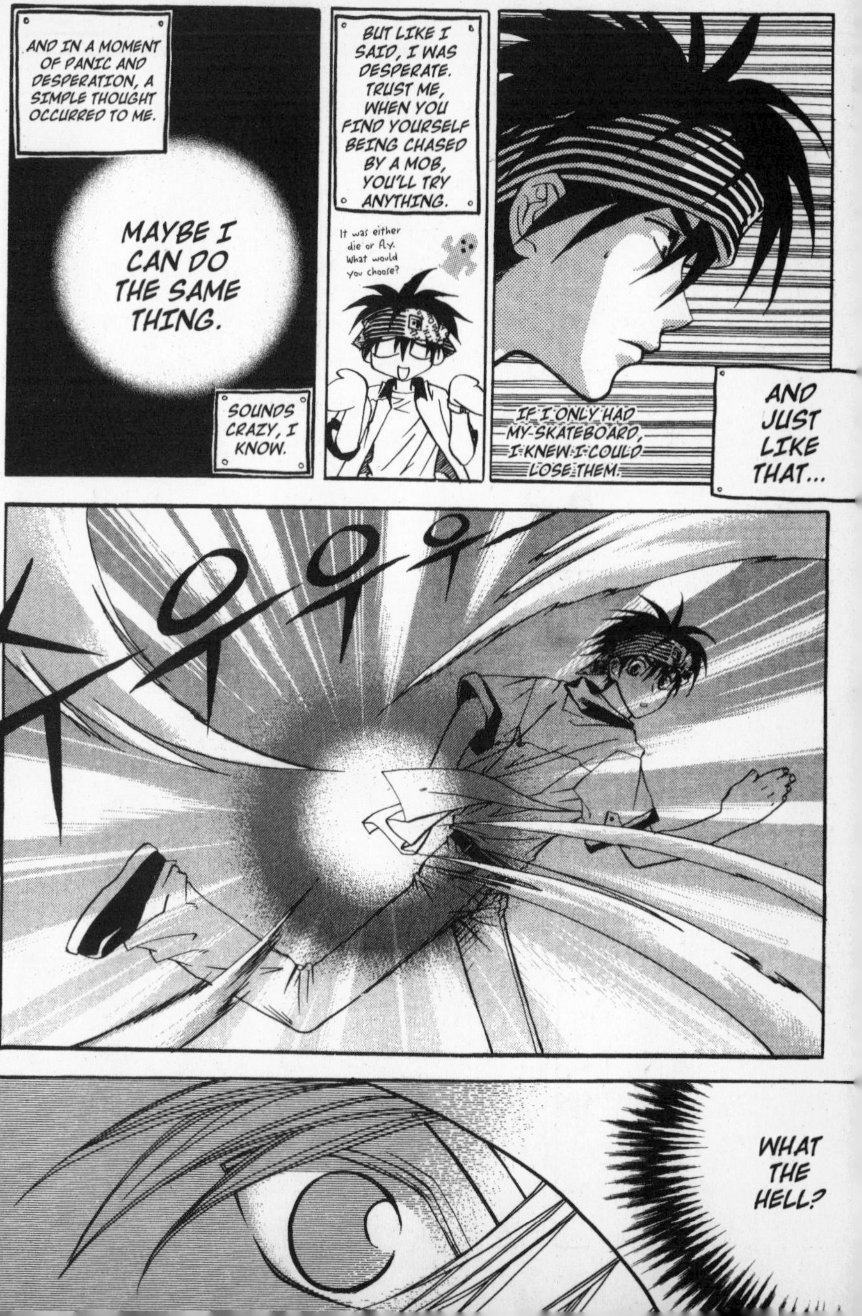
AND IN A MOMENT OF PANIC AND DESPERATION, A SIMPLE THOUGHT OCCURRED TO ME.
MAYBE I CAN DO THE SAME THING.
SOUNDS CRAZY, I KNOW.
BUT LIKE I SAID, I WAS DESPERATE. TRUST ME, WHEN YOU FIND YOURSELF BEING CHASED BY A MOB, YOU'LL TRY ANYTHING.
It was either die or fly. What would you choose?
IF I ONLY HAD MY SKATEBOARD, I KNEW I COULD LOSE THEM.
AND JUST LIKE THAT...
WHAT THE HELL?

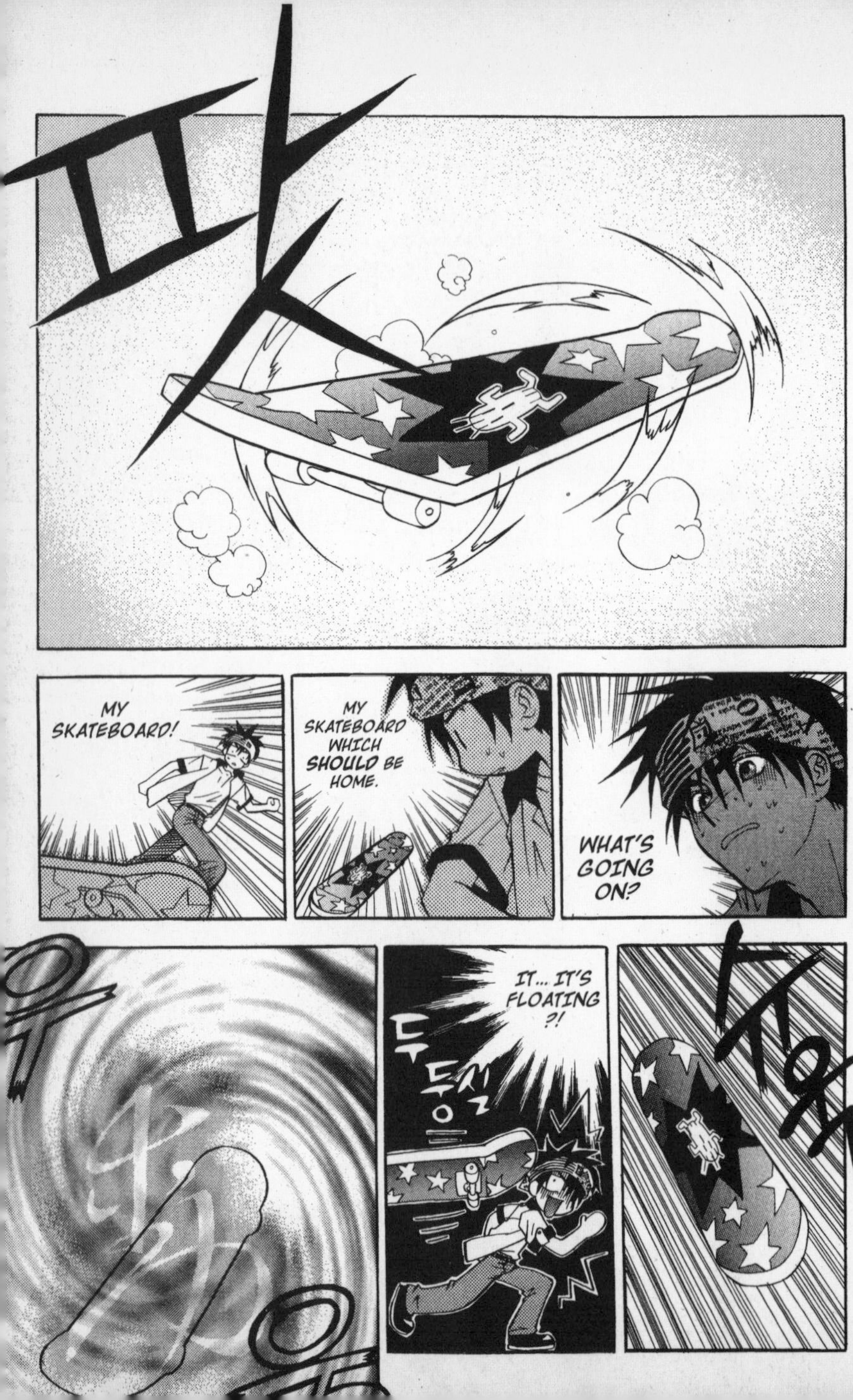
MY SKATEBOARD!
MY SKATEBOARD WHICH SHOULD BE HOME.
WHAT'S GOING ON?
IT... IT'S FLOATING ?!

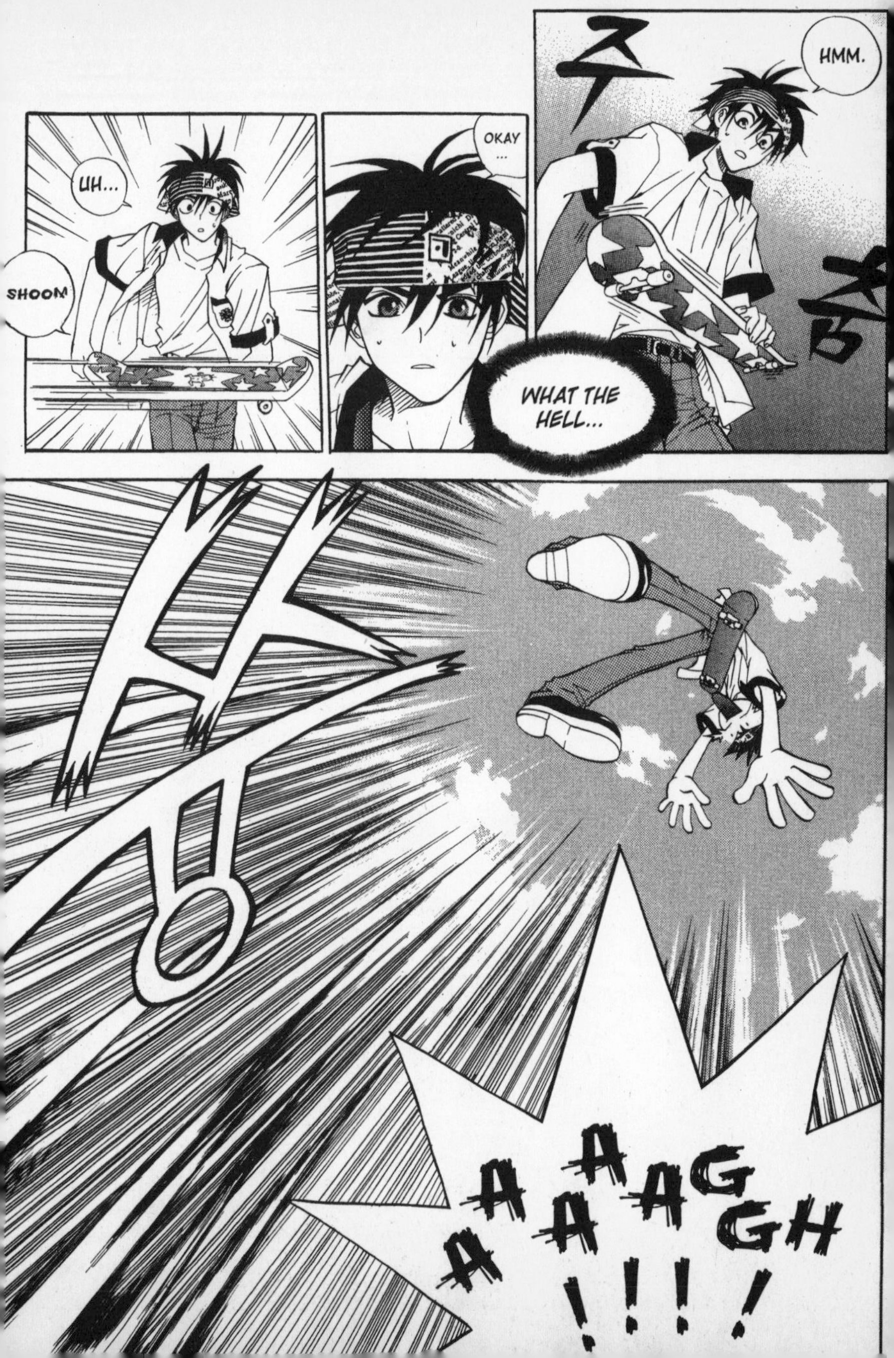
UH...
SHOOM
OKAY ...
WHAT THE HELL...
HMM.
AAAAAAGH!!!!

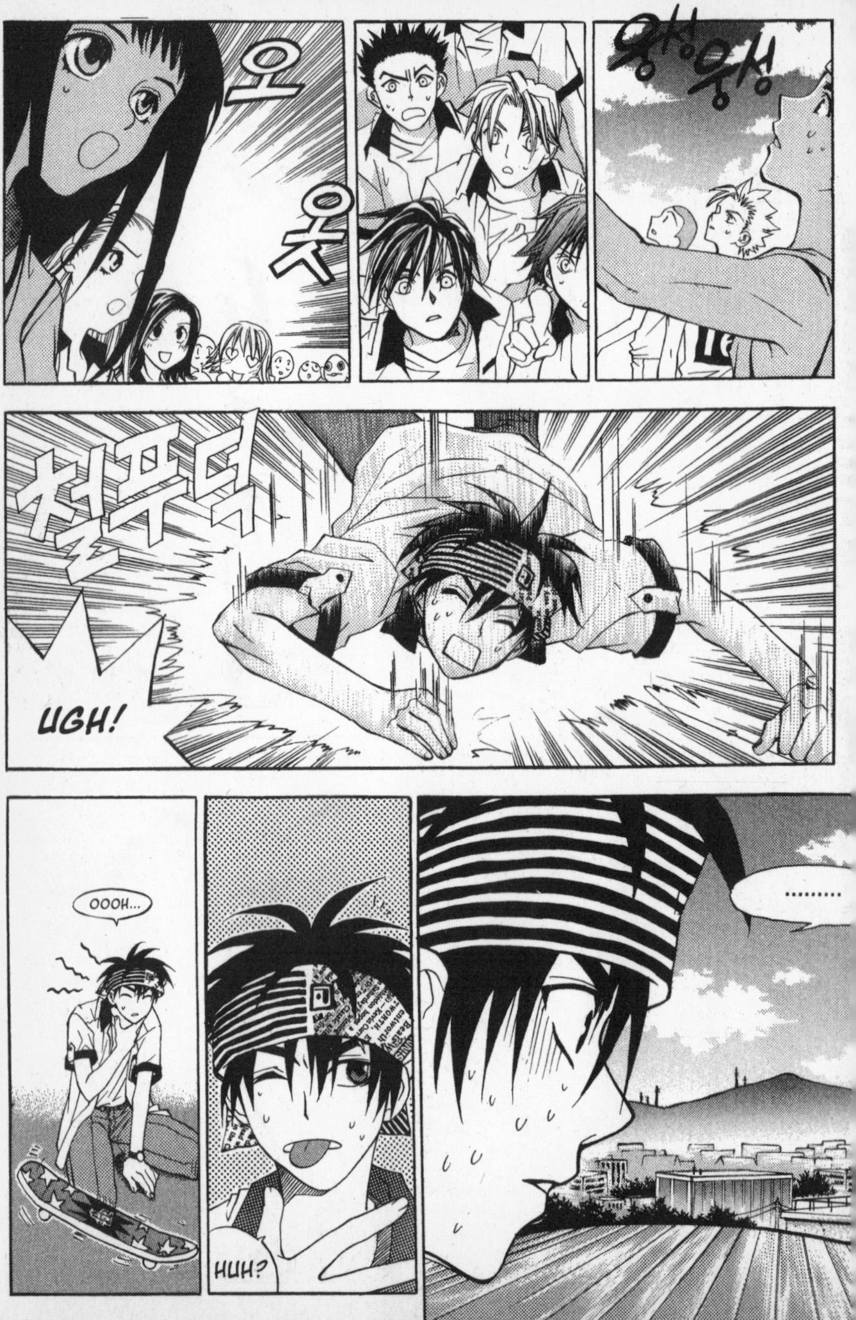
오
옷
웅성 웅성
철푸덕
UGH!
OOOH...
HUH?
....

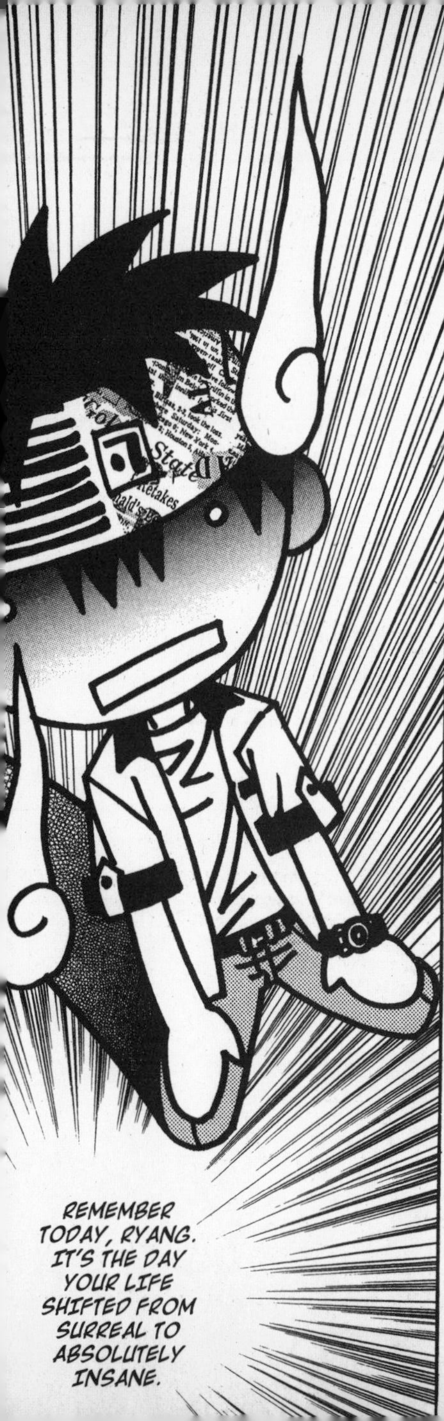
REMEMBER TODAY, RYANG. IT'S THE DAY YOUR LIFE SHIFTED FROM SURREAL TO ABSOLUTELY INSANE.

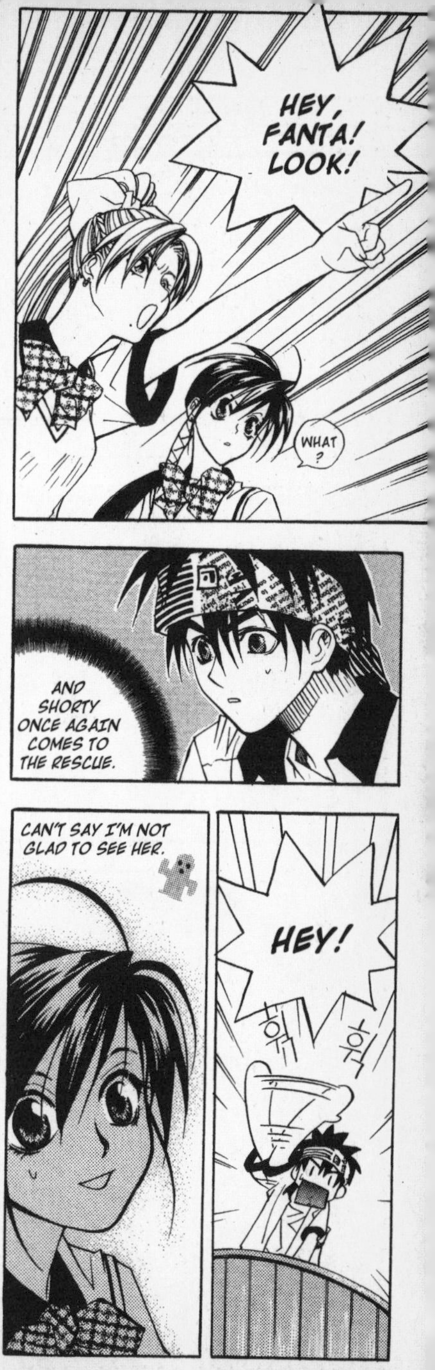
HEY, FANTA! LOOK!
WHAT?
AND SHORTY ONCE AGAIN COMES TO THE RESCUE.
CAN'T SAY I'M NOT GLAD TO SEE HER.
HEY!

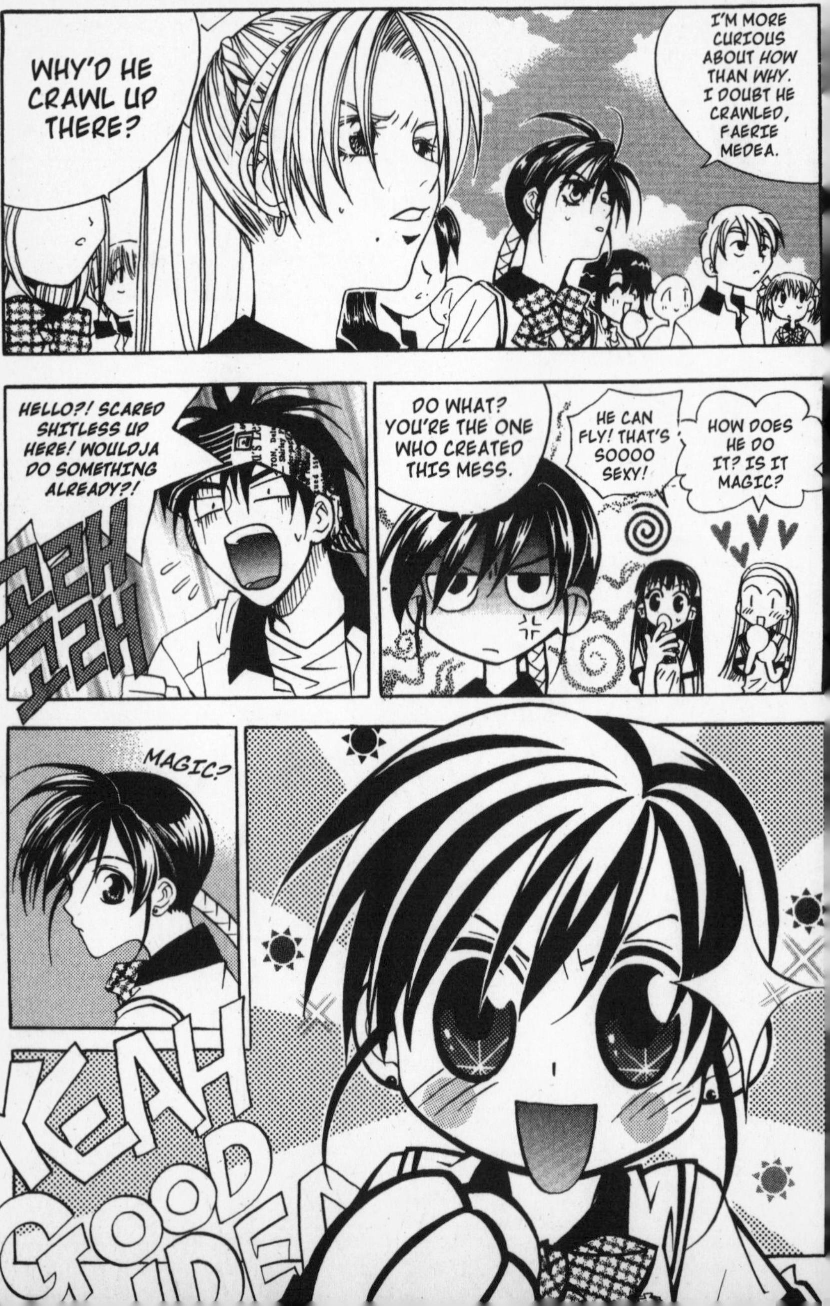
WHY'D HE CRAWL UP THERE?
I'M MORE CURIOUS ABOUT HOW THAN WHY. I DOUBT HE CRAWLED, FAERIE MEDEA.
HELLO?! SCARED SHITLESS UP HERE! WOULDJA DO SOMETHING ALREADY?!
DO WHAT? YOU'RE THE ONE WHO CREATED THIS MESS.
HE CAN FLY! THAT'S SOOOO SEXY!
HOW DOES HE DO IT? IS IT MAGIC?
MAGIC?
YEAH GOOD IDE

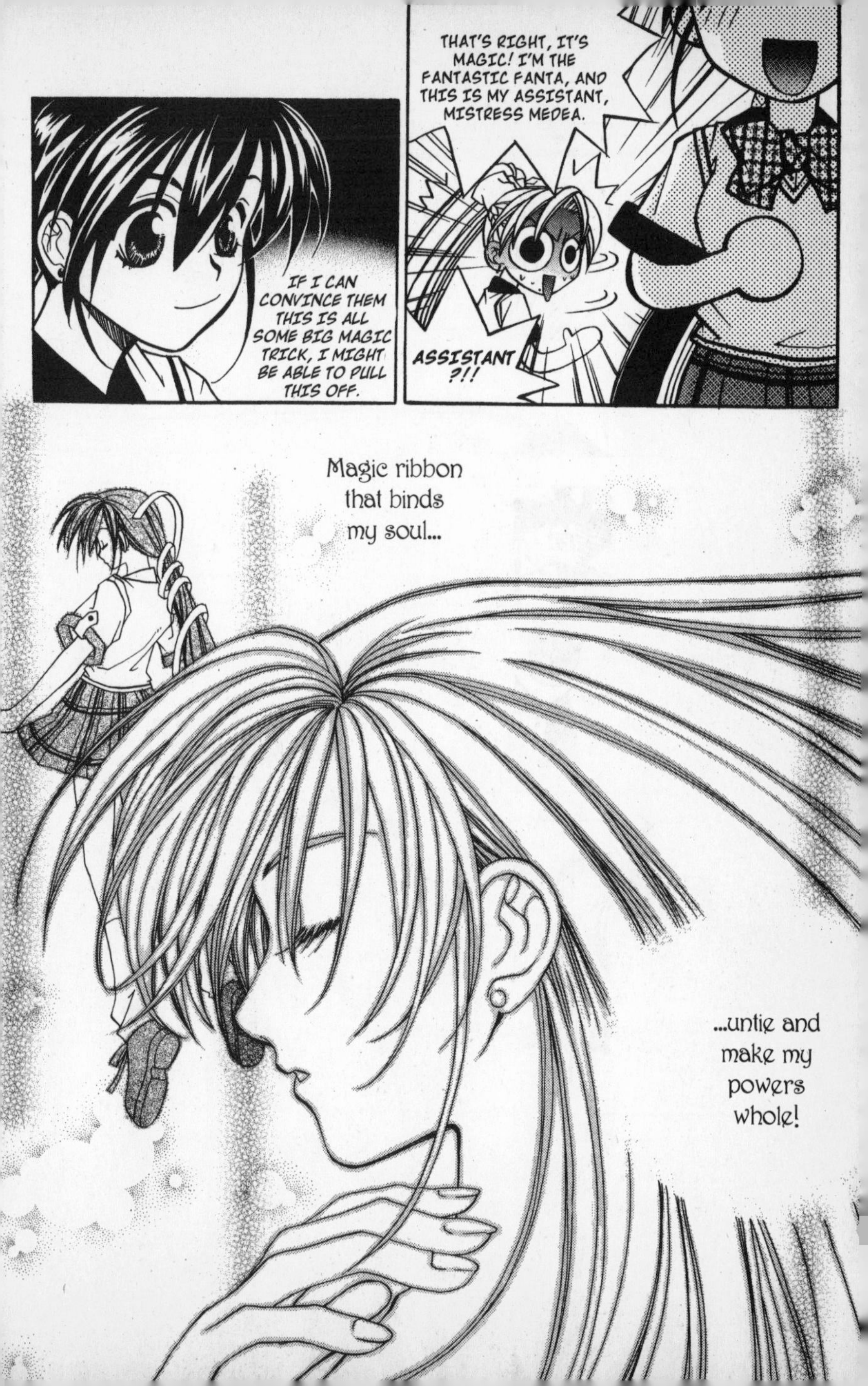
IF I CAN CONVINCE THEM THIS IS ALL SOME BIG MAGIC TRICK, I MIGHT BE ABLE TO PULL THIS OFF.
THAT'S RIGHT, IT'S MAGIC! I'M THE FANTASTIC FANTA, AND THIS IS MY ASSISTANT, MISTRESS MEDEA.
ASSISTANT ?!!
Magic ribbon that binds my soul...
...untie and make my powers whole!

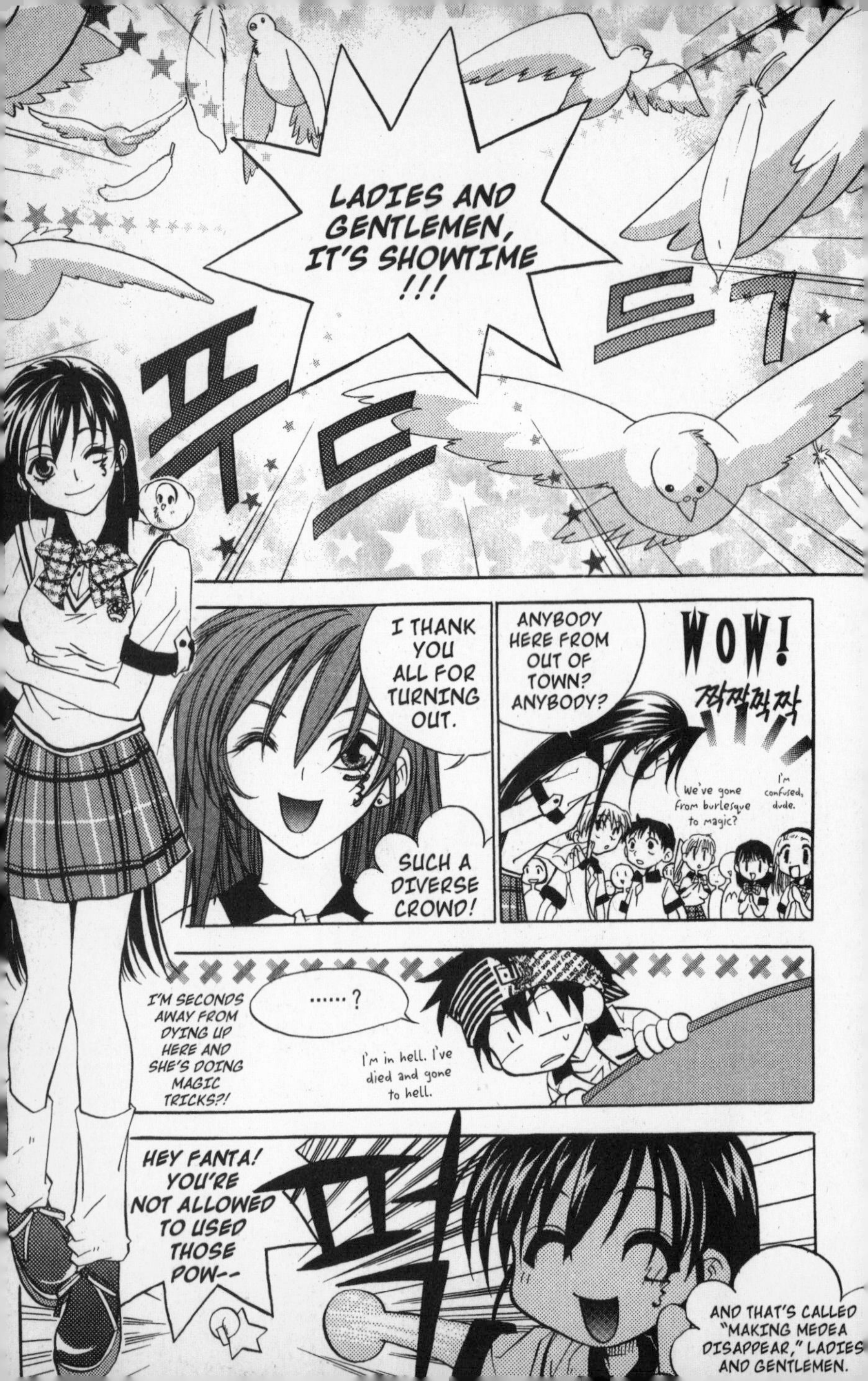
LADIES AND GENTLEMEN, IT'S SHOWTIME!!!
푸드득
I THANK YOU ALL FOR TURNING OUT.
SUCH A DIVERSE CROWD!
ANYBODY HERE FROM OUT OF TOWN? ANYBODY?
WOW!
짝짝짝짝
We've gone from burlesque to magic?
I'm confused, dude.
I'M SECONDS AWAY FROM DYING UP HERE AND SHE'S DOING MAGIC TRICKS?!
......?
I'm in hell. I've died and gone to hell.
HEY FANTA! YOU'RE NOT ALLOWED TO USED THOSE POW--
AND THAT'S CALLED "MAKING MEDEA DISAPPEAR," LADIES AND GENTLEMEN.

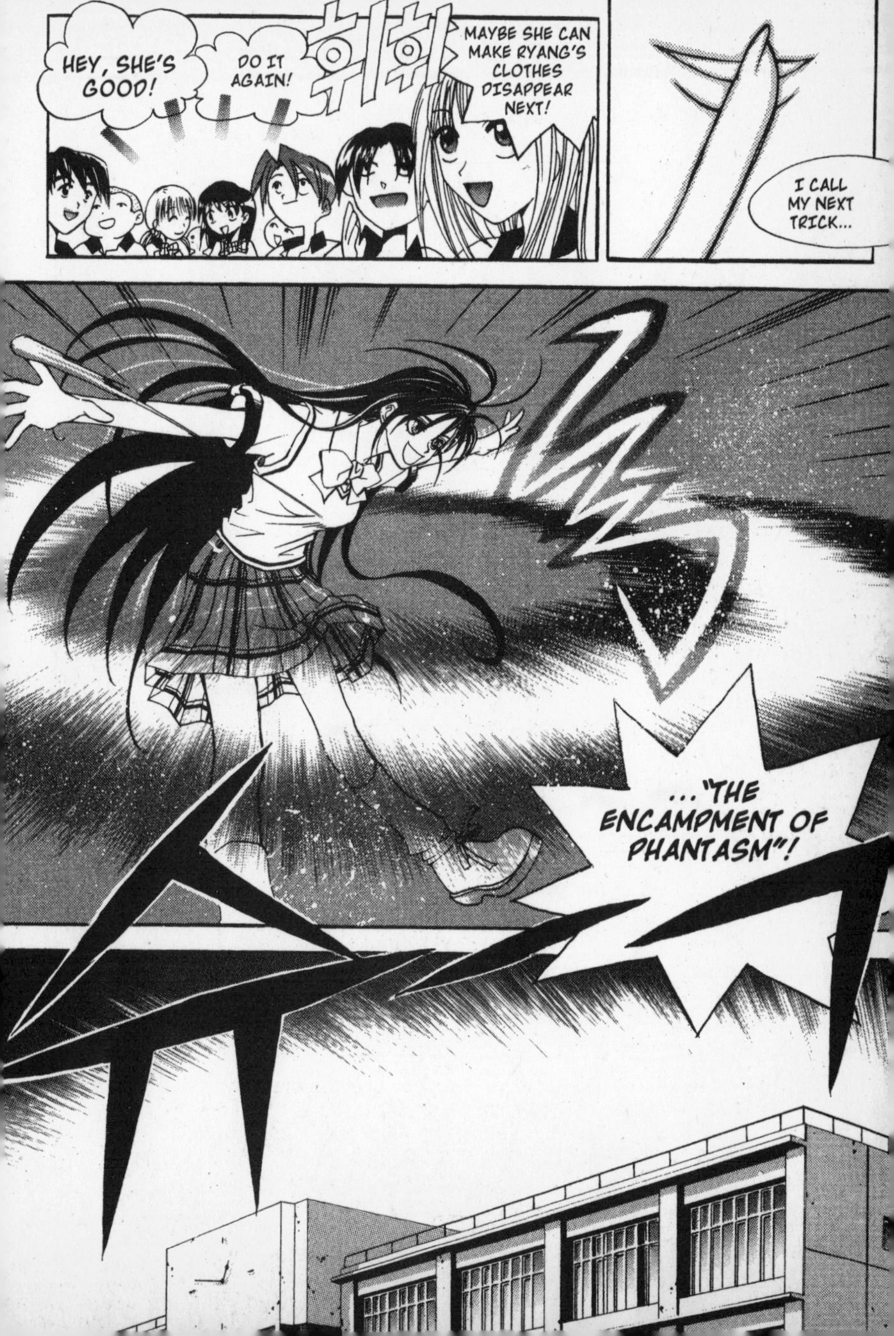
HEY, SHE'S GOOD!
DO IT AGAIN!
휘휘
MAYBE SHE CAN MAKE RYANG'S CLOTHES DISAPPEAR NEXT!
I CALL MY NEXT TRICK...
..."THE ENCAMPMENT OF PHANTASM"!

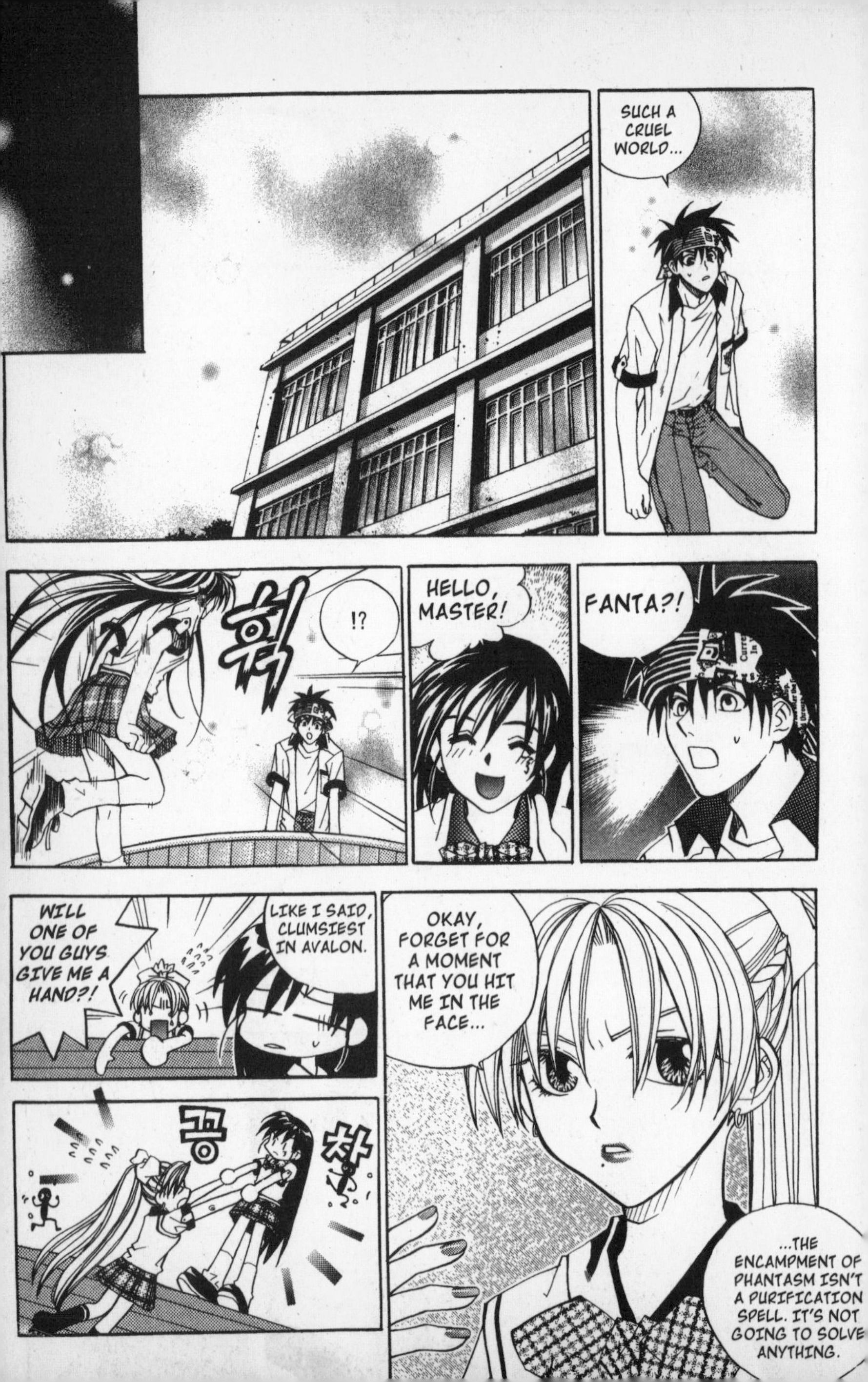
SUCH A CRUEL WORLD...
휙
!?
HELLO, MASTER!
FANTA?!
WILL ONE OF YOU GUYS GIVE ME A HAND?!
LIKE I SAID, CLUMSIEST IN AVALON.
꿍
착
OKAY, FORGET FOR A MOMENT THAT YOU HIT ME IN THE FACE...
...THE ENCAMPMENT OF PHANTASM ISN'T A PURIFICATION SPELL. IT'S NOT GOING TO SOLVE ANYTHING.

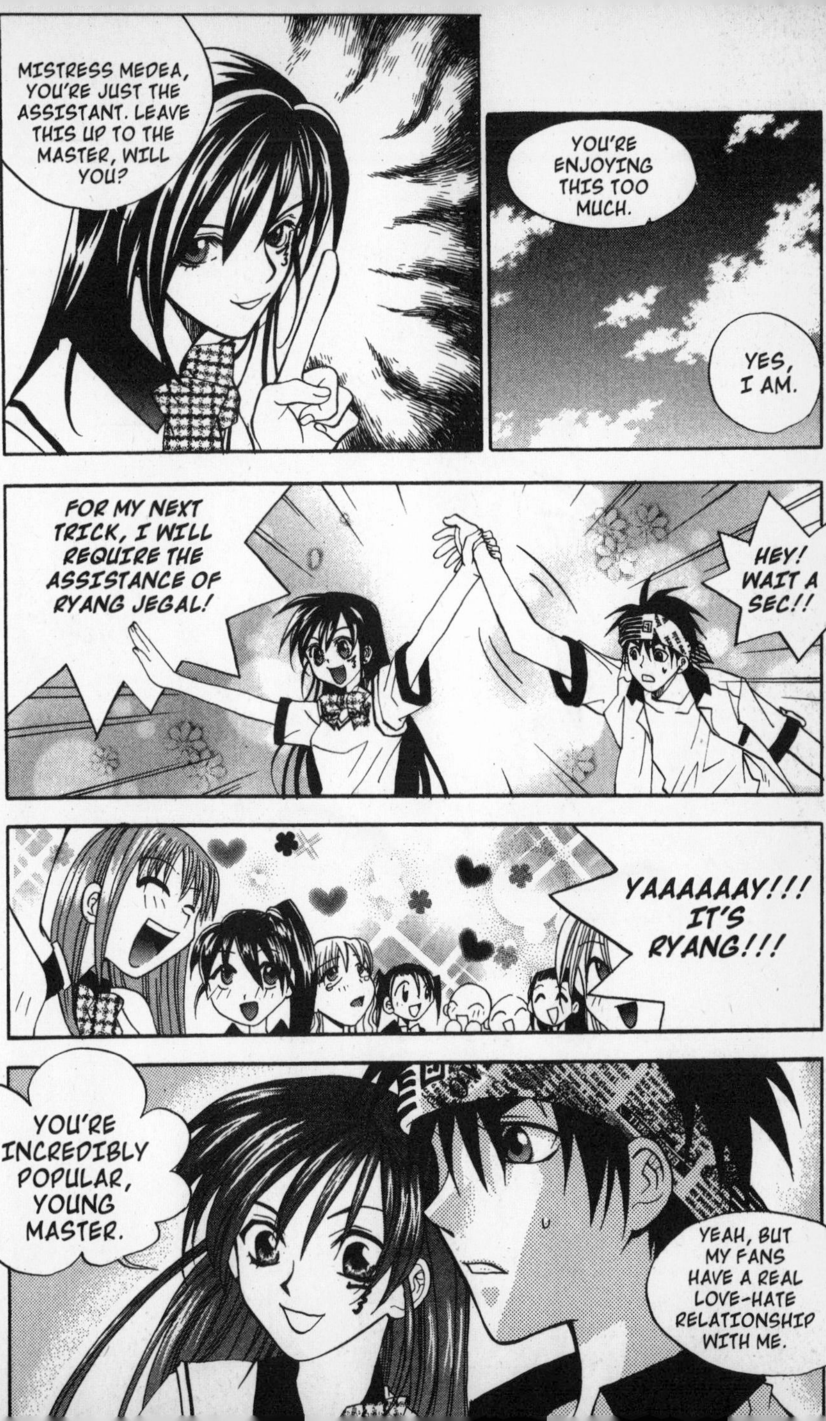
MISTRESS MEDEA, YOU'RE JUST THE ASSISTANT. LEAVE THIS UP TO THE MASTER, WILL YOU?
YOU'RE ENJOYING THIS TOO MUCH.
YES, I AM.
FOR MY NEXT TRICK, I WILL REQUIRE THE ASSISTANCE OF RYANG JEGAL!
HEY! WAIT A SEC!!
YAAAAAAY!!! IT'S RYANG!!!
YOU'RE INCREDIBLY POPULAR, YOUNG MASTER.
YEAH, BUT MY FANS HAVE A REAL LOVE-HATE RELATIONSHIP WITH ME.

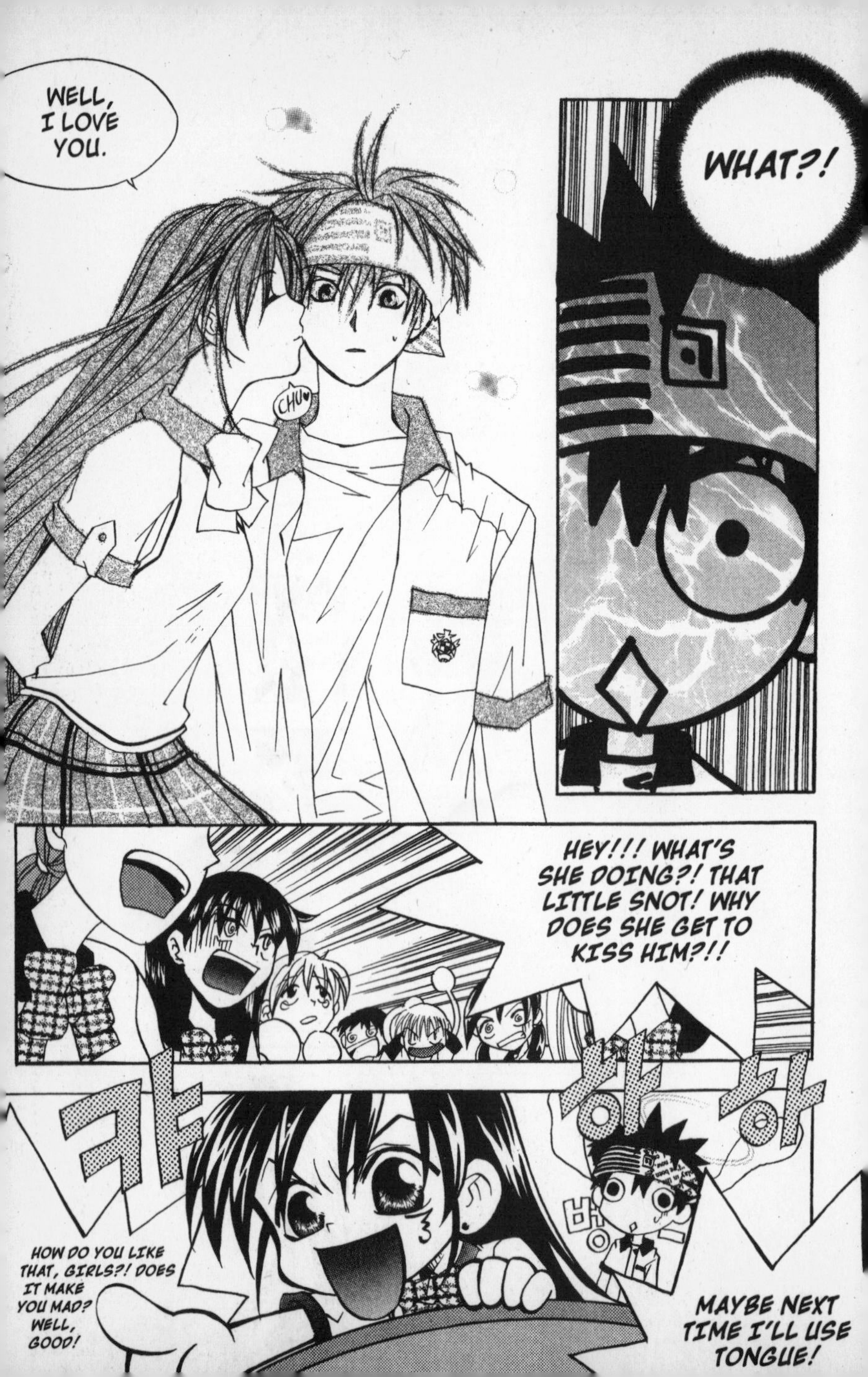
WELL, I LOVE YOU.
CHU♥
WHAT?!
HEY!!! WHAT'S SHE DOING?! THAT LITTLE SNOT! WHY DOES SHE GET TO KISS HIM?!!
HOW DO YOU LIKE THAT, GIRLS?! DOES IT MAKE YOU MAD? WELL, GOOD!
MAYBE NEXT TIME I'LL USE TONGUE!

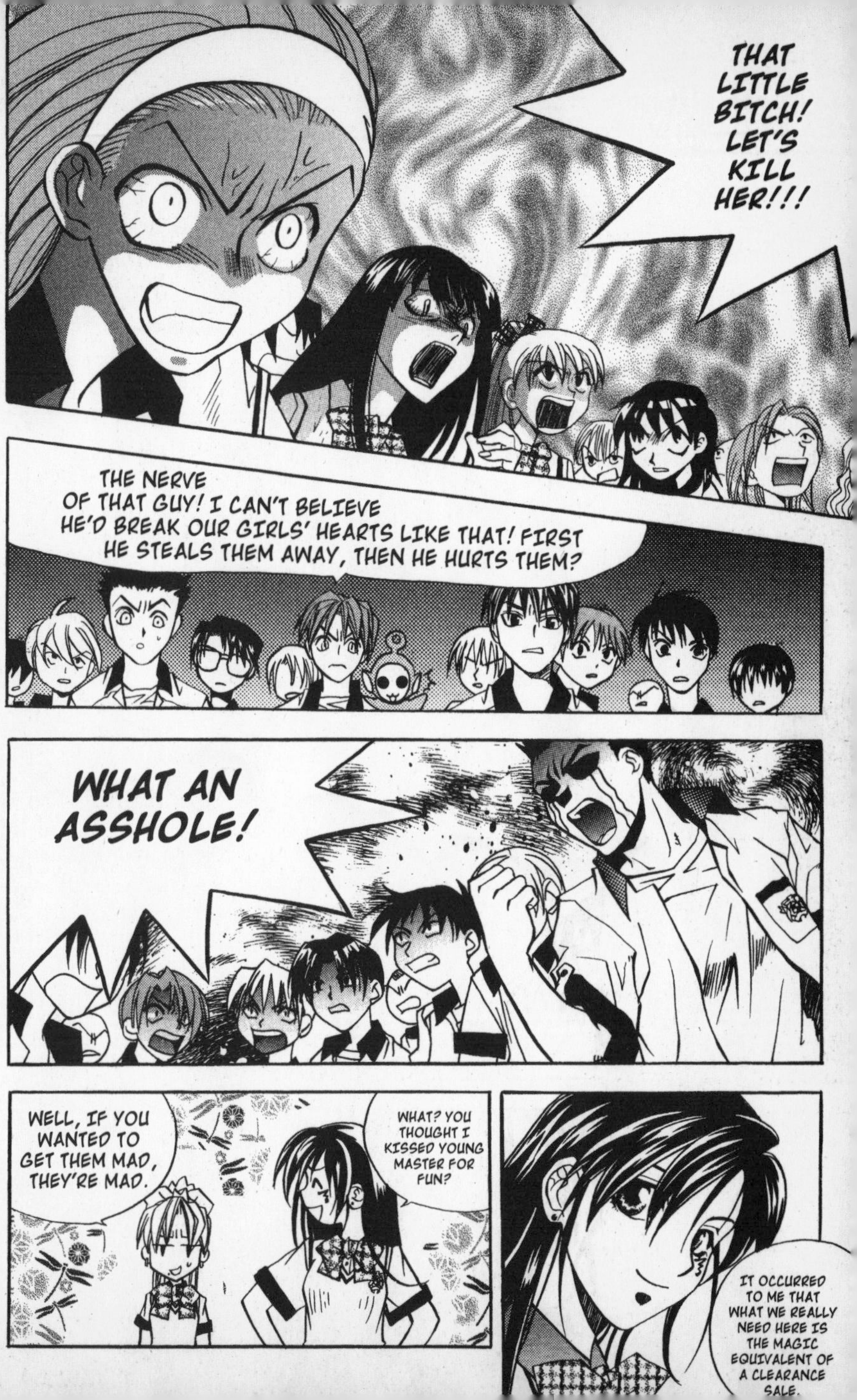
THAT LITTLE BITCH! LET'S KILL HER!!!
THE NERVE OF THAT GUY! I CAN'T BELIEVE HE'D BREAK OUR GIRLS' HEARTS LIKE THAT! FIRST HE STEALS THEM AWAY, THEN HE HURTS THEM?
WHAT AN ASSHOLE!
WELL, IF YOU WANTED TO GET THEM MAD, THEY'RE MAD.
WHAT? YOU THOUGHT I KISSED YOUNG MASTER FOR FUN?
IT OCCURRED TO ME THAT WHAT WE REALLY NEED HERE IS THE MAGIC EQUIVALENT OF A CLEARANCE SALE.

Clearance Corps, Infantry Div.
AND JUDGING BY THE FORM THE EVIL AFFINITIES HAVE TAKEN, I'D SAY THE GODS AGREE!
Karma shaped like toys that no one wants to buy, leave behind your wretched forms...

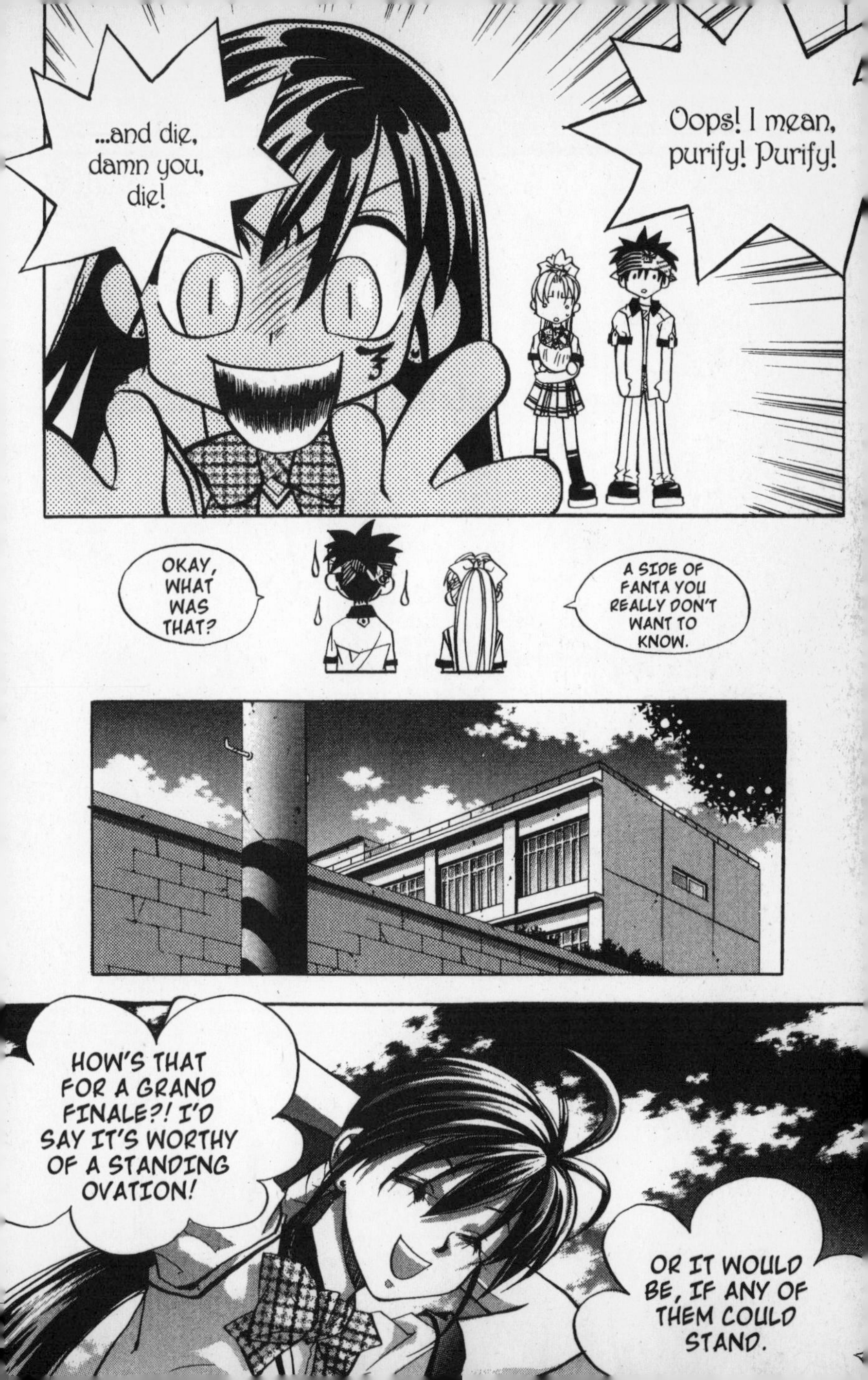
...and die, damn you, die!
Oops! I mean, purify! Purify!
OKAY, WHAT WAS THAT?
A SIDE OF FANTA YOU REALLY DON'T WANT TO KNOW.
HOW'S THAT FOR A GRAND FINALE?! I'D SAY IT'S WORTHY OF A STANDING OVATION!
OR IT WOULD BE, IF ANY OF THEM COULD STAND.

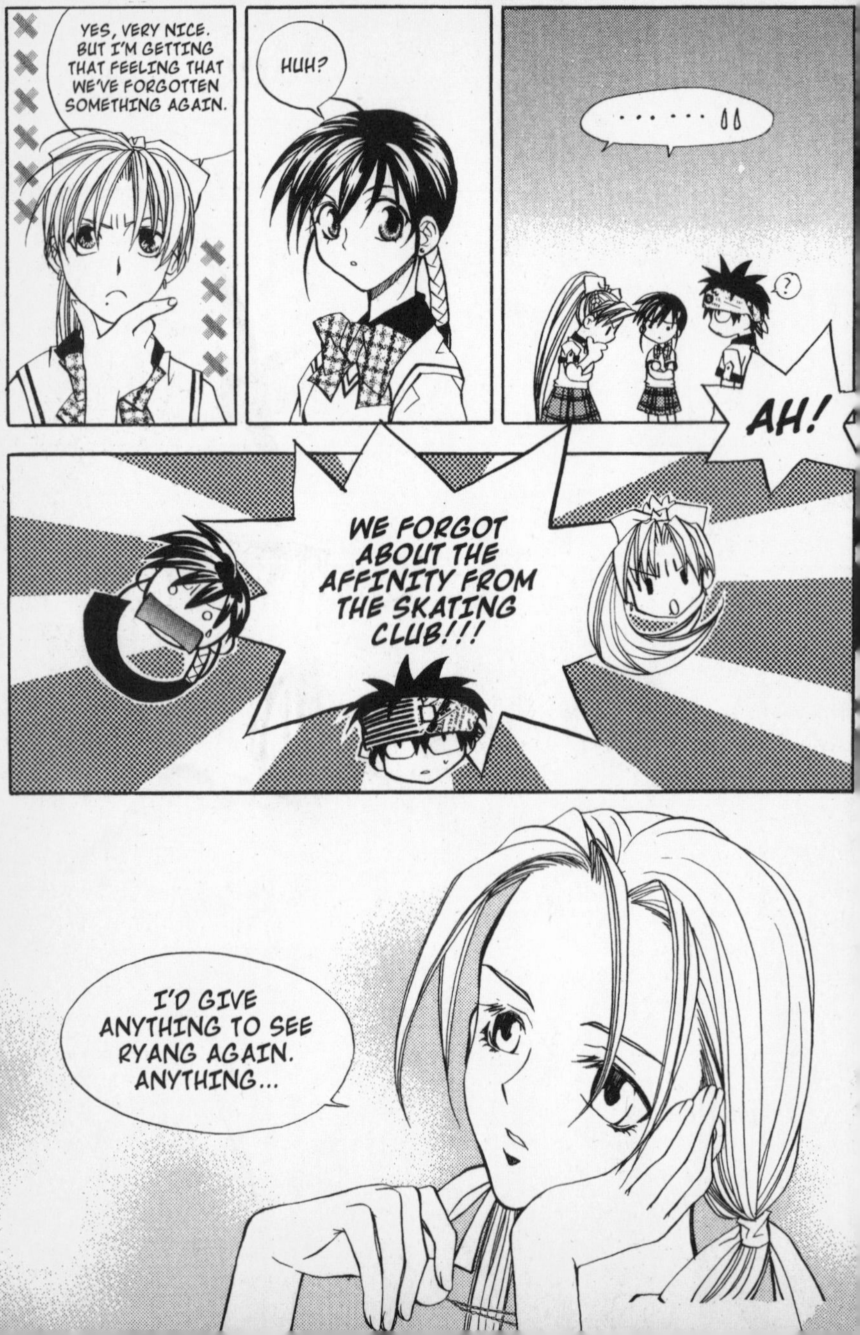
YES, VERY NICE. BUT I'M GETTING THAT FEELING THAT WE'VE FORGOTTEN SOMETHING AGAIN.
HUH?
......
?
AH!
WE FORGOT ABOUT THE AFFINITY FROM THE SKATING CLUB!!!
I'D GIVE ANYTHING TO SEE RYANG AGAIN. ANYTHING...

Faeries Crashing

A Love Story

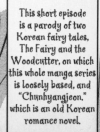

This short episode
is a parody of two
Korean fairy tales,
The Fairy and the
Woodcutter, on which
this whole manga series
is loosely based, and
"Chunhyangjeon,"
which is an old Korean
romance novel.

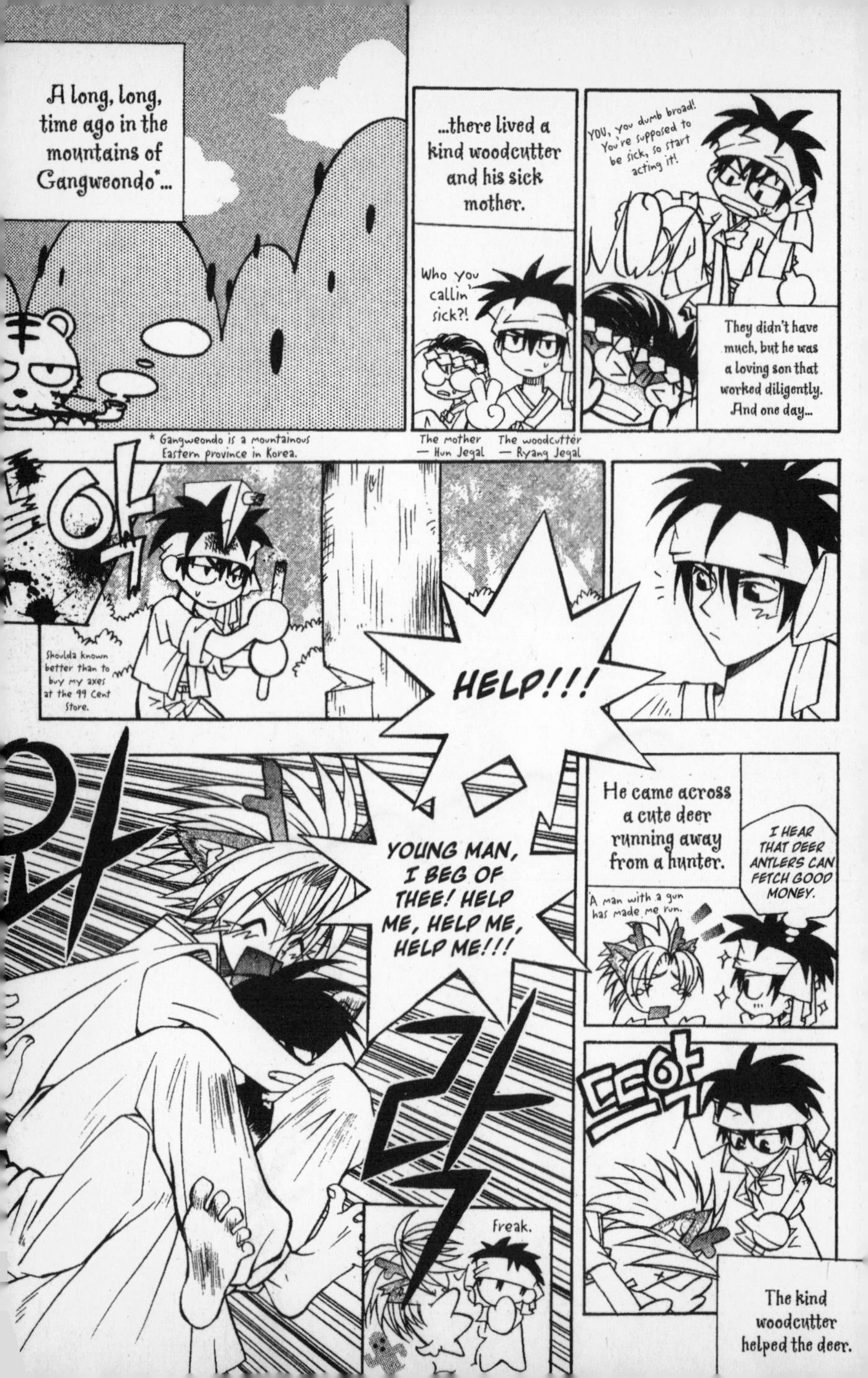
A long, long, time ago in the mountains of Gangweondo*...
...there lived a kind woodcutter and his sick mother.
Who you callin' sick?!
YOU, you dumb broad! You're supposed to be sick, so start acting it!
They didn't have much, but he was a loving son that worked diligently. And one day...
* Gangweondo is a mountainous Eastern province in Korea.
The mother — Hun Jegal
The woodcutter — Ryang Jegal
Shoulda known better than to buy my axes at the 99 Cent Store.
HELP!!!
YOUNG MAN, I BEG OF THEE! HELP ME, HELP ME, HELP ME!!!
He came across a cute deer running away from a hunter.
I HEAR THAT DEER ANTLERS CAN FETCH GOOD MONEY.
A man with a gun has made me run.
freak.
The kind woodcutter helped the deer.

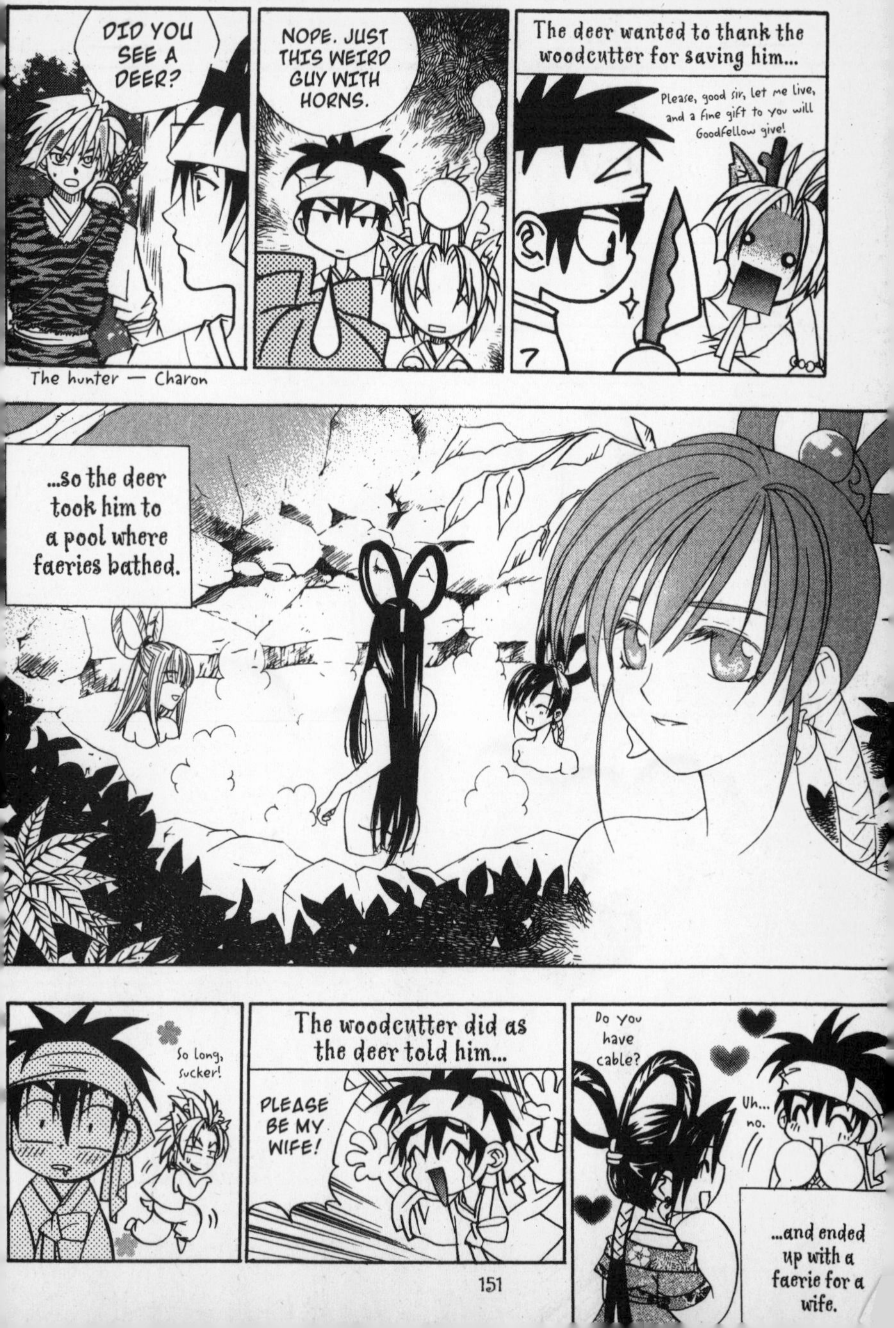

DID YOU SEE A DEER?
The hunter — Charon
NOPE. JUST THIS WEIRD GUY WITH HORNS.
The deer wanted to thank the woodcutter for saving him...
Please, good sir, let me live, and a fine gift to you will Goodfellow give!
7
...so the deer took him to a pool where faeries bathed.
So long, sucker!
The woodcutter did as the deer told him...
PLEASE BE MY WIFE!
Do you have cable?
Uh... no.
...and ended up with a faerie for a wife.

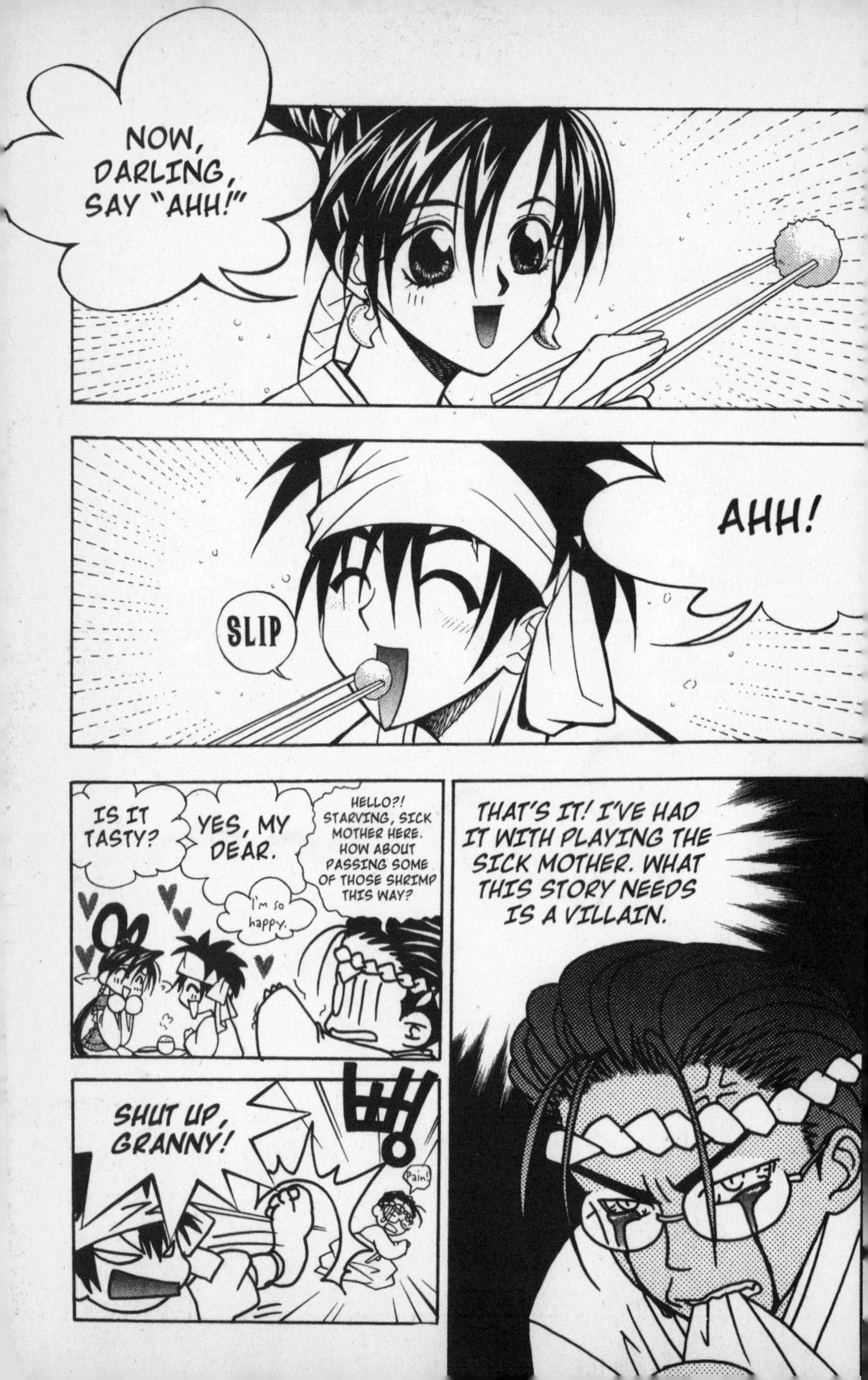
NOW, DARLING, SAY "AHH!"
SLIP
AHH!
IS IT TASTY?
YES, MY DEAR.
HELLO?! STARVING, SICK MOTHER HERE. HOW ABOUT PASSING SOME OF THOSE SHRIMP THIS WAY?
I'm so happy.
SHUT UP, GRANNY!
Pain!
THAT'S IT! I'VE HAD IT WITH PLAYING THE SICK MOTHER. WHAT THIS STORY NEEDS IS A VILLAIN.

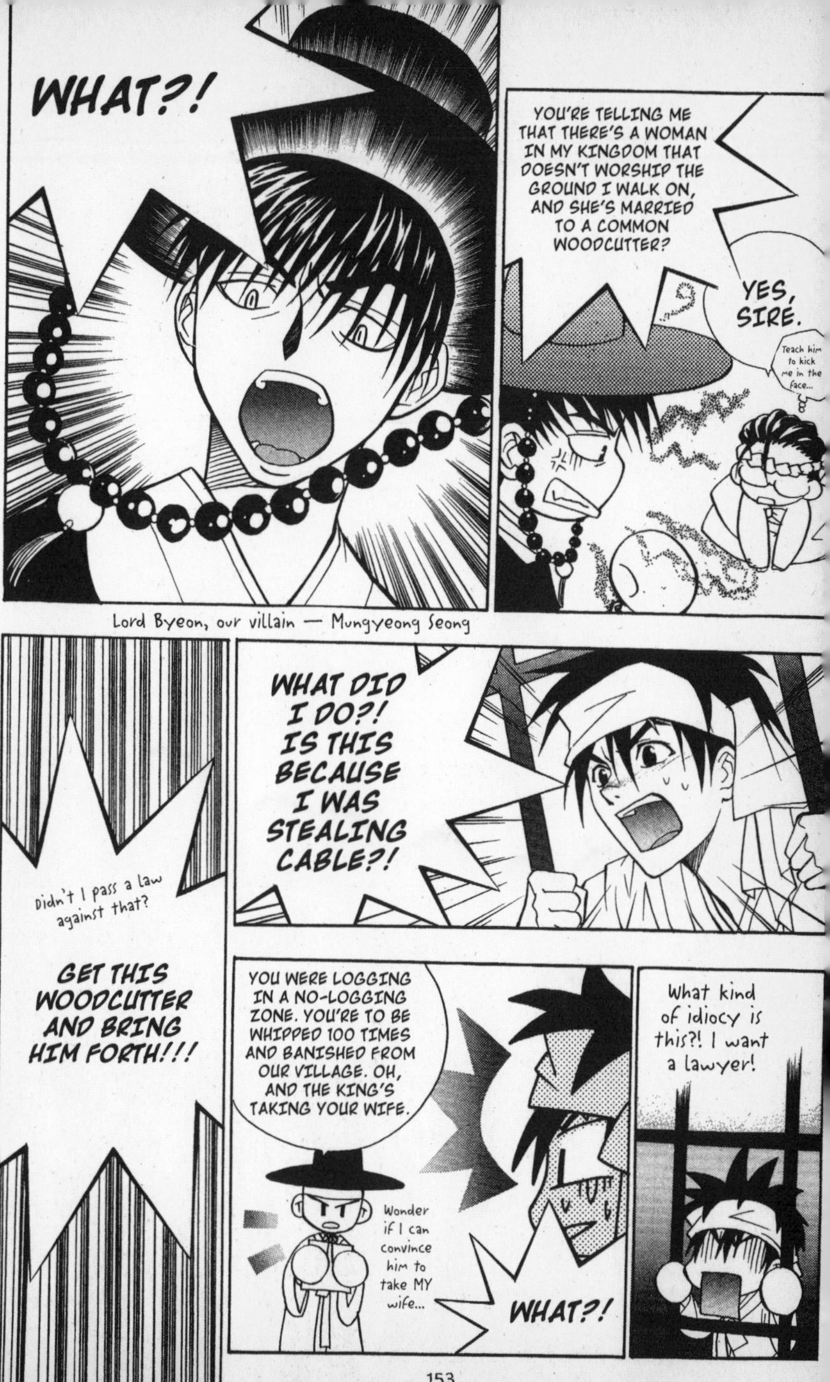
WHAT?!
YOU'RE TELLING ME THAT THERE'S A WOMAN IN MY KINGDOM THAT DOESN'T WORSHIP THE GROUND I WALK ON, AND SHE'S MARRIED TO A COMMON WOODCUTTER?
YES, SIRE.
Teach him to kick me in the face...
Lord Byeon, our villain — Mungyeong Seong
Didn't I pass a law against that?
GET THIS WOODCUTTER AND BRING HIM FORTH!!!
WHAT DID I DO?! IS THIS BECAUSE I WAS STEALING CABLE?!
YOU WERE LOGGING IN A NO-LOGGING ZONE. YOU'RE TO BE WHIPPED 100 TIMES AND BANISHED FROM OUR VILLAGE. OH, AND THE KING'S TAKING YOUR WIFE.
Wonder if I can convince him to take MY wife...
WHAT?!
What kind of idiocy is this?! I want a lawyer!

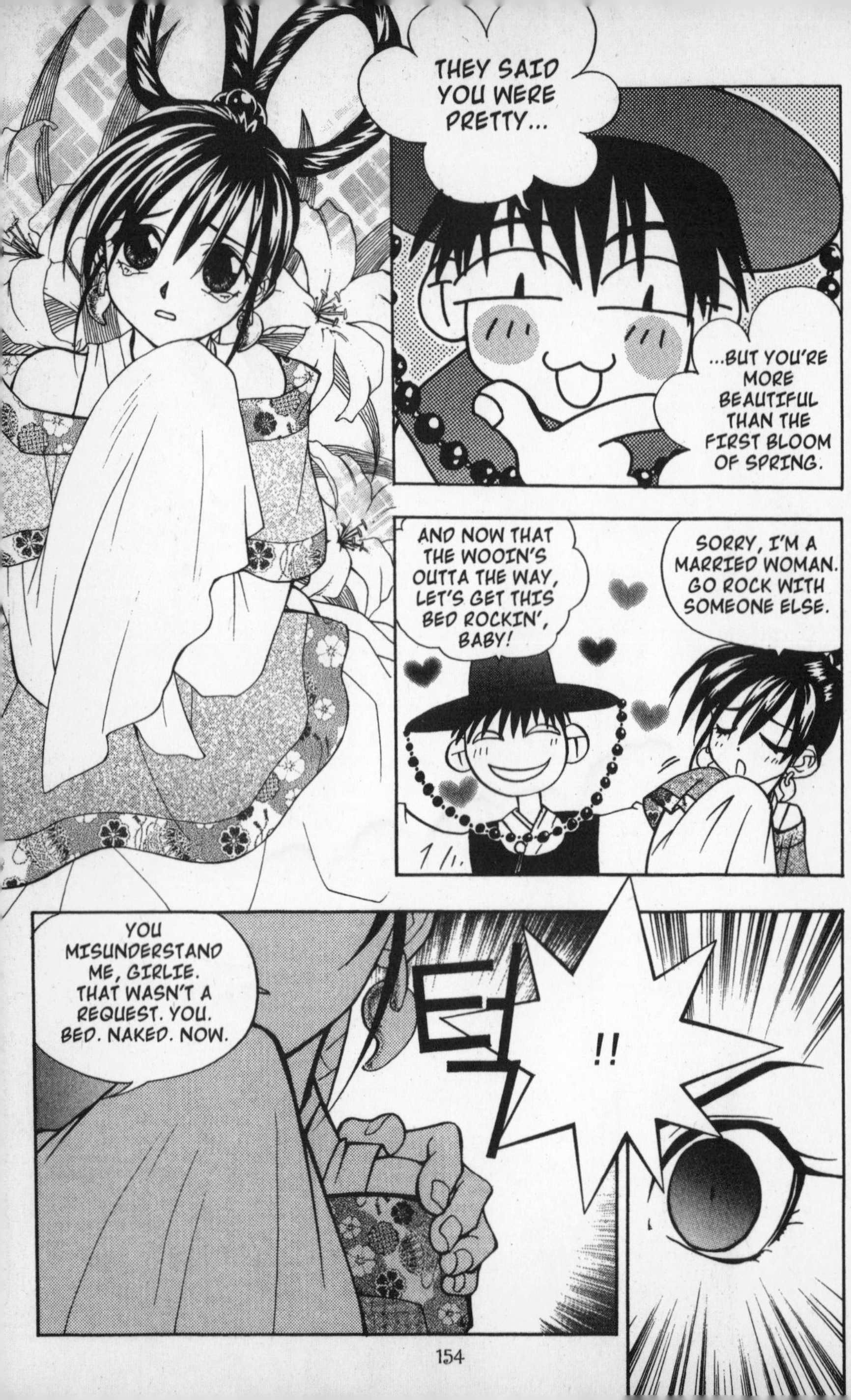
THEY SAID YOU WERE PRETTY...
...BUT YOU'RE MORE BEAUTIFUL THAN THE FIRST BLOOM OF SPRING.
AND NOW THAT THE WOOIN'S OUTTA THE WAY, LET'S GET THIS BED ROCKIN', BABY!
SORRY, I'M A MARRIED WOMAN. GO ROCK WITH SOMEONE ELSE.
YOU MISUNDERSTAND ME, GIRLIE. THAT WASN'T A REQUEST. YOU. BED. NAKED. NOW.
!!

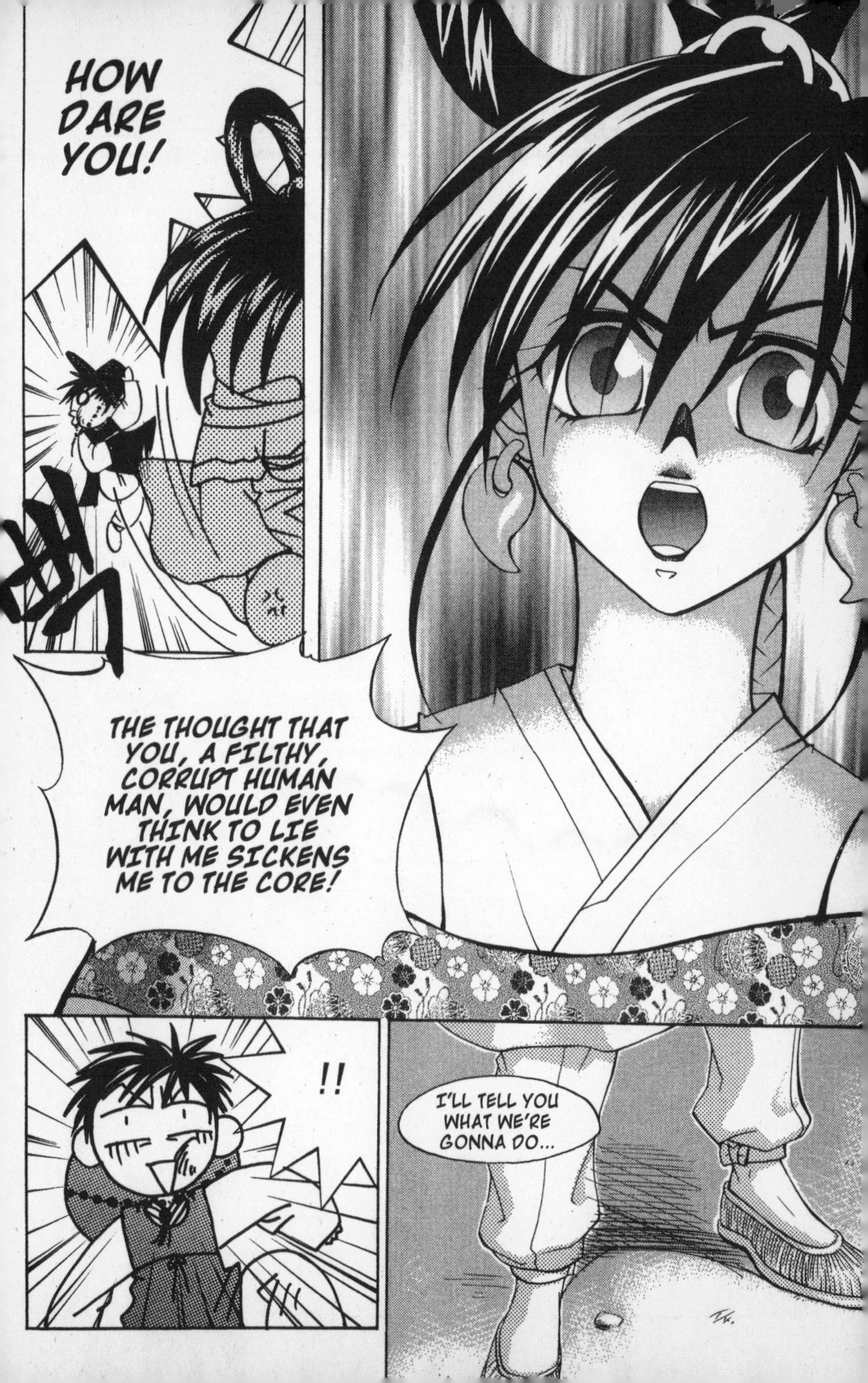
HOW DARE YOU!
THE THOUGHT THAT YOU, A FILTHY, CORRUPT HUMAN MAN, WOULD EVEN THINK TO LIE WITH ME SICKENS ME TO THE CORE!
!!
I'LL TELL YOU WHAT WE'RE GONNA DO...

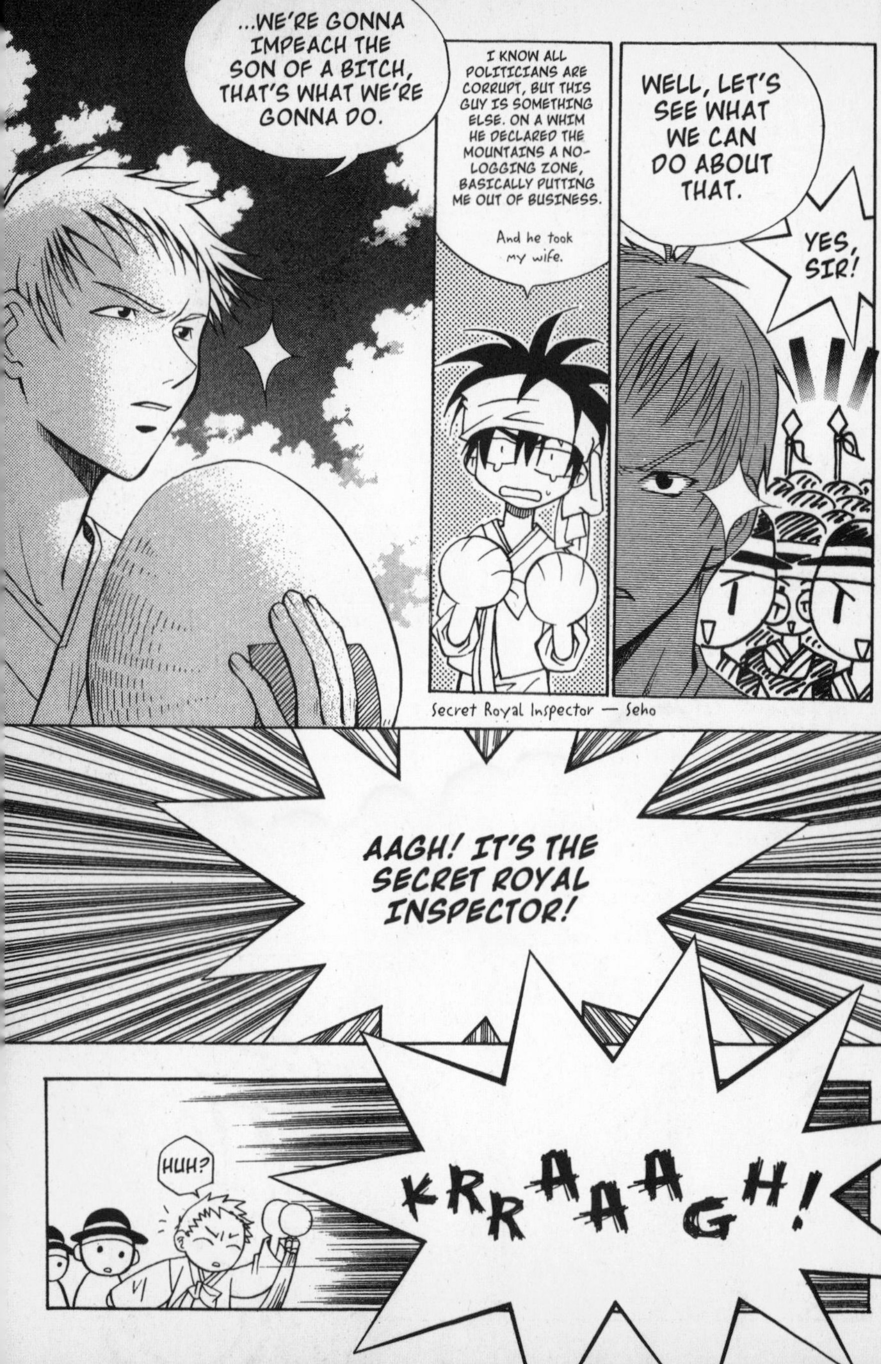
...WE'RE GONNA IMPEACH THE SON OF A BITCH, THAT'S WHAT WE'RE GONNA DO.
I KNOW ALL POLITICIANS ARE CORRUPT, BUT THIS GUY IS SOMETHING ELSE. ON A WHIM HE DECLARED THE MOUNTAINS A NO-LOGGING ZONE, BASICALLY PUTTING ME OUT OF BUSINESS.
And he took my wife.
Secret Royal Inspector — Seho
WELL, LET'S SEE WHAT WE CAN DO ABOUT THAT.
YES, SIR!
AAGH! IT'S THE SECRET ROYAL INSPECTOR!
HUH?
KRRAAAGH!

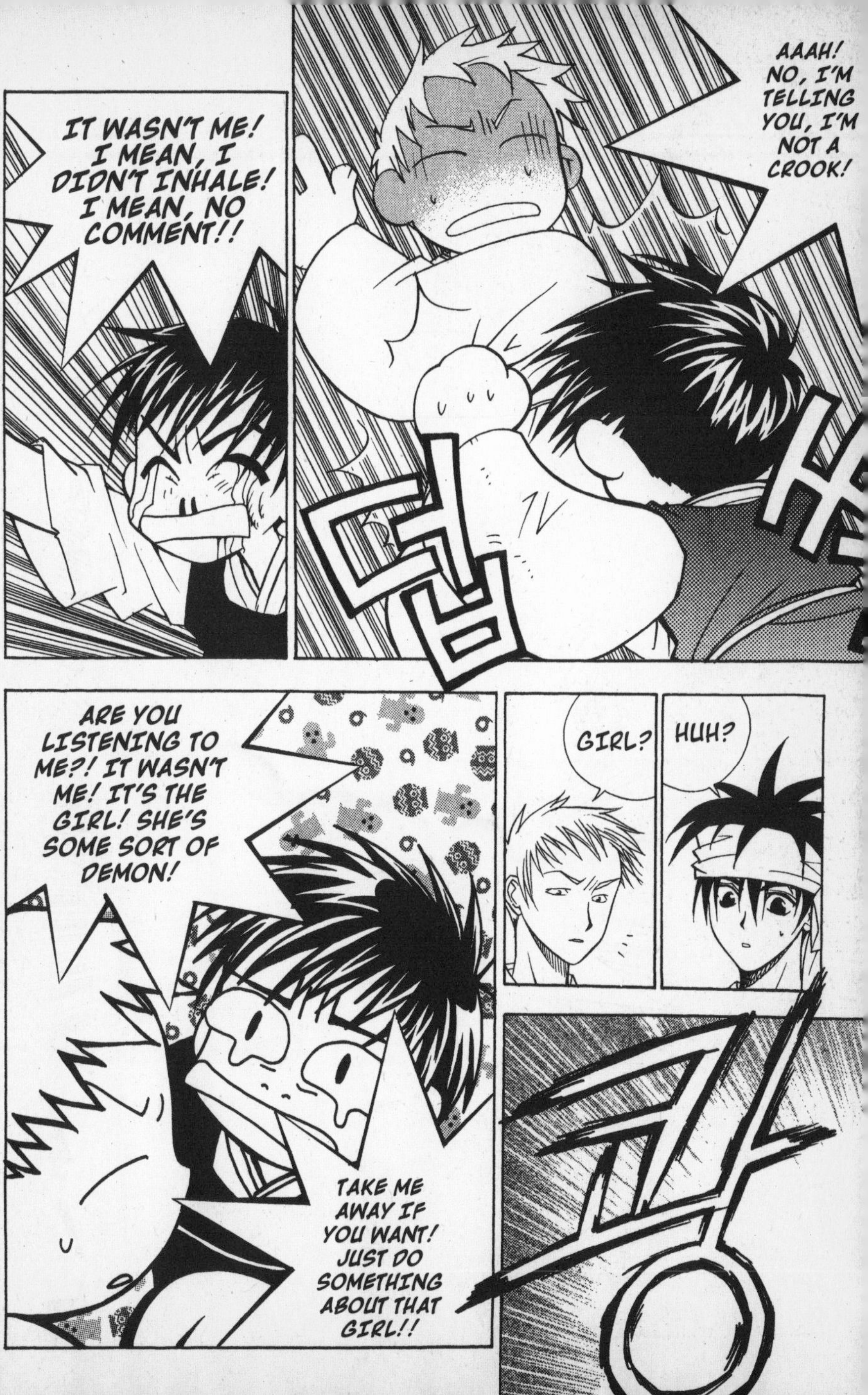
IT WASN'T ME! I MEAN, I DIDN'T INHALE! I MEAN, NO COMMENT!!
AAAH! NO, I'M TELLING YOU, I'M NOT A CROOK!
ARE YOU LISTENING TO ME?! IT WASN'T ME! IT'S THE GIRL! SHE'S SOME SORT OF DEMON!
TAKE ME AWAY IF YOU WANT! JUST DO SOMETHING ABOUT THAT GIRL!!
GIRL?
HUH?

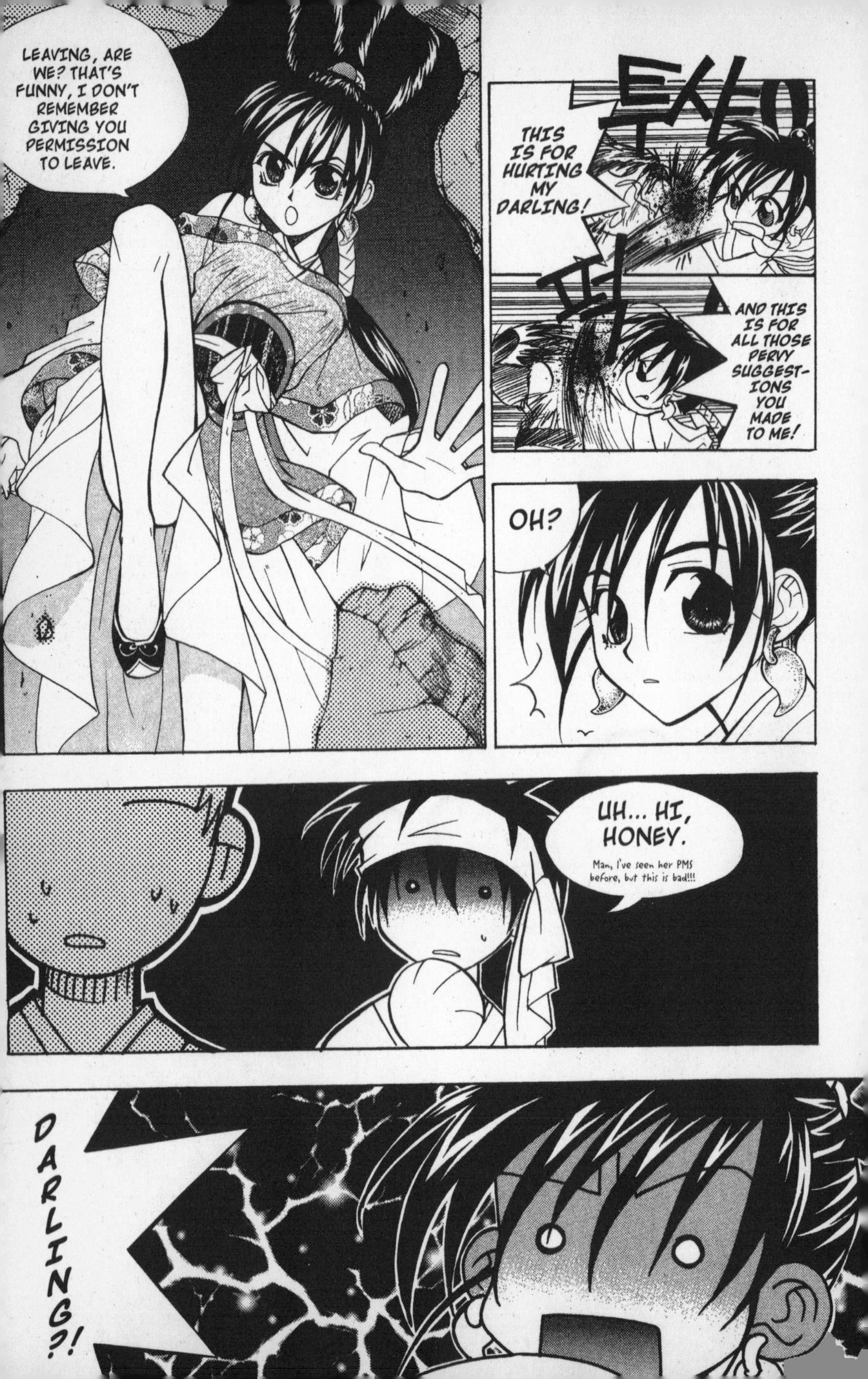
LEAVING, ARE WE? THAT'S FUNNY, I DON'T REMEMBER GIVING YOU PERMISSION TO LEAVE.
THIS IS FOR HURTING MY DARLING!
AND THIS IS FOR ALL THOSE PERVY SUGGEST-IONS YOU MADE TO ME!
OH?
UH... HI, HONEY.
Man, I've seen her PMS before, but this is bad!!!
DARLING?!

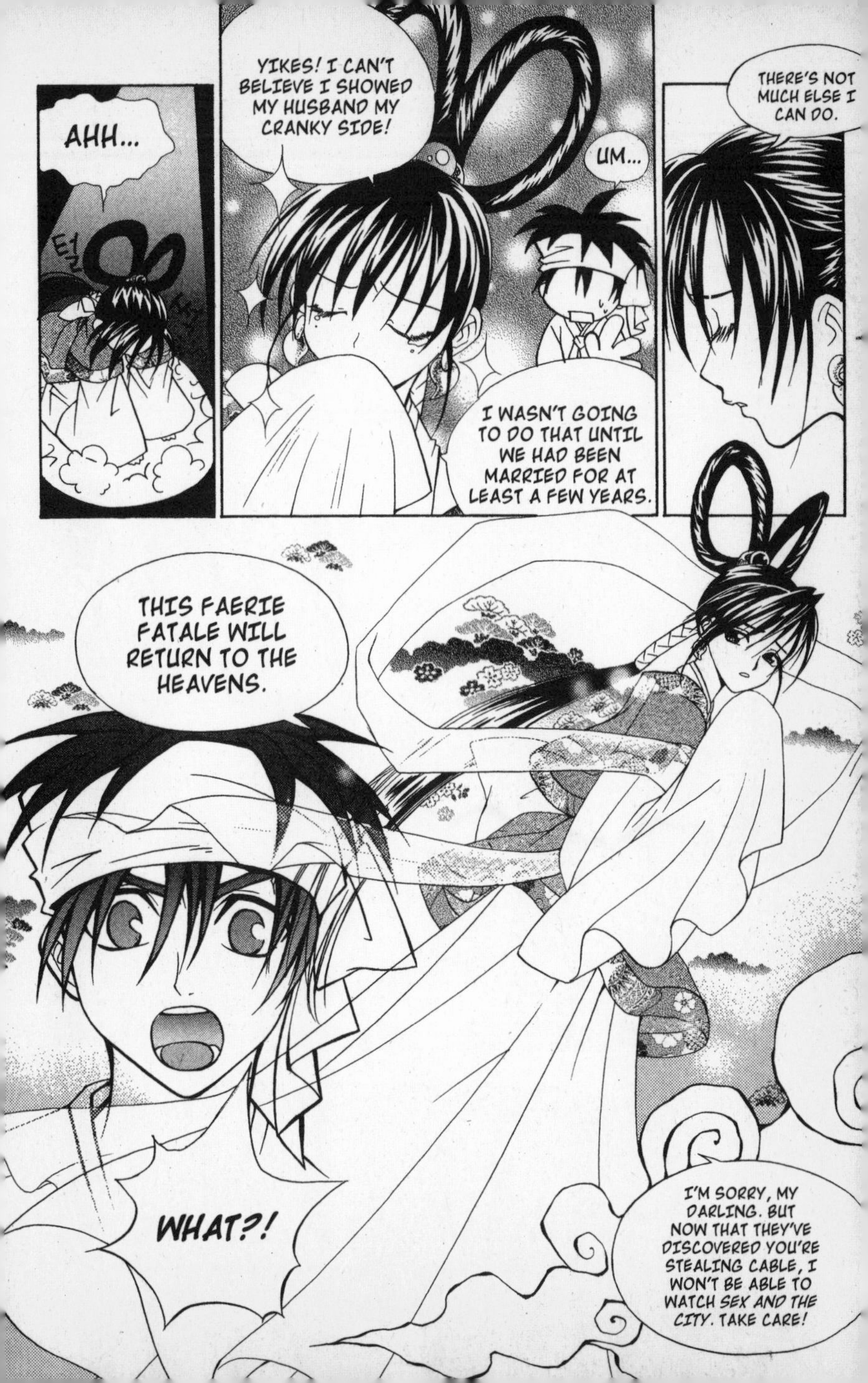
AHH...
털
YIKES! I CAN'T BELIEVE I SHOWED MY HUSBAND MY CRANKY SIDE!
UM...
I WASN'T GOING TO DO THAT UNTIL WE HAD BEEN MARRIED FOR AT LEAST A FEW YEARS.
THERE'S NOT MUCH ELSE I CAN DO.
THIS FAERIE FATALE WILL RETURN TO THE HEAVENS.
WHAT?!
I'M SORRY, MY DARLING. BUT NOW THAT THEY'VE DISCOVERED YOU'RE STEALING CABLE, I WON'T BE ABLE TO WATCH SEX AND THE CITY. TAKE CARE!

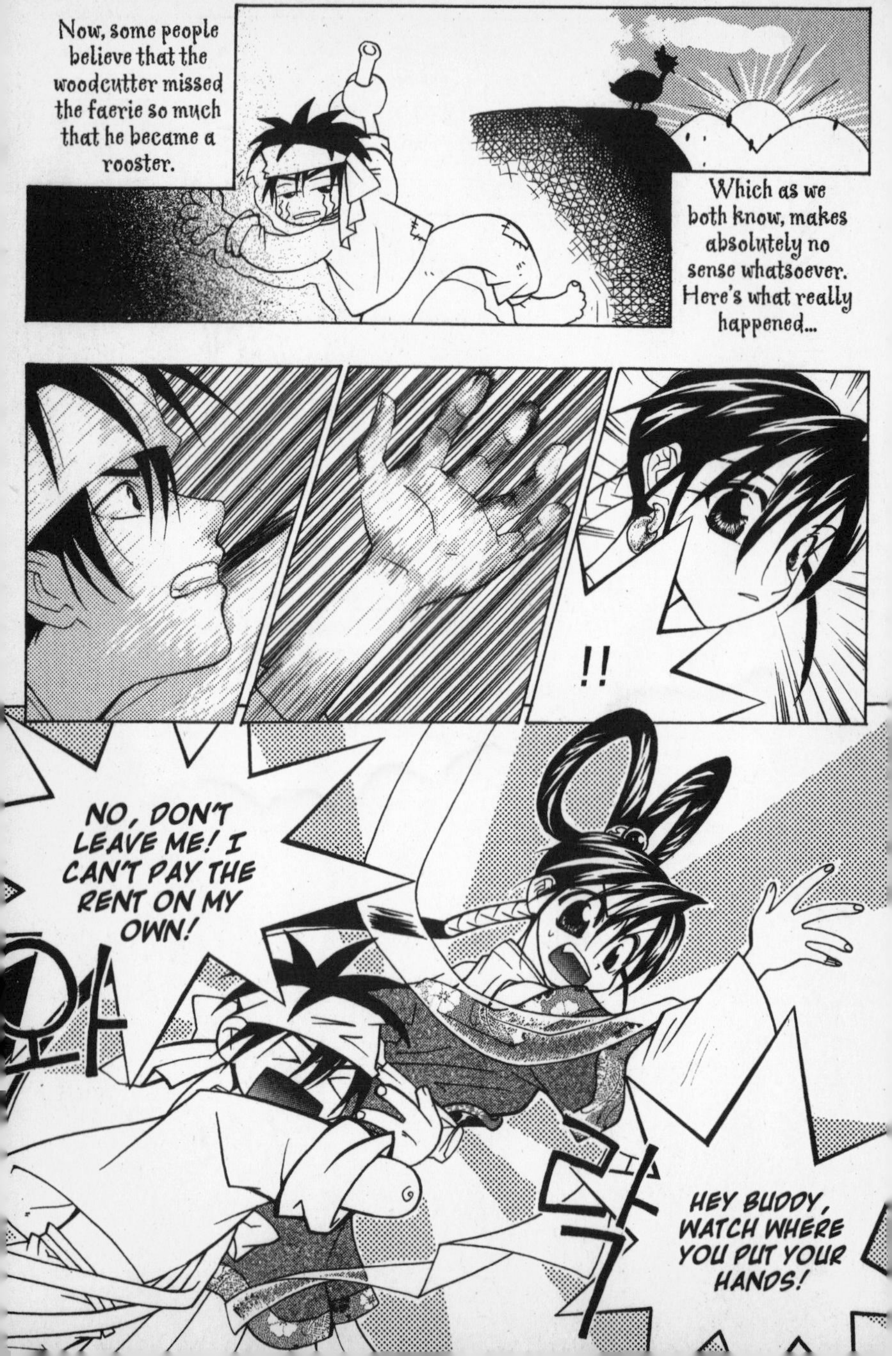
Now, some people believe that the woodcutter missed the faerie so much that he became a rooster.
Which as we both know, makes absolutely no sense whatsoever. Here's what really happened...
!!
NO, DON'T LEAVE ME! I CAN'T PAY THE RENT ON MY OWN!
HEY BUDDY, WATCH WHERE YOU PUT YOUR HANDS!

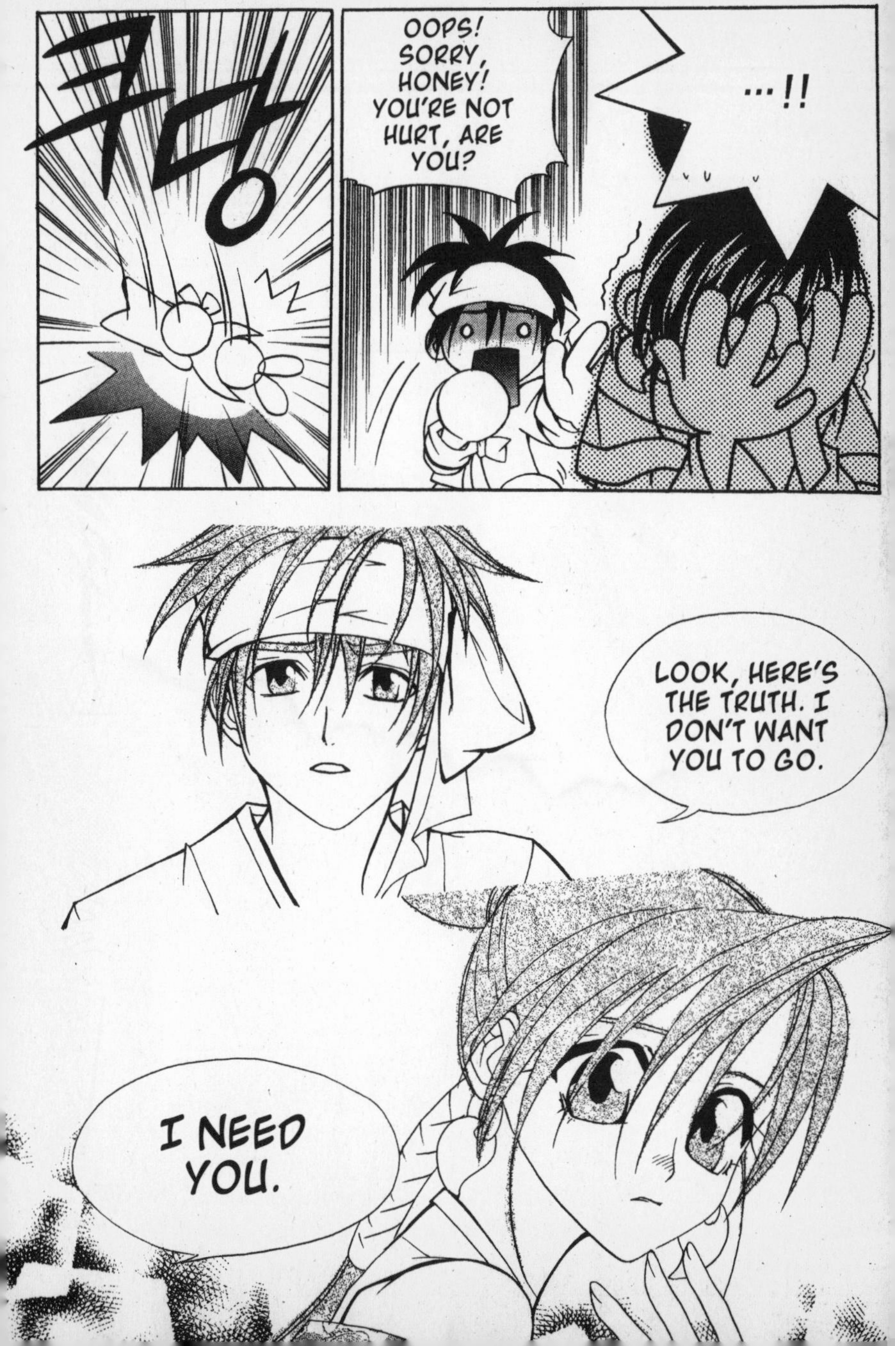
OOPS! SORRY, HONEY! YOU'RE NOT HURT, ARE YOU?
...!!
LOOK, HERE'S THE TRUTH. I DON'T WANT YOU TO GO.
I NEED YOU.

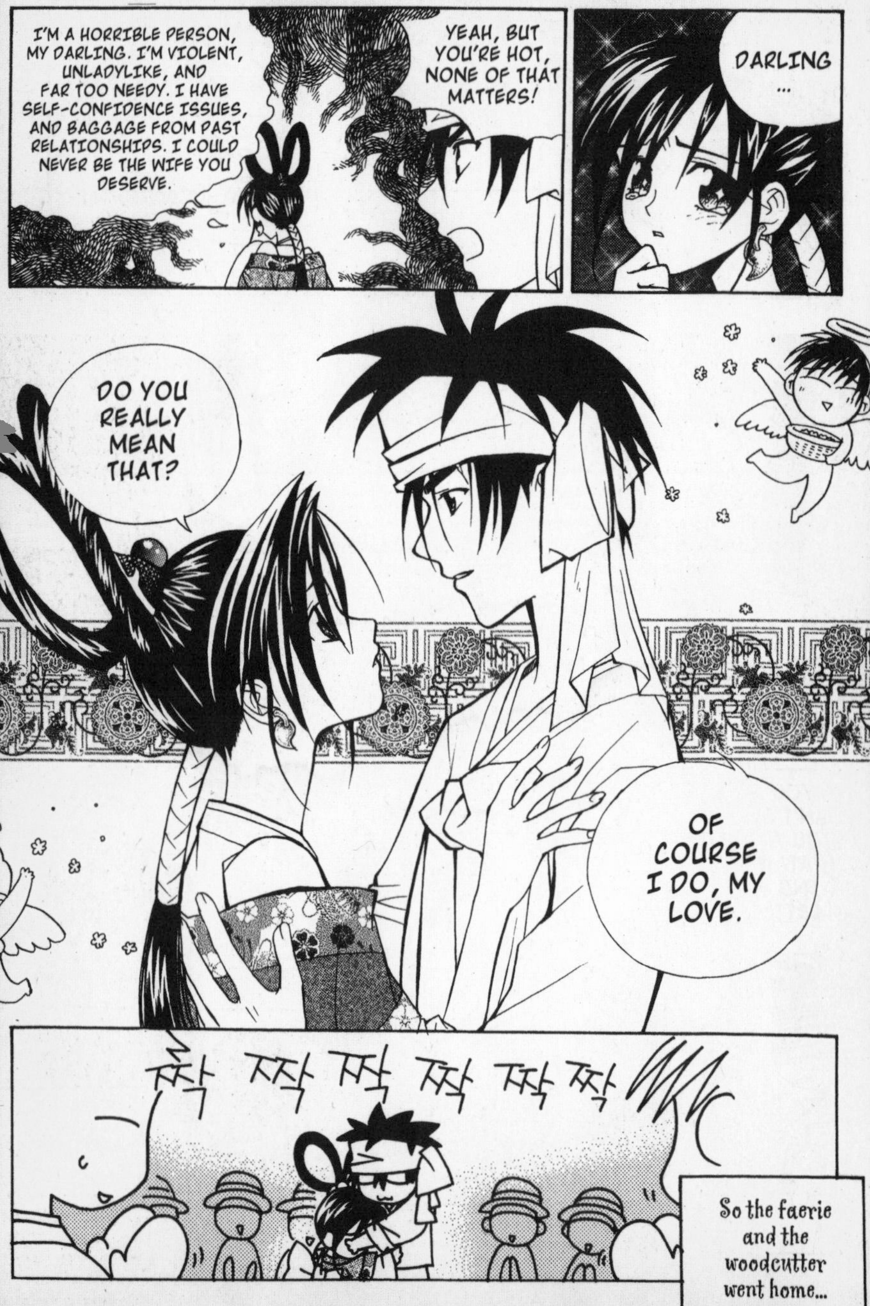
I'M A HORRIBLE PERSON, MY DARLING. I'M VIOLENT, UNLADYLIKE, AND FAR TOO NEEDY. I HAVE SELF-CONFIDENCE ISSUES, AND BAGGAGE FROM PAST RELATIONSHIPS. I COULD NEVER BE THE WIFE YOU DESERVE.
YEAH, BUT YOU'RE HOT, NONE OF THAT MATTERS!
DARLING ...
DO YOU REALLY MEAN THAT?
OF COURSE I DO, MY LOVE.
짝 짝 짝 짝 짝 짝
So the faerie and the woodcutter went home...

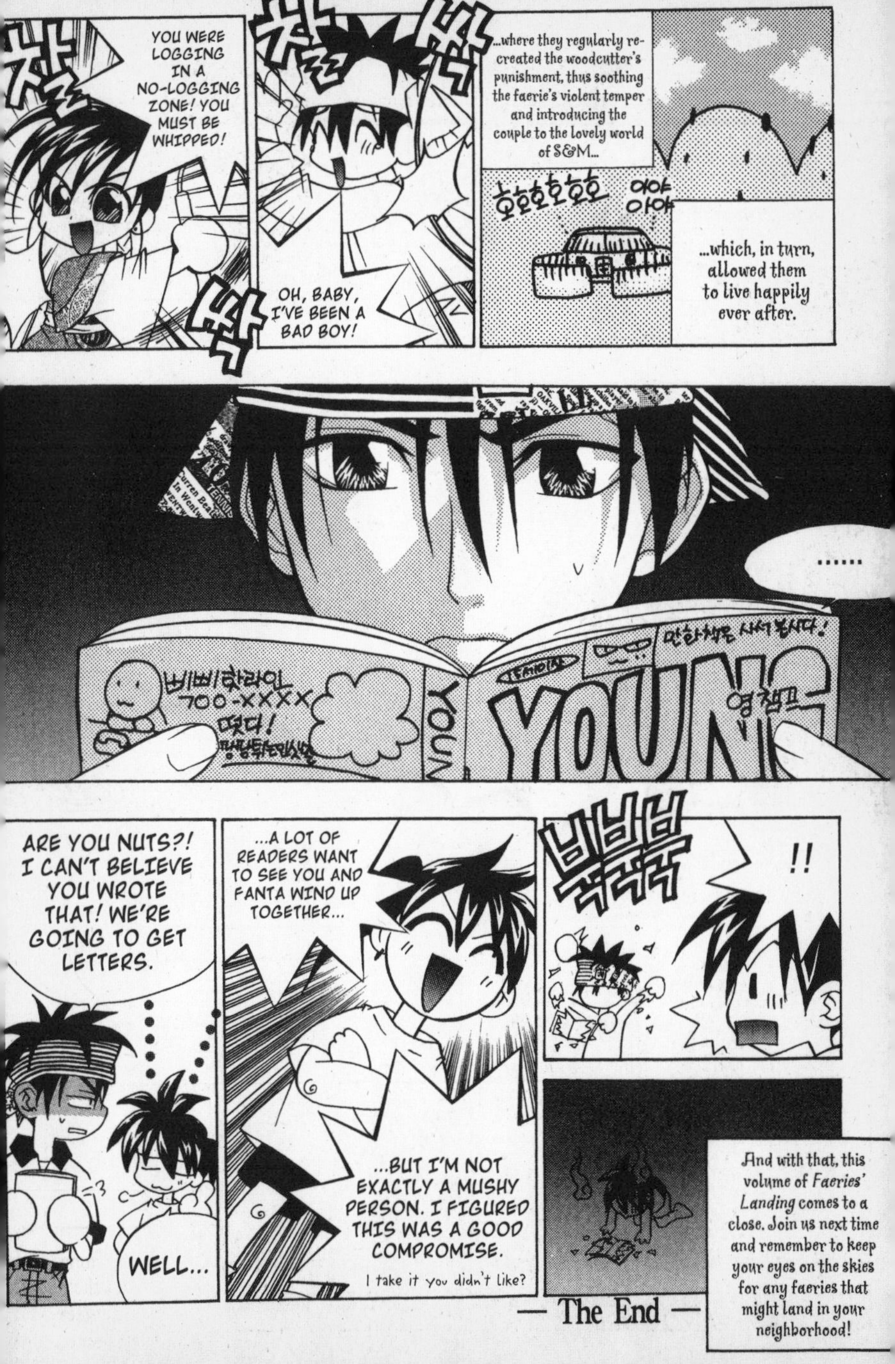
YOU WERE LOGGING IN A NO-LOGGING ZONE! YOU MUST BE WHIPPED!
OH, BABY, I'VE BEEN A BAD BOY!
...where they regularly re-created the woodcutter's punishment, thus soothing the faerie's violent temper and introducing the couple to the lovely world of S&M...
호호호호호호
아야 아야
...which, in turn, allowed them to live happily ever after.
......
만화책은 사서 봅시다!
YOUNG
영챔프
ARE YOU NUTS?! I CAN'T BELIEVE YOU WROTE THAT! WE'RE GOING TO GET LETTERS.
WELL...
...A LOT OF READERS WANT TO SEE YOU AND FANTA WIND UP TOGETHER...
...BUT I'M NOT EXACTLY A MUSHY PERSON. I FIGURED THIS WAS A GOOD COMPROMISE.
I take it you didn't like?
!!
And with that, this volume of *Faeries' Landing* comes to a close. Join us next time and remember to keep your eyes on the skies for any faeries that might land in your neighborhood!
— The End —

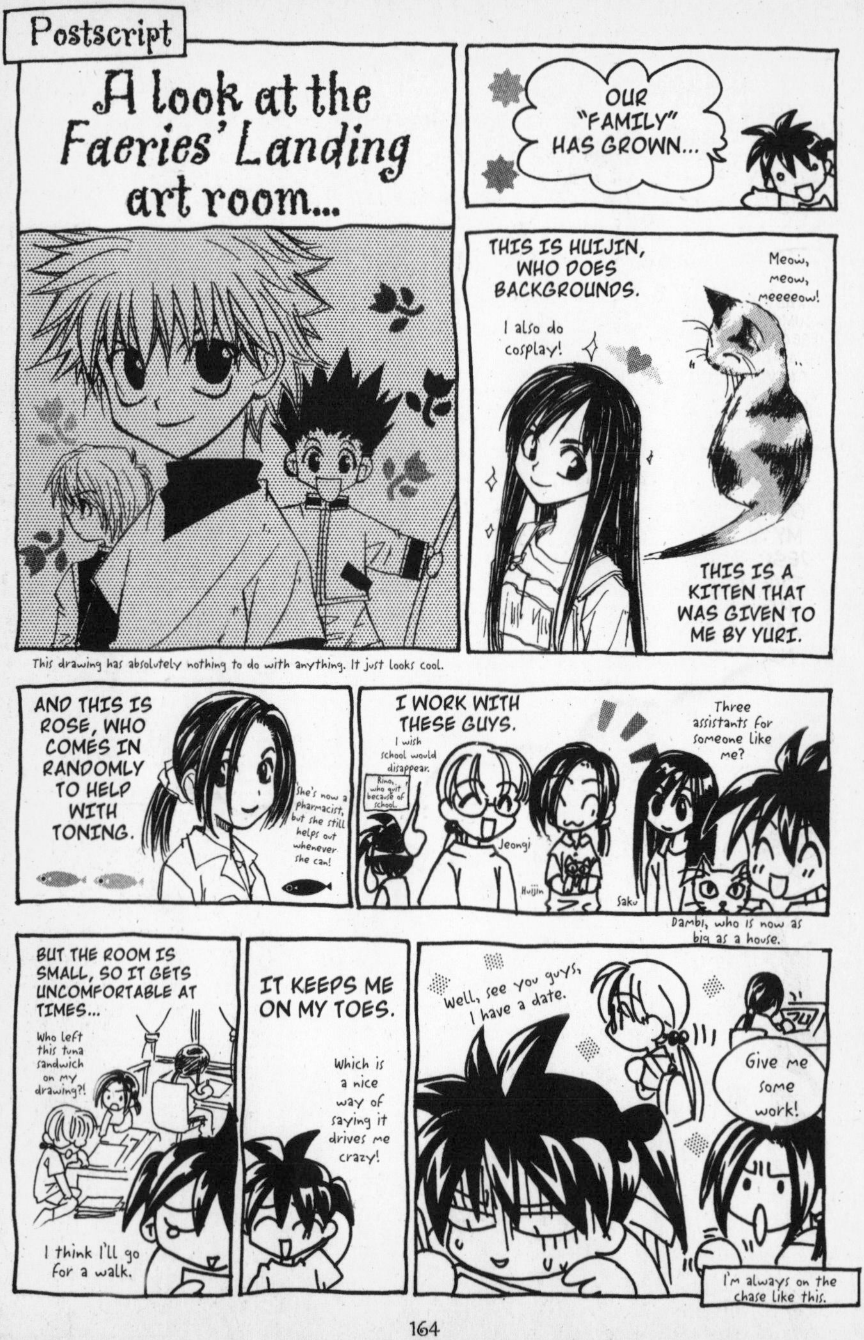
Postscript
A look at the Faeries' Landing art room...
OUR "FAMILY" HAS GROWN...
This drawing has absolutely nothing to do with anything. It just looks cool.
THIS IS HUIJIN, WHO DOES BACKGROUNDS.
I also do cosplay!
Meow, meow, meeeeow!
THIS IS A KITTEN THAT WAS GIVEN TO ME BY YURI.
AND THIS IS ROSE, WHO COMES IN RANDOMLY TO HELP WITH TONING.
She's now a pharmacist, but she still helps out whenever she can!
I WORK WITH THESE GUYS.
I wish school would disappear.
Rino, who quit because of school.
Jeongi
Huijin
Saku
Three assistants for someone like me?
Dambi, who is now as big as a house.
BUT THE ROOM IS SMALL, SO IT GETS UNCOMFORTABLE AT TIMES...
Who left this tuna sandwich on my drawing?!
I think I'll go for a walk.
IT KEEPS ME ON MY TOES.
Which is a nice way of saying it drives me crazy!
Well, see you guys, I have a date.
Give me some work!
I'm always on the chase like this.

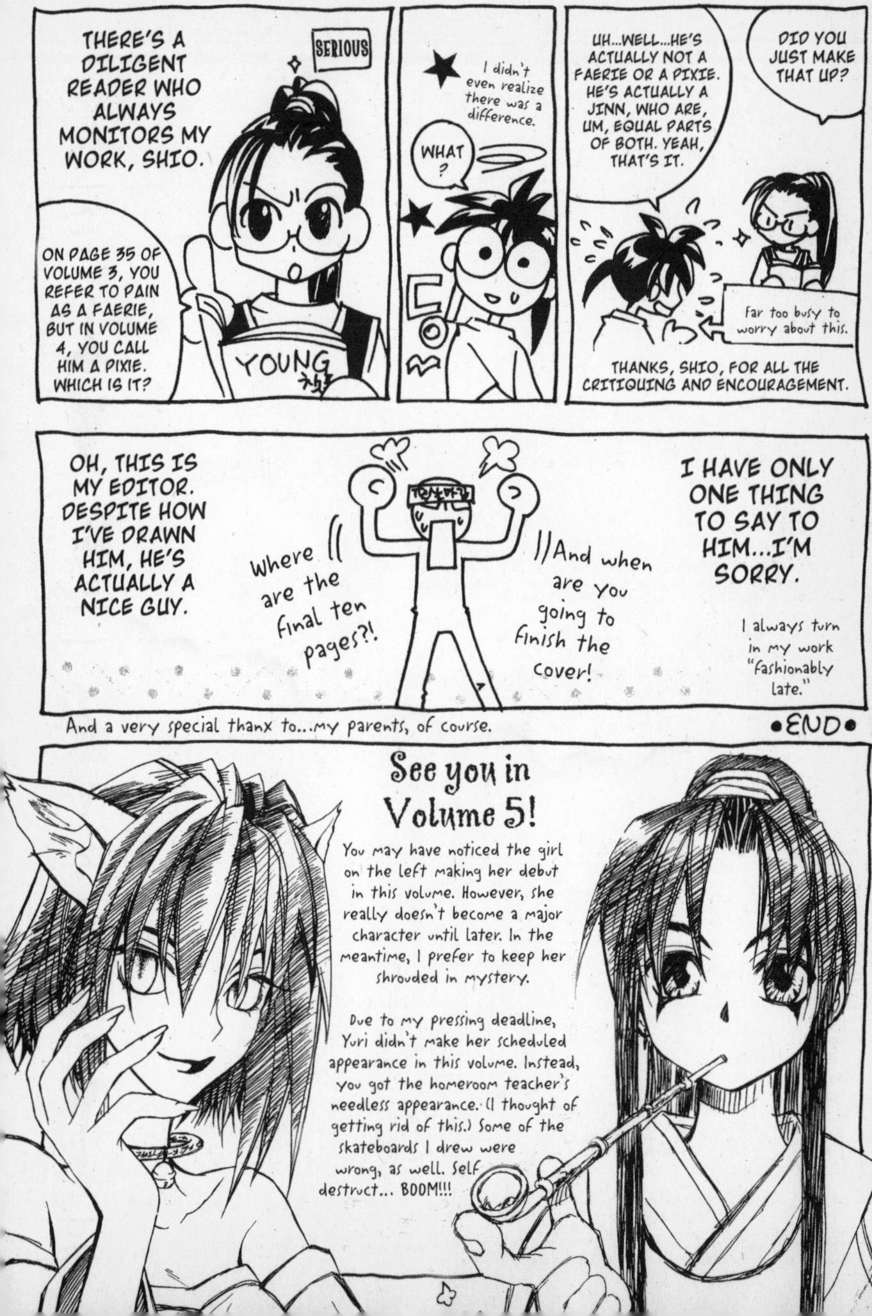
THERE'S A DILIGENT READER WHO ALWAYS MONITORS MY WORK, SHIO.
SERIOUS
ON PAGE 35 OF VOLUME 3, YOU REFER TO PAIN AS A FAERIE, BUT IN VOLUME 4, YOU CALL HIM A PIXIE. WHICH IS IT?
YOUNG
I didn't even realize there was a difference.
WHAT?
UH...WELL...HE'S ACTUALLY NOT A FAERIE OR A PIXIE. HE'S ACTUALLY A JINN, WHO ARE, UM, EQUAL PARTS OF BOTH. YEAH, THAT'S IT.
DID YOU JUST MAKE THAT UP?
Far too busy to worry about this.
THANKS, SHIO, FOR ALL THE CRITIQUING AND ENCOURAGEMENT.
OH, THIS IS MY EDITOR. DESPITE HOW I'VE DRAWN HIM, HE'S ACTUALLY A NICE GUY.
Where are the final ten pages?!
And when are you going to finish the cover!
I HAVE ONLY ONE THING TO SAY TO HIM...I'M SORRY.
I always turn in my work "fashionably late."
And a very special thanx to...my parents, of course.
•END•
See you in Volume 5!
You may have noticed the girl on the left making her debut in this volume. However, she really doesn't become a major character until later. In the meantime, I prefer to keep her shrouded in mystery.
Due to my pressing deadline, Yuri didn't make her scheduled appearance in this volume. Instead, you got the homeroom teacher's needless appearance. (I thought of getting rid of this.) Some of the skateboards I drew were wrong, as well. Self destruct... BOOM!!!

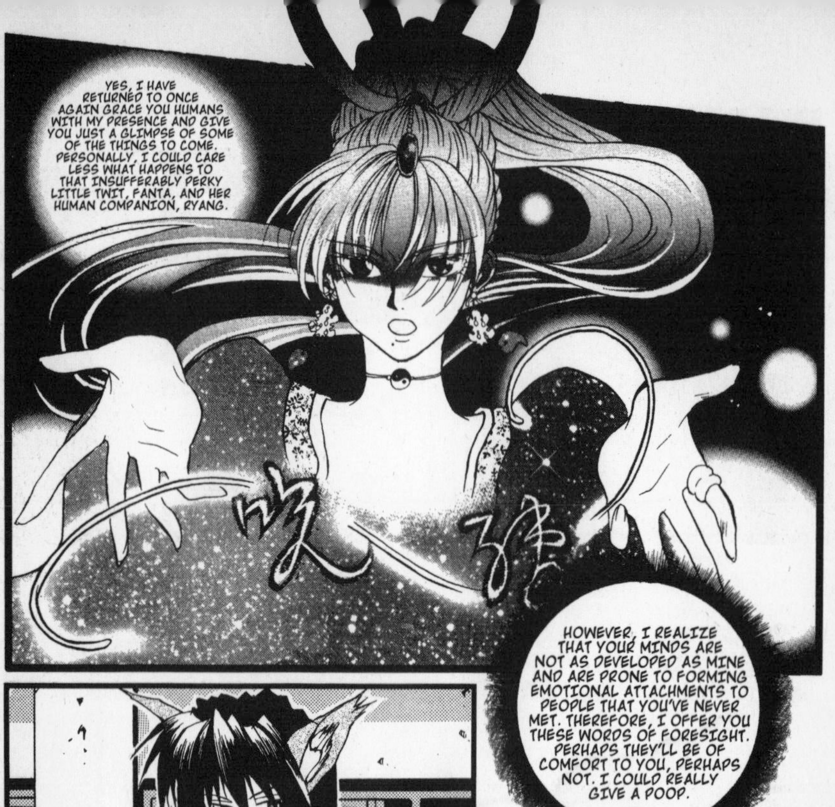
YES, I HAVE RETURNED TO ONCE AGAIN GRACE YOU HUMANS WITH MY PRESENCE AND GIVE YOU JUST A GLIMPSE OF SOME OF THE THINGS TO COME. PERSONALLY, I COULD CARE LESS WHAT HAPPENS TO THAT INSUFFERABLY PERKY LITTLE TWIT, FANTA, AND HER HUMAN COMPANION, RYANG.
HOWEVER, I REALIZE THAT YOUR MINDS ARE NOT AS DEVELOPED AS MINE AND ARE PRONE TO FORMING EMOTIONAL ATTACHMENTS TO PEOPLE THAT YOU'VE NEVER MET. THEREFORE, I OFFER YOU THESE WORDS OF FORESIGHT. PERHAPS THEY'LL BE OF COMFORT TO YOU, PERHAPS NOT. I COULD REALLY GIVE A POOP.

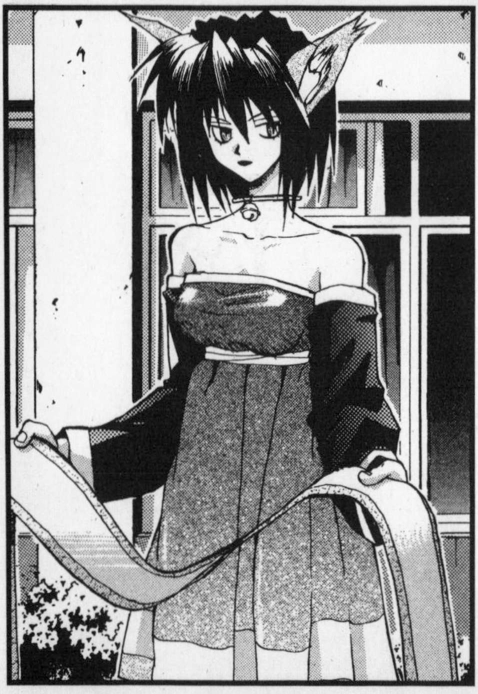

IT APPEARS THAT BAST, THE GODDESS OF CATS, WILL BE PAYING US A VISIT. BE FOREWARNED, THAT LITTLE TART IS TROUBLE. HOPEFULLY, SHE DOESN'T EXPECT A WARM WELCOME, BECAUSE THIS IS ONE LITTLE KITTY THAT RUBS ALL OF US THE WRONG WAY.

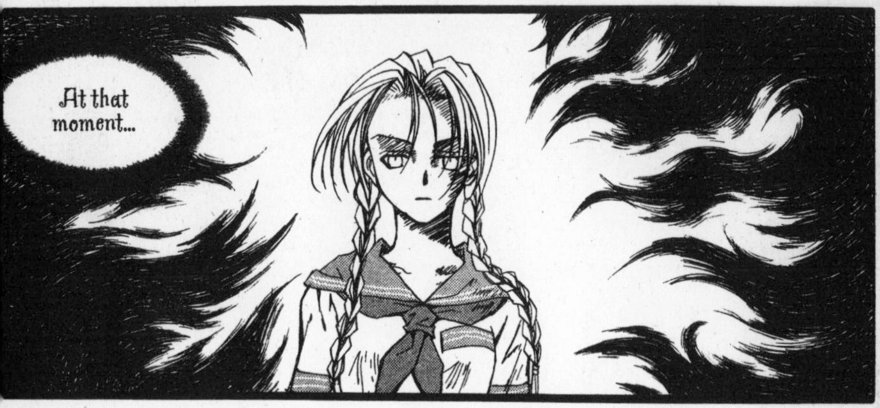
At that moment...

IT LOOKS LIKE OUR LITTLE LOOSE THREAD IS ABOUT TO RETURN WITH A VENGEANCE. JINHUI AND HANSU MAY HAVE SURVIVED A ROCKY RELATIONSHIP, BUT CAN THEY SURVIVE PLAYING HOST TO AN EVIL AFFINITY? BUT, WAIT! WE'RE NOT JUST TALKING ABOUT AN ORDINARY AFFINITY HERE. NO, THIS IS SOMETHING FAR, FAR WORSE.

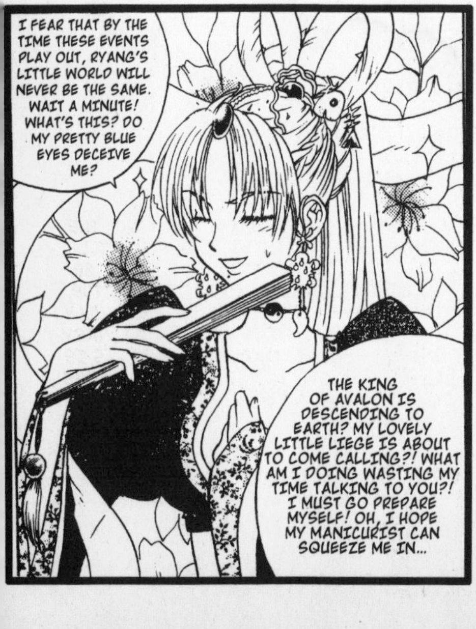
I FEAR THAT BY THE TIME THESE EVENTS PLAY OUT, RYANG'S LITTLE WORLD WILL NEVER BE THE SAME. WAIT A MINUTE! WHAT'S THIS? DO MY PRETTY BLUE EYES DECEIVE ME?
THE KING OF AVALON IS DESCENDING TO EARTH? MY LOVELY LITTLE LIEGE IS ABOUT TO COME CALLING?! WHAT AM I DOING WASTING MY TIME TALKING TO YOU?! I MUST GO PREPARE MYSELF! OH, I HOPE MY MANICURIST CAN SQUEEZE ME IN...

Faeries' Landing

Volume 5

July 2004

MANGA

.HACK//LEGEND OF THE TWILIGHT
@LARGE
ABENOBASHI: MAGICAL SHOPPING ARCADE
A.I. LOVE YOU
AI YORI AOSHI
ANGELIC LAYER
ARM OF KANNON
BABY BIRTH
BATTLE ROYALE
BATTLE VIXENS
BRAIN POWERED
BRIGADOON
B'TX
CANDIDATE FOR GODDESS, THE
CARDCAPTOR SAKURA
CARDCAPTOR SAKURA - MASTER OF THE CLOW
CHOBITS
CHRONICLES OF THE CURSED SWORD
CLAMP SCHOOL DETECTIVES
CLOVER
COMIC PARTY
CONFIDENTIAL CONFESSIONS
CORRECTOR YUI
COWBOY BEBOP
COWBOY BEBOP: SHOOTING STAR
CRAZY LOVE STORY
CRESCENT MOON
CROSS
CULDCEPT
CYBORG 009
D•N•ANGEL
DEMON DIARY
DEMON ORORON, THE
DEUS VITAE
DIABOLO
DIGIMON
DIGIMON TAMERS
DIGIMON ZERO TWO
DOLL
DRAGON HUNTER
DRAGON KNIGHTS
DRAGON VOICE
DREAM SAGA
DUKLYON: CLAMP SCHOOL DEFENDERS
EERIE QUEERIE!
ERICA SAKURAZAWA: COLLECTED WORKS
ET CETERA
ETERNITY
EVIL'S RETURN
FAERIES' LANDING
FAKE
FLCL
FLOWER OF THE DEEP SLEEP
FORBIDDEN DANCE
FRUITS BASKET
G GUNDAM

GATEKEEPERS
GETBACKERS
GIRL GOT GAME
GIRLS' EDUCATIONAL CHARTER
GRAVITATION
GTO
GUNDAM BLUE DESTINY
GUNDAM SEED ASTRAY
GUNDAM WING
GUNDAM WING: BATTLEFIELD OF PACIFISTS
GUNDAM WING: ENDLESS WALTZ
GUNDAM WING: THE LAST OUTPOST (G-UNIT)
GUYS' GUIDE TO GIRLS
HANDS OFF!
HAPPY MANIA
HARLEM BEAT
HONEY MUSTARD
I.N.V.U.
IMMORTAL RAIN
INITIAL D
INSTANT TEEN: JUST ADD NUTS
ISLAND
JING: KING OF BANDITS
JING: KING OF BANDITS - TWILIGHT TALES
JULINE
KARE KANO
KILL ME, KISS ME
KINDAICHI CASE FILES, THE
KING OF HELL
KODOCHA: SANA'S STAGE
LAMENT OF THE LAMB
LEGAL DRUG
LEGEND OF CHUN HYANG, THE
LES BIJOUX
LOVE HINA
LUPIN III
LUPIN III: WORLD'S MOST WANTED
MAGIC KNIGHT RAYEARTH I
MAGIC KNIGHT RAYEARTH II
MAHOROMATIC: AUTOMATIC MAIDEN
MAN OF MANY FACES
MARMALADE BOY
MARS
MARS: HORSE WITH NO NAME
MINK
MIRACLE GIRLS
MIYUKI-CHAN IN WONDERLAND
MODEL
MY LOVE
NECK AND NECK
ONE
ONE I LOVE, THE
PARADISE KISS
PARASYTE
PASSION FRUIT
PEACH GIRL
PEACH GIRL: CHANGE OF HEART
PET SHOP OF HORRORS

PITA-TEN
PLANET LADDER
PLANETES
PRIEST
PRINCESS AI
PSYCHIC ACADEMY
QUEEN'S KNIGHT, THE
RAGNAROK
RAVE MASTER
REALITY CHECK
REBIRTH
REBOUND
REMOTE
RISING STARS OF MANGA
SABER MARIONETTE J
SAILOR MOON
SAINT TAIL
SAIYUKI
SAMURAI DEEPER KYO
SAMURAI GIRL REAL BOUT HIGH SCHOOL
SCRYED
SEIKAI TRILOGY, THE
SGT. FROG
SHAOLIN SISTERS
SHIRAHIME-SYO: SNOW GODDESS TALES
SHUTTERBOX
SKULL MAN, THE
SNOW DROP
SORCERER HUNTERS
STONE
SUIKODEN III
SUKI
THREADS OF TIME
TOKYO BABYLON
TOKYO MEW MEW
TOKYO TRIBES
TRAMPS LIKE US
UNDER THE GLASS MOON
VAMPIRE GAME
VISION OF ESCAFLOWNE, THE
WARRIORS OF TAO
WILD ACT
WISH
WORLD OF HARTZ
X-DAY
ZODIAC P.I.

NOVELS

CLAMP SCHOOL PARANORMAL INVESTIGATORS
KARMA CLUB
SAILOR MOON
SLAYERS

ART BOOKS

ART OF CARDCAPTOR SAKURA
ART OF MAGIC KNIGHT RAYEARTH, THE
PEACH: MIWA UEDA ILLUSTRATIONS

ANIME GUIDES

COWBOY BEBOP
GUNDAM TECHNICAL MANUALS
SAILOR MOON SCOUT GUIDES

TOKYOPOP KIDS

STRAY SHEEP

CINE-MANGA™

ALADDIN
CARDCAPTORS
DUEL MASTERS
FAIRLY ODDPARENTS, THE
FAMILY GUY
FINDING NEMO
G.I. JOE SPY TROOPS
GREATEST STARS OF THE NBA
JACKIE CHAN ADVENTURES
JIMMY NEUTRON: BOY GENIUS, THE ADVENTURES OF
KIM POSSIBLE
LILO & STITCH: THE SERIES
LIZZIE MCGUIRE
LIZZIE MCGUIRE MOVIE, THE
MALCOLM IN THE MIDDLE
POWER RANGERS: DINO THUNDER
POWER RANGERS: NINJA STORM
PRINCESS DIARIES 2
RAVE MASTER
SHREK 2
SIMPLE LIFE, THE
SPONGEBOB SQUAREPANTS
SPY KIDS 2
SPY KIDS 3-D: GAME OVER
THAT'S SO RAVEN
TOTALLY SPIES
TRANSFORMERS: ARMADA
TRANSFORMERS: ENERGON
VAN HELSING

**For more
information visit
www.TOKYOPOP.com**

03.30.04T

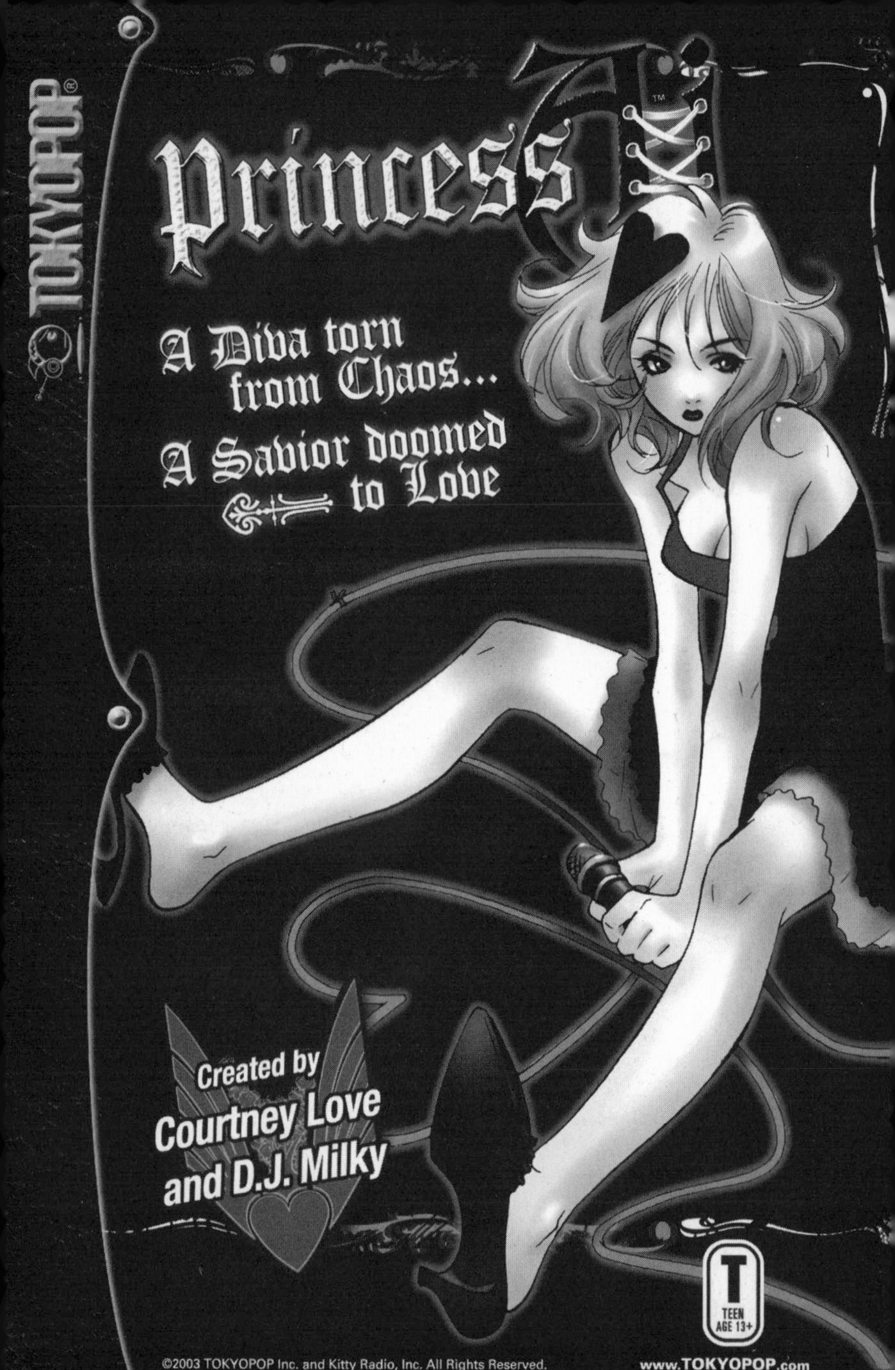
TOKYOPOP
Princess Ai™
A Diva torn from Chaos...
A Savior doomed to Love
Created by
Courtney Love
and D.J. Milky
T
TEEN
AGE 13+

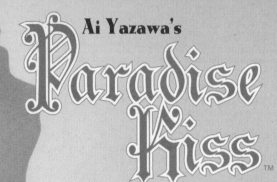

PITA-TEN™

By Koge-Donbo · Creator of Digicharat

The girl next door is
bringing a touch of heaven
to the neighborhood.

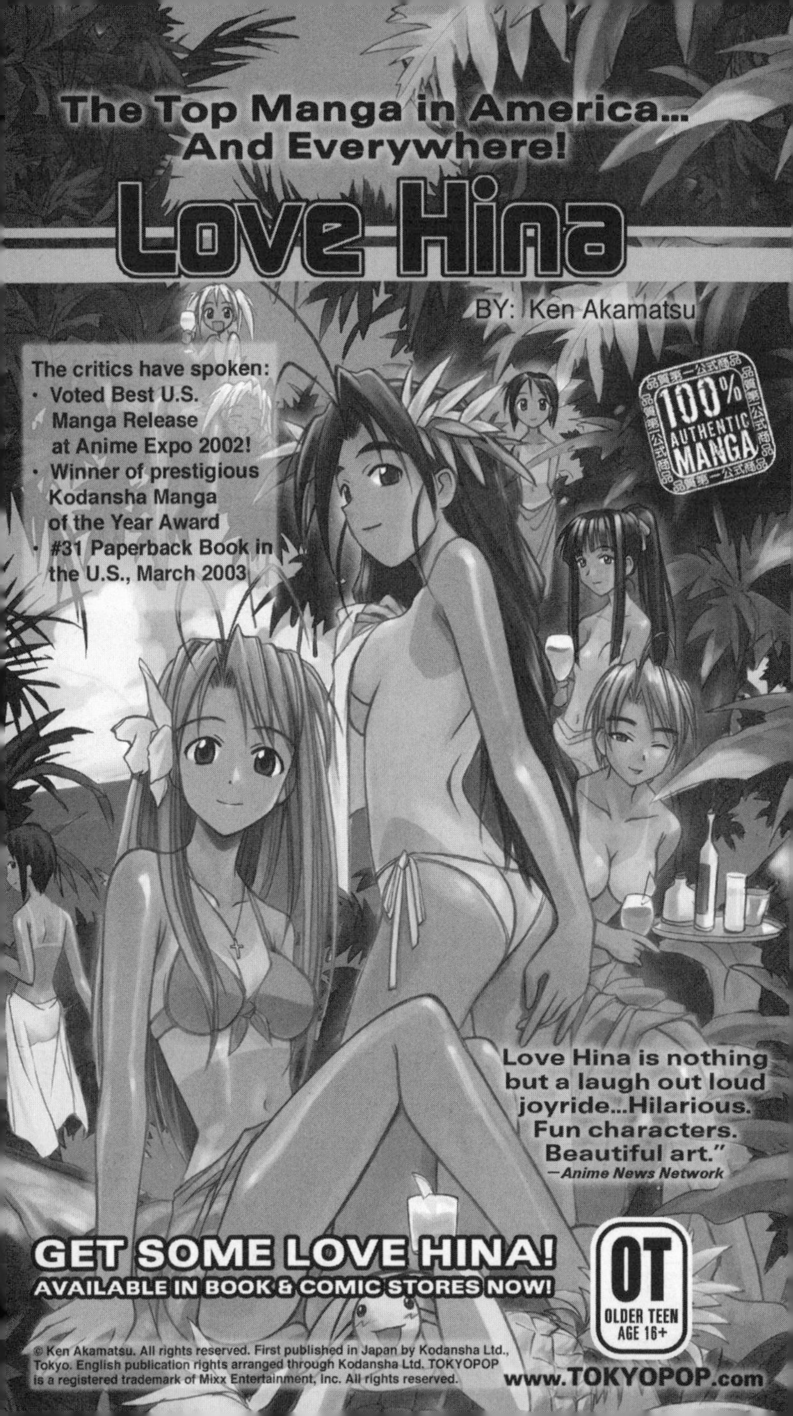
The Top Manga in America...
And Everywhere!
Love Hina
BY: Ken Akamatsu
The critics have spoken:
• Voted Best U.S. Manga Release at Anime Expo 2002!
• Winner of prestigious Kodansha Manga of the Year Award
• #31 Paperback Book in the U.S., March 2003
100% AUTHENTIC MANGA
Love Hina is nothing but a laugh out loud joyride...Hilarious. Fun characters. Beautiful art."
—Anime News Network
GET SOME LOVE HINA!
AVAILABLE IN BOOK & COMIC STORES NOW!
OT
OLDER TEEN AGE 16+
© Ken Akamatsu. All rights reserved. First published in Japan by Kodansha Ltd., Tokyo. English publication rights arranged through Kodansha Ltd. TOKYOPOP is a registered trademark of Mixx Entertainment, Inc. All rights reserved.
www.TOKYOPOP.com

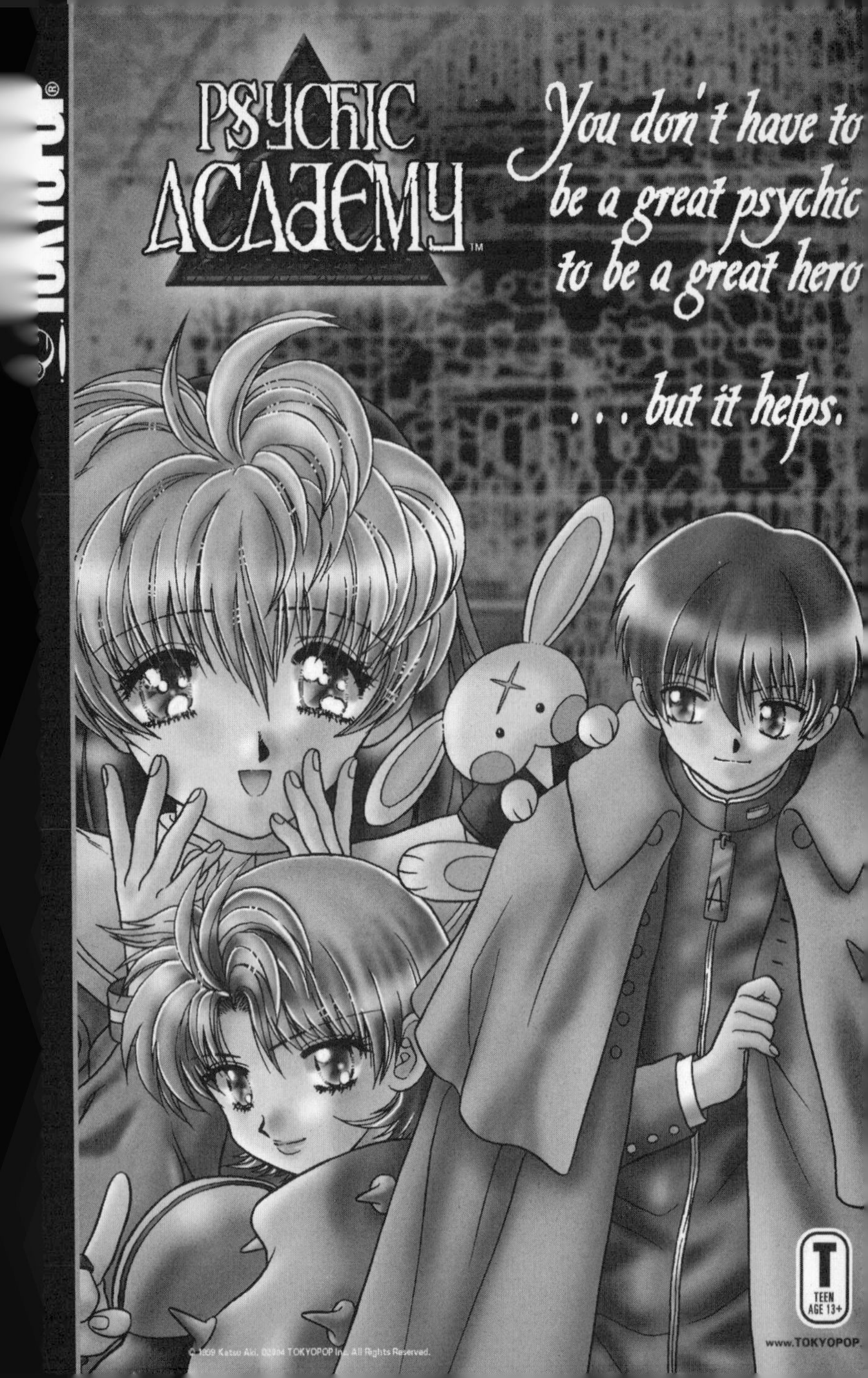
PSYCHIC ACADEMY™
You don't have to be a great psychic to be a great hero
. . . but it helps.
T TEEN AGE 13+
www.TOKYOPOP.
All Rights Reserved.

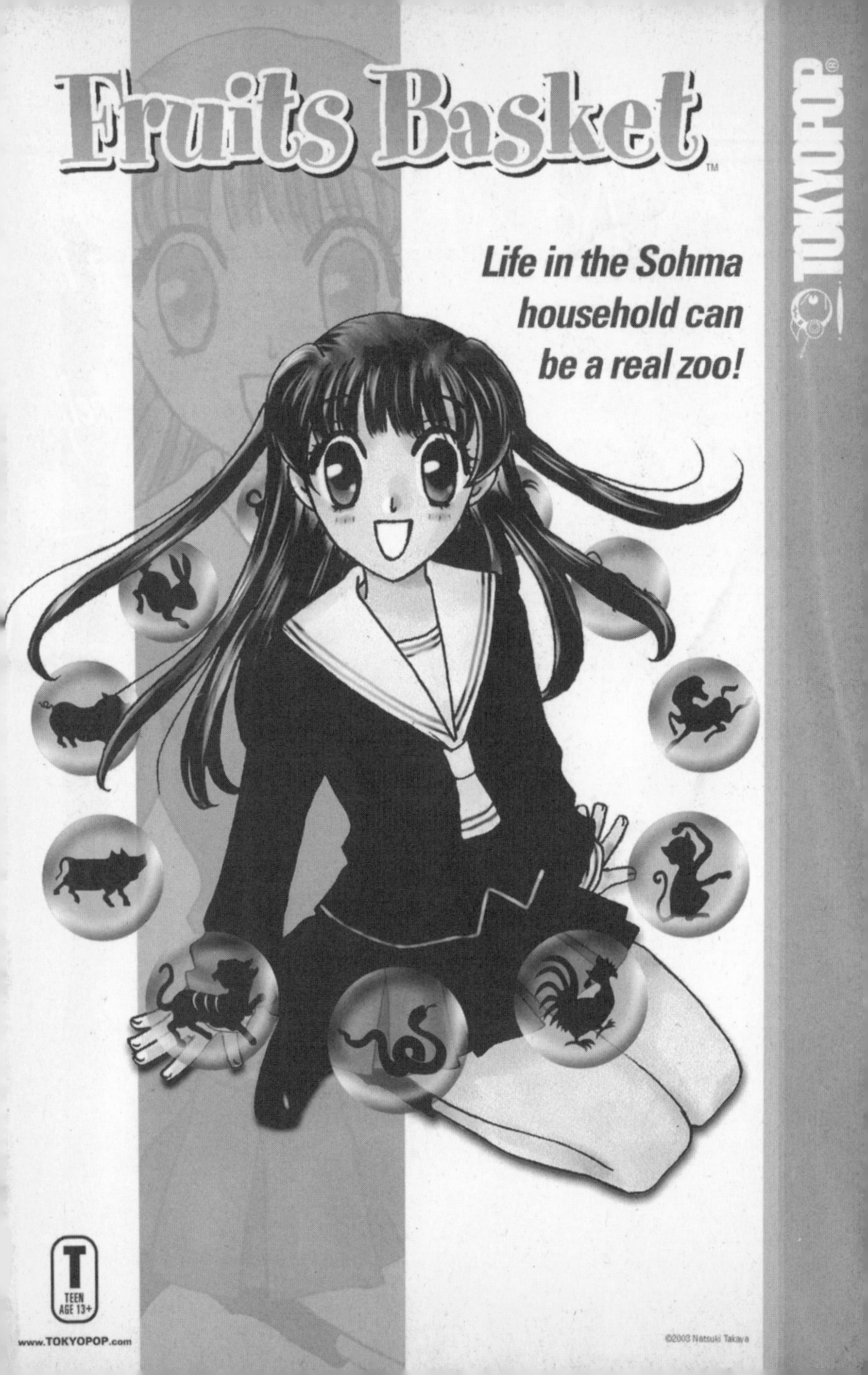
Fruits Basket™
Life in the Sohma household can be a real zoo!
TOKYOPOP®
T
TEEN
AGE 13+
www.TOKYOPOP.com
©2003 Natsuki Takaya